Microsoft® Official Academic Course

Microsoft Access 2010, EXAM 77-885

WILEY

EDITOR	Bryan Gambrel
DIRECTOR OF SALES	Mitchell Beaton
EXECUTIVE MARKETING MANAGER	Chris Ruel
ASSISTANT MARKETING MANAGER	Debbie Martin
MICROSOFT STRATEGIC RELATIONSHIPS MANAGER	Colin Klein of Microsoft Learning
EDITORIAL PROGRAM ASSISTANT	Jennifer Lartz
CONTENT MANAGER	Micheline Frederick
PRODUCTION EDITOR	Amy Weintraub
CREATIVE DIRECTOR	Harry Nolan
COVER DESIGNER	Jim O'shea
INTERIOR DESIGNER	Amy Rosen
PHOTO EDITORS	Sheena Goldstein, Jennifer MacMillan
EXECUTIVE MEDIA EDITOR	Tom Kulesa
MEDIA EDITOR	Wendy Ashenberg

This book was set in Garamond by Aptara, Inc. and printed and bound by Courier Kendallville. The covers were printed by Lehigh Phoenix.

Microsoft, ActiveX, Access, Excel, InfoPath, Microsoft Press, MSDN, OneNote, Outlook, PivotChart, PivotTable, PowerPoint, SharePoint, SQL Server, Visio, Windows, Windows Mobile, and Windows Server are either registered trademarks or trademarks of Microsoft Corporation in the United States and/or other countries. Other product and company names mentioned herein may be the trademarks of their respective owners.

The example companies, organizations, products, domain names, e-mail addresses, logos, people, places, and events depicted herein are fictitious. No association with any real company, organization, product, domain name, e-mail address, logo, person, place, or event is intended or should be inferred.

The book expresses the author's views and opinions. The information contained in this book is provided without any express, statutory, or implied warranties. Neither the authors, John Wiley & Sons, Inc., Microsoft Corporation, nor their resellers or distributors will be held liable for any damages caused or alleged to be caused either directly or indirectly by this book.

Founded in 1807, John Wiley & Sons, Inc. has been a valued source of knowledge and understanding for more than 200 years, helping people around the world meet their needs and fulfill their aspirations. Our company is built on a foundation of principles that include responsibility to the communities we serve and where we live and work. In 2008, we launched a Corporate Citizenship Initiative, a global effort to address the environmental, social, economic, and ethical challenges we face in our business. Among the issues we are addressing are carbon impact, paper specifications and procurement, ethical conduct within our business and among our vendors, and community and charitable support. For more information, please visit our website: www.wiley.com/go/citizenship.

ISBN 978-0-470-90768-9

Printed in the United States of America

10 9 8 7 6 5 4 3 2 1

Foreword from the Publisher

Wiley's publishing vision for the Microsoft Official Academic Course series is to provide students and instructors with the skills and knowledge they need to use Microsoft technology effectively in all aspects of their personal and professional lives. Quality instruction is required to help both educators and students get the most from Microsoft's software tools and to become more productive. Thus our mission is to make our instructional programs trusted educational companions for life.

To accomplish this mission, Wiley and Microsoft have partnered to develop the highest quality educational programs for Information Workers, IT Professionals, and Developers. Materials created by this partnership carry the brand name "Microsoft Official Academic Course," assuring instructors and students alike that the content of these textbooks is fully endorsed by Microsoft, and that they provide the highest quality information and instruction on Microsoft products. The Microsoft Official Academic Course textbooks are "Official" in still one more way—they are the officially sanctioned courseware for Microsoft IT Academy members.

The Microsoft Official Academic Course series focuses on *workforce development*. These programs are aimed at those students seeking to enter the workforce, change jobs, or embark on new careers as information workers, IT professionals, and developers. Microsoft Official Academic Course programs address their needs by emphasizing authentic workplace scenarios with an abundance of projects, exercises, cases, and assessments.

The Microsoft Official Academic Courses are mapped to Microsoft's extensive research and job-task analysis, the same research and analysis used to create the Microsoft Office Specialist (MOS) exams. The textbooks focus on real skills for real jobs. As students work through the projects and exercises in the textbooks, they enhance their level of knowledge and their ability to apply the latest Microsoft technology to everyday tasks. These students also gain resume-building credentials that can assist them in finding a job, keeping their current job, or in furthering their education.

The concept of lifelong learning is today an utmost necessity. Job roles, and even whole job categories, are changing so quickly that none of us can stay competitive and productive without continuously updating our skills and capabilities. The Microsoft Official Academic Course offerings, and their focus on Microsoft certification exam preparation, provide a means for people to acquire and effectively update their skills and knowledge. Wiley supports students in this endeavor through the development and distribution of these courses as Microsoft's official academic publisher.

Today educational publishing requires attention to providing quality print and robust electronic content. By integrating Microsoft Official Academic Course products, *WileyPLUS*, and Microsoft certifications, we are better able to deliver efficient learning solutions for students and teachers alike.

Joseph Heider
General Manager and Senior Vice President

Preface

Welcome to the Microsoft Official Academic Course (MOAC) program for Microsoft Access 2010. MOAC is the collaboration between Microsoft Learning and John Wiley & Sons, Inc. publishing company. Microsoft and Wiley teamed up to produce a series of textbooks that deliver compelling and innovative teaching solutions to instructors and superior learning experiences for students. Infused and informed by in-depth knowledge from the creators of Microsoft Office and Windows, and crafted by a publisher known worldwide for the pedagogical quality of its products, these textbooks maximize skills transfer in minimum time. Students are challenged to reach their potential by using their new technical skills as highly productive members of the workforce.

Because this knowledgebase comes directly from Microsoft, architect of Office 2010 and creator of the Microsoft Office Specialist (MOS) exams (http://www.microsoft.com/learning/en/us/certification/mos.aspx), you are sure to receive the topical coverage that is most relevant to your personal and professional success. Microsoft's direct participation not only assures you that MOAC textbook content is accurate and current; it also means that students will receive the best instruction possible to enable their success on certification exams and in the workplace.

THE MICROSOFT OFFICIAL ACADEMIC COURSE PROGRAM

The *Microsoft Official Academic Course* series is a complete program for instructors and institutions to prepare and deliver great courses on Microsoft software technologies. With MOAC, we recognize that, because of the rapid pace of change in the technology and curriculum developed by Microsoft, there is an ongoing set of needs beyond classroom instruction tools for an instructor to be ready to teach the course. The MOAC program endeavors to provide solutions for all these needs in a systematic manner in order to ensure a successful and rewarding course experience for both instructor and student—technical and curriculum training for instructor readiness with new software releases; the software itself for student use at home for building hands-on skills, assessment, and validation of skill development; and a great set of tools for delivering instruction in the classroom and lab. All are important to the smooth delivery of an interesting course on Microsoft software, and all are provided with the MOAC program. We think about the model below as a gauge for ensuring that we completely support you in your goal of teaching a great course. As you evaluate your instructional materials options, you may wish to use the model for comparison purposes with available products.

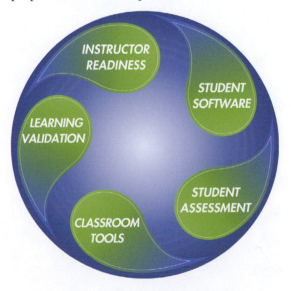

www.wiley.com/college/microsoft
or call the MOAC Toll-Free Number: 1+(888) 764-7001 (U.S. & Canada only)

PEDAGOGICAL FEATURES

The MOAC textbooks for Microsoft Office 2010 are designed to cover all the learning objectives for that MOS exam, which is referred to as its exam objective. The Microsoft Office Specialist (MOS) exam objectives are highlighted throughout the textbooks. Many pedagogical features have been developed specifically for *Microsoft Official Academic Course* programs. Unique features of our task-based approach include a Lesson Skill Matrix that correlates skills taught in each lesson to the MOS objectives; Certification, Workplace, and Internet Ready exercises; and three levels of increasingly rigorous lesson-ending activities: Competency, Proficiency, and Mastery Assessment.

Presenting the extensive procedural information and technical concepts woven throughout the textbook raises challenges for the student and instructor alike. The Illustrated Book Tour that follows provides a guide to the rich features contributing to *Microsoft Official Academic Course* program's pedagogical plan. Following is a list of key features in each lesson designed to prepare students for success on the certification exams and in the workplace:

- Each lesson begins with a **Lesson Skill Matrix**. More than a standard list of learning objectives, the skill matrix correlates each software skill covered in the lesson to the specific MOS exam objective domain.

- Each lesson features a real-world **Business Case** scenario that places the software skills and knowledge to be acquired in a real-world setting.

- **Software Orientation** provides an overview of the software features students will be working with in the lesson. The orientation will detail the general properties of the software or specific features, such as a ribbon or dialog box; and it includes a large, labeled screen image.

- Concise and frequent **Step-by-Step** instructions teach students new features and provide an opportunity for hands-on practice. Numbered steps give detailed step-by-step instructions to help students learn software skills. The steps also show results and screen images to match what students should see on their computer screens.

- **Illustrations** provide visual feedback as students work through the exercises. The images reinforce key concepts, provide visual clues about the steps, and allow students to check their progress.

- When the text instructs a student to click a particular button, **button images** are shown in the margin or in the text.

- Important technical vocabulary is listed in the **Key Terms** section at the beginning of the lesson. When these terms are used later in the lesson, they appear in bold italic type with yellow highlighter and are defined. The Glossary contains all of the key terms and their definitions.

- Engaging point-of-use **Reader aids**, located throughout the lessons, tell students why this topic is relevant (*The Bottom Line*), provide students with helpful hints (*Take Note*), or show alternate ways to accomplish tasks (*Another Way*), or point out things to watch out for or avoid (*Troubleshooting*). Reader aids also provide additional relevant or background information that adds value to the lesson.

- **Certification Ready** features throughout the text signal students where a specific certification objective is covered. They provide students with a chance to check their understanding of that particular MOS exam objective and, if necessary, review the section of the lesson where it is covered. MOAC provides complete preparation for MOS certification.

- The **New Feature** icon appears near any software feature that is new to Access 2010.
- Each lesson ends with a **Skill Summary** recapping the MOS exam skills covered in the lesson.
- The **Knowledge Assessment** section provides a total of 20 questions from a mix of True/False, Fill in the Blank, Matching, or Multiple Choice, testing students on concepts learned in the lesson.
- **Competency, Proficiency, and Mastery Assessment** sections provide progressively more challenging lesson-ending activities.
- **Internet Ready** projects combine the knowledge that students acquire in a lesson with Web-based task research.
- **Integrated Circling Back** projects provide students with an opportunity to renew and practice skills learned in previous lessons.
- **Workplace Ready** features preview how Microsoft Access 2010 applications are used in real-world situations.
- The student companion website contains the **online files** needed for each lesson. These data files are indicated by the @ icon in the margin of the textbook.

Illustrated Book Tour

LESSON FEATURES

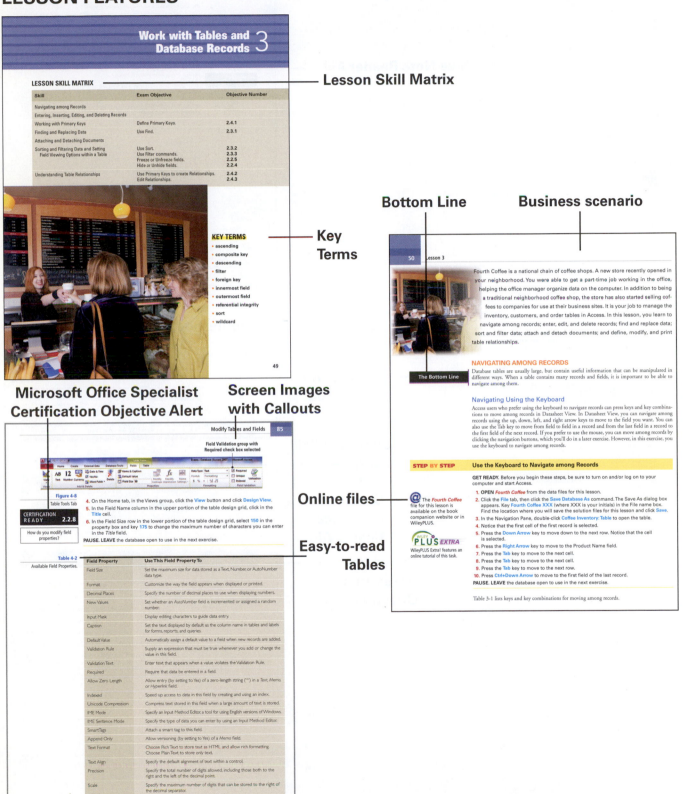

Lesson Skill Matrix

Key Terms

Bottom Line

Business scenario

Microsoft Office Specialist Certification Objective Alert

Screen Images with Callouts

Online files

Easy-to-read Tables

Step-by-Step Exercises

Take Note Reader Aid

Troubleshooting Reader Aid

Another Way Reader Aid

Summary Skill Matrix

Cross Reference Reader Aid

Knowledge Assessment Questions

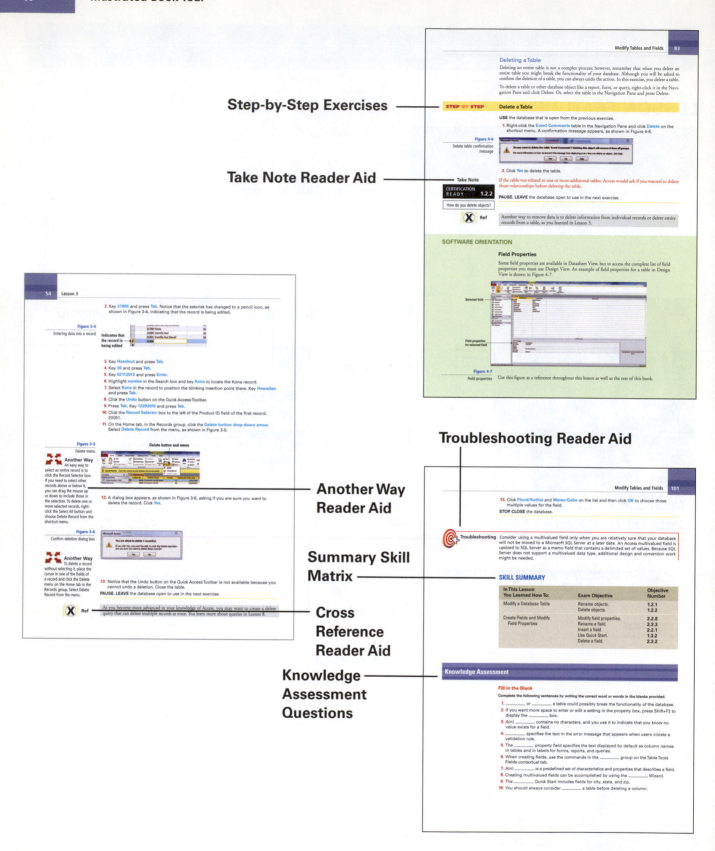

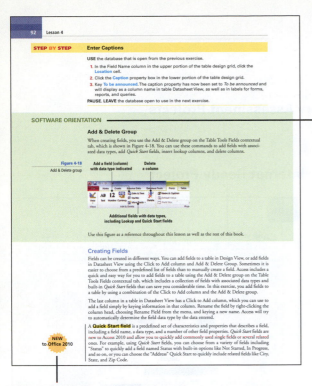

Software Orientation

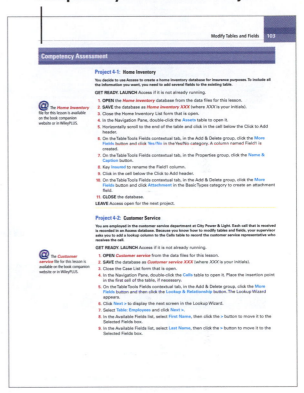

Competency Assessment Projects

New to Office 2010 Feature

Proficiency Assessment Projects

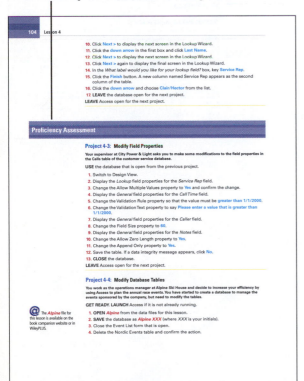

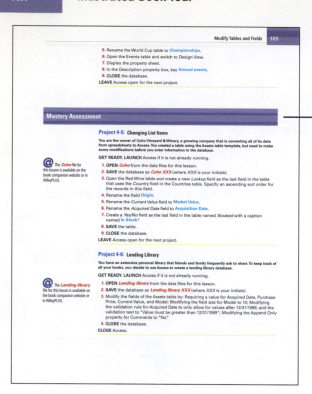

Mastery Assessment Projects

Internet Ready Project

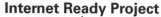

Circling Back Exercises

Workplace Ready

Conventions and Features Used in This Book

This book uses particular fonts, symbols, and heading conventions to highlight important information or to call your attention to special steps. For more information about the features in each lesson, refer to the Illustrated Book Tour section.

NEW to Office 2010

This icon indicates a new or greatly improved Windows feature in this version of the software.

The Bottom Line

This feature provides a brief summary of the material to be covered in the section that follows.

CLOSE

Words in all capital letters indicate instructions for opening, saving, or closing files or programs. They also point out items you should check or actions you should take.

CERTIFICATION READY

This feature signals the point in the text where a specific certification objective is covered. It provides you with a chance to check your understanding of that particular MOS objective and, if necessary, review the section of the lesson where it is covered.

Take Note

Take Note reader aids, set in red text, provide helpful hints related to particular tasks or topics.

Another Way

Another Way provides an alternative procedure for accomplishing a particular task.

Ref

These notes, set in gray shaded boxes, provide pointers to information discussed elsewhere in the textbook or describe interesting features that are not directly addressed in the current topic or exercise.

ALT + Tab

A plus sign (+) between two key names means that you must press both keys at the same time. Keys that you are instructed to press in an exercise will appear in the font shown here.

Key terms

Key terms appear in bold italic with highlighting.

Key **My Name is**

Any text you are asked to key appears in **color**.

Click **OK**

Any button on the screen you are supposed to click on or select will also appear in **color**.

BudgetWorksheet1

The names of data files will appear in bold, italic, and red for easy identification.

Instructor Support Program

The *Microsoft Official Academic Course* programs are accompanied by a rich array of resources that incorporate the extensive textbook visuals to form a pedagogically cohesive package. These resources provide all the materials instructors need to deploy and deliver their courses. The following resources are available online for download.

- The **Instructor's Guide** contains Solutions to all the textbook exercises as well as chapter summaries and lecture notes. The Instructor's Guide and Syllabi for various term lengths are available from the Instructor's Book Companion site (www.wiley.com/college/microsoft).

- The **Solution Files** for all the projects in the book are available online from our Instructor's Book Companion site (www.wiley.com/college/microsoft).

- The **Test Bank** contains hundreds of questions organized by lesson in multiple-choice, true-false, short answer, and essay formats and is available to download from the Instructor's Book Companion site (www.wiley.com/college/microsoft). A complete answer key is provided.

  This title's test bank is available for use in Respondus' easy-to-use software. You can download the test bank for free using your Respondus, Respondus LE, or StudyMate Author software.

  Respondus is a powerful tool for creating and managing exams that can be printed to paper or published directly to Blackboard, WebCT, Desire2Learn, eCollege, ANGEL, and other eLearning systems.

- A complete set of **PowerPoint Presentations** is available on the Instructor's Book Companion site (www.wiley.com/college/microsoft) to enhance classroom presentations. Tailored to the text's topical coverage and Skills Matrix, these presentations are designed to convey key Microsoft Access 2010 concepts addressed in the text.

  All **images** from the text are on the Instructor's Book Companion site (www.wiley.com/college/microsoft). You can incorporate them into your PowerPoint presentations, or create your own overhead transparencies and handouts.

  By using these visuals in class discussions, you can help focus students' attention on key elements of Access 2010 and help them understand how to use it effectively in the workplace.

- The **MSDN Academic Alliance** is designed to provide the easiest and most inexpensive developer tools, products, and technologies available to faculty and students in labs, classrooms, and on student PCs. A free three-year membership is available to qualified MOAC adopters.

  Note: Microsoft Access 2010 can be downloaded from MSDN AA for use by students in this course.

- **Office Grader** automated grading system allows you to easily grade student data files in Word, Excel, PowerPoint, or Access format, against solution files. Save tens or hundreds of hours each semester with automated grading. More information on OfficeGrader is available from the Instructor's Book Companion site (www.wiley.com/college/microsoft).

- The **Student Data Files** are available online on both the Instructor's Book Companion Site and for students on the Student Book Companion Site.

- Microsoft Official Academic Course books can be bundled with MOS exam vouchers from Certiport and MOS practice tests from GMetrix LLC or Certiport, available as a single bundle from Wiley to create a **complete certification solution**. Instructors who use MOAC courseware in conjunction with a practice MOS exam find their students best-prepared for the MOS certification exam. Providing your students with the MOS exam voucher in addition, is the ultimate workforce preparation.

www.wiley.com/college/microsoft
or call the MOAC Toll-Free Number: 1+(888) 764-7001 (U.S. & Canada only)

- When it comes to improving the classroom experience, there is no better source of ideas and inspiration than your fellow colleagues. The **Wiley Faculty Network** connects teachers with technology, facilitates the exchange of best practices, and helps to enhance instructional efficiency and effectiveness. Faculty Network activities include technology training and tutorials, virtual seminars, peer-to-peer exchanges of experiences and ideas, personal consulting, and sharing of resources. For details visit www.WhereFacultyConnect.com.

WILEYPLUS

Broad developments in education over the past decade have influenced the instructional approach taken in the Microsoft Official Academic Course programs. The way that students learn, especially about new technologies, has changed dramatically in the Internet era. Electronic learning materials and Internet-based instruction is now as much a part of classroom instruction as printed textbooks. WileyPLUS provides the technology to create an environment where students reach their full potential and experience academic success that will last a lifetime.

WileyPLUS is a powerful and highly integrated suite of teaching and learning resources designed to bridge the gap between what happens in the classroom and what happens at home and on the job. WileyPLUS provides instructors with the resources to teach their students new technologies and guide them to reach their goals of getting ahead in the job market by having the skills to become certified and advance in the workforce. For students, WileyPLUS provides the tools for study and practice that are available to them 24/7, wherever and whenever they want to study. WileyPLUS includes a complete online version of the student textbook; Power-Point presentations; homework and practice assignments and quizzes; image galleries; test bank questions; gradebook; and all the instructor resources in one easy-to-use website.

New to WileyPLUS for Access 2010 are:

- In addition to the hundreds of questions included in the WileyPLUS courses that are not included in the testbank or textbook, we've added over a dozen additional projects that can be assigned to students.
- Many more animated tutorials, videos, and audio clips to support students as they learn the latest Access 2010 features.

MSDN ACADEMIC ALLIANCE

Free Three-Year Membership Available to Qualified Adopters!

The Microsoft Developer Network Academic Alliance (MSDN AA) is designed to provide the easiest and most inexpensive way for universities to make the latest Microsoft developer tools, products, and technologies available in labs, classrooms, and on student PCs. MSDN AA is an annual membership program for departments teaching Science, Technology, Engineering, and Mathematics (STEM) courses. The membership provides a complete solution to keep academic labs, faculty, and students on the leading edge of technology.

Software available in the MSDN AA program is provided at no charge to adopting departments through the Wiley and Microsoft publishing partnership.

As a bonus to this free offer, faculty will be introduced to Microsoft's Faculty Connection and Academic Resource Center. It takes time and preparation to keep students engaged while giving them a fundamental understanding of theory, and the Microsoft Faculty Connection is designed to help STEM professors with this preparation by providing articles, curriculum, and tools that professors can use to engage and inspire today's technology students.

Contact your Wiley rep for details.

For more information about the MSDN Academic Alliance program, go to: **msdn.microsoft.com/academic/**

IMPORTANT WEB ADDRESSES AND PHONE NUMBERS

To locate the Wiley Higher Education Rep in your area go to www.wiley.com/college, select Instructors under Resources, and click on the Who's My Rep link, or call the MOAC toll-free number: 1 + (888) 764-7001 (U.S. and Canada only).

To learn more about becoming a Microsoft Certified Professional and exam availability, visit www.microsoft.com/learning/mcp.

WHY MOS CERTIFICATION?

Microsoft Office Specialist (MOS) 2010 is a valuable credential that recognizes the desktop computing skills needed to use the full features and functionality of the Microsoft Office 2010 suite.

In the worldwide job market, Microsoft Office Specialist is the primary tool companies use to validate the proficiency of their employees in the latest productivity tools and technology, helping them select job candidates based on globally recognized standards for verifying skills. The results of an independent research study show that businesses with certified employees are more productive compared to non-certified employees and that certified employees bring immediate value to their jobs.

In academia, as in the business world, institutions upgrading to Access 2010 may seek ways to protect and maximize their technology investment. By offering certification, they validate that decision—because powerful Access 2010 applications such as Word, Excel and PowerPoint can be effectively used to demonstrate increases in academic preparedness and workforce readiness.

Individuals seek certification to increase their own personal sense of accomplishment and to create advancement opportunities by establishing a leadership position in their school or department, thereby differentiating their skill sets in a competitive college admissions and job market.

BOOK COMPANION WEBSITE

The students' book companion site for the MOAC series, www.wiley.com/college/microsoft, includes any resources, exercise files, and web links that will be used in conjunction with this course.

WILEY DESKTOP EDITIONS

Wiley MOAC Desktop Editions are innovative, electronic versions of printed textbooks. Students buy the desktop version for 50% off the U.S. price of the printed text and get the added value of permanence and portability. Wiley Desktop Editions provide students with numerous additional benefits that are not available with other e-text solutions.

Wiley Desktop Editions are NOT subscriptions; students download the Wiley Desktop Edition to their computer desktops. Students own the content they buy and keep it for as long as they want. Once a Wiley Desktop Edition is downloaded to the computer desktop, students have instant access to all of the content without being online. Students can also print the sections they prefer to read in hard copy. Students also have access to fully integrated resources within their Wiley Desktop Edition. From highlighting their e-text to taking and sharing notes, students can easily personalize their Wiley Desktop Edition as they are reading or following along in class.

COURSESMART

CourseSmart goes beyond traditional expectations providing instant, online access to the textbooks and course materials you need at a lower cost option. You can save time and hassle with a digital eTextbook that allows you to search for the most relevant content at the very moment you need it. To learn more go to: www.coursesmart.com.

PREPARING TO TAKE THE MICROSOFT OFFICE SPECIALIST (MOS) EXAM

The Microsoft Office Specialist credential has been upgraded to validate skills with the Microsoft Office 2010 system. The MOS certifications target information workers and cover the most popular business applications such as Word 2010, PowerPoint 2010, Excel 2010, Access 2010, and Outlook 2010.

By becoming certified, you demonstrate to employers that you have achieved a predictable level of skill in the use of a particular Office application. Employers often require certification either as a condition of employment or as a condition of advancement within the company or other organization. The certification examinations are sponsored by Microsoft but administered through exam delivery partners like Certiport.

To learn more about becoming a Microsoft Certified Application Specialist and exam availability, visit www.microsoft.com/learning/msbc.

Preparing to Take an Exam

Unless you are a very experienced user, you will need to use a test preparation course to prepare for the test and to complete it correctly and within the time allowed. The *Microsoft Official Academic Course* series is designed to prepare you with a strong knowledge of all exam topics. With some additional review and practice on your own, you should feel confident in your ability to pass the appropriate exam.

After you decide which exam to take, review the list of objectives for the exam. This list can be found in Appendix A at the back of this book. You can also easily identify tasks that are included in the objective list by locating the Lesson Skill Matrix at the start of each lesson and the Certification Ready sidebars in the margin of the lessons in this book.

To take the MOS test, visit http://www.microsoft.com/learning/en/us/certification/mos.aspx to locate your nearest testing center. Then call the testing center directly to schedule your test. The amount of advance notice you should provide will vary for different testing centers, and it typically depends on the number of computers available at the testing center, the number of other testers who have already been scheduled for the day on which you want to take the test, and the number of times per week that the testing center offers MOS testing. In general, you should call to schedule your test at least two weeks prior to the date on which you want to take the test.

When you arrive at the testing center, you might be asked for proof of identity. A driver's license or passport is an acceptable form of identification. If you do not have either of these items of documentation, call your testing center and ask what alternative forms of identification will be accepted. If you are retaking a test, bring your MOS identification number, which will have been given to you when you previously took the test. If you have not prepaid or if your organization has not already arranged to make payment for you, you will need to pay the test-taking fee when you arrive.

Test Format

All MOS certification tests are live, performance-based tests. There are no multiple-choice, true/false, or short-answer questions. Instructions are general: you are told the basic tasks to perform on the computer, but you aren't given any help in figuring out how to perform them. You are not permitted to use reference material other than the application's Help system.

As you complete the tasks stated in a particular test question, the testing software monitors your actions. Following is an example question.

Open the file named *Wiley Guests* and select the word *Welcome* in the first paragraph. Change the font to 12 point, and apply bold formatting. Select the words at *your convenience* in the second paragraph, move them to the end of the first paragraph using drag and drop, and then center the first paragraph.

When the test administrator seats you at a computer, you will see an online form that you use to enter information about yourself (name, address, and other information required to process your exam results). While you complete the form, the software will generate the test from a master test bank and then prompt you to continue. The first test question will appear in a window. Read the question carefully, and then perform all the tasks stated in the test question. When you have finished completing all tasks for a question, click the Next Question button.

You have 45 to 60 minutes to complete all questions, depending on the test that you are taking. The testing software assesses your results as soon as you complete the test, and the test administrator can print the results of the test so that you will have a record of any tasks that you performed incorrectly. A passing grade is 75 percent or higher. If you pass, you will receive a certificate in the mail within two to four weeks. If you do not pass, you can study and practice the skills that you missed and then schedule to retake the test at a later date.

Tips for Successfully Completing the Test

The following tips and suggestions are the result of feedback received from many individuals who have taken one or more MOS tests:

- **Make sure that you are thoroughly prepared**: If you have extensively used the application for which you are being tested, you might feel confident that you are prepared for the test. However, the test might include questions that involve tasks that you rarely or never perform when you use the application at your place of business, at school, or at home. You must be knowledgeable in all the MOS objectives for the test that you will take.

- **Read each exam question carefully**: An exam question might include several tasks that you are to perform. A partially correct response to a test question is counted as an incorrect response. In the example question on the previous page, you might apply bold formatting and move the words at *your convenience* to the correct location, but forget to center the first paragraph. This would count as an incorrect response and would result in a lower test score.

- **Use the Help system only when necessary**: You are allowed to use the application's Help system, but relying on the Help system too much will slow you down and possibly prevent you from completing the test within the allotted time.

- **Keep track of your time**: The test does not display the amount of time that you have left, so you need to keep track of the time yourself by monitoring your start time and the required end time on your watch or a clock in the testing center (if there is one). The test program displays the number of items that you have completed along with the total number of test items (for example, "35 of 40 items have been completed"). Use this information to gauge your pace.

- **You cannot return to a question once you've skipped it**: If you skip a question, you cannot return to it later. You should skip a question only if you are certain that you cannot complete the tasks correctly.

• **Make sure you understand the instructions for each question**: As soon as you are finished reading a question and you click in the application window, a condensed version of the instruction is displayed in a corner of the screen. If you are unsure whether you have completed all tasks stated in the test question, click the Instructions button on the test information bar at the bottom of the screen and then reread the question. Close the instruction window when you are finished. Do this as often as necessary to ensure you have read the question correctly and that you have completed all the tasks stated in the question.

If You Do Not Pass the Test

If you do not pass, you can use the assessment printout as a guide to practice the items that you missed. There is no limit to the number of times that you can retake a test; however, you must pay the fee each time that you take the test. When you retake the test, expect to see some of the same test items on the subsequent test; the test software randomly generates the test items from a master test bank before you begin the test. Also expect to see several questions that did not appear on the previous test.

Office 2010 Professional Six-Month Trial Software (Available in Some Editions)

Some editions of the MOAC Office 2010 series come with six-month trial editions of Office 2010 Professional. If your book included a trial, there would have been a CD glued into the front or back cover of your book. This section pertains only to those editions that came with an Office 2010 Professional trial.

STEP BY STEP Installing the Microsoft Office System 2010 Six-Month Trial

1. Insert the trial software CD-ROM into the CD drive on your computer. The CD will be detected, and the Setup.exe file should automatically begin to run on your computer.
2. When prompted for the Office Product Key, enter the Product Key provided with the software, and then click **Next**.
3. Enter your name and organization user name, and then click **Next**.
4. Read the End-User License Agreement, select the *I Accept the Terms in the License Agreement* check box, and then click **Next**.
5. Select the install option, verify the installation location or click **Browse** to change the installation location, and then click **Next**.
6. Verify the program installation preferences, and then click **Next**.

Click **Finish** to complete the setup.

UPGRADING MICROSOFT OFFICE PROFESSIONAL 2010 SIX-MONTH TRIAL SOFTWARE TO THE FULL PRODUCT

You can convert the software into full use without removing or reinstalling software on your computer. When you complete your trial, you can purchase a product license from any Microsoft reseller and enter a valid Product Key when prompted during setup.

UNINSTALLING THE TRIAL SOFTWARE AND RETURNING TO YOUR PREVIOUS OFFICE VERSION

If you want to return to your previous version of Office, you need to uninstall the trial software. This should be done through the Add or Remove Programs icon in Control Panel (or Uninstall a program in the Control Panel of Windows Vista).

STEP BY STEP Uninstall Trial Software

1. Quit any programs that are running.
2. In Control Panel, click **Programs and Features** (**Add or Remove Programs** in Windows XP).
3. Click **Microsoft Office Professional 2010**, and then click **Uninstall** (**Remove** in Windows XP).

Take Note If you selected the option to remove a previous version of Office during installation of the trial software, you need to reinstall your previous version of Office. If you did not remove your previous version of Office, you can start each of your Office programs either through the Start menu or by opening files for each program. In some cases, you may have to re-create some of your shortcuts and default settings.

STUDENT DATA FILES

All of the practice files that you will use as you perform the exercises in the book are available for download on our student companion site. By using the practice files, you will not waste time creating the samples used in the lessons, and you can concentrate on learning how to use Microsoft Office 2010. With the files and the step-by-step instructions in the lessons, you will learn by doing, which is an easy and effective way to acquire and remember new skills.

Copying the Practice Files

Your instructor might already have copied the practice files before you arrive in class. However, your instructor might ask you to copy the practice files on your own at the start of class. Also, if you want to work through any of the exercises in this book on your own at home or at your place of business after class, you may want to copy the practice files.

STEP BY STEP	Copy the Practice Files

OPEN Internet Explorer.

1. In Internet Explorer, go to the student companion site: www.wiley.com.
2. Search for your book title in the upper-right hand corner.
3. On the Search Results page, locate your book and click on the **Visit the Companion Sites** link.
4. Select **Student Companion Site** from the pop-up box.
5. In the left-hand column, under "Browse by Resource" select **Student Data Files**.
6. Now select **Student Data Files** from the center of the screen.
7. On the File Download dialog box, select **Save** to save the data files to your external drive (often called a ZIP drive or a USB drive or a thumb drive) or a local drive.
8. In the Save As dialog box, select a local drive in the left-hand panel that you'd like to save your files to; again, this should be an external drive or a local drive. Remember the drive name that you saved it to.

Acknowledgments

We'd like to thank the many reviewers who pored over the manuscript, providing invaluable feedback in the service of quality instructional materials.

Access 2010

Tammie Bolling, *Tennessee Technology Center—Jacksboro*
Mary Corcoran, *Bellevue College*
Trish Culp, *triOS College—Business Technology Healthcare*
Jana Hambruch, *Lee County School District*
Aditi Mukherjee, *University of Florida—Gainesville*

Excel 2010

Tammie Bolling, *Tennessee Technology Center—Jacksboro*
Mary Corcoran, *Bellevue College*
Trish Culp, *triOS College—Business Technology Healthcare*
Dee Hobson, *Richland College*
Christie Hovey, *Lincoln Land Community College*
Ralph Phillips, *Central Oregon Community College*
Rajeev Sachdev, *triOS College—Business Technology Healthcare*

Outlook 2010

Mary Harnishfeger, *Ivy Tech State College—Bloomington*
Sandra Miller, *Wenatchee Valley College*
Bob Reeves, *Vincennes University*
Lourdes Sevilla, *Southwestern College—Chula Vista*
Phyllis E. Traylor, *St. Philips College*

PowerPoint 2010

Natasha Carter, *SUNY—ATTAIN*
Dr. Susan Evans Jennings, *Stephen F. Austin State University*
Sue Van Lanen, *Gwinnett Technical College*
Carol J. McPeek, *SUNY—ATTAIN*
Michelle Poertner, *Northwestern Michigan College*
Tim Sylvester, *Glendale Community College (AZ)*

Project 2010

Tatyana Pashnyak, *Bainbridge College*
Debi Griggs, *Bellevue College*

Word 2010

Portia Hatfield, *Tennessee Technology Center—Jacksboro*
Terri Holly, *Indian River State College*
Pat McMahon, *South Suburban College*
Barb Purvis, *Centura College*
Janet Sebesy, *Cuyahoga Community College*

We would also like to thank Lutz Ziob, Jason Bunge, Ben Watson, David Bramble, Merrick Van Dongen, Don Field, Pablo Bernal, Colin Klein, and Wendy Johnson at Microsoft for their encouragement and support in making the Microsoft Official Academic Course program the finest instructional materials for mastering the newest Microsoft technologies for both students and instructors. Finally, we would like to thank Lorna Gentry of Content LLC for development editing and Jeff Riley and his team at Box Twelve Communications for technical editing.

About the Author

KEITH HOELL

Keith Hoell is a professor and Chair of Business and Technology at Briarcliffe College in Long Island, New York. An experienced academic technology professional, he has served as an instructor, dean, and technology consultant for several schools. He has a broad range of experience in various areas of technology, including database management, network administration, and Internet technologies. He also served on the Microsoft Official Academic Curriculum (MOAC) Advisory Board and helped develop other MOAC textbooks.

Besides his interest in technology, he is also an avid runner, having run in several marathons including New York and Boston.

Brief Contents

Contents

1 Database Essentials   1

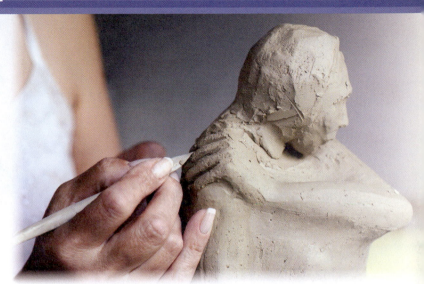

2 Create Database Tables 30

3 Work with Tables and Database Records 49

4 Modify Tables and Fields 78

5   Create Forms   107

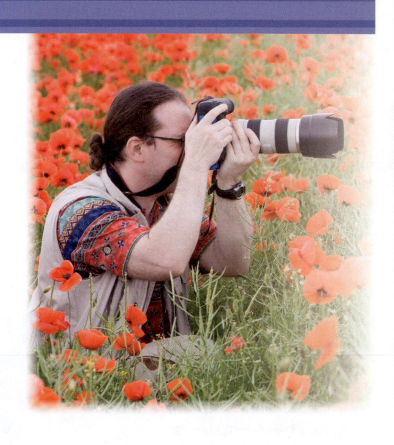

6   Create Reports   134

7   Create and Modify Queries   155

8 Use Controls in Reports and Forms 183

9 Advanced Tables 224

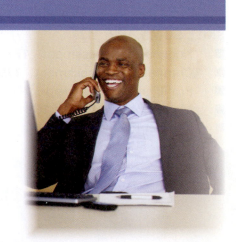

www.wiley.com/college/microsoft
or call the MOAC Toll-Free Number: 1+(888) 764-7001 (U.S. & Canada only)

12   Advanced Queries   286

13 Display and Share Data 325

14 Import and Export Data 350

www.wiley.com/college/microsoft
or call the MOAC Toll-Free Number: 1+(888) 764-7001 (U.S. & Canada only)

15   Database Tools   382

LESSON SKILL MATRIX

Skill	Exam Objective	Objective Number
Getting Started	Use Open.	**1.1.2**
Working in the Access Window	Set Navigation options.	**1.2.3**
Using the On-Screen Tools		
Using the Backstage View		
Using the Microsoft Office Access Help Button		
Defining Data Needs and Types	Modify data types.	**2.2.6**

KEY TERMS

- **Backstage view**
- **badges**
- **Connection Status menu**
- **database**
- **database management system (DBMS)**
- **datasheet**
- **data type**
- **desktop**
- **dialog box launcher**
- **field**
- **File tab**
- **form**
- **groups**
- **KeyTip**
- **normal forms**
- **normalization**
- **objects**
- **primary key**
- **query**
- **Quick Access Toolbar**
- **record**
- **redundant data**
- **relational database**
- **report**
- **Ribbon**
- **tab**
- **table**

The School of Fine Art in Poughkeepsie, New York, is the brainchild of two profes-sional artists—Shaun Beasley, a printmaker, and Jane Clayton, a sculptor. Last year, the new private high school opened with an enrollment of 12 students and with Jane and Shaun as the only full-time instructors. All academic and busi-ness records were maintained manually by the founders. This year, however, you were hired as an executive assistant to help them manage an increasing amount of information. Enrollment is climbing, new full-time faculty members are being hired, and the school is receiving scholarship funds from local patrons. With the help of an Access database, you will organize the school's academic and business data. In this lesson, you will learn basic database concepts and how to define data needs and types.

SOFTWARE ORIENTATION

Microsoft Access' Opening Screen

Before you begin working in Microsoft Access, you need to be familiar with the primary user interface. In the next section, you will be asked to open a new blank database in Access. When you do so, a screen appears that is similar to the one shown in Figure 1-1.

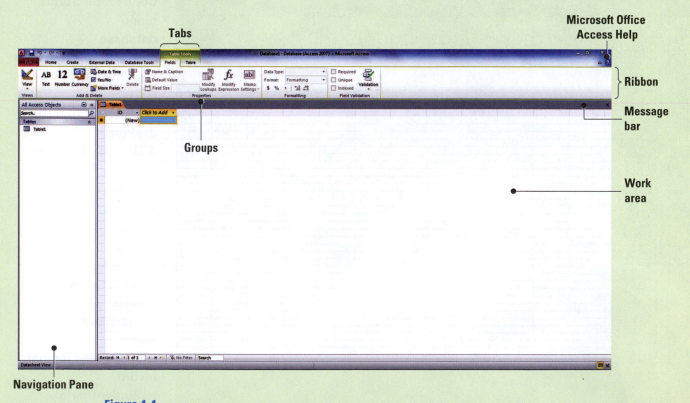

Figure 1-1

Opening screen for new blank Access database

When you create a blank database in Microsoft Access, the opening screen provides you with a workspace in which to build a database. Understanding the screen elements helps orient you to important tools and information. The elements and features of your screen may vary if default settings have been changed or if other preferences have been set. Use Figure 1-1 as a reference throughout this lesson as well as the rest of this book.

GETTING STARTED

The Bottom Line

A **database** is a tool for collecting and organizing information. For example, as a database, a phone book organizes a large amount of data—names, addresses, and phone numbers—so you can access it by name in alphabetic order. Even a grocery list is a simple type of database. A computerized **database management system (DBMS)**, such as Microsoft Office Access, enables you to easily collect large volumes of data organized into categories of related information. This type of database allows you to store, organize, and manage your data, no matter how complex it is, and then retrieve and present it in various formats and reports. As with any program, however, the first tasks are the most basic. This section shows you how to start Access and open an existing database.

Starting Access

The **Backstage view** appears when you start Access. From here, you can create a new blank database, create a database from a template, or open a recent database (if you have already created one). You can also access Microsoft Office Online for featured content and more information about the 2010 Microsoft Office system and Office Access 2010. In this exercise, you learn to start Access from the Microsoft Office menu.

 Ref

You learn to use Backstage view in a later section of this lesson.

STEP BY STEP   **Start Access**

GET READY. Before you begin these steps, be sure to turn on and/or log on to your computer.

1. On the Windows taskbar, click the **Start button** and click **All Programs**. A menu of installed programs appears.
2. Click **Microsoft Office**. Another menu appears as shown in Figure 1-2.

Figure 1-2

Start button and Microsoft Office menu

Microsoft
Office menu

Start button

3. Click **Microsoft Access 2010**. Access opens displaying the Backstage view, as shown in Figure 1-3.

Search Office.com for templates

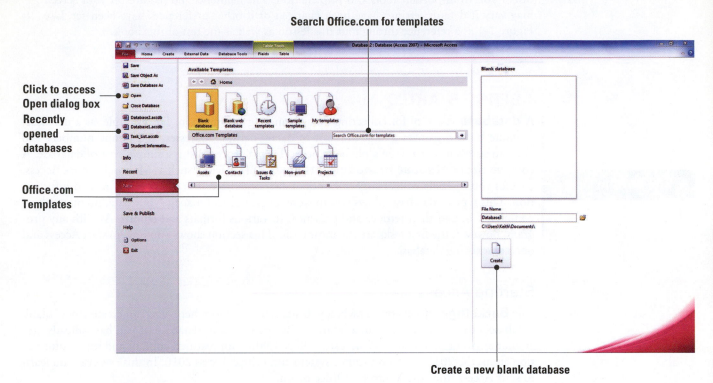

Click to access Open dialog box

Recently opened databases

Office.com Templates

Create a new blank database

Figure 1-3

Backstage view

PAUSE. LEAVE Microsoft Access open to use in the next exercise.

Another Way
When Office was installed on your computer, a shortcut icon might have been added to the Start menu or to your **desktop**—the screen you see when you start Windows. Click the shortcut to start Access without having to go through the Start menu.

Opening an Existing Database

When you open an existing database, you access not only your previously entered and saved data, but also the elements you created to organize that data. In this exercise, you open a database that is in the beginning stages of development.

The Open command displays the Open dialog box used to find and open files wherever they may be located—on the desktop, in a folder on your computer, on a network drive, or on a CD or other removable media. The Look in box lists the available locations, such as a folder, drive, or Internet location. Click the location, and the folders will be displayed in the folder list. From this list, you can double-click the folder you want to open. When you find the file you want, double-click the filename to open it or click it once to select it and then click the Open button.

STEP BY STEP   **Open an Existing Database**

GET READY. The blank database in Backstage view should be on the screen from the previous exercise.

1. Click the **Open** command on the left side of the Backstage View screen. The Open dialog box appears, as shown in Figure 1-4.

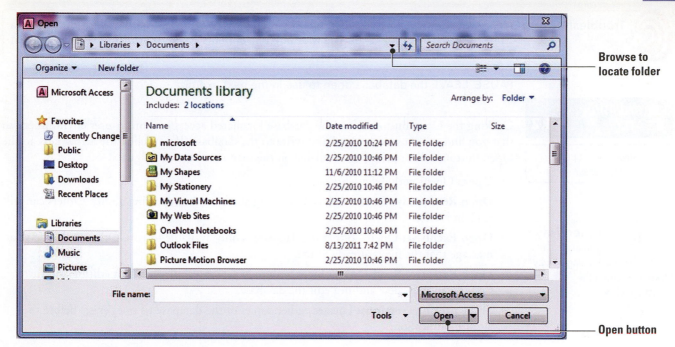

Figure 1-4

Open dialog box

Take Note

Another Way
Press Ctrl+O to display the Open dialog box.

@ The *Student Information* file for this lesson is available on the book companion website or in WileyPLUS.

If the database you want to use is listed under the Close Database command on the left panel of the Backstage view, simply click to open it.

2. Navigate to the data files for this lesson and select *Student Information*.
3. Click the **Open** button in the Open dialog box, as shown in Figure 1-4. The existing database opens, as shown in Figure 1-5.

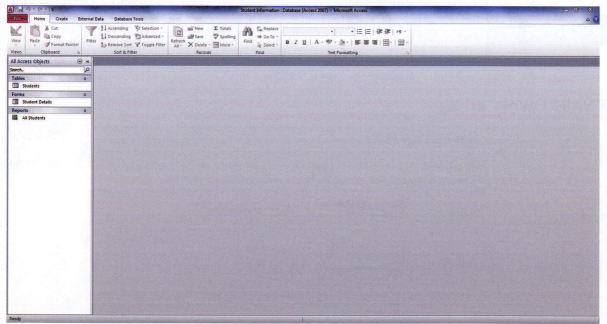

Figure 1-5

Existing database open in Access

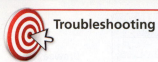

Troubleshooting As part of the Office Access 2010 security model, when you open a database outside of a trusted location, a tool called the Message Bar appears to warn you that certain content has been disabled. If you know you can trust the database, click Enable Content.

PAUSE. LEAVE the database open to use in the next exercise.

CERTIFICATION
R E A D Y   **1.1.2**

How do you open databases?

Clicking the Open button opens the database for shared access in a multi-user environment so that you and other users can read and write to the database. If you click the arrow next to the Open button, other options are available on the menu as shown in Figure 1-6:

- **Open:** Opens with default access.
- **Open Read-Only:** Opens with only viewing ability and not editing ability. Others can still read and write.
- **Open Exclusive:** Opens so that the database is only available to you. Others will receive a message that the file is already in use.
- **Open Exclusive Read-Only:** Opens with only viewing ability and not editing ability. Others can only view and not edit the database.
- **Show previous versions:** Locates earlier copies of the database (if ones exist) before the latest modification.

Another Way
You can also display the Open dialog box by clicking Recent in the Backstage view.

Figure 1-6

Open button menu

Take Note

Each time you start Access, you open a new instance of Access. You can only have one database open at a time in a single instance of Access. In other words, you cannot start Access, open one database, and then open another database without closing the first database. However, you can open multiple databases at the same time by opening another instance of Access. For example, to have two Access databases open, start Access and open the first Access database, and then start a new instance of Access and open the second database.

WORKING IN THE ACCESS WINDOW

The Bottom Line

The Access 2010 Window user interface was designed to help you find the commands you need quickly so that you can successfully perform your tasks. You will start using the Navigation Pane and exploring the Ribbon across the top right away. Also in this lesson, you will practice using other on-screen tools and features, such as the Backstage view and Access Help.

SOFTWARE ORIENTATION

Navigation Pane

By default, the Navigation Pane, shown in Figure 1-7, appears on the left side of the Access screen each time you create or open a database.

Figure 1-7

Navigation Pane

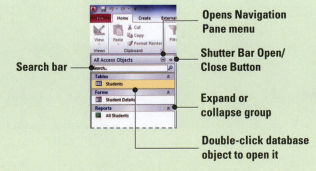

The Navigation Pane enables you to open, copy, and delete tables and other database **objects**. It also lists all the objects in your database, including: **tables**—the most basic database object that stores data in categories; **queries**—allow you to search and retrieve the data you have stored; **forms**—control data entry and data views, and provide visual cues that make data easier to work with; and **reports**—present your information in ways that are most useful to you. You learn more about managing database objects such as forms, queries, and reports in later lessons of this book. For now, just familiarize yourself with the Navigation Pane. Use Figure 1-7 as a reference throughout this lesson as well as the rest of this book.

CERTIFICATION READY 1.2.3

How do you set navigation options?

Using the Navigation Pane

Before you can create a database, you need to understand its most basic elements. This section introduces you to some of the elements in a database that help you organize data and navigate using the Navigation Pane, object tabs, and different views.

STEP BY STEP   **Use the Navigation Pane**

USE the database from the previous exercise.

1. In the Navigation Pane, double-click **Students** to display the table in the Access work area, as shown in Figure 1-8.

Double-click object in Navigation Pane to display it in the work area

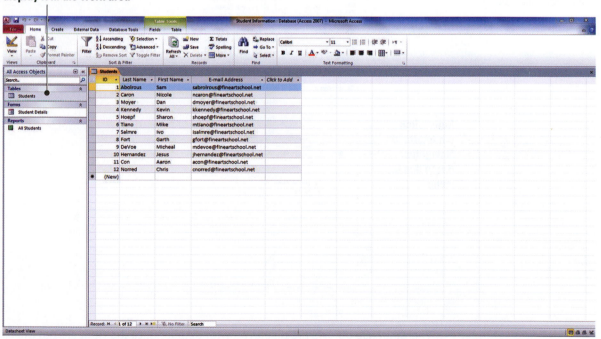

Figure 1-8

Table open in Access work area

Take Note   The Navigation Pane replaces an older tool, the Database window, which appeared in earlier versions of Access.

2. Click the **down arrow** next to All Access Objects at the top of the Navigation Pane to display the menu, as shown in Figure 1-9.

Figure 1-9

Navigation Pane menu

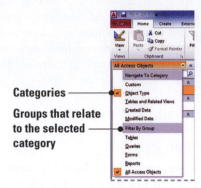

Categories ──────

Groups that relate to the selected ────── category

3. Click **Tables and Related Views**. The default group in this category is All Tables, which appears in the menu at the top of the Navigation Pane. Notice the Students table and all other objects related to it are displayed under the Students header.

4. Click the **down arrow** next to All Tables at the top of the Navigation Pane to display the menu again, and click **Object Type** to return to the original view.

5. Right-click in the white area of the Navigation Pane to display a shortcut menu. Click **View By** and then **Details**, as shown in Figure 1-10.

Figure 1-10

Navigation Pane shortcut menu

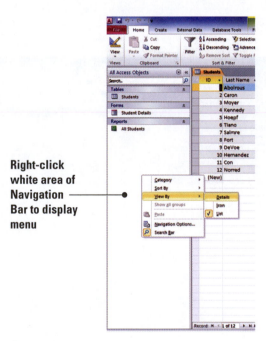

Right-click white area of Navigation ────── Bar to display menu

6. The database objects are displayed with details. Click the right side of the Navigation Pane and drag to make it wider so all the information can be read, as shown in Figure 1-11.

Figure 1-11

Widen the Navigation Pane

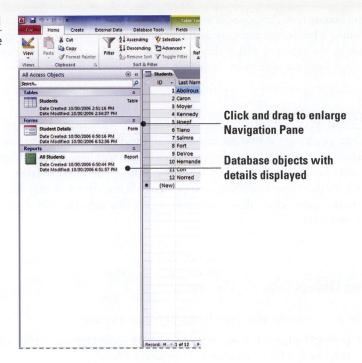

Click and drag to enlarge Navigation Pane

Database objects with details displayed

7. If the search bar does not appear at the top of the Navigation Pane, right-click on the **Tables** header of the Navigation Pane. On the shortcut menu, click **Search Bar**. A search bar is now displayed at the top of the Navigation Pane. You can toggle the search bar display by clicking the Search Bar option.

8. Display the Navigation Pane shortcut menu, click **View By** and then **List** to display the database objects in a list.

9. Click the **Shutter Bar Open/Close Button** to collapse the Navigation Pane. Notice it is not entirely hidden, as shown in Figure 1-12.

Figure 1-12

Navigation Pane collapsed

Navigation Pane collapsed

10. Click the **Shutter Bar Open/Close Button** to expand the Navigation Pane again.

PAUSE. LEAVE the database open to use in the next exercise.

The Navigation Pane divides your database objects into categories, and those categories contain groups. The default category is Tables and Related Views, which groups the objects in a database by the tables to which they are related. You can change the category to Object Type, which groups database objects by their type—tables, forms, reports, and so on.

Using Object Tabs

When you create a database in Access, all the objects in that database—including forms, tables, reports, and queries—are displayed in a single window separated by tabs. Tabs help keep open objects visible and accessible. To move among the open objects, click a tab. To close a tab, click its Close button. You can also right-click a tab to display the shortcut menu where you can save, close, close all, or switch views. In this exercise, you practice opening and displaying object tabs.

STEP BY STEP	Use Object Tabs

USE the database you used in the previous exercise.

1. In the Navigation Pane, double-click **Student Details**. A new object tab opens to display the form, as shown in Figure 1-13.

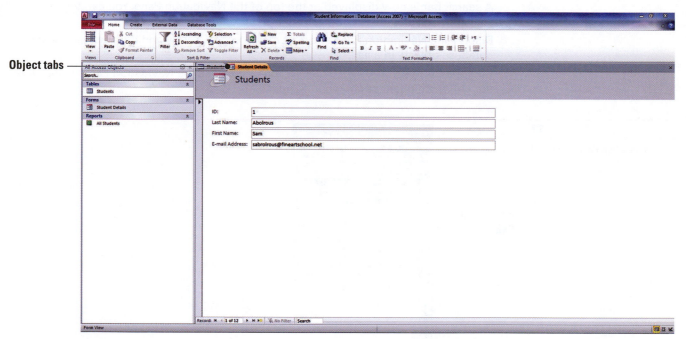

Figure 1-13

Tab with form

2. In the Navigation Pane, double-click **All Students**. A new object tab opens to display the report, as shown in Figure 1-14.

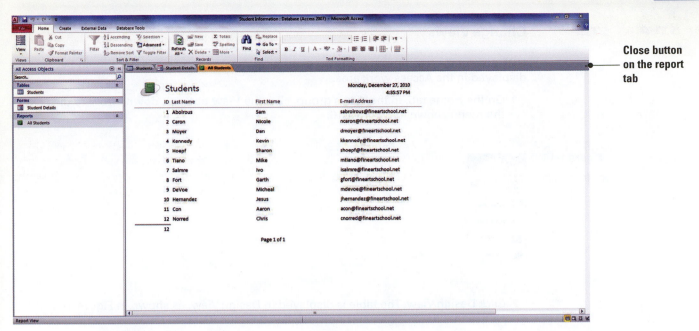

Close button
on the report
tab

Figure 1-14

Tab with report

3. Click the **Close** button on the Report tab to close it.

4. Right-click the **Student Details** tab to display the shortcut menu shown in Figure 1-15.

Figure 1-15

Tab shortcut menu

Right-click tab to display shortcut menu

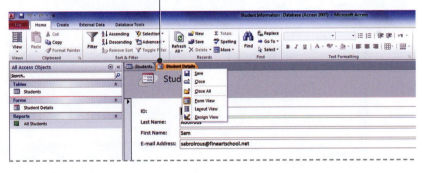

5. Click **Close** to close the form.

PAUSE. LEAVE the database open to use in the next exercise.

Changing Views

Each database object can be viewed several different ways. The main views for a table are Datasheet View and Design View. Datasheet View can be used to perform most table design tasks, so you will probably use it most often. A **datasheet** is the visual representation of the data contained in a table or of the results returned by a query. A query is simply a question you can ask a table or another query.

To change the view, click the View button's down arrow and then choose a view from the menu. When you change views, the commands available on the **Ribbon** change to match the tasks you will be performing in that view. You learn more about the Ribbon in the next section.

Change Views

USE the database you used in the previous exercise. The Students table should be displayed in the Access work area.

1. On the Home tab, in the Views group, click the **View button's down arrow** to display the menu shown in Figure 1-16.

Figure 1-16

View menu for a table

2. Click **Design View**. The table is displayed in Design View, as shown in Figure 1-17. Notice that the Design tab is now displayed on the Ribbon.

Contextual design commands

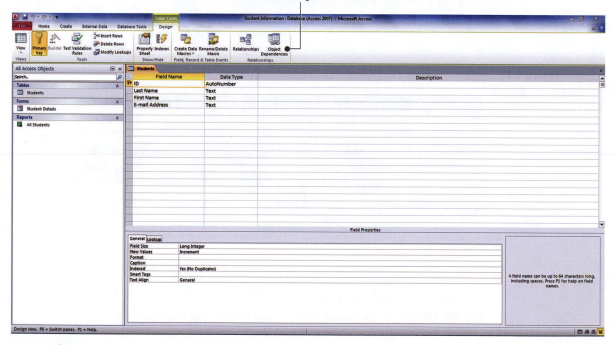

Figure 1-17

Table in Design View

3. On the Design tab, in the Views group, click the **View button's down arrow**, and then click **Datasheet View**.

4. Click the **Fields** tab under the Table Tools tab on the Ribbon to display the contextual commands for that view, as shown in Figure 1-18.

Contextual datasheet commands

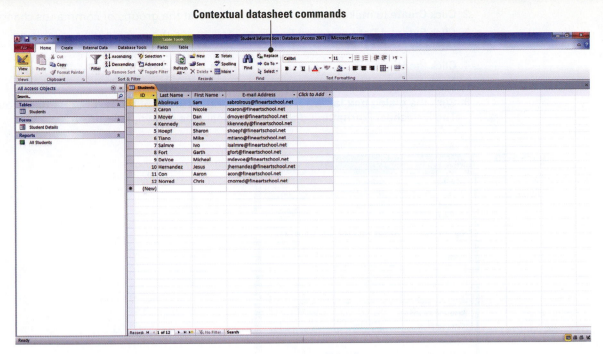

Figure 1-18

Table in Datasheet View

PAUSE. LEAVE the database open to use in the next exercise.

USING THE ON-SCREEN TOOLS

Access has many tools to help with your database needs. In this section, you explore the Ribbon, which displays common commands in **groups** arranged by tabs. You'll also learn about other on-screen tools to help you get your work done faster, such as the **Quick Access Toolbar** and KeyTips.

The Bottom Line

Using the Ribbon

The Ribbon is located across the top of the screen and contains tabs and groups of commands. It is divided into five tabs, or areas of activity. Each tab contains groups of related commands. The Ribbon is contextual, which means it offers you commands related to the object that you are working on or the task that you are performing.

Some groups have a **dialog box launcher**, which is a small arrow in the lower-right corner of the group that you click to launch a dialog box that displays additional options or information. Some commands on the Ribbon have small arrows pointing down. These arrows indicate that a menu is available that lists more options from which you can choose.

In the next exercise you practice using the Ribbon.

STEP BY STEP **Use the Ribbon**

USE the database you used in the previous exercise.

1. Click the **Home** tab to make it active. As shown in Figure 1-19, the Ribbon is divided into groups of commands.

Figure 1-19

The Ribbon

2. Click **Create** to make it the active tab. Notice that the groups of commands change.

3. Click **External Data** and then **Database Tools** to see the commands available on those tabs.

4. Click the **Home** tab.

5. Click the **ID** column header to select it.

6. Click the **dialog box launcher** in the lower-right corner of the Text Formatting group. The Datasheet Formatting dialog box appears, as shown in Figure 1-20.

Figure 1-20

Datasheet formatting dialog box

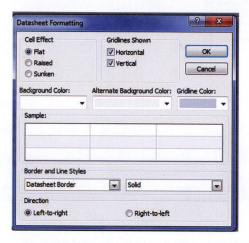

7. Click **Cancel** to close the dialog box.

8. Double-click the **Home** tab. Notice the groups are hidden to give you more screen space to work with your database.

9. Double-click **Home** again to display the groups.

PAUSE. LEAVE the database open to use in the next exercise.

NEW to Office 2010

New to Access 2010 is the ability to customize the Ribbon to have greater control over the commands that appear on it by turning off tabs and groups you rarely use, moving and/or duplicating groups from one tab to another, creating custom groups, and even creating custom tabs.

Using the Quick Access Toolbar

The Quick Access Toolbar contains the commands that you use most often, such as Save, Undo, and Redo.

Located on the Quick Access Toolbar is the Customize Quick Access Toolbar button that presents you with a menu that allows you to quickly add commonly used commands to the Quick Access Toolbar, as shown in Figure 1-21. You can also use this menu to choose an option to show the Quick Access Toolbar above or below the Ribbon, or click the More Commands button to open the Customize screen in the Access Options dialog box, as shown in Figure 1-22.

Figure 1-21

Customize Quick Access Toolbar menu

Customize Quick Access Toolbar button and menu

Figure 1-22

Customize the Quick Access
Toolbar screen of the Access
Options dialog box

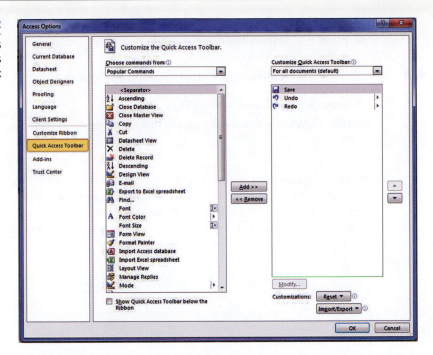

Use this dialog box to customize the Quick Access Toolbar by adding buttons from a greater variety of commands that you need the most so they are always just one click away.

In this exercise, you use the Customize Quick Access Toolbar menu to place the toolbar below the Ribbon.

Use the Quick Access Toolbar

USE the database you used in the previous exercise.

1. On the Quick Access Toolbar, click the **Customize Quick Access Toolbar** button. A menu appears.
2. Click **Show Below the Ribbon**. The toolbar is moved.
3. Click the **Customize Quick Access Toolbar** button again. Click **Show Above the Ribbon**.

PAUSE. LEAVE the database open to use in the next exercise.

Using KeyTips

When you press the Alt key, small letters and numbers called **KeyTips** appear on the Ribbon in small square labels, called **badges**. To execute a command using KeyTips, press the Alt key then press the KeyTip or sequence of KeyTips that corresponds to the command you want to use. Every command on the Ribbon has a KeyTip. You display KeyTips in the next exercise.

Use KeyTips

USE the database you used in the previous exercise.

1. Press **Alt**. Letters and numbers appear on the Ribbon to let you know which key to use to access commands or tabs. See Figure 1-23.

KeyTips

Figure 1-23

KeyTips

2. Press **C** to activate the Create tab.

3. Press **P** to display the Application Parts menu.

 Ref   You learn more about Application Parts in Lessons 2 and 10.

4. Press **Alt** to remove the KeyTips.

PAUSE. LEAVE the database open to use in the next exercise.

Take Note   Shortcut keys are keys or combinations of keys pressed together to perform a command. Shortcut keys provide a quick way to give commands without having to move your hands off the keyboard and reach for a mouse. Keyboard shortcuts from previous versions of Access that begin with Ctrl are the same. However, those that begin with Alt are different and require the use of KeyTips.

SOFTWARE ORIENTATION

Introducing the Backstage View

NEW to Office 2010

In Office 2010, Microsoft introduces the Backstage view. The Backstage view is on the File **tab** and contains many of the commands that were on the File menu in previous versions of Microsoft Access. The Backstage view enables you to do things to a database file including creating a new database, creating a database from a template, opening an existing database, and performing many database maintenance tasks. The Backstage view is the default view when you first open Microsoft Access. See Figure 1-24.

Search Office.com for templates

Click to access Open dialog box
Recently opened databases

Office.com Templates

Create a new blank database

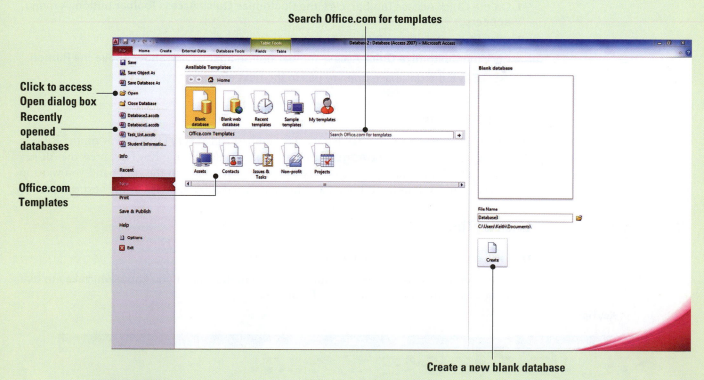

Figure 1-24

Backstage view

USING THE BACKSTAGE VIEW

The **File tab** on the Ribbon accesses the Backstage view—a menu of commands that you use for the common tasks performed with your database files—such as opening, saving, and printing. It also contains commands for managing and publishing your database.

Using the Backstage View

The File tab opens the Backstage view (Figure 1-24), a menu of basic commands and tabs for opening, saving, and printing files, as well as more advanced options. You can click commands to view related dialog boxes, as well as tabs to view more options within the Backstage view window.

The following is an overview of the commands and tabs in the Backstage view:

- **Save Object As:** Save the current object (such as a table, query, form, or report) as a new object.
- **Save Database As:** Save the current database object as a new object or save the database in another format that is compatible with earlier versions of Access.
- **Open:** Open an existing database.
- **Close Database:** Close the open database.
- **Info:** Compact and repair the database and encrypt the database with a password to restrict access.
- **Recent:** View a list of recently accessed databases.
- **New:** Create a new database from scratch or from available templates.
- **Print:** Quick print straight to the printer, open a dialog box from which to choose print options, or preview your document before printing.
- **Save & Publish:** Save the database to a document management server for sharing, or package the database and apply a digital signature.
- **Help:** View Microsoft Office support resources, the Options menu, and check for updates.
- **Options:** View the Options menu to customize language, display, and other settings.
- **Exit:** Exit the Access application.

You practice using the Backstage view in the next exercise.

Use the Backstage View

1. **USE** the database you used in the previous exercise.

   Click the **File** tab. Backstage view opens, displaying a menu of commands and tabs down the left side of the window, as shown in Figure 1-25.

Print command used to view print options

Save & Publish command used to save databases and objects and publish to Access services

Figure 1-25

Backstage view's Print and Save & Publish commands

2. Click the **Save & Publish** command to view the options available.

3. Click the **Print** command to view more options.

4. Click the **File** tab again to remove the menu.

PAUSE. LEAVE the database open to use in the next exercise.

USING THE MICROSOFT OFFICE ACCESS HELP BUTTON

The Bottom Line

If you have questions, Microsoft Access Help has answers. In fact, you can choose whether you want to use the help topics on your computer that were installed with Office, or if you are connected to the Internet, you can choose to use the help that is available online. Either way, you can key in search words, browse help topics, or choose a topic from the Table of Contents to get your answers. In this exercise, you use the Help button to access the Help information installed on your computer with Access 2010.

Using the Help Button and Connection Status Command

The **Connection Status menu** in the lower-right corner of Access Help lets you choose between the help topics that are available online and the help topics installed in your computer offline. If you are usually connected to the Internet, you might prefer to set the Connection Status to Show content from Office Online to get the most updated help available. But there may be times when you can't or don't want to be online; in those instances you can choose Show content only from this computer to get offline help topics. You practice using Access Help and the Connection Status menu in the next exercise.

STEP BY STEP   **Use the Help Button and Connection Status Command**

Take Note   When you rest the mouse pointer over a command on the Ribbon, a ScreenTip appears displaying the name of the command. Access 2010 also has Enhanced ScreenTips, which give more information about the command, as well as a Help button you can click to get more help.

USE the database you used in the previous exercise.

1. Click the **Microsoft Office Access Help** button. 🔘 The Access Help dialog box appears, as shown in Figure 1-26. Notice the Search button and Search menu button. The Search menu is used to specify the scope of topics you want to search, such as All Access, Access Templates, Access Training, and so on. Also notice the Connection Status command in the lower-right corner indicates that Access is set to Connected to Office Online to search online for help topics. If your Connection Status is set to Offline, the screen will look different.

Figure 1-26

Access Help dialog box when connected to Office online

Search button

Connection Status command

2. Click the **Connection Status** button. A menu appears, as shown in Figure 1-27.

Figure 1-27

Access Help dialog box and
Connection Status menu

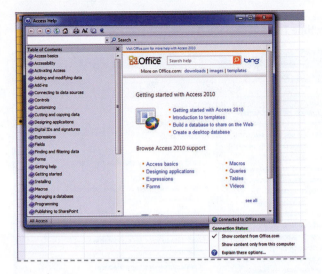

3. Click **Show content only from this computer**. Access Help appears, as shown in Figure 1-28.

Figure 1-28

Access Help dialog box
when Offline

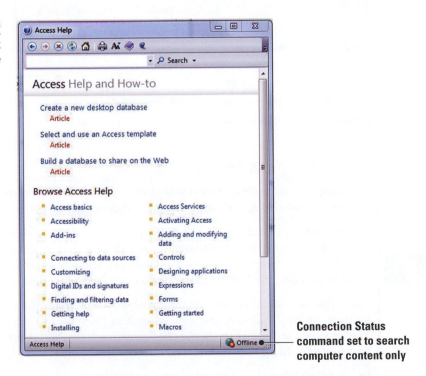

**Connection Status
command set to search
computer content only**

4. Key **ribbon** in the text box and click **Search**. A list of possible topics appears.

5. Click the **Customize the Ribbon** link in the search results that appear. The help topic appears.

6. Click the **Show Table of Contents** button 📖. The Table of Contents pane appears.

7. Click the **Getting started** option in the Table of Contents pane to expand it and then click the **What's new in Microsoft Access** link. The text for the topic appears in the window.

8. Click the **Home** button  and then the **Access basics** link that appears. The text for the topic appears in the window, as shown in Figure 1-29.

Figure 1-29

Access Help with Table of Contents and topics displayed

Show/Hide Table of Contents button

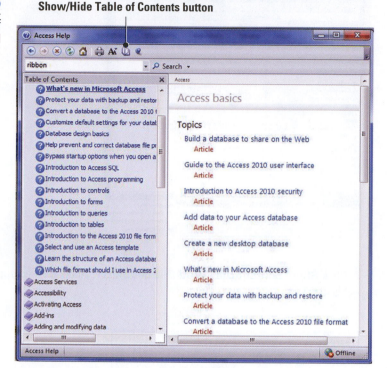

Another Way
The Access Help button is positioned in some dialog boxes and ScreenTips for quick access to context-related help. Click it wherever you see it to launch Access Help.

9. Click the **Home** button.

10. Click the **Close** button to close Microsoft Access Help.

STOP. CLOSE the database.

DEFINING DATA NEEDS AND TYPES

The Bottom Line

To create a database that achieves your goals and provides you with up-to-date, accurate information, you need to spend time planning and designing it.

When planning a database, the first step is to consider the purpose of your database. You need to design the database so that it accommodates all your data processing and reporting needs. You should gather and organize all the information that you want to include, starting with any existing forms or lists, and think about the reports and mailings you might want to create using the data.

Once you have decided how the information will be used, the next step is to categorize the information by dividing it into subjects such as Products or Orders, which become the tables in your database. Each table should only contain information that relates to that subject. If you find yourself adding extra information, create a new table.

In a database table, data is stored in rows and columns—similar in appearance to a spreadsheet. Each row in a table is called a **record**. Each column in a table is called a **field**. For example, if a table is named "Student List," each record (row) contains information about a different student and each field (column) contains a different type of information, such as last name or email address.

To create the columns within the table, you then need to determine what information you want to store in the table—such as Color, Year, or Cost. Break each piece of information into the smallest useful part—for example, use First Name and Last Name instead of just Name if you want to sort, search, calculate, or report using the separate pieces of information.

For each table, you will choose a primary key. A **primary key** is a column that uniquely identifies each row, such as Item Number.

Defining Table Fields

To define table fields, you establish which data needs to be stored in the table. Planning is an important part of creating a database. In this exercise, you open a database that is further along in the process of being developed to see what a more advanced database looks like.

Define Table Fields

 The *Student Data* file for this lesson is available on the book companion website or in WileyPLUS.

OPEN the *Student Data* database from the data files for this lesson.

1. On the Student List form, click the **ID** for record 5 to display the Student Details dialog box for Sharon Hoepf, as shown in Figure 1-30.

Figure 1-30

Student Details

WileyPLUS Extra! features an online tutorial of this task.

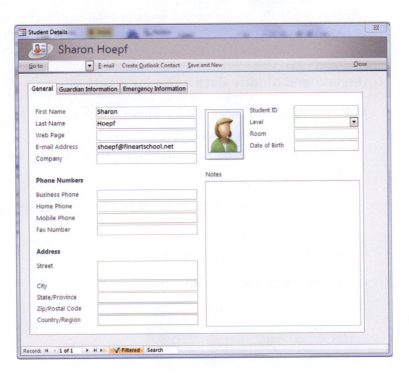

2. Click the **Guardian Information** tab and then the **Emergency Information** tab. Each of the fields on these tabs is an example of the type of information that could be contained in a database table.

3. Click **Close** to close the Student Details dialog box.

PAUSE. LEAVE the database open to use in the next exercise.

(X) Ref   You learn more about defining and modifying a primary key in Lesson 3.

Defining and Modifying Data Types for Fields

When designing the database, you set a **data type** for each field (column) that you create to match the information it will store. A data type controls the type of data a field will contain—whether it is text, number, date/time, or some other type. When defining table fields, it is important to define them as specifically as possible. For example, if you are using a number, you should determine whether you need to use the Currency or Number data type. Or, if you need to store large amounts of text, you may need to use the Memo data type instead of Text. Sometimes you may also need to modify data types for preexisting fields. In this exercise, you practice reviewing and modifying data types.

When you create a new field in a table and then enter data in it, Office Access 2010 automatically tries to detect the appropriate data type for the new column. For example, if you key a price, such as $10, Access recognizes the data as a price, and sets the data type for the field to Currency. If Access doesn't have enough information from what you enter to guess the data type, the data type is set to Text.

NEW to Office 2010

New to Access 2010 is the calculated data type. The calculated data type creates a new field that can store formulas and expressions, which can perform logical, text, or mathematical calculations on existing fields within the same table and make it easy to add the calculated field to a form, query, or report. For example, you can easily create a calculated field named *FullName* that concatenates the *First Name* and *Last Name* fields into one string. Then, the *FullName* field can easily be added to a form, query, or report without having to create a new expression within the object.

Take Note   Most database management systems can store only a single value in a field, but with Microsoft Office Access 2010, you can create a field that holds multiple values, which may be appropriate in certain situations.

STEP BY STEP   **Review and Modify Data Types for Fields**

USE the database you used in the previous exercise.

1. Close the **Student List** form.
2. In the Navigation Pane, in the Supporting Objects group, double-click the **Students** table to open it.
3. Click the **Date of Birth** field header.
4. On the Ribbon, click the **Fields** tab. Notice in the Formatting group that the Data Type is Date/Time.
5. Click the **down arrow** in the Format box to display the menu of formatting options for that type, as shown in Figure 1-31.

Figure 1-31

Format options for Date/Time data type

CERTIFICATION READY   2.2.6

How do you modify data types?

6. Click the **Last Name** header. Notice that the Data Type is Text and that no formatting options are available for that data type.
7. Scroll to the right and click the **Address** header.
8. In the Data Type box, click the **down arrow** and click **Text** to modify the data type. When a warning message appears, click **Yes**.

Take Note   Be aware that changing a data type might cut off some or all of the data in a field, and in some cases may remove the data entirely.

9. Scroll to the far right and click the **Click to Add** [Click to Add ▾] **column header**. In the Data Type box, click **Yes/No**.
10. Click the **down arrow** in the Format box to display the menu of formatting options for the Yes/No data type, as shown in Figure 1-32.

Figure 1-32

Format options for Yes/No data type

11. Click outside the menu to close it.

PAUSE. LEAVE the database open to use in the next exercise.

Access provides eleven different data types, each with its own purpose. The list in Table 1-1 describes the types of data that each field can be set to store.

Table 1-1

Types of data stored in fields

Data Type	Example	Description
Text	Last Name: Zimmerman Street: 6789 Walker Street	The most common data type for fields. Can store up to 255 characters of text, numbers, or a combination of both.
Memo	Comments: Student will make monthly payments on the 15th of each month of $247.	Stores large amounts of text—up to 64,000 characters of text, numbers, or a combination (although if you use that much space, your database will run slowly).
Number	Age: 19	Stores numeric data that can be used in mathematical calculations.
Date/Time	Birthday: December 1, 1987	Stores date and/or time data.
Currency	Registration Fee: $50.00	Stores monetary data with precision to four decimal places. Use this data type to store financial data and when you don't want Access to round values.
AutoNumber	Student ID: 56	Unique values created by Access when you create a new record. Tables often contain an *AutoNumber* field used as the primary key.
Yes/No	Insurance: Yes	Stores Boolean (true or false) data. Access uses 1 for all Yes values and 0 for all No values.
OLE Object	Photo	Stores images, documents, graphs, and other objects from Office and Windows-based programs.
Hyperlink	Web addresses	Stores links to websites, sites or files on an intranet or Local Area Network (LAN), and sites or files on your computer.
Attachment	Any supported type of file	You can attach images, spreadsheet files, documents, charts, and other types of supported files to the records in your database, much like you attach files to email messages.
Calculated	FullName: John Derenzo	Stores an expression based on two or more fields within the same table.

Take Note   The Number data type should only be used if the numbers will be used in mathematical calculations. For numbers such as phone numbers, use the Text data type.

 Ref   You learn more about multivalued fields in Lesson 4.

Defining Database Tables

Tables are the most basic organizational element of a database. Not only is it important to plan the tables to hold the type of data you need, but also to plan how the tables and information will be connected.

STEP BY STEP   **Define Database Tables**

USE the database you used in the previous exercise.

1. On the Database Tools tab, in the Relationships section, click **Relationship** to display a visual representation of the relationship between the Students and Guardians tables, as shown in Figure 1-33.

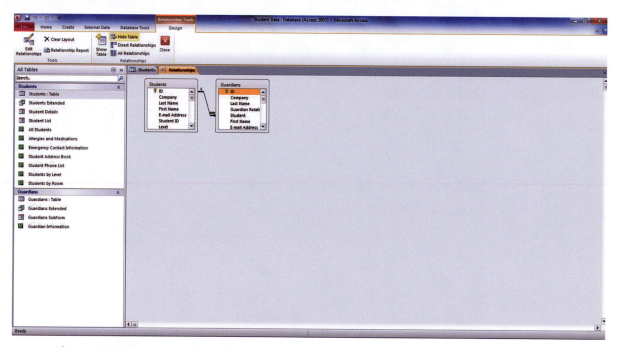

Figure 1-33

Relationship between tables

2. Close the **Relationships** tab.
3. Close the **Students** tab.

STOP. CLOSE the database.

In a simple database, you might only have one table, but most databases will have more. The tables you include in a database will be based on the data available. For example, a database of students might have a table for contact information, one for grades, and one for tuition and fees.

In database applications like Access, you can create a relational database. A **relational database** stores information in separate tables that are connected or linked by a defined relationship that ties the data together.

 Ref   You learn more about table relationships in Lesson 3.

An important principle to consider when planning a database is to try to record each piece of information only once. Duplicate information, or **redundant data**, wastes space and increases the likelihood of errors. Relationships among database tables help ensure consistency and reduce repetitive data entry.

As you create each table, keep in mind how the data in the tables are related to each other. Enter test data and then add fields to tables or create new tables as necessary to refine the database. The last step is to apply data normalization rules to see if your tables are structured correctly and make adjustments as needed. **Normalization** is the process of applying rules to your database design to ensure that you have divided your information items into the appropriate tables.

Database design principles include standards and guidelines that can be used to determine if your database is structured correctly. These are referred to as **normal forms**. There are five normal forms, but typically only the first three are applied, because that is usually all that is required. The following is a summary of the first three normal forms:

- **First Normal Form (1NF):** Break each field down into the smallest meaningful value, remove repeating groups of data, and create a separate table for each set of related data.
- **Second Normal Form (2NF):** Each nonkey column should be fully dependent on the entire primary key. Create new tables for data that applies to more than one record in a table and add a related field to the table.
- **Third Normal Form (3NF):** Remove fields that do not relate to, or provide a fact about, the primary key.

Data can be brought into an Access database in a number of ways, including linking and importing. When defining tables, you have to decide whether data should be linked to or imported from external sources. When you import data, Access creates a copy of the data or objects in the destination database without altering the source. Linking lets you connect to data from another source without importing it, so that you can view and modify the latest data in both the source and destination databases without creating and maintaining two copies of the same data. Any changes you make to the data in the source are reflected in the linked table in the destination database, and vice versa.

 Ref   You learn more about importing data and linking to an external data source in Lesson 14.

SKILL SUMMARY

In This Lesson You Learned How To:	Exam Objective	Objective Number
Get Started	Use Open.	1.1.2
Work in the Access Window	Set Navigation options.	1.2.3
Use the On-Screen Tools		
Use the Backstage View		
Use the Microsoft Office Access Help Button		
Define Data Needs and Types	Modify data types.	2.2.6

Knowledge Assessment

Matching

Match the term in Column 1 to its description in Column 2.

Column 1	Column 2
1. record	**a.** most basic database object; stores data in categories
2. field	**b.** database object that presents information in a format that is easy to read and print
3. redundant data	**c.** duplicate information in a database
4. primary key	**d.** row in a database table
5. database	**e.** database object that enables stored data to be searched and retrieved
6. table	**f.** column in a database that uniquely identifies each row
7. query	**g.** database object that simplifies the process of entering, editing, and displaying data
8. report	**h.** column in a database table
9. form	**i.** kind of information a field contains
10. data type	**j.** tool for collecting and organizing information

True/False

Circle T if the statement is true or F if the statement is false.

T   F   **1.** Any list you make for a specific purpose can be considered a simple database, even a grocery list.

T   F   **2.** By default, the Navigation Pane appears on the right side of the Access screen each time you create or open a database.

T   F   **3.** Forms, queries, and reports are examples of database objects.

T   F   **4.** The dialog box launcher contains the commands that you use most often, such as Save, Undo, and Redo.

T   F   **5.** When you press the Shift key, small letters and numbers called KeyTips appear on the Ribbon.

T   F   **6.** The Connection Status menu lets you choose between the help topics that are available online and the help topics installed in your computer offline.

T   F   **7.** In a database table, data is stored in rows and columns—similar in appearance to a spreadsheet.

T   F   **8.** Each field in a table must be designated for a particular data type.

T   F   **9.** An important principle to consider when planning a database is to try to record each piece of information as many times as possible for easy access.

T   F   **10.** Normalization is the process of applying rules to your database design to ensure that you have divided your information items into the appropriate tables.

Competency Assessment

Project 1-1: Personalizing Access

When working in Access or another Microsoft Office application, it is useful to personalize your copy of the software. Personalizing your software helps credit you as the creator of the Access database or other Office application.

GET READY. LAUNCH Access if it is not already running.

1. Click the **File** tab.
2. Click the **Options** button to display the Access Options dialog box.

Take Note   Throughout this lesson you will see information that appears in black text within brackets, such as [Press **Enter**], or [your e-mail address]. The information contained in the brackets is intended to be directions for you rather than something you actually type word-for-word. It will instruct you to perform an action or substitute text. Do **not** type the actual text that appears within brackets.

3. In the *Personalize your copy of Microsoft Office* section of the dialog box, key [your name] in the User name box and key [your initials] in the Initials box.
4. Click **OK** to close the dialog box.

LEAVE Access open for the next project.

Project 1-2: Using the Navigation Pane

As a busy editor at Lucerne Publishing, you use Access to organize and manage your task list.

GET READY. LAUNCH Access if it is not already running.

@ The *task_list* file for this lesson is available on the book companion website or in WileyPLUS.

1. **OPEN** *task_list* from the data files for this lesson.
2. Click the **Shutter Bar Open/Close Button** to display the Navigation Pane.
3. Click the **Contacts** group header in the Navigation Pane to display those database objects.
4. Click the **Supporting Objects** group header to display those database objects.
5. In the Supporting Objects group, double-click **Tasks** to open that table.
6. In the Tasks group, double-click **Tasks By Assigned To** to open that report.
7. In the Navigation Pane, click the **Tasks Navigation** header to display the menu and then click **Object Type**.
8. **CLOSE** the database.

LEAVE Access open for the next project.

Proficiency Assessment

Project 1-3: Understanding Database Design

You work at Margie's Travel, a full-service travel agency that specializes in providing services to senior citizens. You plan to create a database of tours, cruises, adventure activities, group travel, and vacation packages geared toward seniors, but first you want to learn more about database design.

GET READY. LAUNCH Access if it is not already running.

1. Open Access Help.
2. Search for database design.
3. Read the article about database design basics.

4. **OPEN** a new Word document.

5. List the steps that should be taken when designing a database with a short description of each.

6. **SAVE** the document as *database_design* and then **CLOSE** the file.

LEAVE Access open for the next project.

Project 1-4: Planning Table Fields

You are a volunteer for the Tech Terrace Neighborhood Association that holds an annual March Madness 5K Run. In the past, all data has been kept on paper, but you decide it would be more efficient to create a database. Decide what fields would make sense for a table holding data about the runners.

GET READY. LAUNCH Access if it is not already running.

1. Think about what fields would be useful in a database table that contains information about the runners in an annual 5K road race.

2. **OPEN** a new Word document.

3. In the document, key a list of the names of at least six possible field names.

4. **SAVE** the document as *race_fields* and keep the file open.

LEAVE Access open for the next project.

Mastery Assessment

Project 1-5: Planning Data Types for Fields

Now that you have decided what fields to use in a database table containing information about runners in an annual 5K road race, you need to determine what data type should be used for each field.

USE the document you used in the previous project.

1. Beneath the name of each possible field name for the table about runners in the annual 5K road race, key the data type that would be used with a short explanation of why you chose that type.

2. **SAVE** the document as *data_type* and then **CLOSE** the file.

LEAVE Access open for the next project.

Project 1-6: What's New in Microsoft Access 2010

Your supervisor at Margie's Travel has suggested that you research what's new in Access 2010 before you begin to create a database.

GET READY. LAUNCH Access if it is not already running.

1. Open the Backstage view and access the Help menu.

2. Use Access Help to locate the article "What's New in Microsoft Access."

3. Read the overview.

CLOSE Access.

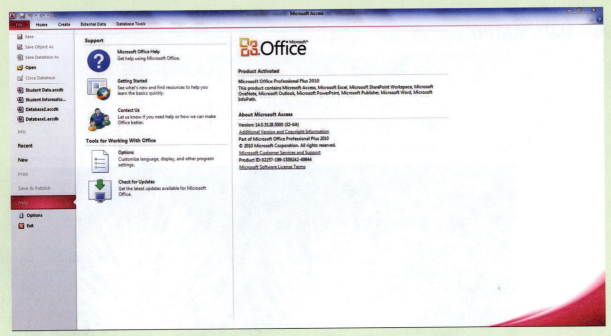

INTERNET READY
On the Help menu in the Backstage view there is a Getting Started option, as shown in Figure 1-34.

Use Access Help to find out what this section offers and how to get the latest online content while working in Office 2010 by turning on automatic updates.

Figure 1-34

Backstage view Help menu

Workplace *Ready*

WORKING WITH TEMPLATES IN ACCESS

In today's business world, it can be overwhelming to keep up with the different types of data that a company needs to collect, organize, and report. Sales invoices, client contacts, employee files, vendor information—the list seems endless. You can customize the templates available in Access to meet your business needs and save the time it would take to create database objects from scratch.

In your position as the technical support director for the A. Datum Corporation, you are responsible for coordinating technical support for the company. You can streamline your work by downloading an Access template to use as a starting point and then modifying it to track critical data. Using the Issues database, you can set up, organize, and track technical service requests submitted by people in your organization. You can then assign, prioritize, and follow the progress of issues from start to finish.

The database template contains various predefined tables—such as Issues and Contacts—that you can use to enter data. Such tables may be functional just as they are. But, as you work, chances are that you will need to create tables that are more specific to the needs of your company.

The Issues database template, like all others in Microsoft Office Access 2010, also includes predesigned forms, reports, and queries that can be used as they are. This not only saves time, but also enables you to see a complete database system developed by professionals so you can be sure you are capturing essential business information in a logical and efficient manner.

2 Create Database Tables

LESSON SKILL MATRIX

Skill	Exam Objective	Objective Number
Creating a Database	Create a database from a template.	1.1.6
Creating a Table	Use user templates.	1.3.3
Saving a Database Object	Use Save Object As.	1.1.1

KEY TERMS
- Application Parts
- Quick Start
- template

As an assistant curator at the Baldwin Museum of Science, you are responsible for the day-to-day management of the insect collection, including duties such as sorting and organizing specimens, as well as supervising the mounting and labeling of the insects. The insect collection catalog has never been transferred to an electronic database. Because you have experience with database management, part of your responsibility is to create a database to store the information about the specimens and collections, as well as museum exhibits and events, a task perfectly suited to Access 2010. In this lesson, you learn how to create a blank database and how to use a template to create a database. You also learn how to create a table from a template, how to create a table by copying the structure from another table, and how to save a database object.

SOFTWARE ORIENTATION

Getting Started with Microsoft Access

The New tab in the Backstage view, shown in Figure 2-1, provides options for creating a database. This is the default view after starting Access. The Backstage view is also where you can create a new, blank database. Use this figure as a reference throughout this lesson as well as the rest of this book.

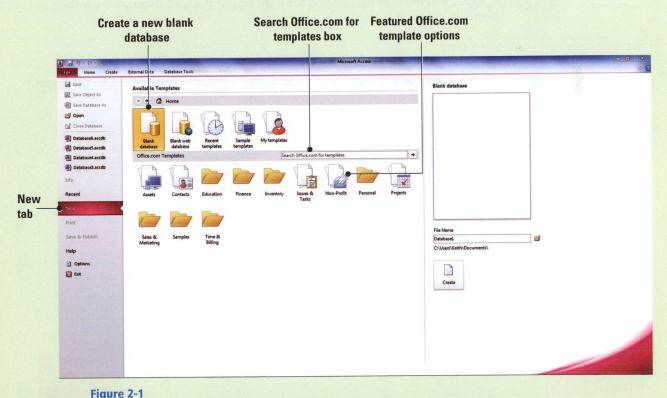

Figure 2-1

New tab in Backstage view

CREATING A DATABASE

In Microsoft Office Access 2010, the process of creating a new database is easier than ever. You can create a database using one of the many available **templates** (ready-to-use databases that contain all of the tables, queries, forms, and reports needed for performing specific tasks) or by creating a new blank database.

Using a Template to Create a Database

Access offers a variety of templates to help get you started. Some templates are immediately available for your use since they are built into Access, while you can easily download others from Office.com. Microsoft or users have created the templates found at Office.com. User-submitted templates have a specific thumbnail associated with them, as outlined in Figure 2-4. Built-in and Office.com templates are available that can be used to track issues, manage contacts, or keep a record of expenses. Some templates contain a few sample records to help demonstrate their use. You can use templates as is, or you can customize them to better suit your purposes. In this exercise, you use one of the many available templates to create a database.

STEP BY STEP | **Use a Template to Create a Database**

GET READY. Before you begin these steps, be sure that you are logged on to the Internet. **LAUNCH** Microsoft Access to display the Backstage view.

1. In the center of the Backstage view window, in the *Search Office.com for Templates* box, key **Personal** and press **Enter** on the keyboard.

2. In the list of Office.com Personal templates that appears in the middle of the Backstage view results pane, click **Home inventory**. A preview of the selected template appears in the preview pane on the right side of the Backstage view window, as shown in Figure 2-2.

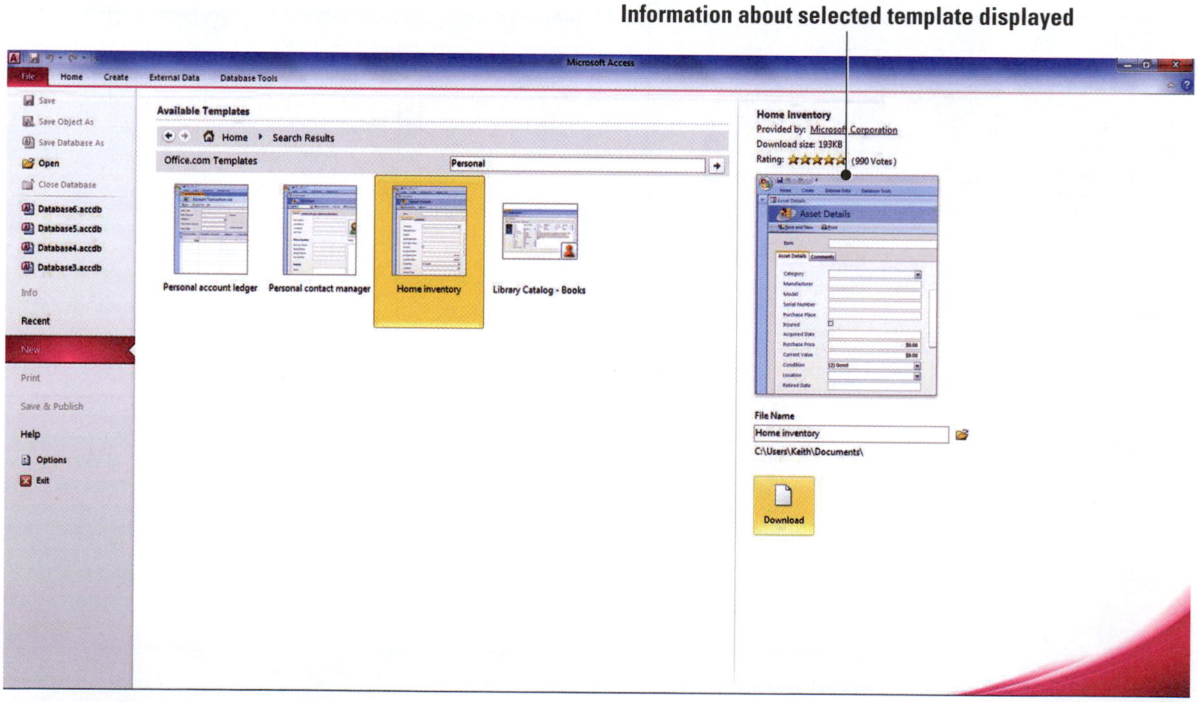

Information about selected template displayed

Figure 2-2

Office.com Personal templates

3. In the Office.com templates search box, key **Education** and press **Enter** on the keyboard.

4. In the list of Office.com Education templates that appears, click **Faculty**. Your screen should look similar to Figure 2-3.

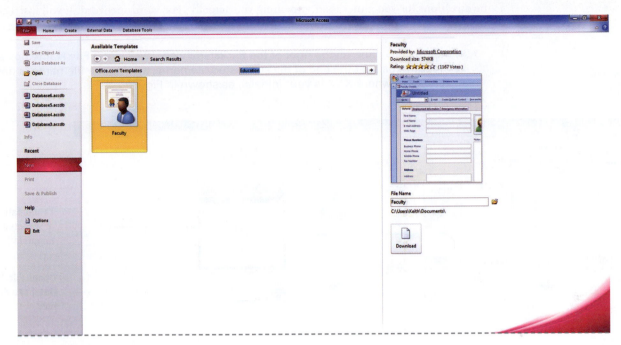

Figure 2-3

Office.com Faculty template

5. In the Office.com templates search box, key in **Assets** and press **Enter** on the keyboard. Your screen should look similar to Figure 2-4.

Office.com
user-submitted template

Office.com
Microsoft template

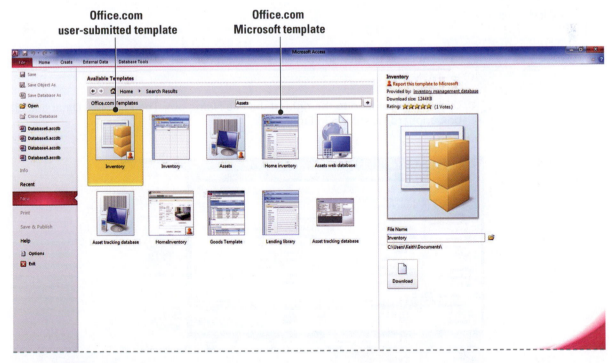

Figure 2-4

Office.com Assets templates

6. In the list of Office.com Business templates in the middle, click **Asset tracking database**.

Take Note Throughout this lesson you will see information that appears in black text within brackets, such as [Press **Enter**], or [your e-mail address]. The information contained in the brackets is intended to be directions for you rather than something you actually type word-for-word. It will instruct you to perform an action or substitute text. Do **not** type the actual text that appears within brackets.

7. In the preview pane on the right of the Backstage view, click in the **File Name** box and key [your initials] at the end of the suggested file name, so that the file name is now **Assets XXX** (where XXX is your initials), as shown in Figure 2-5.

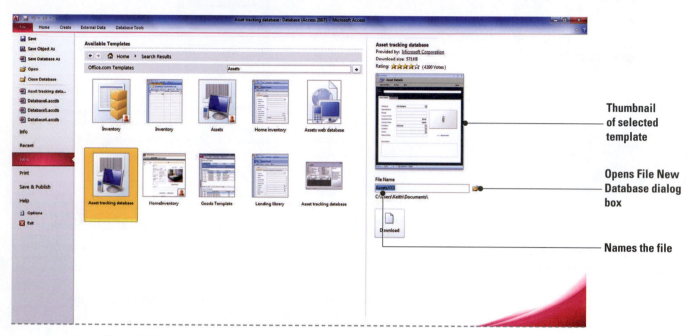

Thumbnail of selected template

Opens File New Database dialog box

Names the file

Figure 2-5

File Name box and folder icon

Take Note If you do not add an extension to your database file name, Access does it for you—for example, *AccessXXX.accdb*.

8. Click the **folder** icon to the right of the File Name box. The File New Database dialog box appears, as shown in Figure 2-6.

Figure 2-6

File New Database dialog box

9. Navigate to the location where you want to save the file and click **OK**.

Take Note   You should save your files in a separate directory from where your data files are stored. This will ensure that you don't overwrite the original data files with your updated files. Check with your instructor to see if she wants you to save your work on a flash drive or in a particular network directory.

10. Click the **Download** button at the bottom of the Preview pane. The Downloading Template dialog box opens and indicates that the template is being downloaded, as shown in Figure 2-7. When the download is complete, the dialog box closes.

Figure 2-7

Downloading Template dialog box

11. Access creates and then opens the AccessXXX database. Getting Started and Access 2007 Help windows may appear, which contain helpful videos and links about using the Asset tracking database. Close these windows, if necessary, to return to the AccessXXX database with the Asset List table active, as shown in Figure 2-8. Click to place the insertion point in the first cell of the *Item* field and key **Canon EOS Rebel 300D**.

Access 2007 on the title bar specifies format of databases created with Access 2010, not the version

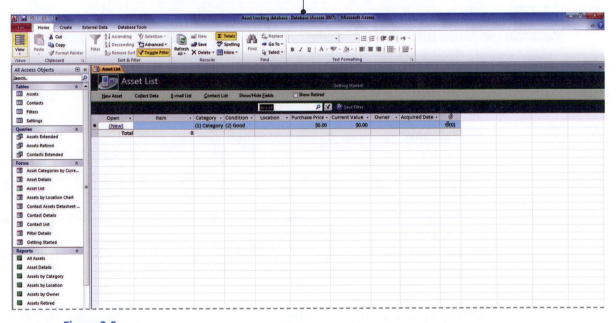

Figure 2-8

Assets template database

Take Note   When you open an Access database template that was created in Access 2007 (such as the Asset tracking database), Access may open the Access 2007 Help menu as well.

 **Troubleshooting**   If you are asked to enable the content, click the Enable Content button on the Security Warning Message Bar. By default, Access blocks potentially harmful content that might contain viruses or present other security issues. This content should only be enabled if the database is downloaded from a trustworthy site, like Microsoft Office Online.

12. Click the **Shutter Bar Open/Close Button**, if necessary, to display the Navigation Pane, as shown in Figure 2-9, to see all the objects in the database.

Shutter Bar
Open/Close Button

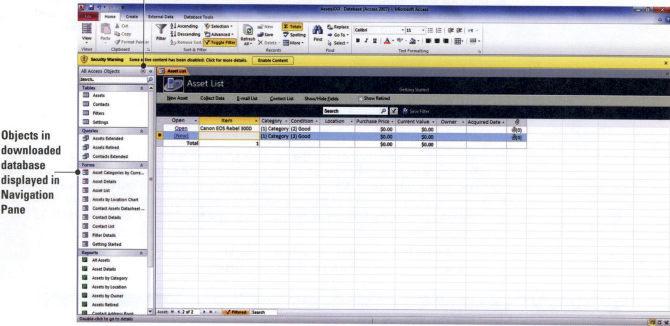

Objects in
downloaded
database
displayed in
Navigation
Pane

Figure 2-9

Assets database with
Navigation Pane displayed

13. CLOSE the database.

PAUSE. LEAVE Access open to use in the next exercise.

Take Note   Unless you choose a different folder, Access uses the following default locations to store your databases:

- Microsoft Windows Server 2008, Microsoft Windows 7, and Microsoft Windows Vista— c:\Users\user name\Documents

- Microsoft Windows Server 2003 or Microsoft Windows XP—c:\Documents and Settings\ user name\My Documents

Creating a Blank Database

If you have existing data, you may decide that it is easier to create a blank database rather than using a template, because it would require a lot of work to adapt your existing data to the template's defined data structure. When you create a new blank database, Access opens a database that contains a table where you can enter data, but it creates no other database objects. By default, Access creates a primary key field named "ID" for all new datasheets, and it sets the data type for the field to AutoNumber. In this exercise, you create a new blank database.

STEP BY STEP   **Create a Blank Database**

GET READY. The Backstage view should be on the screen from the previous exercise.

1. Click the **Blank database** icon in the Available Templates section of Backstage view. A Blank database thumbnail image appears in the Preview pane, as shown in Figure 2-10.

Blank Database pane

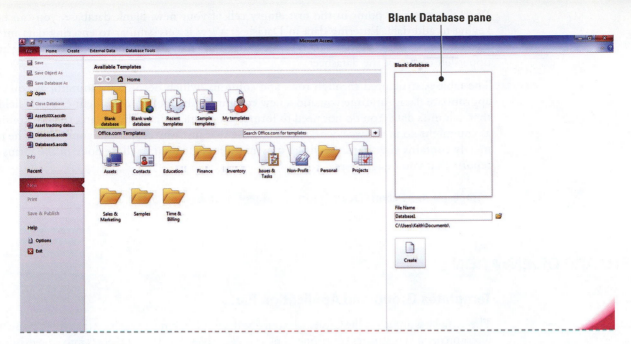

Figure 2-10

Blank database pane

2. In the File Name box below the thumbnail, key **Blank Database XXX** (where XXX is your initials).

3. If you want to save the file in a location other than the one shown beneath the File Name box, click the folder icon to the right of the File Name box and browse to a different location.

4. Click the **Create** button to create the blank database in your chosen location. Access creates the database, and then opens an empty table named Table1 in Datasheet View, as shown in Figure 2-11.

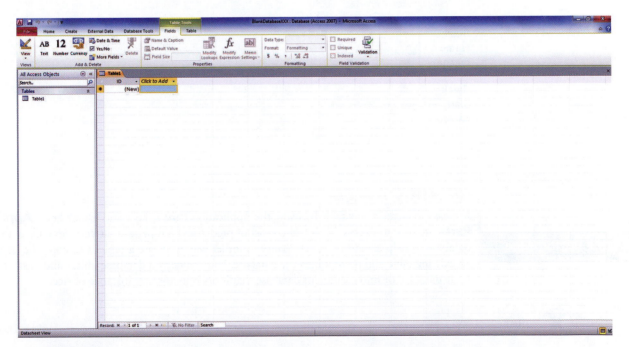

Figure 2-11

New blank database

PAUSE. LEAVE the database open to use in the next exercise.

 Ref   You learn more about defining and modifying a primary key in Lesson 3.

With the insertion point in the first empty cell of your new, blank database, you can begin keying to add data. Entering data in Datasheet View is very similar to entering data into an Excel worksheet, except that data must be entered in related rows and columns, starting at the upper-left corner of the datasheet.

The table is structured through rows and columns, which become meaningful as you enter appropriate data. Anytime you add a new column to the table, Access defines a new field for that column's data. You do not need to format your data by including blank rows or columns, as you might do in an Excel worksheet, because that just wastes space in your table. The table merely contains your data. All visual presentation of that data will be done in the forms and reports that you design later.

 Ref You learn more about creating forms and reports in Lessons 5 and 6.

SOFTWARE ORIENTATION

Templates Group and Application Parts

The Templates group on the Create tab contains the Application Parts gallery that you can use to insert predefined templates consisting of objects like tables, forms, and reports into a preexisting database. Use Figure 2-12 as a reference throughout this lesson as well as the rest of this book.

Figure 2-12

Application Parts gallery

Application Parts button accesses gallery

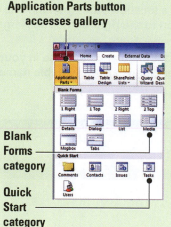

Blank Forms category

Quick Start category

CREATING A TABLE

The Bottom Line

It is easy to create a new table by using the Application Parts gallery and Quick Start. **Application Parts** are new to Access 2010 and consist of predefined templates that you can add to an existing database to help extend its functionality. Another way to create a table is to copy the structure of an existing table and paste it into the database. You can copy a database object and paste it into the same database or into a different database that is open in another instance of Access.

 Ref You learn more about creating forms using the Application Parts gallery in Lesson 10.

Using the Application Parts Gallery and Quick Start

NEW
to Office 2010

Application parts vary from a single table to a collection of database objects like tables, forms, and reports. The Application Parts gallery consists of two categories, Blank Forms and Quick Start. The Blank Forms category contains a collection of form parts that allows you to add predefined forms to a database. The **Quick Start** category of these templates contains a collection of predefined objects arranged by parts for tracking things such as comments, contacts, and issues. In this exercise, you will quickly create a table using the Application Parts Gallery and Quick Start.

STEP BY STEP   **Create a Table Using the Application Parts Gallery and Quick Start**

USE the database that is open from the previous exercise.

1. On the Create tab, in the Templates group, click the **Application Parts** button to display the gallery shown in Figure 2-13.

Figure 2-13

Application Parts gallery

2. In the Quick Start section of the gallery, click **Comments**. Click **Yes** on the Microsoft Access dialog box that appears asking to close all open objects before instantiating this application part to close the empty table that appeared when you created the blank database in the previous exercise, and return to the Blank database screen with the Comments table open.

3. In the Navigation Pane, double-click **Comments** to display the newly created table with fields for comments, as shown in Figure 2-14. Close the Comments table by clicking on the Comments table close button.

Comments table tab

New table object named Comments in Navigation Pane

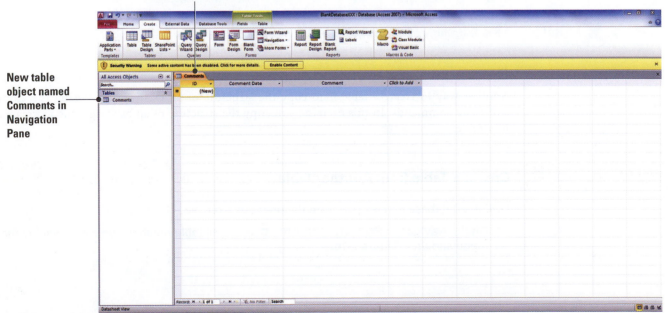

Figure 2-14

New Comments table
for comments

4. On the Application Parts menu, click **Contacts**. In the Create Relationship dialog box that appears, select the **There is no relationship** radio button then click **Create**. A new table is created along with supporting forms and report objects, as shown in Figure 2-15.

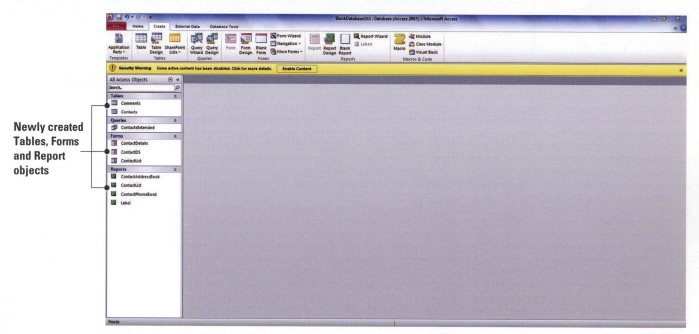

Newly created Tables, Forms and Report objects

Figure 2-15

New table, forms, and reports for contacts

PAUSE. LEAVE the database open to use in the next exercise.

CERTIFICATION READY   1.3.3

How do you create tables by using user templates?

    Ref   You learn how to create a custom table in Lesson 9.

Creating a Table from Another Table

Another way to create a table is to copy the structure of an existing table using the Copy and Paste commands. In this exercise, you copy the structure of an existing table to create a new table.

STEP BY STEP   **Create a Table from Another Table**

USE the database that is open from the previous exercise.

1. On the Navigation Pane, right-click the **Comments** table database object to display the menu shown in Figure 2-16.

Figure 2-16

Database object menu

Right-click to display menu

Another Way
You can also copy a database object by selecting it in the Navigation Pane and pressing Ctrl+C. Or on the Home tab, in the Clipboard group, you can click the Copy button.

Figure 2-17

Shortcut menu

2. Click **Copy**.

3. Right-click in a blank area of the Navigation Pane and, in the shortcut menu that appears, click **Paste** (see Figure 2-17).

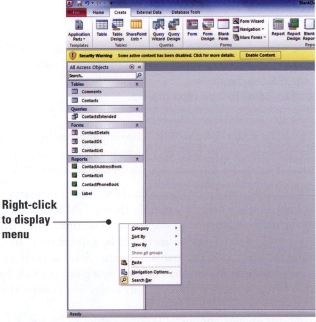

Right-click to display menu

Another Way
You can also paste a database object by selecting the destination location in the Navigation Pane and pressing Ctrl+V. Or on the Home tab, in the Clipboard group, you can click the Paste button.

Figure 2-18

Paste Table As dialog box

4. The Paste Table As dialog box appears, as shown in Figure 2-18. Notice the default name, **Copy Of Comments**, in the Table Name box.

5. In the Paste Options section, select the **Structure Only** radio button, to paste only the table's structure, rather than pasting a copy of the table's data along with its structure.

6. Click **OK**.

7. The new table appears at the end of the list of database table objects in the Navigation Pane, as shown in Figure 2-19.

Figure 2-19

New table copied from existing table

New copied table appears at the end of the list of database objects

8. Double-click **Copy Of Comments** to open the new table. Notice that the structure of the new table is the same as the table from which it was copied.

PAUSE. CLOSE the database.

LEAVE Access open for the next project.

When you create a copy of a table by copying and pasting, you have the option of re-creating just the table's structure, or both its structure and data. To paste just the structure of the table, click Structure Only. To also paste the data, click Structure and Data.

As you learned in Lesson 1, a relational database stores information in separate tables that are connected or linked by a defined relationship that ties the data together. When you add a new table to an existing database, that new table stands alone until you relate it to your existing tables. For example, say you need to track orders placed by a distributor. To do that, you add a table named Distributor Contacts to a sales database. To take advantage of the power that a relational database can provide—to search for the orders placed by a given contact, for example—you must create a relationship between the new table and any tables that contain the order data.

 Ref   You learn more about defining table relationships in Lesson 3.

SAVING A DATABASE OBJECT

The Bottom Line

Access automatically saves data that you have entered any time you add an Application Part like a Quick Start template, move to a new record, close an object or database, or quit the application. But you will need to save the design of a table, or any other database object, after it is created. Additionally, using the Save Object As command in the Backstage view, you can create a duplicate of a database object (like a table, query, or report) by specifying an alternate name.

CERTIFICATION
READY   1.1.1

How do you use Save
Object As?

Saving a Table

When you save a new table for the first time, give it a name that describes the information it contains. You can use up to 64 characters (letters or numbers), including spaces. For example, you might name a table Orders 2011, Clients, Tasks, Inventory Parts, or Comments. In this exercise, you save a database table and then use the Save Object As command to create a duplicate of the same table.

STEP BY STEP   **Save a Table**

GET READY. The Backstage view should be on the screen from the previous exercise.

1. If necessary, click the **New** command, then click the **Blank database** icon; a Blank Database thumbnail appears in the Preview pane.
2. In the Blank database preview's File Name box, keep the default name.
3. If you want to save the file in a location other than the one shown beneath the File Name box, click the **folder icon** and browse to a different location.
4. Click the **Create** button. A new blank database appears with the default table labeled Table1 displayed, as shown in Figure 2-20.

Figure 2-20

New blank database with default table

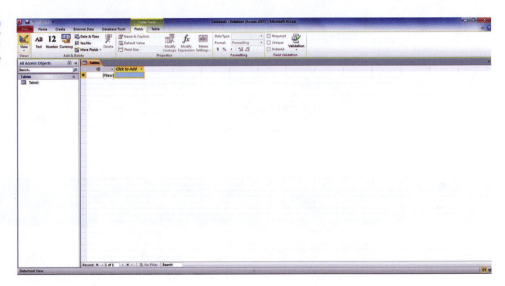

5. Click to place the insertion point in the cell under the Click to add field and key **Sample Data**.
6. Right-click on the **Table1** tab to display the shortcut menu, as shown in Figure 2-21.

Figure 2-21

Shortcut menu

Right-click to display menu

7. Click **Save**. The Save As dialog box appears, as shown in Figure 2-22.

Figure 2-22

Save As dialog box

Another Way

You can also save a table by pressing Ctrl+S. You do not need to save new data that you enter. Access automatically saves a record when you move to a different record or close the object or database.

Access also automatically saves changes to your data whenever you quit the program. However, if you have made changes to the design of any database objects since you last saved them, Access asks whether you want to save these changes before quitting.

8. In the Table Name box, key **Sample Table**.

9. Click **OK** to close the dialog box and return to the table, which now is labeled Sample Table.

10. Click the **File** tab to display the Backstage view.

11. Click **Save Object As** to display the Save As dialog box.

12. In the Table Name box, key **Backup of Sample Table**.

13. Click **OK**.

14. Click the **Home** tab.

15. Notice the new table object named Backup of Sample Table in the Navigation Pane.

16. **CLOSE** the database.

CLOSE Access.

SKILL SUMMARY

In This Lesson You Learned How To:	Exam Objective	Objective Number
Create a Database	Create a database from a template.	**1.1.6**
Create a Table	Use user templates.	**1.3.3**
Save a Database Object	Use Save Object As.	**1.1.1**

Knowledge Assessment

Fill in the Blank

Complete the following sentences by writing the correct word or words in the blanks provided.

1. You can create a database using one of the many templates available or by creating a new _____ database.

2. By default, Access creates a(n) _____ field named "ID" for all new datasheets.

3. Entering data in Datasheet View is very similar to entering data in a(n) _____.

4. The _____ contains predefined templates included in two categories, Blank Forms and Quick Start.

5. One way to create a table is to copy the _____ of an existing table and paste it into the database.

6. When you add a new table to an existing database, that new table stands alone until you _____ it to your existing tables.

7. You can use up to _____ characters (letters or numbers), including spaces, to name a database object.

8. Several options for creating a database are provided on the _____ tab in the Backstage view.

9. The _____ category in the Application Parts gallery contains a collection of predefined database objects for tracking comments, contacts, and issues.

10. After you add _____ to a table, you should save its design.

Multiple Choice

Select the best response for the following statements.

1. In Access, a template is
   a. A database to manage contacts
   b. Where a database is stored
   c. Two tables linked together
   d A ready-to-use database

2. When you create a new blank database, Access opens a database that contains
   a. One of each type of database object
   b. A table
   c. Sample data
   d. A template

3. To save a database file in a location other than the default, click the
   a. Folder icon
   b. Blank database icon
   c. File name button
   d. Help button

4. The table structure is created when you
   a. Format the data
   b. Enter data
   c. Insert blank rows and columns
   d. Switch to Design View

5. The Templates group commands are located on which tab?
   a. Home
   b. Create
   c. Database Tools
   d. Datasheet

6. To copy a table, you must first select it in
   a. The Clipboard
   b. Microsoft Office Online
   c. The Navigation Pane
   d. Datasheet View

7. When you paste a table, which dialog box is displayed?
   a. Table Structure
   b. Copy Table
   c. Paste Data
   d. Paste Table As

8. After you have created a table or other database object, you should
   a. Save it with a descriptive name
   b. Copy it to create a backup
   c. Link it to an external data source
   d. Insert a blank column at the end

9. When you quit the program, Access automatically
   a. Creates a link between all tables
   b. Leaves the Navigation Pane open
   c. Saves the data
   d. Renames the file

10. Which is *not* a way to create a new database table?

    a. Use Quick Start

    b. Choose Create on the Table menu

    c. Copy the structure of another table

    d. Create a new blank database

Competency Assessment

Project 2-1: Contacts Database

You want to use Access to store, organize, and manage the contact information for the wholesale coffee suppliers used by Fourth Coffee, where you work as a buyer for the 15 stores in the northeast region. Use a template to create a database for the contacts.

GET READY. LAUNCH Access if it is not already running.

1. Open Backstage view and in the Office.com Templates section of the New tab, select the **Contacts** category.
2. On the next screen that displays, select the **Call Tracker** template.
3. Key **Call tracker XXX** (where XXX is your initials) in the File Name box.
4. If necessary, click the folder icon and choose a different location for the file.
5. Click **Download** (or click **Create** if not logged on to the Internet) to create and open the database.
6. Close the **Access 2007 Help** window that appears.
7. Click the **Shutter Bar Open/Close Button** to open the Navigation Pane.
8. Click the **Supporting** Objects header to display the database objects in that group.
9. Right-click the **Customers** table under the Customers header to display the menu and click **Copy**.
10. Right-click in the white area of the Navigation Pane and click Paste on the menu.
11. In the Paste Table As dialog box, key **Customers structure**.
12. Click the **Structure Only** radio button.
13. Click **OK**.
14. **CLOSE** the *Call trackerXXX* database.

LEAVE Access open for the next project.

Project 2-2: Database for Restaurants

As a regional manager for a franchise restaurant chain, you want to keep track of restaurant locations and customer comments. You decide to create a database to store the necessary information.

GET READY. LAUNCH Access if it is not already running.

1. In the Backstage view's New tab, click the **Blank Database** icon.
2. In the Blank Database pane on the right, key **Restaurants XXX** (where XXX is your initials) in the File Name box.
3. If necessary, click the folder icon and choose a different location for the file.
4. Click the **Create** button.
5. Right-click the **Table1** tab and click **Save**.
6. In the Save As dialog box, key **Locations**.
7. Click **OK**.

LEAVE Access open for the next project.

Proficiency Assessment

Project 2-3: Adding Tables

You need to add some tables to the database that you just created for information about the restaurants.

USE the database that is open from the previous project.

1. Use the Application Parts gallery to create a table for comments.
2. In the Create Relationship window that appears, click the **Cancel** button.
3. Rename the table *Uptown Comments*.
4. Copy the structure of the Uptown Comments table to create a new table.
5. Name the new table *Downtown Comments*.
6. **CLOSE** the database.

LEAVE Access open for the next project.

Project 2-4: Nutrition Tracker

You have become health conscious and want to track your activity, exercise, and food logs using Access.

GET READY. LAUNCH Access if it is not already running.

1. If necessary, log on to the Internet.
2. In the *Search Office.com For Templates* box, search for, download, and save the Nutrition template with the file name *Nutrition XXX* (where XXX is your initials).
3. Key your information in the My Profile form that is displayed to see your body mass index and recommended calorie consumption. (If the My Profile form is not displayed, open it first.)
4. Click **OK**.
5. Open the **Tips** table to view the tips stored in the database.
6. Explore the other useful forms and information available.
7. **CLOSE** the database.

LEAVE Access open for the next project.

Mastery Assessment

Project 2-5: Northwind Traders

You have just joined the sales force at Northwind Traders. To familiarize yourself with the information available in the company database, open the file and browse through the objects.

GET READY. LAUNCH Access if it is not already running.

1. In the Sample templates category, download the Northwind database using the name *Northwind 2010 XXX* (where XXX is your initials).
2. Enable the content.
3. Log in as a sales representative, Jan Kotas, by selecting that name from the Select Employee drop-down menu and clicking the **Log In** button.
4. Open the Navigation Pane and open each group to view all the objects that are part of the database.
5. **CLOSE** the database.

LEAVE Access open for the next project.

Project 2-6: Customer Service Database

Southridge Video has a large membership of customers that rent new release and film library movies, as well as video games. As the store manager, customer complaints are directed to you. Create an Access database for the purpose of tracking customer service issues.

GET READY. LAUNCH Access if it is not already running.

1. Choose an Application Parts template to create a database called *Southridge XXX* (where XXX is your initials) that will store information about customer service issues. Make no changes to the default Application Parts template.

2. **CLOSE** the database.

LEAVE Access open for the next project.

INTERNET READY

If you want to read more about Access templates, you can explore the Office Online website. Search Access Help for "Access templates." Click the search results link titled "Introduction to the Access 2010 templates," as shown in Figure 2-23, to read more about the templates that are included with Access 2010 and on Office.com.

Figure 2-23

Search results for Access templates

LESSON SKILL MATRIX

Skill	Exam Objective	Objective Number
Navigating among Records		
Entering, Inserting, Editing, and Deleting Records		
Working with Primary Keys	Define Primary Keys.	2.4.1
Finding and Replacing Data	Use Find.	2.3.1
Attaching and Detaching Documents		
Sorting and Filtering Data and Setting Field Viewing Options within a Table	Use Sort. Use Filter commands. Freeze or Unfreeze fields. Hide or Unhide fields.	2.3.2 2.3.3 2.2.5 2.2.4
Understanding Table Relationships	Use Primary Keys to create Relationships. Edit Relationships.	2.4.2 2.4.3

KEY TERMS

- ascending
- composite key
- descending
- filter
- foreign key
- innermost field
- outermost field
- referential integrity
- sort
- wildcard

Fourth Coffee is a national chain of coffee shops. A new store recently opened in your neighborhood. You were able to get a part-time job working in the office, helping the office manager organize data on the computer. In addition to being a traditional neighborhood coffee shop, the store has also started selling coffees to companies for use at their business sites. It is your job to manage the inventory, customers, and order tables in Access. In this lesson, you learn to navigate among records; enter, edit, and delete records; find and replace data; sort and filter data; attach and detach documents; and define, modify, and print table relationships.

NAVIGATING AMONG RECORDS

The Bottom Line

Database tables are usually large, but contain useful information that can be manipulated in different ways. When a table contains many records and fields, it is important to be able to navigate among them.

Navigating Using the Keyboard

Access users who prefer using the keyboard to navigate records can press keys and key combinations to move among records in Datasheet View. In Datasheet View, you can navigate among records using the up, down, left, and right arrow keys to move to the field you want. You can also use the Tab key to move from field to field in a record and from the last field in a record to the first field of the next record. If you prefer to use the mouse, you can move among records by clicking the navigation buttons, which you'll do in a later exercise. However, in this exercise, you use the keyboard to navigate among records.

STEP BY STEP   **Use the Keyboard to Navigate among Records**

GET READY. Before you begin these steps, be sure to turn on and/or log on to your computer and start Access.

@ The *Fourth Coffee* file for this lesson is available on the book companion website or in WileyPLUS.

WileyPLUS Extra! features an online tutorial of this task.

1. **OPEN** *Fourth Coffee* from the data files for this lesson.
2. Click the **File** tab, then click the **Save Database As** command. The Save As dialog box appears. Key **Fourth Coffee XXX** (where XXX is your initials) in the File name box. Find the location where you will save the solution files for this lesson and click **Save**.
3. In the Navigation Pane, double-click **Coffee Inventory: Table** to open the table.
4. Notice that the first cell of the first record is selected.
5. Press the **Down Arrow** key to move down to the next row. Notice that the cell is selected.
6. Press the **Right Arrow** key to move to the Product Name field.
7. Press the **Tab** key to move to the next cell.
8. Press the **Tab** key to move to the next cell.
9. Press the **Tab** key to move to the next row.
10. Press **Ctrl+Down Arrow** to move to the first field of the last record.

PAUSE. LEAVE the database open to use in the next exercise.

Table 3-1 lists keys and key combinations for moving among records.

Table 3-1

Keyboard Commands for Navigating Records

Commands	Results
Tab or Right Arrow	Moves cursor to the next field
End	Moves cursor to the last field in the current record
Shift+Tab or Left Arrow	Moves cursor to the previous field
Home	Moves cursor to the first field in the current record
Down Arrow	Moves cursor to the current field in the next record
Ctrl+Down Arrow	Moves cursor to the current field in the last record
Ctrl+End	Moves cursor to the last field in the last record
Up Arrow	Moves cursor to the current field in the previous record
Ctrl+Up Arrow	Moves cursor to the current field in the first record
Ctrl+Home	Moves cursor to the first field in the first record

Using Navigation Buttons

Access users who prefer to use the mouse can move among records by clicking the navigation buttons. In this exercise, you use the mouse to navigate among records.

The record navigation buttons are displayed at the bottom of the screen in Datasheet View. Click the First, Previous, Next, Last, and New (blank) Record buttons to go to those records. Key a record number into the Current Record box and press Enter to go to that record. Key data into the Search box to find a match in the table. The Filter Indicator shows whether a filter has been applied to the table, which will be covered later in this lesson.

STEP BY STEP   **Use Navigation Buttons**

USE the database open from the previous exercise.

1. Click the **First record** button, shown in Figure 3-1. The selection moves to the first record.

Figure 3-1

Record navigation buttons

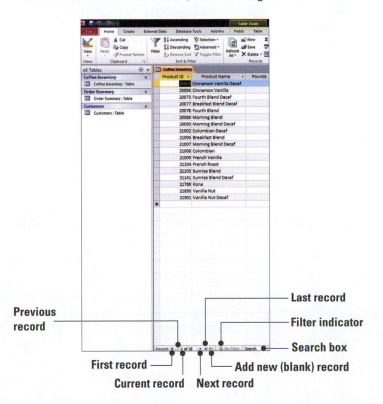

2. Click the **Next record** button. The selection moves to the next record.

3. Select and then delete the number **2** in the Current Record box. Key **5** and press **Enter**. The selection moves to the fifth record.

4. Click the **Search** box to position the insertion point. Key **sunrise** into the Search box. Notice that the selection moves to the first occurrence of the word Sunrise.

5. Press **Enter**. The selection moves to the next occurrence of the word Sunrise.

6. Click the **New (blank) record** button. The insertion point moves to the first column and last row of the table.

PAUSE. LEAVE the database open to use in the next exercise.

SOFTWARE ORIENTATION

Records Group, Record Selector Box, and Record Shortcut Menu

There are a few ways you can enter record data, delete data from individual fields of records, and insert and delete entire records, using the Records group, Record Selector box, and commands in the Record Shortcut menu, as shown in Figure 3-2. Refer to this figure as a reference throughout this lesson as well as the rest of this book.

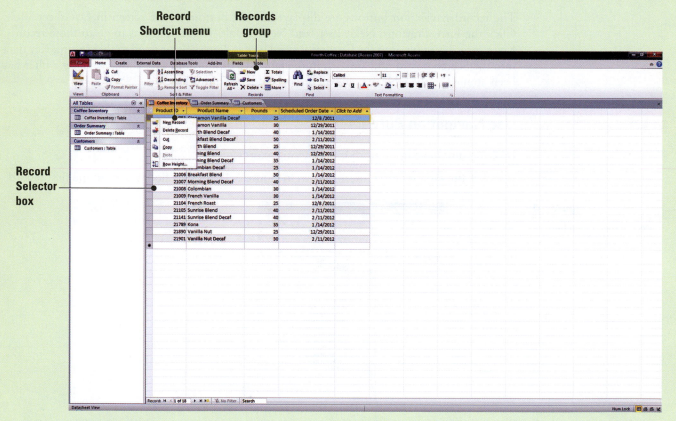

Figure 3-2

Records group, Record Selector box, and Record Shortcut menu

Use the commands in the Records group and the Record Shortcut menu, as well as the Record Selector box (a blank square to the left of a record), to assist you in entering record data and inserting and deleting records.

ENTERING, INSERTING, EDITING, AND DELETING RECORDS

The Bottom Line

Keeping a database up-to-date and useful is an ongoing process. You can easily enter data by positioning the insertion point in the table cell where you want to add data and begin keying. To insert a new record, select any record in the table and click the New button on the Home tab in the Records group. You can also click the Record Selector box then right-click the selected record and select New Record from the shortcut menu. A new record is added to the end of the table. Select existing data to edit or delete it.

Entering, Editing, and Deleting Records

To enter new data, in Datasheet View, position the insertion point in the first empty cell of a record and begin keying the data. After you enter data and move to a new field, Access automatically saves the data in the table. Each field in a table is formatted with a specific data type, so you must enter that kind of data in the field. If you do not, you will get an error message. To delete information from an individual field of a record, highlight the field data and press the Delete key or click the Delete button on the Home tab in the Records group. If you change your mind after you delete information from a field, you can undo the action by clicking the Undo button on the Quick Access Toolbar. In this exercise, you enter a new record as well as edit and delete existing records.

You can delete an entire record or several records at once from a database. Just select the row or rows using the Record Selector box and press the Delete key or click the Delete button on the Home tab in the Records group. You can also right-click and select Delete Record from the shortcut menu. After you delete a record, you cannot undo it.

STEP BY STEP | **Enter, Edit, and Delete Records**

USE the database you used in the previous exercise.

1. The insertion point should be positioned in the first field of the new, blank row at the bottom of the datasheet, as shown in Figure 3-3. Notice the asterisk in the Record Selector box, which indicates that this is a new record, ready for data.

Figure 3-3

Blank record in Datasheet View

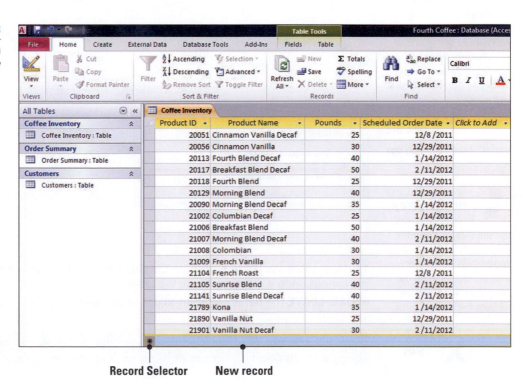

Record Selector box

New record

2. Key **21905** and press **Tab**. Notice that the asterisk has changed to a pencil icon, as shown in Figure 3-4, indicating that the record is being edited.

Figure 3-4

Entering data into a record

Indicates that the record is being edited ——

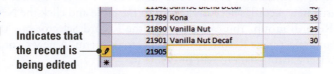

3. Key **Hazelnut** and press **Tab**.

4. Key **30** and press **Tab**.

5. Key **02112012** and press **Enter**.

6. Highlight **sunrise** in the Search box and key **Kona** to locate the Kona record.

7. Select **Kona** in the record to position the blinking insertion point there. Key **Hawaiian** and press **Tab**.

8. Click the **Undo** button on the Quick Access Toolbar.

9. Press **Tab**. Key **12292010** and press **Tab**.

10. Click the **Record Selector** box to the left of the Product ID field of the first record, 20051.

11. On the Home tab, in the Records group, click the **Delete button drop-down arrow**. Select **Delete Record** from the menu, as shown in Figure 3-5.

Figure 3-5

Delete menu

Another Way
An easy way to select an entire record is to click the Record Selector box. If you need to select other records above or below it, you can drag the mouse up or down to include those in the selection. To delete one or more selected records, right-click the Select All button and choose Delete Record from the shortcut menu.

Delete button and menu

12. A dialog box appears, as shown in Figure 3-6, asking if you are sure you want to delete the record. Click **Yes**.

Figure 3-6

Confirm deletion dialog box

Another Way
To delete a record without selecting it, place the cursor in one of the fields of a record and click the Delete menu on the Home tab in the Records group. Select Delete Record from the menu.

13. Notice that the Undo button on the Quick Access Toolbar is not available because you cannot undo a deletion. Close the table.

PAUSE. LEAVE the database open to use in the next exercise.

 Ref

As you become more advanced in your knowledge of Access, you may want to create a delete query that can delete multiple records at once. You learn more about queries in Lesson 8.

WORKING WITH PRIMARY KEYS

The Bottom Line

As you learned in Lesson 1, a primary key is a column that uniquely identifies a record or row in a table. Customer IDs, serial numbers, or product IDs usually make good primary keys. Each table should have a primary key, and some tables might have two or more. When you divide information into separate tables, the primary keys help Access bring the information back together again.

Defining a Primary Key

You can define a primary key for a field in Design View by selecting the row that contains the field for which you want to assign a primary key and clicking the Primary Key button on the Design tab in the Tools group on the Ribbon. When you create a new database, Access creates a primary key field named "ID" by default and sets the data type for the field to AutoNumber. If you don't have a field in an existing database that you think will make a good primary key, you can use a field with the AutoNumber data type. It doesn't contain factual information (such as a telephone number) about a record and it is not likely to change. In this exercise, you define a primary key.

Once a primary key is defined, you can use it in other tables to refer back to the table with the primary key. When a primary key from one table is used in another table, it is called the **foreign key.** The foreign key is used to reference the data from the primary key to help avoid redundancy.

You can modify a primary key by deleting it from one field and adding it to another field. To remove a primary key in Design View, select the row and click the Primary Key button on the Design tab in the Tools group on the Ribbon to remove it.

STEP BY STEP   **Define a Primary Key**

USE the database you used in the previous exercise.

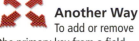
Another Way
To add or remove the primary key from a field, you can also select the row, right-click, and select Primary Key from the shortcut menu.

1. In the Navigation Pane, double-click **Order Summary: Table** to open the table.
2. On the Home tab, in the Views group, click the **View button drop-down arrow**, and from the menu that appears, select **Design View**.
3. Click the **Row Selector** box beside the Order ID row to select the row.
4. On the Design tab, in the Tools group, click the **Primary Key** button. The Primary Key button is highlighted in orange and appears to be pushed in. A key icon appears on the Order ID row to designate the field as a primary key, as shown in Figure 3-7.

Figure 3-7

Primary Key

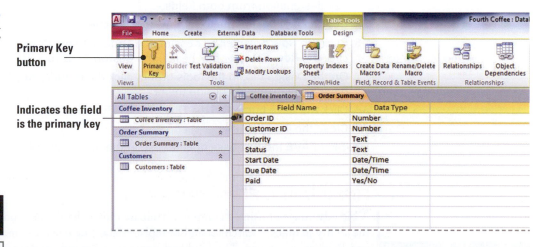

CERTIFICATION READY   2.4.1

How do you designate a primary key in an Access table?

PAUSE. LEAVE the table open to use in the next exercise.

Defining and Modifying a Multifield Primary Key

In some cases, you may want to use two or more fields that, together, provide the primary key of a table. In Design View, select the rows you want to designate as primary keys and click the Primary Key button. To remove multiple primary keys, select the rows and click the Primary Key button. In this exercise, you practice defining and modifying a multifield primary key.

Two or more primary keys in a table are called the **composite key.** Composite keys are useful in unique situations when a combination of data from two fields needs to provide a unique identifier in a table.

STEP BY STEP   **Define and Modify a Multifield Primary Key**

USE the database open from the previous exercise.

1. Press and hold the **Ctrl** key.

2. Click the **Row Selector** box beside the Paid row. Continue to hold down the **Ctrl** key and click the **Order ID Row Selector** box. Both fields should be selected, as shown in Figure 3-8. If not, continue to hold the **Ctrl** key and click the **Paid Row Selector** box again.

Figure 3-8

Primary Key row and another row selected

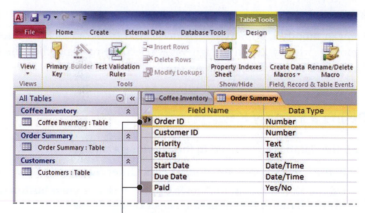

Both fields are selected

3. On the Design tab, in the Tools group, click the **Primary Key** button. A key icon should be displayed beside both of the two selected fields.

4. With the rows still selected, click the **Primary Key** button again to remove the primary key designation from both fields.

5. Click on any field name to remove the selection.

6. Click the **Row Selector** box beside the Order ID row. Press and hold the **Ctrl** key and click the **Row Selector** box beside the Customer ID row. Both fields should be selected.

7. On the Design tab, in the Tools group, click the **Primary Key** button. Both rows should have a key displayed beside them.

8. Click the **Save** button on the Quick Access Toolbar.

9. Close the Design View.

PAUSE. LEAVE the database open to use in the next exercise.

FINDING AND REPLACING DATA

The Bottom Line

A big advantage of using a computer database rather than paper and pencil for recordkeeping is the ability to quickly search for and/or replace data. These features may be accessed from the Find and Replace dialog box. The Find and Replace commands in Access work very much like those in Word or other Office applications you might have used. You can use the Find command to search for specific text in a table or to move quickly to a particular word or number in the table. The Replace command can be used to automatically replace a word or number with another.

In the Find and Replace dialog box, key the text or numbers that you want to search for into the Find What box and click Find Next to locate the record containing the data. If you want to replace the data, key the new data into the Replace With box and click Replace or Replace All.

Take Note When replacing data, it is usually a good practice to click Replace instead of Replace All so that you can confirm each replacement to make sure that it is correct.

Finding and Replacing Data

The Find and Replace dialog box searches only one table at a time; it does not search the entire database. The Look In menu allows you to choose to search by field or to search the entire table. By default, Access searches the field that was selected when you opened the Find and Replace dialog box. If you want to search a different field, select the field while the dialog box is open; you don't have to close it first. In the next exercise, you find and replace table data.

Remember these points when finding and replacing data in Access 2010:

- In the Match menu, you can specify where you want Access to look in a field. Select Any Part of Field for the broadest search.

- Sometimes Access selects the Search Fields As Formatted check box. When it does, do not clear the check box, or your search probably will not return any results.

- Click the Match Case box to search for text with the same uppercase and/or lowercase capitalization of text.

- You can use **wildcard** characters such as a question mark or asterisk to find words or phrases that contain specific letters or combinations of letters. Key a question mark (?) to represent a single character—for example, keying *b?t* will find *bat, bet, bit,* and *but.* Key an asterisk (*) to represent a string of characters—for example, *m*t* will find *mat, moment,* or even *medium format.*

- If you key a wildcard character in the Replace With box, Access will insert that character just as you keyed it.

STEP BY STEP **Find and Replace Data**

USE the database open from the previous exercise.

1. Open the **Customers** table.

2. On the Home tab, in the Find group, click the **Find** button. The Find and Replace dialog box appears with the Find tab displayed.

3. Click the **Replace** tab in the Find and Replace dialog box.

4. Key **Elm** into the Find What box.

5. Key **Little Elm** into the Replace With box.

6. Click the **down arrow** beside the Look In menu and select **Current document**, so that the entire table will be searched **instead** of just the Customer ID field.

7. Click the **down arrow** beside the Match menu and select **Any Part of Field** if it isn't already selected to broaden the search. See Figure 3-9.

Figure 3-9

Find and Replace dialog box

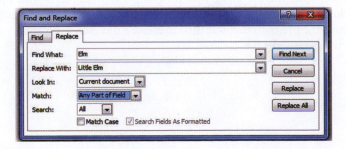

CERTIFICATION READY 2.3.1

How do you find data within a table?

Another Way To open the Find tab in the Find and Replace dialog box using the keyboard, press Ctrl+F. To open the Replace tab, press Ctrl+H.

8. Click the **Find Next** button. Access searches the table and finds and selects the word *Elm*.

9. Click the **Replace** button. Access replaces *Elm* with *Little Elm*.

10. Click the **Find Next** button. Access finds *Elm* in the new text that was just inserted.

11. Click **Find Next** again. Access displays a message saying that no more occurrences of the word have been found. Click **OK**.

12. Click **Cancel** to close the Find and Replace dialog box.

13. Press the **down arrow** to remove the selection and allow Access to save the change.

14. Close the table.

PAUSE. LEAVE the database open to use in the next exercise.

Take Note   If you want to use the Find and Replace dialog box to search for characters that are used as wildcards, such as a question mark, you must enclose that character in brackets, for example [?]. Follow this rule when searching for all wildcard characters except exclamation points (!) and closing brackets (]).

ATTACHING AND DETACHING DOCUMENTS

The Bottom Line   Access 2010 allows you to attach documents, such as Word documents or photo files, to records in a database. For example, the human resources department of a large company could keep a photo, a resume, and employee evaluation documents with each employee record. These attached files can also be easily detached, if necessary. The Attachments dialog box allows you to manage the documents attached to records.

Take Note   You cannot attach files to databases created in versions of Access prior to Access 2007. You cannot share attachments with a database created in these prior versions of Access.

Attaching and Detaching Documents

Before you can start attaching documents, you must create a field in a table and format it with the Attachment data type. You can add the field in Datasheet View or in Design View. Access displays a paper clip icon in the header row and in every record in the field along with a number in parentheses indicating the number of attached files in the field. In this exercise, you create a new field and format it with the Attachment data type, then remove the attachment from your database records.

Double-click the record in the Attachments field to display the Attachments dialog box where you can add, remove, open, or save multiple attachments, such as images, documents, and spreadsheets, for a single record. You can save attached files to your hard disk or network drive so that you can save changes to documents there before saving them to the database.

Take Note   You can attach a maximum total of 2 gigabytes of data, but each individual file cannot exceed 256 megabytes in size.

Another Way You can also right-click in the Attachments field to display a shortcut menu. Select Manage Attachments from the menu to display the Attachments dialog box.

If the program that was used to create the attached file is installed on your computer, you can open and edit the file using that program. For example, if you open a Word resume that is attached to a record, the Word program starts and you view the document in Word. If you do not have the program that was used to create a file, Access prompts you to choose a program you do have to view the file.

USE the database open from the previous exercise.

1. Open the **Order Summary** table.
2. Click the header row of the Due Date field to select it.
3. In the Add & Delete group on the Table Tools Fields contextual tab, click the **More Fields** button. The More Fields menu appears.
4. Click **Attachment** under Basic Types, as shown in Figure 3-10. The Attachment field is inserted in the table.

Figure 3-10

More Fields menu

@ The *invoice 100* file for this lesson is available on the book companion website or in WileyPLUS.

5. Double-click the first row of the Attachments field. The Attachments dialog box appears.
6. Click the **Add** button. Navigate to the data files for this lesson and select *Invoice100.docx*. Click **Open**. The document appears in the Attachments dialog box, as shown in Figure 3-11.

Figure 3-11

Attachments dialog box

7. Click **OK**. The number of attachments in the first record changes to 1, as shown in Figure 3-12.

Figure 3-12

Attachments field displaying the number of attachments

8. Double-click the **attachment number** in the Attachment field. The Attachments dialog box appears.

9. Click the **Open** button. The attachment, an invoice document, opens in Microsoft Word.

10. Click the **Close** button to close the invoice document.

11. Click the **Access** button on the taskbar, if necessary, to return to Access.

12. In the Attachments dialog box, click the **Remove** button, and click **OK**. The attachment is removed from the record.

13. Close the Order Summary table.

PAUSE. LEAVE the database open to use in the next exercise.

Take Note   Once a field has been set to the Attachment data type, it cannot be converted to another data type.

SORTING AND FILTERING DATA AND SETTING FIELD VIEWING OPTIONS WITHIN A TABLE

The Bottom Line   It is often helpful to display data in order, display similar records, or hide and freeze certain fields without affecting the preexisting data. Sorting allows you to order records. For example, an office contact list that displays employees in alphabetical order by last name would help the user find information for a particular employee quickly. If you wanted to view only the records of employees in a particular department, you could create a filter to display only those records. You could also hide or freeze certain fields. For example, in a table that has several fields, you can hide or freeze fields to help you concentrate on certain data.

SOFTWARE ORIENTATION

Sort & Filter Group

The Sort & Filter group is located on the Home tab in the Ribbon (Figure 3-13). Use the Sort & Filter group of commands to sort and filter records in tables.

Figure 3-13

Sort & Filter group

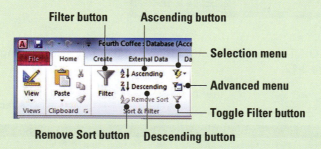

Filter button   Ascending button

Selection menu

Advanced menu

Toggle Filter button

Remove Sort button   Descending button

Sorting Data within a Table

To **sort** data means to arrange it alphabetically, numerically, or chronologically. Sorting within a table displays all the records in the table in the order that you select. You can easily sort by one or more fields to achieve the order that you want. Access can sort text, numbers, or dates in ascending or descending order. **Ascending** order sorts data from beginning to end, such as from A to Z, 1 to 10, and January to December. **Descending** order sorts data from the end to the beginning, such as from Z to A, 10 to 1, and December to January. In this exercise, you sort data using multiple fields and then remove the sort.

To sort text, numbers, dates, or other data types in a column, you first need to select the column. Then click the Ascending or Descending button in the Sort & Filter group of the Home tab. You can also right-click a selected column and choose a Sort command from the shortcut menu. The available sort commands in the shortcut menu vary depending on the type of data in the column, as shown in Table 3-2.

Table 3-2

Sort Commands on the Shortcut Menu

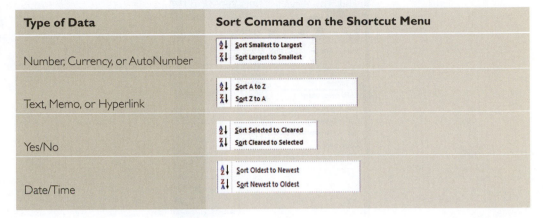

Type of Data	Sort Command on the Shortcut Menu
Number, Currency, or AutoNumber	Sort Smallest to Largest / Sort Largest to Smallest
Text, Memo, or Hyperlink	Sort A to Z / Sort Z to A
Yes/No	Sort Selected to Cleared / Sort Cleared to Selected
Date/Time	Sort Oldest to Newest / Sort Newest to Oldest

You can also sort records on multiple fields. When you are using multiple fields, determine which order you want them to be sorted in. The primary sort field is called the **outermost field**. A secondary sort field is called an **innermost field**. For example, if you want to sort a contact list so that each employee's last name is sorted primarily and first name is sorted secondarily, Last Name would be the outermost field and First Name would be the innermost field. In your completed sort, Wright, David, would be listed before Wright, Steven, in an A to Z (ascending) sort. When designating the sort order, however, you select the innermost field first and choose the type of sort you want from the shortcut menu. Then select the outermost field and select the type of sort that you want.

After you sort one or more columns, Access inserts sort arrows in the header row to show that the field is sorted. These sort commands remain with the table until you remove them. When you want to remove a sort order, click the Remove Sort button from the Sort & Filter group on the Home tab. This removes the sorting commands from all the fields in the table. In a table with more than one sorted field, you cannot remove just one sort.

STEP BY STEP   **Sort Data within a Table**

USE the database you used in the previous exercise.

1. Open the **Customers** table.
2. Click the header row of the Customer ID field to select it.
3. Right-click in the field to display the shortcut menu, shown in Figure 3-14. Select **Sort Largest to Smallest**.

Figure 3-14

Shortcut menu

4. The data is sorted and an arrow is inserted in the header row, as shown in Figure 3-15, indicating that the data is displayed in sort order.

Figure 3-15

Sorted column

Sort arrow

5. On the Home tab, in the Sort & Filter group, click the **Remove Sort** button. The sort is removed from the Customer ID field.

6. Select the **First Name** field. On the Home tab, in the Sort & Filter group, click the **Ascending** button. The data in the First Name field is sorted in ascending order.

7. Select the **Last Name** field. On the Home tab, in the Sort & Filter group, click the **Ascending** button. The data in the Last Name field is sorted in ascending order.

8. On the Home tab, in the Sort & Filter group, click the **Remove Sort** button. The sort is removed from both the First Name and Last Name fields.

9. Close the table. If a dialog box appears asking if you want to save changes to the table, click **No**.

PAUSE. LEAVE the database open to use in the next exercise.

CERTIFICATION
R E A D Y   **2.3.2**

How do you sort data
within a table?

Filtering Data within a Table

A **filter** is a set of rules for determining which records will be displayed. When you apply a filter, Access displays only the records that meet your filter criteria; the other records are hidden from view. Once the filtered records are displayed, you can edit and navigate the records just as you would without a filter applied. Filters remain in effect until you close the object. You can switch between views, and the filter settings will stay in effect. To make the filter available the next time you open the object, save the object before closing it. In this exercise, you practice creating filters in several different ways.

STEP BY STEP   **Apply a Filter**

USE the database you used in the previous exercise.

1. Open the **Coffee Inventory** table.

2. Select the **Product Name** field. On the Home tab, in the Sort & Filter group, click the **Filter** button. A menu appears.

3. Point to Text Filters. A second menu appears. Select **Contains**, as shown in Figure 3-16.

Figure 3-16

Filter menu with
Contains selected

4. The Custom Filter box appears. Key **Decaf**, as shown in Figure 3-17, and click **OK**. Access filters the database to display only the records containing the word Decaf. A filter icon is displayed in the header row of the field, as shown in Figure 3-18.

Figure 3-17

Custom filter box

Figure 3-18

Filtered records

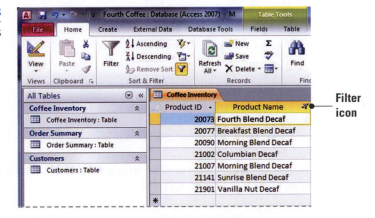

5. Click the **Toggle Filter** button in the Sort & Filter group to display the records without the filter.

6. In the second record in the Product Name field, double-click the word **Decaf** to select it.

7. Right-click the word **Decaf** to display the shortcut menu. Select **Does Not Contain "Decaf,"** as shown in Figure 3-19. Notice that the records are filtered to show only those that do not contain the word Decaf.

Figure 3-19

Shortcut menu with Does
Not Contain "Decaf"
option selected

8. Click in the **Pounds** field of the first record.

9. On the Home tab, in the Sort & Filter group, click the **Filter** button.

10. Click the check boxes to remove the check marks beside 30, 35, 40, and 50, as shown in Figure 3-20. Only the check mark beside 25 should remain.

Figure 3-20

Filter menu selected
to show only 25 in the
pounds column

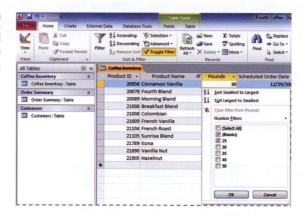

11. Click **OK**. Access filters the records to show only those containing the number 25 in the pounds field.

12. Click the **Toggle Filter** button.

13. In the second row of the Scheduled Order Date field, highlight **1/14/2012** by clicking and dragging the mouse.

14. On the Home tab, in the Sort & Filter group, click the **Selection** button. A menu appears, as shown in Figure 3-21.

Figure 3-21

Selection button and menu

Selection button and menu

CERTIFICATION
R E A D Y   **2.3.3**

How do you filter
table records?

15. Select **On or After 1/14/2012**. The data is filtered to show only those records with content in the Scheduled Order Date field that matches the filter selection.

16. In the seventh row of the Pounds field, select **30**.

17. On the Home tab, in the Sort & Filter group, click the **Selection** button. Select **Less Than or Equal to 30**. The records are filtered.

PAUSE. LEAVE the database open to use in the next exercise.

Take Note   Only one filter can be applied per column. When you apply a filter to a column that is already filtered, the previous filter is removed and the new filter is applied.

Removing a Filter

After applying a filter, you may need to return to records not displayed by the filter. The Toggle Filter button lets you switch between viewing the filtered records and viewing the table without the filter. Note that the purpose of this button changes accordingly—when the records are filtered the button is used to remove the filter, and when the filter is removed the button is used to apply the filter. When you are finished using the filter, you can permanently remove it. In this exercise, you permanently remove the filter you previously applied.

STEP BY STEP   Remove a Filter

USE the table you used in the previous exercise.

1. Select the **Pounds** field. On the Home tab, in the Sort & Filter group, click the **Filter** button. A menu appears.
2. Select **Clear Filter from Pounds**, as shown in Figure 3-22.

Figure 3-22

Removing filter from the pounds column

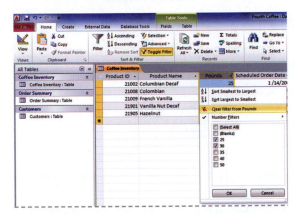

3. On the Home tab, in the Sort & Filter group, click the **Advanced Filter Options** button. A menu appears.
4. Select **Clear All Filters** from the menu, as shown in Figure 3-23.

Figure 3-23

Advanced filter Options button and menu

Advanced filter Options button

5. Save and close the table.

PAUSE. LEAVE the database open to use in the next exercise.

Freezing/Unfreezing and Hiding/Unhiding Fields

Sometimes you may need to change the view of a table's data to more efficiently find the information you're looking for. For example, it may be helpful to freeze First Name and Last Name fields so you can keep them fixed on the screen and then horizontally scroll and view other pertinent fields, like E-mail or Telephone Number to get a better view of your data. You can also hide those fields that may distract you from getting a better view of the data. For example, if you're interested in viewing just a person's name and telephone number, you may decide to hide all fields except First Name, Last Name, and Phone Number. In this exercise, you practice freezing and unfreezing fields, as well as hiding and unhiding them.

STEP BY STEP   **Freeze/Unfreeze and Hide/Unhide Fields**

USE the database you used in the previous exercise.

1. Open the **Customers** table.
2. Select the **Last Name** field. On the Home tab, in the Records group, click the **More** button. A menu appears, as shown in Figure 3-24.

Figure 3-24

More button menu

More button menu

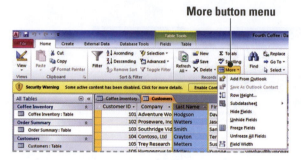

3. Select **Freeze Fields**. Notice that the Last Name field moves to the first field position in the table.
4. Click the **Restore Down** button in the top, right corner of the application window, as shown in Figure 3-25. The Restore Down button now becomes the Maximize button. Press the **Right Arrow** key to scroll the table's fields to the left, and stop when you reach the ZIP/Postal Code field. Notice that the Last Name field stays fixed as the other fields scroll.

Restore down button

Figure 3-25

Restore down button

5. Click the **More** button again and select **Unfreeze All Fields**. Notice how the Last Name field remains in the table's first field position. Press the **Right Arrow** key several times until the Last Name field scrolls off from view. Notice how the Last Name field moved with the other fields when the Right Arrow key was pressed several times.

Take Note   Fields can be rearranged in Datasheet View by clicking on the field name headers and dragging them to where you want to move them.

6. Click the **Maximize** button on the application window.
7. Select the **Customer ID** field. Click the **More** button and select **Hide Fields**. Notice the Customer ID field is now hidden from view, as shown in Figure 3-26.

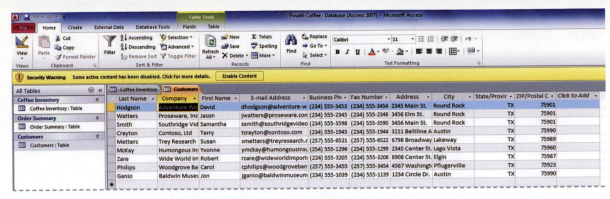

Figure 3-26

Hidden Customer ID field

8. Click the **More** button and select **Unhide Fields**. The Unhide Columns dialog box should appear as shown in Figure 3-27. Notice the check mark is missing from the Customer ID check box, signifying that it's hidden.

Figure 3-27

Unhide Columns dialog box

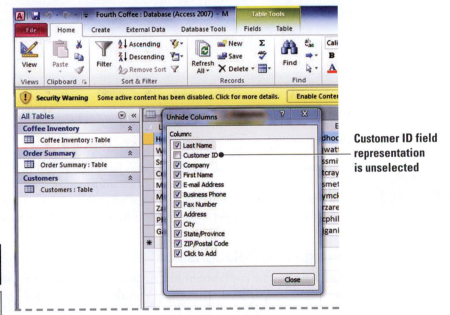

Customer ID field
representation
is unselected

CERTIFICATION
READY   **2.2.5**

How do you freeze or
unfreeze fields?

CERTIFICATION
READY   **2.2.4**

How do you hide or
unhide fields?

9. Deselect the check boxes next to all the other field representations except Last Name and Business Phone, and then click the **Close** button in the Unhide Columns dialog box. Notice the only fields now displayed in Datasheet View are the Last Name and Business Phone fields.

10. Close the Customers table without saving the changes to the layout.

PAUSE. LEAVE the database open to use in the next exercise.

Take Note   You can save your table so it retains your formatting the next time you open it.

Take Note   To select more than one field to freeze or hide, hold down the shift key while selecting adjacent fields.

Another Way
You can also access
the Hide/Unhide and Freeze/
Unfreeze options from the
shortcut menu that appears
after you right-click a field name.

SOFTWARE ORIENTATION

Relationship Tools on the Ribbon

When you click the Relationships button on the Database Tools tab, the Relationship window appears and the Relationship Tools are displayed in the Ribbon (Figure 3-28).

Figure 3-28

Use the Relationship Tools to define and modify table relationships

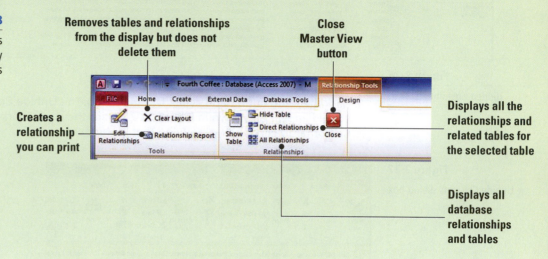

Removes tables and relationships from the display but does not delete them

Close Master View button

Creates a relationship you can print

Displays all the relationships and related tables for the selected table

Displays all database relationships and tables

UNDERSTANDING TABLE RELATIONSHIPS

The Bottom Line

As you have already learned, most databases have more than one table. Creating relationships among these tables allows Access to bring that information back together again through objects such as reports and queries so that you can display information from several tables at once. This is why it is a good idea to define table relationships before you start creating reports and queries.

Defining Table Relationships

In relational database applications like Access, you can store information in separate tables that are connected by a defined relationship that ties the data together. You define a table relationship in the Relationships window. To create that relationship, you place common fields in tables and define the relationships between the tables. Common fields used in different tables do not have to have the same names, but they usually do. They must have the same data type, though. In this exercise, you use a table that already has a primary key field to create a relationship with another table.

You can create three types of relationships in Access tables: one-to-one, one-to-many, and many-to-many.

In a one-to-one relationship, both tables have a common field with the same data. Each record in the first table can only have one matching record in the second table, and each record in the second table can have only one matching record in the first table. This type of relationship is not common because information related in this way is usually stored in the same table.

A one-to-many relationship is more common because each record in the first table can have many records in the second table. For example, in a Customers table and an Orders table, one customer could have many orders. The Customer ID would be the primary key in the Customers table (the one) and the foreign key in the Orders table (the many).

In a third type of relationship, called a many-to-many relationship, many records in the first table can have many records in the second table.

STEP BY STEP   **Define Table Relationships**

USE the database you used in the previous exercise.

1. On the Database Tools tab in the Relationships group, click the **Relationships** button. The Relationships View appears with the Customers table represented.

2. Click the **Show Table** button. The Show Table dialog box appears, as shown in Figure 3-29.

Figure 3-29

Show Table button and dialog box

3. Select **Order Summary** and click **Add**.

4. Click **Close**. The Customer table and Order Summary table are represented in Relationships View.

5. Click the **Customer ID** field in the Customers table and drag it to the Customer ID field of the Order Summary table and release the mouse button. The Customer ID field represents the common field between the two tables. The Edit Relationships dialog box appears, as shown in Figure 3-30.

Figure 3-30

Edit Relationships dialog box

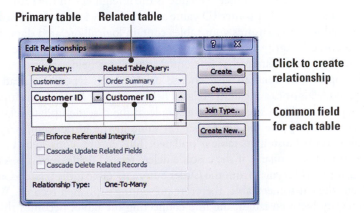

6. Select the *Enforce Referential Integrity* check box. Then select the *Cascade Update Related Fields* and *Cascade Delete Related Records* check boxes.

7. Click **Create**. A relationship line representing the one-to-many table relationship of the Customers and the Order Summary tables is displayed, as shown in Figure 3-31. You just created a one-to-many relationship between these tables using Customer ID, the common field. The one-to-many relationship type signifies that each customer record in the Customers table can have many order records in the Order Summary table.

Figure 3-31

One-to-many relationship

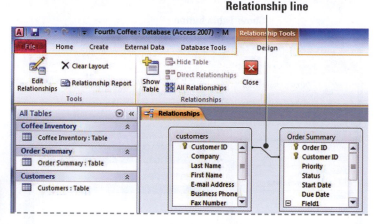

CERTIFICATION READY   2.4.2

How do you use primary keys to create relationships?

PAUSE. LEAVE the database open to use in the next exercise.

Modifying Table Relationships

A table relationship is represented by the line that connects the tables in the Relationship window. To modify the relationship, you can double-click the line to display the Edit Relationships dialog box or delete the line to delete the relationship. The Edit Relationships dialog box allows you to change a table relationship. You can change the tables on either side of the relationship or the fields on either side. You can also perform actions like enforcing referential integrity and choosing cascade options. In the next exercise, you delete the relationship you previously created, and then recreate and edit the relationship to enforce referential integrity.

Referential integrity is an option that you can select in the Edit Relationships dialog box to prevent orphan records. An orphan record is a record in one table that references records in another table that no longer exist. For example, when referential integrity is enforced, Access will not permit a Customer ID value as the foreign key in the Order Summary table that doesn't have a matching Customer ID value as the primary key in the Customers table. In this way, referential integrity ensures your tables contain logically related data. If an operation that violates referential integrity is performed once this option is selected, Access will display a dialog box with a message stating that referential integrity is being violated and therefore will not permit the operation. You can also choose one or both types of cascade options—cascade update related fields or cascade delete related fields—in the Edit Relationships dialog box once referential integrity has been selected. For example, if the cascade update related fields option is selected, Access will update the Customer ID value in the Order Summary table if the Customer ID value in the Customers table is updated. This ensures consistent Customer ID values in the related tables. Similarly, if the cascade delete related fields option is selected, Access will delete all Customer ID records from the Order Summary table if the related Customer ID record is deleted from the Customers table, therefore preventing orphaned records. When you enforce referential integrity between tables, the line connecting the tables becomes thicker. The number 1 is also displayed on the line on the one side of the relationship and an infinity symbol (∞) appears on the other side, to represent the "many" fields that can be included in this side of the relationship.

To remove a table relationship, you must delete the relationship line. You can select the line by pointing to it and clicking it. When the relationship line is selected, it appears thicker. Press the Delete key to delete the line and remove the relationship or right-click the line to display the delete menu.

STEP BY STEP | **Modify Table Relationships**

USE the database you used in the previous exercise.

1. Right-click the center section of the relationship line connecting the two tables. A menu appears, as shown in Figure 3-32.

Figure 3-32

Edit/Delete menu

2. Select **Delete**. A message appears asking if you are sure you want to delete the relationship. Click **Yes**. The line disappears.

3. Select the **Customer ID** field in the first table. Drag the mouse to the Customer ID field in the second table and release the mouse button. The Edit Relationships dialog box appears.

4. Click the **Create** button. A line appears, creating the relationship.

5. Double-click the center section of the relationship line. The Edit Relationships dialog box appears again, listing the tables and the Customer ID fields on each side.

6. Click the **Enforce Referential Integrity** box and click **OK**. The line appears thicker, with the number 1 beside the first table and the infinity symbol (∞) beside the second, as shown in Figure 3-33.

Figure 3-33

Relationship displaying enforced referential integrity

Relationship line with the
number 1 on the "one" side

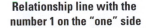
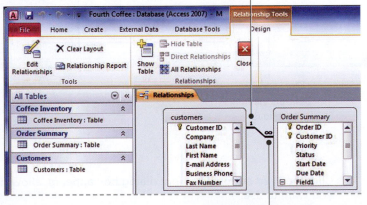

Infinity symbol displayed
on the "many" side

CERTIFICATION
READY **2.4.3**

How do you edit relationships?

PAUSE. LEAVE the database open to use in the next exercise.

Printing Table Relationships

You may want to print a table relationship to save for your records or to discuss with a colleague. The Relationship Report command makes this easy. When you choose to print the relationship report, the Print Preview tab will appear with options for viewing and printing the report. After you make any changes to the layout of the report, click the Print button to start printing. After printing the report, you can choose to save it. In this exercise, you view and print table relationships without saving the relationship report.

STEP BY STEP **Print Table Relationships**

USE the database you used in the previous exercise.

1. In the Tools group of the Relationship Tools Design tab, click the **Relationship Report** button. The report is created and the Print Preview tab appears, as shown in Figure 3-34.

Page Layout group: Controls page orientation and printing options

Data group: Controls all aspects of data exporting

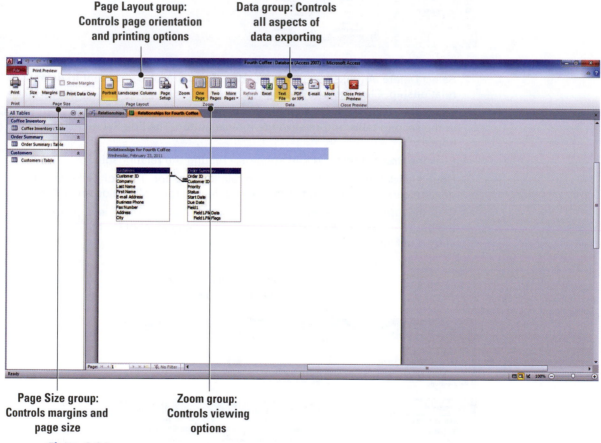

Page Size group: Controls margins and page size

Zoom group: Controls viewing options

Figure 3-34

Print preview of Relationship Report

2. Click the **Print** button. The Print dialog box appears, allowing you to select the printer you want to use.

3. Click **OK** to keep the default settings and print the report.

4. Click the **Close** button to close the Relationships for FourthCoffee tab. A message appears asking if you want to save changes to the report. Click **No**.

5. Close the Relationships tab.

STOP. CLOSE the database.

SKILL SUMMARY

In This Lesson You Learned How To:	Exam Objective	Objective Number
Navigate among Records		
Enter, Insert, Edit, and Delete Records		
Work with Primary Keys	Define Primary Keys.	2.4.1
Find and Replace Data	Use Find.	2.3.1
Attach and Detach Documents		
Sort and Filter Data and Set Field View Options within a Table	Use Sort. Use Filter commands. Freeze or Unfreeze fields. Hide or Unhide fields.	2.3.2 2.3.3 2.2.5 2.2.4
Understand Table Relationships	Use Primary Keys to create Relationships. Edit Relationships.	2.4.2 2.4.3

Knowledge Assessment

Matching

Match the term in Column 1 to its description in Column 2.

Column 1		Column 2
1. foreign key	**a.**	prevents orphan records, to ensure that records do not reference other records that no longer exist
2. composite key	**b.**	sorts data from beginning to end
3. outermost field	**c.**	sorts data from end to beginning
4. referential integrity	**d.**	to arrange data alphabetically, numerically, or chronologically
5. wildcards	**e.**	a primary key from one table that is used in another table
6. ascending order	**f.**	a set of rules for determining which records will be displayed
7. descending order	**g.**	the secondary sort field in a multifield sort
8. filter	**h.**	two or more primary keys in a table
9. sort	**i.**	characters used to find words or phrases that contain specific letters or combinations of letters
10. innermost field	**j.**	the primary sort field in a multifield sort

True/False

Circle T if the statement is true or F if the statement is false.

T F **1.** You can use the Navigation buttons to search for data in a table.

T F **2.** You can enter any kind of data into any field.

T F **3.** After you enter data and move to a new field, Access automatically saves the data for you in the table.

T F **4.** After you delete a record, you can click the Undo button to bring it back.

T F **5.** The Find and Replace dialog box searches all the tables in a database at one time.

T F **6.** An AutoNumber field will usually make a good primary key.

T F **7.** Before you can attach a document, there must be a field in a table formatted with the Attachment data type.

T F **8.** The outermost field is the primary sort field in a multifield sort.

T F **9.** The Toggle Filter button lets you permanently remove a filter and switches you back to the original view.

T F **10.** In a one-to-many relationship, each record in the first table can have many records in the second table.

Competency Assessment

Project 3-1: Charity Event Contacts List

You are working as an intern for Woodgrove Bank. Part of your job is helping your supervisor organize a charity event. Use an Access table to create a contacts list that your supervisor will use to make calls to local businesses requesting sponsorships and donations for the event.

GET READY. LAUNCH Access if it is not already running.

@ The *Charity Event* file for this lesson is available on the book companion website or in WileyPLUS.

1. **OPEN** the *Charity Event* database.
2. **SAVE** the database as *Charity EventXXX* (where XXX is your initials).
3. Open the **Contacts** table.
4. Enter the records shown in the following table:

ID	Company	Last Name	First Name	Business Phone
17	Trey Research	Tiano	Mike	469-555-0182
18	Fourth Coffee	Culp	Scott	469-555-0141
19	Wingtip Toys	Baker	Mary	972-555-0167
20	Margie's Travel	Nash	Mike	972-555-0189

5. Click the **View** menu and choose **Design** View.
6. Select the **ID** row. On the Design tab, on the Tools menu, click the **Primary Key** button.
7. Save the design of the table and return to Datasheet View.
8. On the Home tab, in the Find group, click the **Find** button. The Find and Replace dialog box appears. Key **0177** into the Find What box.
9. Select **Contents** from the Look In menu and select **Any Part of Field** in the Match menu.
10. Click the **Replace** tab. Key **0175** into the Replace With box.
11. Click **Find Next** and then click **Replace**.
12. Click **Cancel** to close the dialog box.
13. Select the **Lucern Publishing** record.
14. On the Home tab, in the Records group, click the **Delete** button. Click **Yes** to delete the record.
15. **CLOSE** the database.

LEAVE Access open for the next project.

Project 3-2: Angels Project Wish List

The four kindergarten classes at the School of Fine Art have adopted one boy and one girl "angel" from the community. Children from the classes may purchase holiday gifts for their angels. As an office assistant at the school, you are working with the Angel Project staff to organize information about each angel.

GET READY. LAUNCH Access if it is not already running.

@ The *Angels* file for this lesson is available on the book companion website or in WileyPLUS.

1. **OPEN** *Angels* from the data files for this lesson.
2. **SAVE** the database as *Angels XXX*, where XXX is your initials.
3. Open the List table.
4. Select the **Gender** field. On the Home tab, in the Sort & Filter group, click the **Ascending** button.
5. Select the **Age** field. On the Home tab, in the Sort & Filter group, click the **Descending** button.
6. On the Home tab, in the Sort & Filter group, click the **Remove Sort** button.
7. In the Gender field, select the **M** in the first record.
8. On the Home tab, in the Sort & Filter group, click the **Selection** button and select **Equals "M."**
9. On the Home tab, in the Sort & Filter group, click the **Toggle Filter** button.
10. Select the Wants field. On the Home tab, in the Sort & Filter group, click the Filter button. Select Text Filters from the menu, select Contains from the next menu, and key Bike in the Custom Filter dialog box and press **Enter.**
11. On the Home tab, in the Sort & Filter group, click the **Advanced Filter Options** button and select **Clear All Filters** from the menu.

LEAVE Access open for the next project.

Proficiency Assessment

Project 3-3: Angel Project Contact Information

GET READY. LAUNCH Access if it is not already running.

1. The Angel database should be open on your screen.
2. Open the **Contact Information** table.
3. Enter the following new records:

ID	Last Name	First Name	Parent's Name	Address	City	State	Zip Code	Home Phone
15	Wright	Steven	Kevin	2309 Monroe Ct	Marietta	GA	34006	770-555-0142
16	Cook	Cathan	Patrick	1268 Oak Dr	Marietta	GA	34006	770-555-0128

4. Switch to Design View. Remove the primary key from the Home Phone field and define the ID field as the primary key.
5. Save the design and return to Datasheet View.
6. Select the **ID** field and sort it in ascending order.
7. On the Database Tools tab, in the Relationships group, click the **Relationships** button.
8. Create a one-to-one relationship between the ID field of the List table and the ID field of the Contact Information table.
9. Save the Relationships View and close it.
10. **CLOSE** the tables and the database.

LEAVE Access open for the next project.

Project 3-4: Wingtip Toys Inventory Table

Wingtip Toys, a small manufacturer of wooden toys, has kept most of its records on paper for the last 20 years. The business has recently expanded, and you have been hired to help the company transfer its entire inventory and other administrative data to Access 2010. Edit the table to include all the latest handwritten data you've found.

GET READY. LAUNCH Access if it is not already running.

@ The *Wingtip Toys* file for this lesson is available on the book companion website or in WileyPLUS.

1. **OPEN** the *Wingtip Toys* database and save it as *Wingtip XXX*, where XXX is your initials.

2. Open the **Inventory** table.

3. On the Home tab, in the Find group, click the **Replace** button to display the Find and Replace dialog box. Change the following prices:

   Find all **14.99** and replace with **29.99**

   Find all **16.99** and replace with **34.99**

   Find all **15.99** and replace with **30.99**

   Find all **24.99** and replace with **34.99**

4. Delete the following records from the database:

   ID = 13

   ID = 19

   ID = 16

5. Edit the following records:

   ID = 30, change the number of items in stock to 3

   ID = 28, change the number of items in stock to 6

   ID = 6, change the number of items in stock to 4

6. Select the **In Stock** field and create a filter to display all the records with a value less than or equal to 10 in the field.

7. Remove the filter.

8. Close the table.

9. **CLOSE** the database.

LEAVE Access open for the next project.

Mastery Assessment

Project 3-5: Soccer Roster

As coach of your son's soccer team, you have created a database in which to store information about the team. Enter, edit, and delete records to update it.

GET READY. LAUNCH Access if it is not already running.

@ The *Soccer* file for this lesson is available on the book companion website or in WileyPLUS.

1. **OPEN** the *Soccer* database from the data files for this lesson.

2. **SAVE** the database as *Soccer XXX*, where *XXX* is your initials.

3. Open the **Roster** table.

4. Enter the following record for a new player:

   Eric Parkinson, 806-555-0170, uniform number 9

5. One player has quit the team, Russell King. Replace his data with this data for the following new player:

   George Jiang, 806-555-0123, uniform number 4

6. In the Size field, enter **XS** for each player, except for uniform numbers 4, 6, and 7, which should be size **S**.

@ The *Medical Alert* file for this lesson is available on the book companion website or in WileyPLUS.

7. Create an Attachment field and attach the Word document *Medical Alert.docx* to the record for Garrett Young.

8. Define the **Uniform** field as the primary key.

9. Save the table design and **CLOSE** the database.

LEAVE Access open for the next project.

Project 3-6: Donations Table

Donations are starting to come in for Woodgrove Bank's charity event. Track the donation commitments received.

GET READY. LAUNCH Access if it is not already running.

1. **OPEN** the *CharityEvent XXX* database you created in Project 3-1.

2. Open the **Donations** table.

3. Create a filter to display the items in the Needs field without Commitments from a company.

4. Remove the filter.

5. Use Find and Replace to find each occurrence of the word Company in the Needs field and replace it with the word Volunteer.

6. Create a relationship between the **ID** field in the Contacts table and the **Committed Company ID** in the Donations table.

7. Print the relationship.

8. Close the relationship without saving.

9. Close the tables.

10. **CLOSE** the database.

CLOSE Access.

INTERNET READY

Search the Internet for at least five coffee shops in your area or a favorite city of your choice. Draw a table on paper or in a Word document with fields for the Company Name, Location, Phone Number, and Hours of Operation. Insert data for the five coffee shops you found. If you feel ready for a challenge, create the table in a new database.

4 Modify Tables and Fields

LESSON SKILL MATRIX

Skill	Exam Objective	Objective Number
Modifying a Database Table	Rename objects.	1.2.1
	Delete objects.	1.2.2
Creating Fields and Modifying Field Properties	Modify field properties.	2.2.8
	Rename a field.	2.2.3
	Insert a field.	2.2.1
	Use Quick Start.	1.3.2
	Delete a field.	2.2.2

KEY TERMS
- input mask
- multivalued field
- properties
- Quick Start field
- validation rule
- validation text
- zero-length string

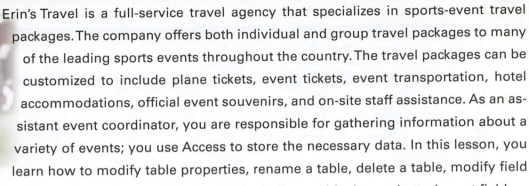

Erin's Travel is a full-service travel agency that specializes in sports-event travel packages. The company offers both individual and group travel packages to many of the leading sports events throughout the country. The travel packages can be customized to include plane tickets, event tickets, event transportation, hotel accommodations, official event souvenirs, and on-site staff assistance. As an assistant event coordinator, you are responsible for gathering information about a variety of events; you use Access to store the necessary data. In this lesson, you learn how to modify table properties, rename a table, delete a table, modify field properties, and create and modify fields—including multivalue and attachment fields.

MODIFYING A DATABASE TABLE

The Bottom Line

After a table has been created, you may need to modify it. You can make many changes to a table—or other database object—using its property sheet. You can also rename or delete a table, but keep in mind that such a change could possibly break the functionality of the database, because in a relational database the various components work together.

Modifying Table Properties

You can set properties that control the appearance or behavior characteristics for an entire table in the table's property sheet. Sometimes it's necessary to describe the purpose of a table by modifying the table's Description property since others who view your table may require more information about its purpose. Other table properties are more advanced and used less often. In this exercise, you modify the description property for a table.

STEP BY STEP   **Modify Table Properties**

GET READY. Before you begin these steps, be sure to launch Microsoft Access.

 The *Events* file for this lesson is available on the book companion website or in WileyPLUS.

1. **OPEN** the *Events* database from the data files for this lesson.
2. **SAVE** the database as *EventsXXX* (where *XXX* is your initials).
3. Click the **Close 'Event List'** button to close the form that displays.
4. In the Navigation Pane, double-click **Events** to open that table.
5. On the Home tab, in the Views group, click the **Views** button and then click **Design View**.
6. On the Design tab, in the Show/Hide group, click **Property Sheet**. The Property Sheet pane appears on the right of the Access window, as shown in Figure 4-1.

WILEY PLUS *EXTRA*

WileyPLUS Extra! features an online tutorial of this task.

Property sheet pane

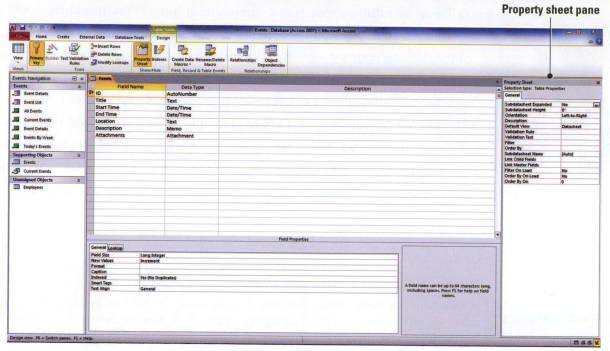

Figure 4-1

Property sheet pane

7. Place the insertion point in the property box for Description.
8. Press **Shift+F2** to open the Zoom box, shown in Figure 4-2, to provide more space.

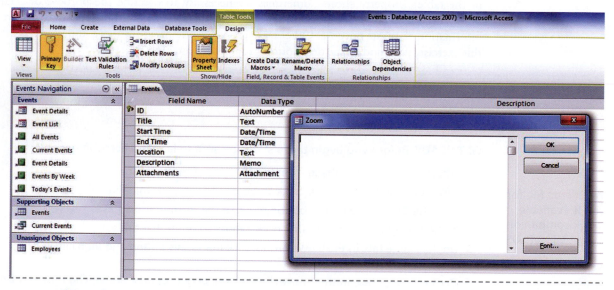

Figure 4-2

Zoom dialog box

Another Way
You can also press
Alt+Enter to display the
property sheet for an object.

9. Key **Most popular events for 2012**.
10. Click **OK**.
11. Click the **Close** button on the Property Sheet pane to close it.
12. Click the **File** tab and click **Save** to save the design changes you've made to the table.
PAUSE. LEAVE the database open to use in the next exercise.

To set the properties for a table, open the table in Design View. On the Design tab, in the Show/Hide group, click Property Sheet. Click the box for the property you want to set and key a setting for the property. Table 4-1 lists the available table properties and what they control.

Table 4-1

Table Properties

Table Property	Use This Table Property To
Subdatasheet Expanded	Specify whether to expand all subdatasheets when you open the table.
Subdatasheet Height	Specify whether to expand to show all available subdatasheet rows (default) when opened or to set the height of the subdatasheet window to show when opened.
Orientation	Set the view orientation, according to whether your language is read left-to-right or right-to-left.
Description	Provide a description of the table.
Default View	Set Datasheet, PivotTable, or PivotChart as the default view when you open the table.
Validation Rule	Supply an expression that must be true whenever you add a record or change a record.
Validation Text	Enter text that appears when a record violates the Validation Rule expression.
Filter	Define criteria to display only matching rows in Datasheet View.
Order By	Select one or more fields to specify the default sort order of rows in Datasheet View.
Subdatasheet Name	Specify whether a subdatasheet should appear in Datasheet View, and, if so, which table or query should supply the rows in the subdatasheet.
Link Child Fields	List the fields in the table or query used for the subdatasheet that match this table's primary key field(s).
Link Master Fields	List the primary key field(s) in this table that match the child fields for the subdatasheet.
Filter On Load	Automatically apply the filter criteria in the Filter property (by setting to Yes) when the table is opened in Datasheet View.
Order By On Load	Automatically apply the sort criteria in the Order By property (by setting to Yes) when the table is opened in Datasheet View.
Order By On	Provide an alternate method to the Order By On Load property by automatically applying the sort criteria in the Order By property when set to -1 (Yes).

Renaming a Table

To rename a table or other database object, you must first close it. In the Navigation Pane, locate and right-click the object that you want to rename, and then click Rename on the shortcut menu that appears. Or, select the table in the Navigation Pane, press F2, key a new name, and press Enter. Think carefully before you rename a table. If existing database objects, such as queries or reports, use data from that table, the name modification might break the functionality of the database. In this exercise, you create a new table and then rename it using the shortcut menu.

STEP BY STEP	Rename a Table

USE the database that is open from the previous exercise.

1. On the Create tab, in the Tables group, click the **Application Parts** button and click **Comments** to create a new table.

2. In the Create Relationship dialog box that appears, select **There is no relationship** and then click **Create**.

3. Open the **Comments** table and right-click **Comments** in the Navigation Pane to display the shortcut menu shown in Figure 4-3. Select **Rename** and a dialog box appears that states *You can't rename the database object 'Comments' while it's open,* as shown in Figure 4-4. Close the dialog box.

Figure 4-3

Rename command on table shortcut menu

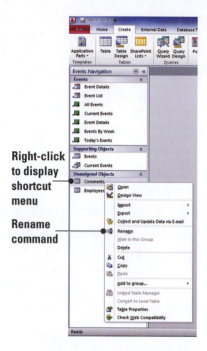

Figure 4-4

Can't rename table dialog box

4. Close the **Comments** table. The table closes.
5. Right-click **Comments** in the Navigation Pane to display the shortcut menu.
6. Click **Rename**. The table name is now selected for renaming, as shown in Figure 4-5.

Figure 4-5

Table name selected for renaming

CERTIFICATION
R E A D Y **1.2.1**

How do you rename a database table?

7. Key **Event Comments** and press **Enter**. The table has been renamed.

PAUSE. LEAVE the database open to use in the next exercise.

Deleting a Table

Deleting an entire table is not a complex process; however, remember that when you delete an entire table you might break the functionality of your database. Although you will be asked to confirm the deletion of a table, you can always undo the action. In this exercise, you delete a table.

To delete a table or other database object like a report, form, or query, right-click it in the Navigation Pane and click Delete. Or, select the table in the Navigation Pane and press Delete.

STEP BY STEP   **Delete a Table**

USE the database that is open from the previous exercise.

1. Right-click the **Event Comments** table in the Navigation Pane and click **Delete** on the shortcut menu. A confirmation message appears, as shown in Figure 4-6.

Figure 4-6

Delete table confirmation message

2. Click **Yes** to delete the table.

Take Note   If the table was related to one or more additional tables, Access would ask if you wanted to delete those relationships before deleting the table.

CERTIFICATION
READY   **1.2.2**

How do you delete objects?

PAUSE. LEAVE the database open to use in the next exercise.

 Ref   Another way to remove data is to delete information from individual records or delete entire records from a table, as you learned in Lesson 3.

SOFTWARE ORIENTATION

Field Properties

Some field properties are available in Datasheet View, but to access the complete list of field properties you must use Design View. An example of field properties for a table in Design View is shown in Figure 4-7.

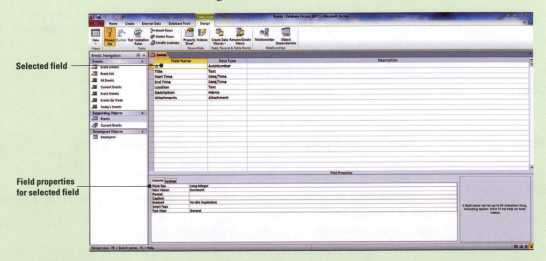

Figure 4-7

Field properties   Use this figure as a reference throughout this lesson as well as the rest of this book.

CREATING FIELDS AND MODIFYING FIELD PROPERTIES

The Bottom Line

A field has certain defining characteristics such as a name that uniquely identifies the field within a table, and a data type that's chosen to match the information to be stored. Every field also has an associated group of settings called **properties** that define the appearance or behavior of the field. In this section, you learn how to create fields and modify field properties.

Access uses the field property settings when you view and edit data. For example, the Format, Input Mask, and Caption properties affect how your information appears in table and query datasheets. In addition, any controls on new forms and reports that are based on the fields in the table inherit these same property settings by default.

Setting Field Properties

You can control the appearance of information, prevent incorrect entries, specify default values, speed up searching and sorting, and control other appearance or behavior characteristics by setting or modifying field properties. For example, you can format numbers to make them easier to read or you can define a validation rule that must be satisfied for information to be entered in a field. In this exercise, you set the *Required* field property in Datasheet View and Field Size property in Design View.

To set a field property in Datasheet View, open the table in Datasheet View. Click in the field for which you want to set the property. In the Field Validation group on the Table Tools Fields contextual tab, select the Unique check box to require the values in the field to be unique for all the records in the table. Or, select the Required check box to make this a required field, where all instances of this field must contain a value. In the Properties group, select the Field Size property box to define the text length for a field, which limits the number of characters allowed for input. You can also select other field properties like Name and Caption, where you can modify a preexisting field or specify a new field name and the associated caption for that field. The field name is what Access uses to reference the field behind the scenes and when you view the field names in Design View. The caption is what appears as column names in tables, and as labels in queries, forms, and reports. Keep in mind that Access will show field names as the column names and labels when no caption property value is specified.

You can set a few of the available field properties in Datasheet View, but to access all of the available field properties (Table 4-2), you must open the table in Design View. For example, you can modify the Field Size property in both Datasheet and Design Views, but can only modify the Smart Tags property—which allows actions to occur when field data is clicked—in Design View.

To set field properties in Design View, open the table in Design View. In the upper portion of the table design grid, click the field for which you want to set properties. The properties for this field are displayed in the lower portion of the table design grid.

Click the box for the field property you want to set. Alternatively, you can press F6 and then move to the property by using the arrow keys. Type a setting for the property or, if an arrow appears at the right side of the property box, click the arrow to choose from a list of settings for the property.

Take Note　The maximum number of characters you can enter into a field is 255.

STEP BY STEP　　**Set a Field Property in Datasheet View and Design View**

USE the database that is open from the previous exercise.

1. Double-click the **Events** table in the Navigation Pane to open the table in Datasheet View, if it is not already open.
2. Click the **Location** column header to select that field.
3. Click the **Required** check box in the Field Validation group on the Table Tools Fields contextual tab, as shown in Figure 4-8. This setting determines that all instances of the *Location* field must contain a value.

**Field Validation group with
Required check box selected**

Figure 4-8

Table Tools Tab

CERTIFICATION
R E A D Y   **2.2.8**

How do you modify field
properties?

4. On the Home tab, in the Views group, click the **View** button and click **Design View**.

5. In the Field Name column in the upper portion of the table design grid, click in the **Title** cell.

6. In the Field Size row in the lower portion of the table design grid, select **150** in the property box and key **175** to change the maximum number of characters you can enter in the *Title* field.

PAUSE. LEAVE the database open to use in the next exercise.

Table 4-2

Available Field Properties.

Field Property	Use This Field Property To
Field Size	Set the maximum size for data stored as a Text, Number, or AutoNumber data type.
Format	Customize the way the field appears when displayed or printed.
Decimal Places	Specify the number of decimal places to use when displaying numbers.
New Values	Set whether an *AutoNumber* field is incremented or assigned a random number.
Input Mask	Display editing characters to guide data entry.
Caption	Set the text displayed by default as the column name in tables and labels for forms, reports, and queries.
Default Value	Automatically assign a default value to a field when new records are added.
Validation Rule	Supply an expression that must be true whenever you add or change the value in this field.
Validation Text	Enter text that appears when a value violates the Validation Rule.
Required	Require that data be entered in a field.
Allow Zero Length	Allow entry (by setting to Yes) of a zero-length string ("") in a *Text, Memo*, or *Hyperlink* field.
Indexed	Speed up access to data in this field by creating and using an index.
Unicode Compression	Compress text stored in this field when a large amount of text is stored.
IME Mode	Specify an Input Method Editor, a tool for using English versions of Windows.
IME Sentence Mode	Specify the type of data you can enter by using an Input Method Editor.
SmartTags	Attach a smart tag to this field.
Append Only	Allow versioning (by setting to Yes) of a *Memo* field.
Text Format	Choose Rich Text to store text as HTML and allow rich formatting. Choose Plain Text to store only text.
Text Align	Specify the default alignment of text within a control.
Precision	Specify the total number of digits allowed, including those both to the right and the left of the decimal point.
Scale	Specify the maximum number of digits that can be stored to the right of the decimal separator.

Defining Input Masks

You use an **input mask** whenever you want users to enter data in a specific way. An input mask can require users to enter dates in a specific format, for example, DD-MM-YYYY, or telephone numbers that follow the conventions for a specific country or region. An input mask is helpful because it can prevent users from entering invalid data (such as a phone number in a date field). In addition, input masks can ensure that users enter data in a consistent way. In this exercise, you specify that the dates in the *Start Time* field be entered in Medium Date format, following the required pattern, *28-Aug-73*.

You can add input masks to table fields by running the Input Mask Wizard or by manually entering masks in the *Input Mask* field property.

Define Input Masks for Fields

USE the database that is open from the previous exercise.

1. In the Field Name column in the upper portion of the table design grid, click in the **Start Time** cell.
2. Click the **Input Mask** property box in the lower portion of the table design grid to display the Input Mask Wizard button (...) on the far right of the cell, as shown in Figure 4-9.

Figure 4-9

Input Mask Wizard button

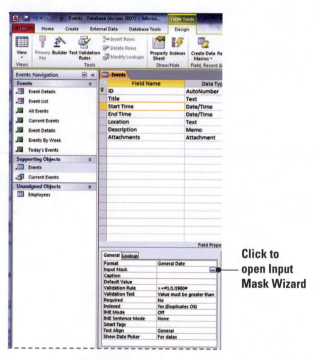

3. Click the **Input Mask Wizard** button. A message box appears asking if you want to save the table now.

4. Click **Yes** to close the message box and display the Input Mask Wizard, as shown in Figure 4-10.

Figure 4-10

Input Mask Wizard

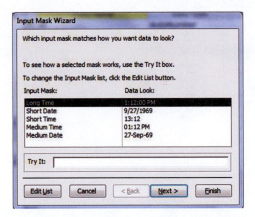

5. Click **Medium Date**, to select the DD-MON-YR date format, and then click **Next >**. The next screen in the Input Mask Wizard appears, as shown in Figure 4-11.

Figure 4-11

Input Mask Wizard, next screen

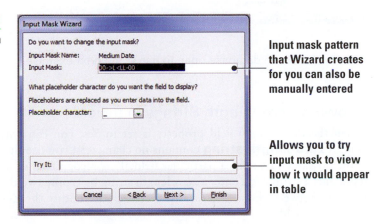

Input mask pattern that Wizard creates for you can also be manually entered

Allows you to try input mask to view how it would appear in table

6. Click **Next** to accept the default settings in this screen and display the final Input Mask Wizard screen, as shown in Figure 4-12.

Figure 4-12

Input Mask Wizard, final screen

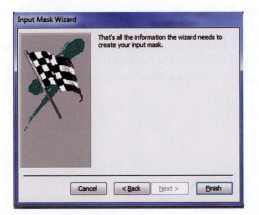

7. Click **Finish**. The input mask appears in the Input Mask row, as shown in Figure 4-13.

Figure 4-13

Input Mask row

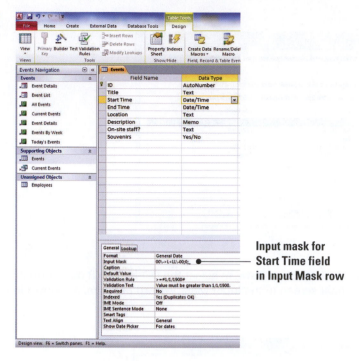

Input mask for
Start Time field
in Input Mask row

PAUSE. LEAVE the database open to use in the next exercise.

Allowing Zero-Length Strings in a Field

When the *Zero Length* field property is set to Yes, you can enter zero-length strings in a field. A **zero-length string** contains no characters; you use the string to indicate that you know no value exists for a particular field. This recognition of a nonexistent value actually represents a string. You enter a zero-length string by typing two double quotation marks with no space between them (""). In this exercise, you modify the Zero Length property for the *Description* field.

Allow Zero Length

USE the database that is open from the previous exercise.

1. In the Field Name column in the upper portion of the table design grid, click in the **Description** cell.
2. Click the **Allow Zero Length** property box in the lower portion of the table design grid to display the down arrow on the far right of the cell.
3. Click the **down arrow** to display the menu, as shown in Figure 4-14.

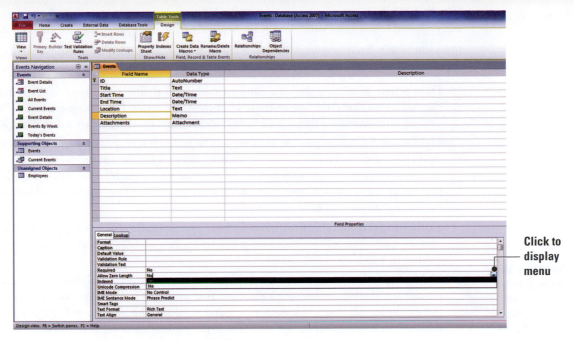

Click to display menu

Figure 4-14

Zero Length property menu

4. Click **Yes**.

PAUSE. LEAVE the database open to use in the next exercise.

Setting Memo Fields as Append Only

A field's data type determines the properties you can set. For example, the Append Only property applies only to a field that is set to the Memo data type. You cannot set this property on a field with any other data type. You use a *Memo* field when you need to store large amounts of text in a database. When the *Append Only* field is enabled, users can add data to the *Memo* field, but they cannot change or remove existing data. This is sometimes necessary if you want to be sure to retain preexisting data and not allow it to be inadvertently deleted. In this exercise, you set the Append Only property for the *Description* field.

STEP BY STEP **Set Memo Field as Append Only**

USE the database that is open from the previous exercise.

1. In the Field Name column in the upper portion of the table design grid, the Description cell should be selected.
2. Click the **Append Only** property box in the lower portion of the table design grid to display the down arrow on the far right of the cell.
3. Click the **down arrow** to display the menu and click **Yes**.

PAUSE. LEAVE the database open to use in the next exercise.

Take Note By default, when you try to position the pointer in a *Memo* field with the Append Only property enabled, Access hides the text.

Setting Data Validation Rules

Validation rules help to ensure that your database users enter the proper types or amounts of data. A **validation rule** is an expression that limits the values that can be entered in the field. The maximum length for the Validation Rule property is 2,048 characters. For example, if the field contains a date, you can require that the date entered in the field be later than June 4, 1977. **Validation text** specifies the text in the error message that appears when a user violates a validation rule. For example, the error message could say "Please enter a date that is later than

June 4, 1977." The maximum length for the Validation Text property is 255 characters. In this exercise, you modify the Validation Rule and Validation Text properties for the *End Time* field.

Data can be validated in several ways, and you will often use multiple methods to define a validation rule. Each of the following can be used to ensure that your users enter data properly:

- **Data types:** When you design a database table, you define a data type for each field in the table, and that data type restricts what users can enter. For example, a *Date/Time* field accepts only dates and times, a *Currency* field accepts only monetary values, and so on.

- **Field sizes:** Field sizes provide another way to validate text. For example, if you create a field that stores first names, you can set it to accept a maximum of 15 characters. This can prevent a malicious user from pasting large amounts of text into the field. It could also prevent an inexperienced user from mistakenly entering a first, middle, and last name in a field designed only to hold a first name.

- **Table properties:** Table properties provide very specific types of validation. For example, you can set the Required property to Yes, and, as a result, force users to enter a value in a field.

- **Field properties:** You can also use field properties, such as the Validation Rule property to require specific values, and the Validation Text property to alert your users to any mistakes. For example, entering a rule such as >1 and <100 in the Validation Rule property forces users to enter values between 1 and 100. Entering text such as "Enter values between 1 and 100" in the Validation Text property tells users when they have made a mistake and how to fix the error.

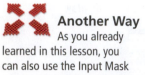

Another Way
As you already learned in this lesson, you can also use the Input Mask property to validate data by forcing users to enter values in a specific way.

STEP BY STEP   **Set Data Validation Rules**

USE the database that is open from the previous exercise.

1. In the Field Name column in the upper portion of the table design grid, click the **End Time** cell.

2. Click the **Validation Rule** property box in the lower portion of the table design grid to display the Expression Builder button (...) on the far right of the cell, as shown in Figure 4-15.

Figure 4-15

Expression Builder button

Click to open the
Expression Builder

3. Click the **Expression Builder** button to display the Expression Builder dialog box, as shown in Figure 4-16.

Figure 4-16

Expression Builder dialog box

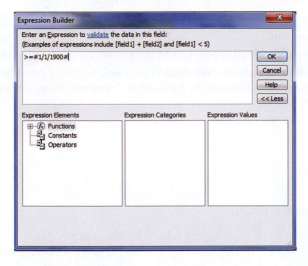

4. Select the number **1900** and replace it by keying **2012**.

5. Click **OK**.

6. Click the **Validation Text** property box in the lower portion of the table design grid.

7. Select the number **1900** and replace it by keying **2012**. The property boxes should look like those shown in Figure 4-17.

Figure 4-17

Modified Validation field properties

PAUSE. LEAVE the database open to use in the next exercise.

Entering Captions

The *Caption property* field specifies the text displayed by default as column names in tables and in labels for forms, reports, and queries. The maximum length for the Caption property is 255 characters. If you don't specify a caption to be displayed, the field name is used as the label. In this exercise, you set the Caption property for the *Location* field.

Enter Captions

USE the database that is open from the previous exercise.

1. In the Field Name column in the upper portion of the table design grid, click the **Location** cell.
2. Click the **Caption** property box in the lower portion of the table design grid.
3. Key **To be announced**. The caption property has now been set to *To be announced* and will display as a column name in table Datasheet View, as well as in labels for forms, reports, and queries.

PAUSE. LEAVE the database open to use in the next exercise.

SOFTWARE ORIENTATION

Add & Delete Group

When creating fields, you use the Add & Delete group on the Table Tools Fields contextual tab, which is shown in Figure 4-18. You can use these commands to add fields with associated data types, add *Quick Start* fields, insert lookup columns, and delete columns.

Figure 4-18

Add & Delete group

Add a field (column) with data type indicated

Delete a column

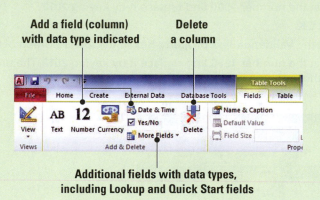

Additional fields with data types, including Lookup and Quick Start fields

Use this figure as a reference throughout this lesson as well as the rest of this book.

Creating Fields

Fields can be created in different ways. You can add fields to a table in Design View, or add fields in Datasheet View using the Click to Add column and Add & Delete Group. Sometimes it is easier to choose from a predefined list of fields than to manually create a field. Access includes a quick and easy way for you to add fields to a table using the Add & Delete group on the Table Tools Fields contextual tab, which includes a collection of fields with associated data types and built-in *Quick Start* fields that can save you considerable time. In this exercise, you add fields to a table by using a combination of the Click to Add column and the Add & Delete group.

The last column in a table in Datasheet View has a Click to Add column, which you can use to add a field simply by keying information in that column. Rename the field by right-clicking the column head, choosing Rename Field from the menu, and keying a new name. Access will try to automatically determine the field data type by the data entered.

A **Quick Start field** is a predefined set of characteristics and properties that describes a field, including a field name, a data type, and a number of other field properties. *Quick Start* fields are new to Access 2010 and allow you to quickly add commonly used single fields or several related ones. For example, using *Quick Start* fields, you can choose from a variety of fields including "Status" to quickly add a field named Status with built-in options like Not Started, In Progress, and so on, or you can choose the "Address" Quick Start to quickly include related fields like City, State, and Zip Code.

To create a new field, you can simply choose from commonly used fields in the Add & Delete group, or click the More Fields button to access a menu with a greater variety of field types. To create a new field using Quick Start, click the More Fields button and then choose a Quick Start field from the menu, as shown in Figure 4-19.

Figure 4-19

More Fields button menu

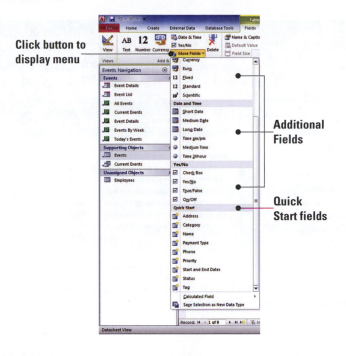

Click button to display menu

Additional Fields

Quick Start fields

STEP BY STEP **Create Fields**

USE the database that is open from the previous exercise.

1. On the Home tab, in the Views group, click the **View** button and click **Datasheet View**. Save the table, if required. If you get a message about data integrity, click **Yes**.

Take Note Whenever you add or modify field validation rules for fields that contain data, the data may violate these new rules. You can allow Access to test the data against the rules and inform you if there are any violations.

2. Scroll to the right of the Events table to display the last column and click in the **first cell below the Click to Add header**, as shown in Figure 4-20. You are going to add a new field in which you can indicate whether or not events will have on-site staff.

Figure 4-20

Click to Add column

Key data to add a new field

3. Key **Yes** and press **Enter**. A new field named Field1 is added, and the Click to Add column becomes the last column in the table, as shown in Figure 4-21.

New field created

Figure 4-21

New field created

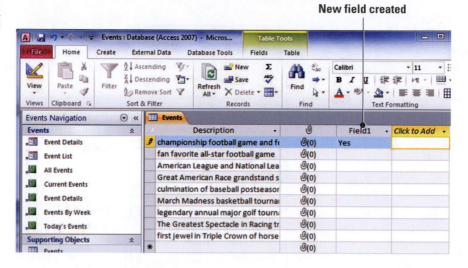

4. Right-click the **Field1** column header to display the shortcut menu and click **Rename Field**, as shown in Figure 4-22.

Right-click to display menu

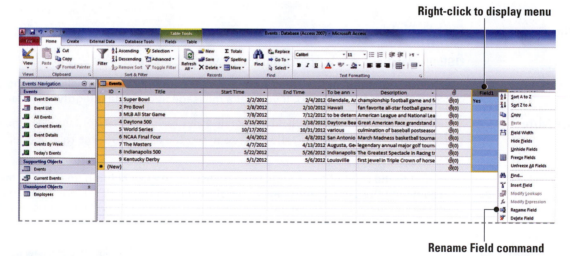

Rename Field command

Figure 4-22

Column shortcut menu

5. Key **On-site staff?** as the column name.

6. Click the **More Fields** button in the Add & Delete group on the Table Tools Fields contextual tab, which is shown in Figure 4-23. The More Fields menu appears.

Figure 4-23

More Fields button and menu

More Fields button displays menu with categories when clicked.

7. In the Yes/No category, click **Check Box**. A new field with check boxes is created in the table, as shown in Figure 4-24.

Figure 4-24

Check box field created

Check box field created for Yes/No values

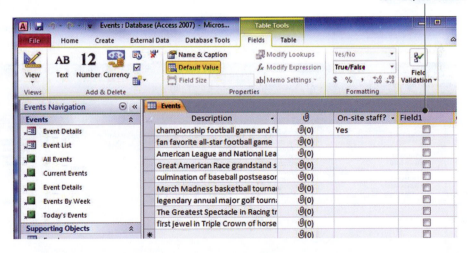

8. Click the **Name & Caption** button in the Properties group, which is shown in Figure 4-25. The Enter Field Properties dialog box appears.

Figure 4-25

Name & Caption button in Properties group

Name & Caption button

9. Key **Souvenirs** in the Name box and press **Enter**. Notice the column has been renamed Souvenirs.

10. Scroll to the right of the Events table to display the last column and click in the first cell below the Click to Add header.

11. Click the **More Fields** button in the Add & Delete group on the Table Tools Fields contextual tab to view the More Fields menu.

12. In the Quick Start category, click **Status**. A new *Quick Start* field named Status, in which you now have options to indicate the status of the event, appears to the right of the *Souvenirs* field, as shown in Figure 4-26.

Status field created

Click down arrow to display list of Status options

Figure 4-26

Status field created

13. Click the **Status field drop-down arrow** button to view the available options, and click **Not Started**, as shown in Figure 4-27.

Click down arrow to display list of Status options

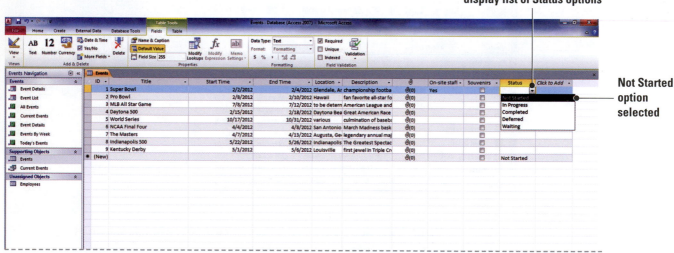

Not Started option selected

Figure 4-27

Status field drop-down box options

14. Click **Close** to close the Field Templates pane.

PAUSE. LEAVE the database open to use in the next exercise.

Deleting a Field

CERTIFICATION
READY   1.3.2

How do you use Quick Start
to add fields?

Another Way
You can also quickly
add fields by accessing the Click
to Add column menu on the
right side of the Click to Add
column header.

Before you delete a column from a datasheet, remember that doing so deletes all the data in the column and that the action cannot be undone. For that reason, you should back up the table before you delete the column. Before you can delete a primary key or a lookup field, you must first delete the relationships for those fields. In this exercise, you learn how to use the shortcut commands to delete a field from an Access 2010 table.

To delete a field in Datasheet View, select the column, right-click, and then click Delete Field from the shortcut menu. Or, on the Table Tools Fields contextual tab in the Add & Delete group, click the Delete button. You will see a confirmation message asking if you are sure you want to delete the column and all the data. Sometimes you may see an additional confirmation message warning you about potential issues when deleting fields. You should always be cautious when deleting fields from a table.

STEP BY STEP | **Delete a Field**

USE the database that is open from the previous exercise.

1. Click the column header for the **Attachment** field, located between the *Description* field and the *On-site staff?* field.
2. Right-click in the column to display the shortcut menu and click **Delete Field**, as shown in Figure 4-28.

Figure 4-28

Delete Field command on field
shortcut menu

Right-click column to display menu

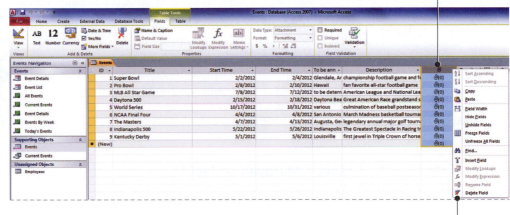

Delete field command

CERTIFICATION
READY   2.2.2

How do you delete a field?

Another Way
You can also delete
a field by clicking the Delete
button on the Table Tools Fields
contextual tab in the Add &
Delete group.

3. A message appears, as shown in Figure 4-29. Click **Yes**.

Figure 4-29

Delete field message

4. A confirmation message appears, as shown in Figure 4-30. Click **Yes**. The field is deleted.

5. Click the column header for the **Status** field.

6. Right-click in the column to display the shortcut menu and click **Delete Field**, and click **Yes** in the message box that appears to delete the *Status* field.

PAUSE. LEAVE the database open to use in the next exercise.

Another Way
You can also delete a field in Design View by selecting the field (row) that you want to delete and clicking Delete Rows on the Table Tools Design contextual tab, in the Tools group.

Creating Multivalued Fields

In Office Access 2010, it is possible to create a **multivalued field** that lets you select more than one choice from a list, without having to create a more advanced database design. You can create a field that holds multiple values, such as a list of employees that you have assigned to a particular event. Use the Lookup Wizard to create multivalued fields. The Lookup Wizard guides you through the process of creating a field or lookup column that can "look up" data that exists in one or more tables to automate the complexity of manually relating tables. In this exercise, you create a multivalued field using the Lookup Wizard in Datasheet View.

Use a multivalued field when you want to store multiple selections from a list of choices that is relatively small. It is also appropriate to use a multivalued field when you will be integrating your database with Windows SharePoint Services, software that allows for information sharing and collaboration—for example, by exporting an Access table to a SharePoint site or linking to a SharePoint list that contains a multivalued field type.

Take Note   You can also create lookup columns that allow for a single selection of a value.

STEP BY STEP   **Create a Multivalued Field**

USE the database that is open from the previous exercise.

1. Place the insertion point in the first cell of the table. Click the **More Fields** button in the Add & Delete group on the Table Tools Fields contextual tab, then click the **Lookup & Relationship** button. The Lookup Wizard appears, as shown in Figure 4-31.

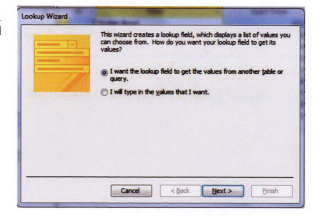

2. Click **Next >** to accept the default setting (*I want the lookup field to get the values from another table or query*) and display the next screen in the Lookup Wizard, as shown in Figure 4-32. Notice you have a choice of two tables to provide the values for the lookup field you're creating. The first table, Employees, should already be selected for you.

Figure 4-32

Lookup Wizard, second screen

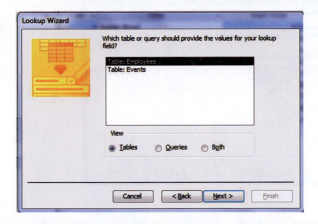

3. Click **Next >** to accept the default settings and display the next screen in the Lookup Wizard, as shown in Figure 4-33. The Available Fields scroll box contains all the fields of the Employees table, two of which you will select since they contain the values you want to eventually look up.

Figure 4-33

Lookup Wizard, third screen

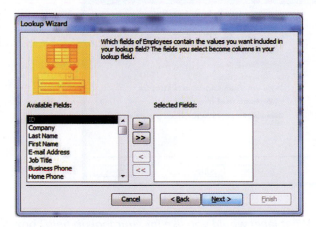

4. In the Available Fields list, select **Last Name**, then click the **>** button to move it to the Selected Fields box.

5. In the Available Fields list, select **First Name**, then click the **>** button to move it to the Selected Fields box.

6. Click **Next >** to accept your settings and display the next screen in the Lookup Wizard.

7. Click the **down arrow** in the first box and click **Last Name**, as shown in Figure 4-34. This will sort the Lookup column in alphabetical order by Last Name.

Figure 4-34

Lookup Wizard, fourth screen

8. Click **Next >** to accept your selection and to display the next screen in the Lookup Wizard, as shown in Figure 4-35.

Figure 4-35

Lookup Wizard, fifth screen

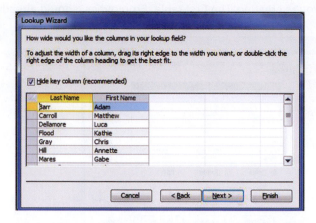

9. Click **Next >** to accept the default selection and to hide the primary key column to ensure only relevant and meaningful data displays in the lookup column later. The final screen of the Lookup Wizard displays, as shown in Figure 4-36.

Figure 4-36

Lookup Wizard, final screen

Another Way
You can also modify the Allow Multiple Values property in the Lookup Field Properties sheet in table Design View.

10. In the *What label would you like for your lookup field?* box, key **Coordinator**. This will create a new label named Coordinator for your column.

11. Select the **Allow Multiple Values** check box to allow for the multiple selection of values.

12. Click the **Finish** button. A new column named Coordinator appears after the *ID* field. Click the **down arrow** in the first cell to display the list of names, as shown in Figure 4-37.

Figure 4-37

Lookup column list

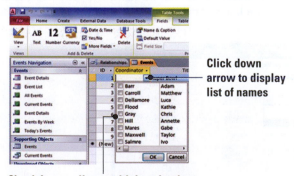

Click down arrow to display list of names

Check boxes allow multiple selections

13. Click **Flood/Kathie** and **Mares/Gabe** on the list and then click **OK** to choose those multiple values for the field.

STOP. CLOSE the database.

Troubleshooting Consider using a multivalued field only when you are relatively sure that your database will not be moved to a Microsoft SQL Server at a later date. An Access multivalued field is upsized to SQL Server as a memo field that contains a delimited set of values. Because SQL Server does not support a multivalued data type, additional design and conversion work might be needed.

SKILL SUMMARY

In This Lesson You Learned How To:	Exam Objective	Objective Number
Modify a Database Table	Rename objects.	1.2.1
	Delete objects.	1.2.2
Create Fields and Modify Field Properties	Modify field properties.	2.2.8
	Rename a field.	2.2.3
	Insert a field.	2.2.1
	Use Quick Start.	1.3.2
	Delete a field.	2.2.2

Knowledge Assessment

Fill in the Blank

Complete the following sentences by writing the correct word or words in the blanks provided.

1. _____ or _____ a table could possibly break the functionality of the database.

2. If you want more space to enter or edit a setting in the property box, press Shift+F2 to display the _____ box.

3. A(n) _____ contains no characters, and you use it to indicate that you know no value exists for a field.

4. _____ specifies the text in the error message that appears when users violate a validation rule.

5. The _____ property field specifies the text displayed by default as column names in tables and in labels for forms, reports, and queries.

6. When creating fields, use the commands in the _____ group on the Table Tools Fields contextual tab.

7. A(n) _____ is a predefined set of characteristics and properties that describes a field.

8. Creating multivalued fields can be accomplished by using the _____ Wizard.

9. The _____ Quick Start includes fields for city, state, and zip.

10. You should always consider _____ a table before deleting a column.

Multiple Choice

Select the best response for the following statements or questions.

1. To rename a table or other database object, first
   a. Save it
   b. Close it
   c. Rename it
   d. Open it

2. If you delete a database table,
   a. You cannot undo the action.
   b. Click Undo to restore the table.
   c. It is still available in the Navigation Pane.
   d. The data is transferred to the Clipboard.

3. A complete list of field properties is available in
   a. The Navigation Pane
   b. Datasheet View
   c. Design View
   d. All of the above

4. Which of the following is *not* a field property?
   a. Column Template
   b. Field Size
   c. Caption
   d. Allow Zero Length

5. Which field property requires users to enter data in a specific format?
   a. Validation Text
   b. Default Value
   c. Required
   d. Input Mask

6. The Append Only property applies only to a field that is set to
   a. Memo
   b. Number
   c. Currency
   d. Text

7. Which of the following is *not* a way to validate data?
   a. Data type
   b. Field sizes
   c. Filtering
   d. Field properties

8. The Caption field property is used for which field?
   a. Text
   b. Attachment
   c. Date/Time
   d. All of the above

9. Which type of field allows you to select more than one choice from a list?
   a. Attachment
   b. Multivalued
   c. Caption
   d. Validation

10. To delete a field in Datasheet view, select the column, right-click, and then click Delete Field from the
    a. Quick Access toolbar
    b. Lookup Wizard
    c. Shortcut menu
    d. Home tab

Competency Assessment

Project 4-1: Home Inventory

You decide to use Access to create a home inventory database for insurance purposes. To include all the information you want, you need to add several fields to the existing table.

GET READY. LAUNCH Access if it is not already running.

1. **OPEN** the *Home inventory* database from the data files for this lesson.
2. **SAVE** the database as *Home inventory XXX* (where *XXX* is your initials).
3. Close the Home Inventory List form that is open.
4. In the Navigation Pane, double-click the **Assets** table to open it.
5. Horizontally scroll to the end of the table and click in the cell below the Click to Add header.
6. On the Table Tools Fields contextual tab, in the Add & Delete group, click the **More Fields** button and click **Yes/No** in the Yes/No category. A column named Field1 is created.
7. On the Table Tools Fields contextual tab, in the Properties group, click the **Name & Caption** button.
8. Key **Insured** to rename the Field1 column.
9. Click in the cell below the Click to Add header.
10. On the Table Tools Fields contextual tab, in the Add & Delete group, click the **More Fields** button and click **Attachment** in the Basic Types category to create an attachment field.
11. **CLOSE** the database.

LEAVE Access open for the next project.

The Home Inventory file for this lesson is available on the book companion website or in WileyPLUS.

Project 4-2: Customer Service

You are employed in the customer service department at City Power & Light. Each call that is received is recorded in an Access database. Because you know how to modify tables and fields, your supervisor asks you to add a lookup column to the Calls table to record the customer service representative who receives the call.

GET READY. LAUNCH Access if it is not already running.

1. **OPEN** *Customer service* from the data files for this lesson.
2. **SAVE** the database as *Customer service XXX* (where *XXX* is your initials).
3. Close the Case List form that is open.
4. In the Navigation Pane, double-click the **Calls** table to open it. Place the insertion point in the first cell of the table, if necessary.
5. On the Table Tools Fields contextual tab, in the Add & Delete group, click the **More Fields** button and then click the **Lookup & Relationship** button. The Lookup Wizard appears.
6. Click **Next >** to display the next screen in the Lookup Wizard.
7. Select **Table: Employees** and click **Next >**.
8. In the Available Fields list, select **First Name**, then click the **>** button to move it to the Selected Fields box.
9. In the Available Fields list, select **Last Name**, then click the **>** button to move it to the Selected Fields box.

The Customer service file for this lesson is available on the book companion website or in WileyPLUS.

10. Click **Next >** to display the next screen in the Lookup Wizard.
11. Click the **down arrow** in the first box and click **Last Name**.
12. Click **Next >** to display the next screen in the Lookup Wizard.
13. Click **Next >** again to display the final screen in the Lookup Wizard.
14. In the *What label would you like for your lookup field?* box, key **Service Rep**.
15. Click the **Finish** button. A new column named Service Rep appears as the second column of the table.
16. Click the **down arrow** and choose **Clair/Hector** from the list.
17. **LEAVE** the database open for the next project.

LEAVE Access open for the next project.

Proficiency Assessment

Project 4-3: Modify Field Properties

Your supervisor at City Power & Light asks you to make some modifications to the field properties in the Calls table of the customer service database.

USE the database that is open from the previous project.

1. Switch to Design View.
2. Display the *Lookup* field properties for the *Service Rep* field.
3. Change the Allow Multiple Values property to **Yes** and confirm the change.
4. Display the *General* field properties for the *Call Time* field.
5. Change the Validation Rule property so that the value must be **greater than 1/1/2000**.
6. Change the Validation Text property to say **Please enter a value that is greater than 1/1/2000**.
7. Display the *General* field properties for the *Caller* field.
8. Change the Field Size property to **60**.
9. Display the *General* field properties for the *Notes* field.
10. Change the Allow Zero Length property to **Yes**.
11. Change the Append Only property to **Yes**.
12. Save the table. If a data integrity message appears, click **No**.
13. **CLOSE** the database.

LEAVE Access open for the next project.

Project 4-4: Modify Database Tables

You work as the operations manager at Alpine Ski House and decide to increase your efficiency by using Access to plan the annual race events. You have started to create a database to manage the events sponsored by the company, but need to modify the tables.

GET READY. LAUNCH Access if it is not already running.

@ The *Alpine* file for this lesson is available on the book companion website or in WileyPLUS.

1. **OPEN** *Alpine* from the data files for this lesson.
2. **SAVE** the database as *Alpine XXX* (where *XXX* is your initials).
3. Close the Event List form that is open.
4. Delete the Nordic Events table and confirm the action.

5. Rename the World Cup table to **Championships**.
6. Open the Events table and switch to Design View.
7. Display the property sheet.
8. In the Description property box, key **Annual events**.
9. **CLOSE** the database.

LEAVE Access open for the next project.

Mastery Assessment

Project 4-5: Changing List Items

You are the owner of Coho Vineyard & Winery, a growing company that is converting all of its data from spreadsheets to Access. You created a table using the Assets table template, but need to make some modifications before you enter information in the database.

GET READY. LAUNCH Access if it is not already running.

@ The *Coho* file for this lesson is available on the book companion website or in WileyPLUS.

1. **OPEN** *Coho* from the data files for this lesson.
2. **SAVE** the database as *Coho XXX* (where *XXX* is your initials).
3. Open the Red Wine table and create a new *Lookup* field as the last field in the table that uses the *Country* field in the Countries table. Specify an ascending sort order for the records in this field.
4. Rename the field **Origin**.
5. Rename the *Current Value* field to **Market Value**.
6. Rename the *Acquired Date* field to **Acquisition Date**.
7. Create a *Yes/No* field as the last field in the table named *Stocked* with a caption named **In Stock?**
8. **SAVE** the table.
9. **CLOSE** the database.

LEAVE Access open for the next project.

Project 4-6: Lending Library

You have an extensive personal library that friends and family frequently ask to share. To keep track of all your books, you decide to use Access to create a lending library database.

GET READY. LAUNCH Access if it is not already running.

@ The *Lending library* file for this lesson is available on the book companion website or in WileyPLUS.

1. **OPEN** *Lending library* from the data files for this lesson.
2. **SAVE** the database as *Lending library XXX* (where *XXX* is your initials).
3. Modify the fields of the Assets table by: Requiring a value for Acquired Date, Purchase Price, Current Value, and Model; Modifying the field size for Model to 10; Modifying the validation rule for Acquired Date to only allow for values after 12/31/1999, and the validation text to "Value must be greater than 12/31/1999"; Modifying the Append Only property for Comments to "No."
4. **CLOSE** the database.

CLOSE Access.

INTERNET READY

A number of online resources can provide solutions to challenges that you might face during a typical workday. Search the Microsoft website for Resources for learning Access 2010, shown in Figure 4-38. This web page is a place where you can find information on how to use Microsoft Access efficiently to perform typical business tasks and activities. Many links to resources are made available here, including links to self-paced training courses, online discussion groups, and Access Power Tips. Explore the resources and content this page has to offer to discover tools or solutions that could be useful on the job and ways you could use Access to be more productive.

Figure 4-38

Access Resource website

LESSON SKILL MATRIX

Skill	Exam Objective	Objective Number
Creating Forms	Use Form Design Tools.	3.1.3
	Create a Blank Form.	3.1.2
	Use the Form Wizard.	3.1.1
	Apply a Theme.	3.2.1
Sorting and Filtering Data within a Form		

KEY TERMS

- Blank Form tool
- common filters
- filter
- filter by form
- Form Design button
- Form tool
- Form Wizard
- Themes

You are the owner of the Graphic Art Institute, a small fine-arts gallery dedicated to presenting challenging and contemporary visual arts and educational programs. The current exhibition is successfully under way; you are now calling for submissions for the next exhibition—a juried art show featuring photographic work from the local region. The competition is open to all regional artists who use photographic processes in their work. This particular event will be open to digital submissions. As each submission is received, you will enter the artist and image information into an Access database for easy retrieval. In this lesson, you learn how to create forms using a variety of methods; how to apply a Theme to a form; and how to sort and filter data within a form.

SOFTWARE ORIENTATION

Forms Group

The Forms group (Figure 5-1) is located on the Create tab in the Ribbon and can be used to create a variety of forms.

Figure 5-1

Forms group

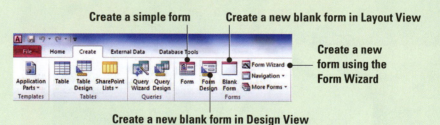

Use this figure as a reference throughout this lesson as well as the rest of this book.

CREATING FORMS

The Bottom Line

A form is a database object that you can use to enter, edit, or display data from a table or query. Forms can be used to control access to data by limiting which fields or rows of data are displayed to users. For example, certain users might need to see only certain fields in a table. Providing those users with a form that contains just those fields makes it easier for them to use the database. Think of forms as windows through which people see and reach your database in a more visually attractive and efficient way.

You can create forms in several different ways, depending on how much control you want over the form's design. Forms that include all fields in a table can be quickly created through a single mouse-click by using the Form tool, or you can control the number of fields you'd like to include on the form as well as the layout of the form by using the Form Wizard. You have the most flexibility with the amount and placement of fields on the form by using Layout or Design View, with Design View giving you the greatest control over field placement and properties. Finally, you can quickly apply a chosen theme to the form to modify its color and font scheme using the Themes command. In this section, you practice creating forms using a variety of these skills.

Creating a Simple Form

You can use the **Form tool** to create a form with a single mouse-click. When you use this tool, all the fields from the underlying data source are placed on the form. Access creates the form and displays it in Layout View. You can begin using the new form immediately, or you can modify it in Layout View or Design View to better suit your needs. In this exercise, you create a simple form by using the Form tool.

To use the Form tool to create a simple form, first click in the Navigation Pane on the table that contains the data you want to see on the form. On the Create tab, in the Forms group, click Form.

To save your form design, click the File tab and click Save. Key a name in the Form Name box and click OK. After you save your form design, you can run the form as often as you want. The design stays the same, but you see current data every time you view the form. If your needs change, you can modify the form design or create a new form that is based on the original.

STEP BY STEP   **Create a Simple Form**

GET READY. Before you begin these steps, be sure to **LAUNCH** Microsoft Access.

1. **OPEN** the *Graphic Art* database from the data files for this lesson.

@ The *Graphic Art* file for this lesson is available on the book companion website or in WileyPLUS.

2. **SAVE** the database as *Graphic Art XXX* (where *XXX* is your initials).
3. In the Navigation Pane, click the **Photo Exhibit** table. This is the table for which you will create a form.
4. On the Create tab, in the Forms group, click the **Form** button. Access creates the form and displays it in Layout View, as shown in Figure 5-2. Your form may be slightly different.

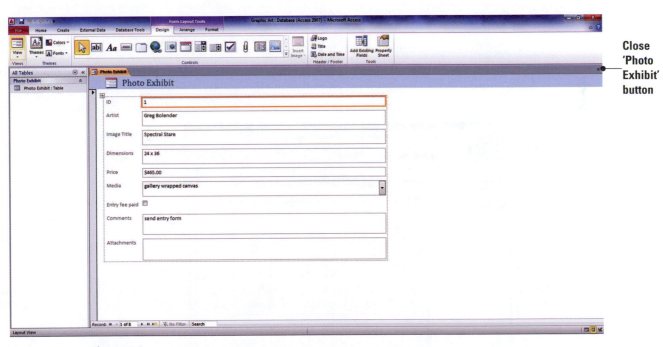

Figure 5-2

Simple form

5. Click the **File** tab and click **Save**. The Save As dialog box appears, as shown in Figure 5-3.

Figure 5-3

Save As dialog box

Take Note   You can use the record navigation buttons at the bottom of a form to navigate among the form's records, just as you used them to navigate among records in a table in Lesson 3.

> 6. Click **OK** to accept the Photo Exhibit form name suggested by Access. The form name appears in the Navigation Pane.
>
> 7. Click the **Close** button on Photo Exhibit to close the form.
>
> 8. **LEAVE** the database open.
>
> **PAUSE. LEAVE** Access open to use in the next exercise.

Creating a Form in Design View

When you click the **Form Design button**, a new blank form is created in Design View. Design View gives you a more detailed view of the structure of your form than Layout View. The form is not actually running when it is shown in Design View, so you cannot see the underlying data while you are making design changes. In this exercise, you create a new blank form in Design View and manually add fields to it.

You can fine-tune your form's design by working in Design View. To switch to Design View, right-click the form name in the Navigation Pane and then click Design View. You can also use the View button on the Home tab on the Ribbon. You can add new controls—used to enter, edit, and find information—and fields to the form by adding them to the design grid. Plus, the property sheet gives you access to a large number of properties that you can set to customize your form.

STEP BY STEP   **Create a Form in Design View**

> **USE** the database that is open from the previous exercise.
>
> 1. On the Create tab, in the Forms group, click the **Form Design** button. A new blank form is created in Design View, as shown in Figure 5-4.

Figure 5-4

New blank form in Design View

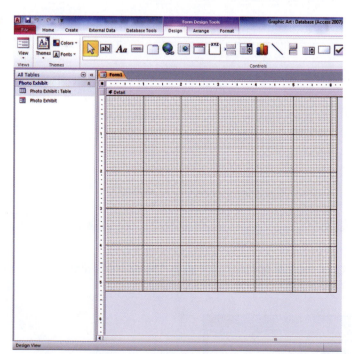

2. On the Form Design Tools Design contextual tab, in the Tools group, click the **Add Existing Fields** button. The Field List pane appears, as shown in Figure 5-5.

Figure 5-5

Field List pane

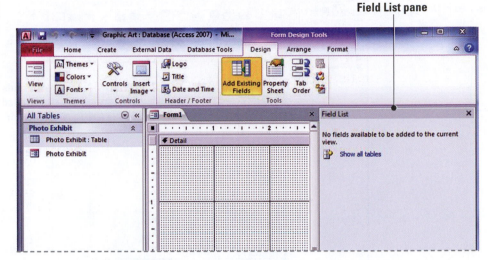

3. Click the **Show all tables** link, then the **expand button** to the left of the table name, as shown in Figure 5-6. The available fields display from the Photo Exhibit table, as shown in Figure 5-7.

Another Way
You can also display the Field List pane by clicking Alt+F8.

Figure 5-6

Field List pane with Show all tables link and expand button

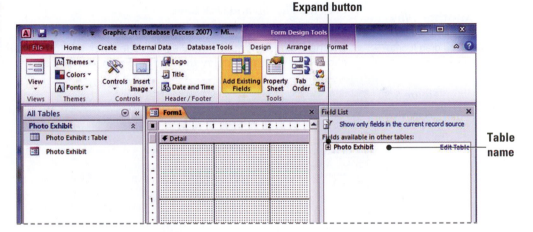

Figure 5-7

Field List pane with available fields

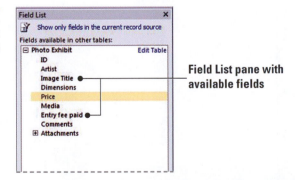

4. In the list of fields, double-click **Artist** to add it to the form.
5. Double-click **Image Title** to add it to the form.

6. Double-click **Price** to add it to the form. Your form should look similar to Figure 5-8.

Figure 5-8

Fields inserted in Design View

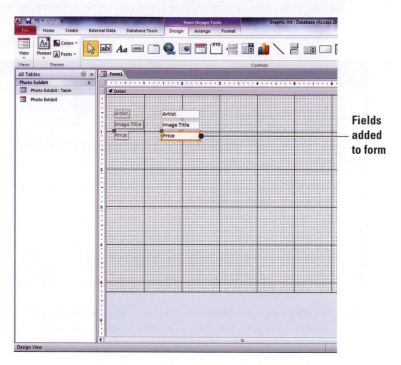

Fields added to form

Another Way
You can also click the field name and drag it onto the form to add a field.

7. Click the **File** tab and click **Save**.

8. In the Save As dialog box, key **Photo Label**, and click **OK**.

9. On the Design menu, in the Views group, click the lower half of the **View** button and click **Form View** to display the form in Form View, as shown in Figure 5-9.

Figure 5-9

Form View

CERTIFICATION
R E A D Y   3.1.3

How do you use form design tools?

10. Click the **Close** button on Photo Label to close the form.

11. LEAVE the database open.

PAUSE. LEAVE the database open to use in the next exercise.

Ref

You learn how to use the commands in the Controls group and a greater variety of form design tools in Lessons 7 and 10.

Creating a Form in Layout View

If other form-building tools do not fit your needs, you can use the Blank Form tool to create a form. The **Blank Form tool** creates a new form in Layout View. This can be a very quick way to build a form, especially if you plan to put only a few fields on your form. Click the Blank Form button to quickly create a new blank form in Layout View; you can make design changes to the form while viewing the underlying data. In this exercise, you use the Blank Form tool to create a form in Layout View.

On the Create tab, in the Forms group, click the Blank Form button. Access opens a blank form in Layout View and displays the Field List pane. To add a field to the form, double-click it or drag it onto the form. In Layout View, you can make design changes to the form while it is displaying data.

STEP BY STEP **Create a Form in Layout View**

USE the database that is open from the previous exercise.

1. On the Create tab, in the Forms group, click the **Blank Form** button. A new blank form is created in Layout View, with the Field List displayed, as shown in Figure 5-10.

Figure 5-10

New blank form in Layout View

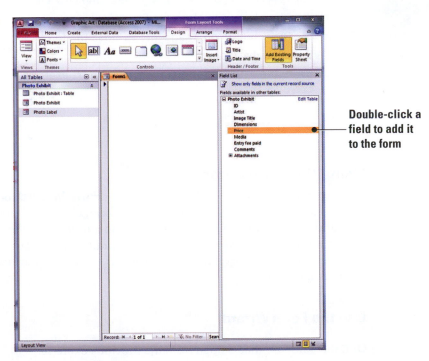

Double-click a field to add it to the form

2. In the list of fields, double-click **Image Title** to add it to the form.
3. Double-click **Dimensions** to add it to the form.
4. Double-click **Media** to add it to the form. Your form should look similar to Figure 5-11.

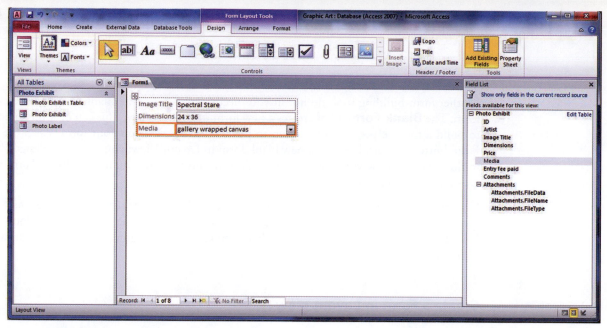

Figure 5-11

Fields inserted in Layout View

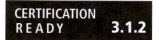

CERTIFICATION
READY   3.1.2

How do you use the Blank
Form tool to create a form?

5. Click the **File** tab and click **Save**.

6. In the Save As dialog box, key **Image Info**, and click **OK**.

7. Click the **Close** button to close the Field List.

8. Click the **Close** button on Image Info to close the form.

9. **LEAVE** the database open.

PAUSE. LEAVE the database open to use in the next exercise.

Take Note   To add more than one field at a time, press Ctrl and click several fields; then, drag them all onto the form at once.

Using the Form Wizard

Another method of building a form is to use the **Form Wizard** tool. The Form Wizard allows you to select the fields that will appear on the form, choose the form layout (which determines the positioning of controls, objects, and data on a form), and also choose a predefined style, if desired. In this exercise, you use the Form Wizard to create a datasheet form. A datasheet form looks very similar to the table upon which it is based and provides a way to enter data using columns and rows.

STEP BY STEP   **Use the Form Wizard**

USE the database that is open from the previous exercise.

1. On the Create tab, in the Forms group, click the **Form Wizard** button, shown in Figure 5-12.

Figure 5-12

Form Wizard button in Forms group

Form Wizard button

2. The Form Wizard displays, as shown in Figure 5-13.

Figure 5-13

Form Wizard

Click to move selected field

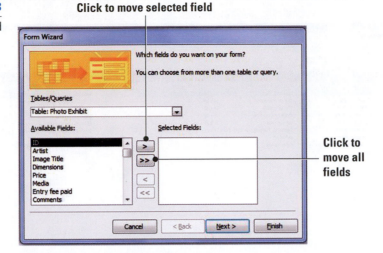

Click to move all fields

3. Click the **>>** button to move all the fields from the Available Fields box to the Selected Fields box.

4. Click the **Next >** button to move to the next screen in the Form Wizard, shown in Figure 5-14.

Figure 5-14

Form Wizard, next screen

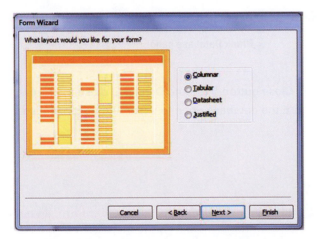

5. Click **Datasheet** as the layout for the form. Form layouts help determine the positioning of controls, objects, and data on a form.

6. Click the **Next >** button to move to the final screen in the Form Wizard, as shown in Figure 5-15.

Figure 5-15

Form Wizard, final screen

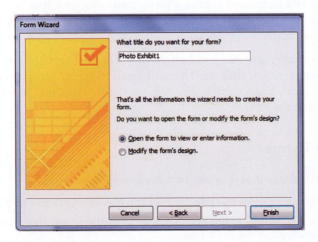

7. Key **Photo Details** as the title of the form.

8. Click the **Finish** button. A datasheet form appears, as shown in Figure 5-16.

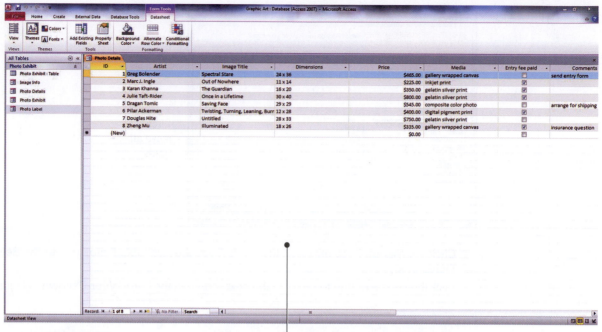

Figure 5-16

Datasheet form

Blank Database pane

9. Click the **Close** button on Photo Details to close the form.

PAUSE. LEAVE the database open to use in the next exercise.

Take Note   To include fields from more than one table on your form, do not click Next or Finish after you select the fields from the first table on the first screen of the Form Wizard. Instead, repeat the steps to select another table, and click any additional fields that you want to include on the form before continuing.

Applying a Theme

The **Themes** command applies a predefined color and font scheme to a form or report. A theme modifies a form by controlling the color and fonts of its text. In this exercise, you apply a Theme to a form.

To apply a theme, first switch to Layout View. On the Form Layout Tools Design contextual tab, in the Themes group, click the Themes button to view a gallery of theme styles from which to choose. You can point to each option to see the name of that format and a live preview before it's applied to the form.

STEP BY STEP   **Apply a Theme**

USE the database that is open from the previous exercise.

1. Double-click the **Image Info** form in the Navigation Pane to open it.

2. On the Home tab, in the Views group, click the lower half of the **View** button, and click **Layout View** on the View menu.

3. On the Form Layout Tools Design contextual tab, in the Themes group, click the **Themes** button, shown in Figure 5-17.

Figure 5-17

Themes button

Themes button accesses Themes gallery

4. A gallery of themes appears, as shown in Figure 5-18.

Figure 5-18

Themes gallery

5. Click the **Couture theme** (fourth row, first column) to apply it to the form. Notice how the form's text has changed, shown in Figure 5-19.

Figure 5-19

Form in Layout View with Couture theme applied

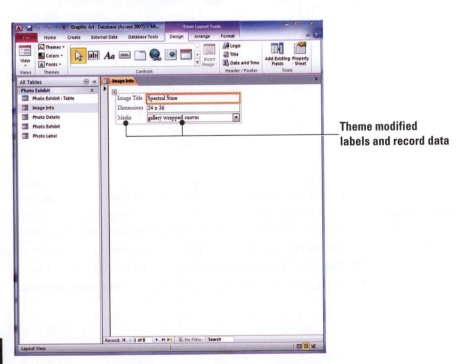

Theme modified labels and record data

6. Click the **Close** button on Image Info to close the form.

PAUSE. LEAVE the database open to use in the next exercise.

SORTING AND FILTERING DATA WITHIN A FORM

The Bottom Line

Sorting data in a form can help make it much more effective and easy to use. Sorting helps users review and locate the records they want without having to browse the data. To find one or more specific records in a form, you can use a filter. A **filter** limits a view of data to specific records without requiring you to alter the design of the form. You also can use a tool called filter by form to filter on several fields in a form or to find a specific record.

Sorting Data within a Form

Data can be sorted in the Form View of a form. The order that is chosen when a form is designed becomes that object's default sort order. But when viewing the form, users can sort the records in whatever way is most useful. You can sort the records in a form on one or more fields. In this exercise, you sort data in a form in ascending order.

STEP BY STEP   **Sort Data within a Form**

USE the database that is open from the previous exercise.

1. Double-click the **Photo Label** form in the Navigation Pane to open it in Form View.
2. Right-click the **Price** field to display the shortcut menu shown in Figure 5-20.

Figure 5-20

Price field shortcut menu

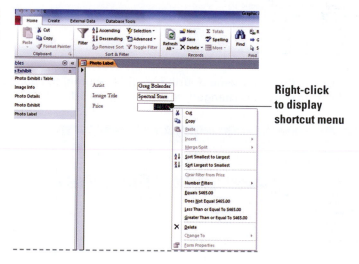

Right-click to display shortcut menu

3. Click **Sort Smallest to Largest**. The form is sorted by price from smallest to largest. The record with the smallest price is displayed first, as shown in Figure 5-21.
4. Click the **Next record** button on the record navigator at the bottom of the form. Continue clicking through all the records to see the records in order according to price.
5. On the Home tab, in the Sort & Filter group, click the **Remove Sort** button.
6. Click the **Close** button on Photo Label to close the form.

PAUSE. LEAVE the database open to use in the next exercise.

Another Way
You can also sort on a field by selecting it and clicking the Ascending or Descending button on the Home tab in the Sort & Filter group.

Figure 5-21

Form sorted by price

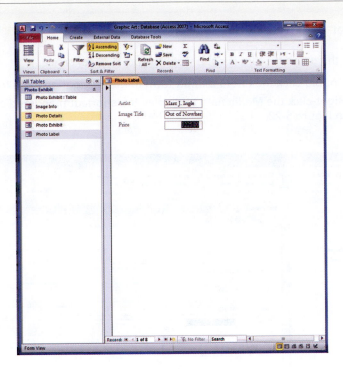

Take Note

You cannot sort on a field that contains attachments. When sorting on a field with the Yes/No data type, a value of "Yes," "True," or "On" is considered "Selected"; a value of "No," "False," or "Off" is considered "Cleared."

You must identify the fields on which you want to sort. To sort on two or more fields, identify the fields that will act as the innermost and outermost sort fields. Right-click anywhere in the column corresponding to the innermost field, and click one of the sort commands. The commands vary based on the type of data that is in the selected field. Repeat the process for each sort field, ending with the outermost sort field. The records are rearranged to match the sort order.

 Ref   You already learned how to sort data within a table in Lesson 3. Sorting in a form is very similar.

The last-applied sort order is automatically saved with the form. If you want it automatically applied the next time you open the form, make sure the Order By On Load property of the form is set to Yes. Remember that you cannot remove a sort order from just a single field. To remove sorting from all sort fields, on the Home tab, in the Sort & Filter group, click Remove Sort.

Filtering Data within a Form

Common filters are built into every view that displays data. The filters available depend on the type and values of the field. When you apply the filter, only records that contain the values that you are interested in are included in the view. The rest are hidden until you remove the filter. In this exercise, you filter form data using common filters.

Filters are easy to apply and remove. Filter settings remain in effect until you close the form, even if you switch to another view. If you save the form while the filter is applied, it will be available the next time you open the form. To permanently remove a filter, on the Home tab, in the Sort & Filter group, click the Advanced button and click Clear All Filters.

Filter Data with Common Filters

USE the database that is open from the previous exercise.

1. Double-click the **Photo Exhibit** form in the Navigation Pane to open it in Form View.

2. Right-click the **Media** field to display the shortcut menu and click **Text Filters**, as shown in Figure 5-22.

Figure 5-22

Media field text filters

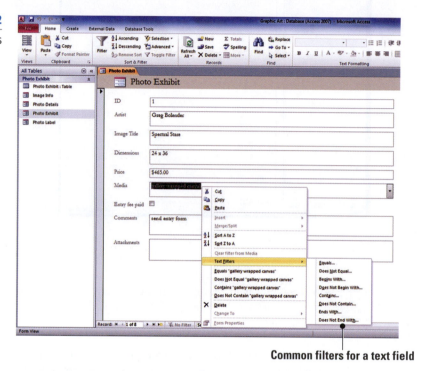

Common filters for a text field

3. Click **Contains . . .** to display the Custom Filter dialog box, as shown in Figure 5-23.

Figure 5-23

Custom Filter dialog box

4. In the *Media contains* box, key **print**, and click **OK**.

5. Click the **Next record** button on the record navigator at the bottom of the form. Continue clicking to see the five records that contain the word "print" in the *Media* field.

6. Right-click the **Price** field to display the shortcut menu and click **Number Filters**, as shown in Figure 5-24.

Figure 5-24

Price field number filters

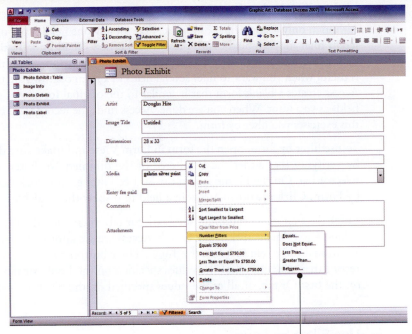

Common filters for a number field

7. Click **Less Than . . .** to display the Custom Filter dialog box shown in Figure 5-25.

Figure 5-25

Custom Filter dialog box

8. In the *Price is less than or equal to* box, key **500**, and click **OK**.
9. Click the **Next record** button on the record navigator at the bottom of the form. Continue clicking to see the three photos that use print media and are less than $500.
10. On the Home tab, in the Sort & Filter group, click the **Advanced Filter Options** button to display the menu shown in Figure 5-26.

Figure 5-26

Advanced Filter Options button menu

11. Click **Clear All Filters**.

PAUSE. LEAVE the database open to use in the next exercise.

Ref

You already learned how to filter data within a table in Lesson 3. Filtering in a form using common filters is very similar.

Using Filter by Form

Although only a single filter can be in effect for any one field at any one time, you can specify a different filter for each field that is present in the view. In addition to the ready-to-use filters for each data type, you can also filter a form by completing an action called filter by form. **Filter by form** is useful when you want to filter several fields in a form or if you are trying to find a specific record. Access creates a blank form that is similar to the original form, you then complete as many of the fields as you want. When you are done, Access finds the records that contain the specified values. In this exercise, you filter by form.

To use filter by form, open the form in Form View and make sure the view is not already filtered by verifying that either the Unfiltered or the dimmed No Filter icon is present on the record selector bar. On the Home tab, in the Sort & Filter group, click Advanced, and then click Filter by Form. Click the down arrow in a field to display the available values.

Enter the first set of values on the Look for tab, then click the Or tab and enter the next set of values. Each time you click the Or tab, Access creates another Or tab so you can continue to add additional filter values. Click the Toggle Filter button to apply the filter. The filter returns any record that contains all of the values specified on the Look for tab, or all of the values specified on the first Or tab, or all of the values specified on the second Or tab, and so on.

STEP BY STEP   **Use Filter by Form**

USE the database that is open from the previous exercise.

1. On the Home tab, in the Sort & Filter group, click the **Advanced Filter Options** button and click **Filter by Form**. A form filter appears, as shown in Figure 5-27.

Figure 5-27

Form filter

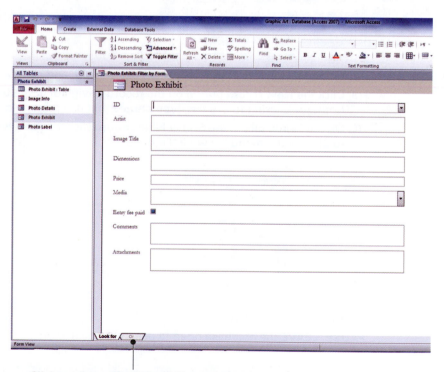

Click or tab to add additional filter values

2. Place the insertion point in the Dimensions box and click the **down arrow** on the right to display the list of options shown in Figure 5-28.

Figure 5-28

Form filter field options

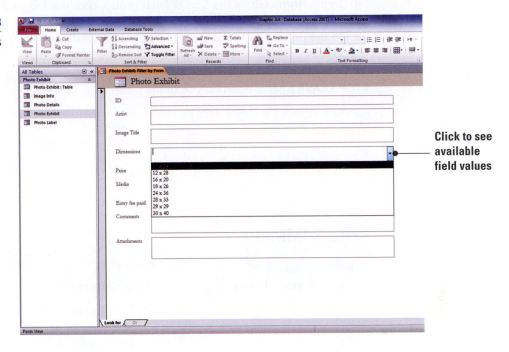

Click to see available field values

3. Click **30 × 40**.

4. Click the **Or** tab at the bottom of the form.

5. Place the insertion point in the Dimensions box, click the **down arrow**, and then click **12 × 28**.

6. On the Home tab, in the Sort & Filter group, click the **Toggle Filter** button to apply the filter. The records containing either the dimensions 30 × 40 or 12 × 28 are displayed, as shown in Figure 5-29.

Figure 5-29

Form filter results

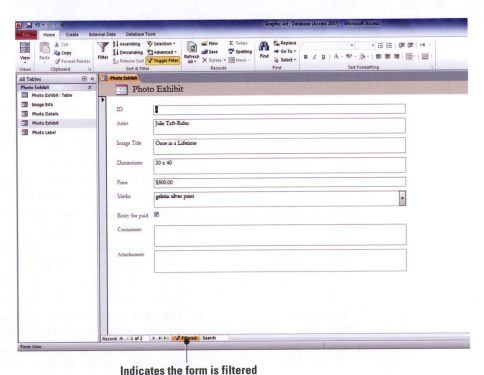

Indicates the form is filtered

7. Click the **Next record** button on the record navigator at the bottom of the form to see the second record in the form filter results.

8. On the Home tab, in the Sort & Filter group, click the **Toggle Filter** button again to remove the filter.

9. On the Home tab, in the Sort & Filter group, click the **Advanced** button and click **Clear All Filters**.

10. Click the **File** tab and click **Close Database**.

STOP. LEAVE Access open for use in the projects.

Take Note   If you want a field value to operate as a filter that is independent of other field values, you must enter that value on the Look for tab and each Or tab. In other words, the Look for tab and each Or tab represents an alternate set of filter values.

SKILL SUMMARY

In This Lesson You Learned How To:	Exam Objective	Objective Number
Create Forms	Use Form Design Tools.	3.1.3
	Create a Blank Form.	3.1.2
	Use the Form Wizard.	3.1.1
	Apply a Theme.	3.2.1
Sort and Filter Data within a Form		

Knowledge Assessment

Matching

Match the term in Column 1 to its description in Column 2.

Column 1		Column 2
1. Form Wizard	a.	useful when you want to filter on several fields in a form or if you are trying to find a specific record
2. Form Design button	b.	creates a simple form with a single mouse-click
3. Theme command	c.	applies a predefined combination of colors and fonts that you select for a form or report
4. Blank Form button	d.	quickly creates a new blank form in Design View
5. form	e.	allows you to select fields for the form, choose the form layout, and also choose a predefined style
6. filter by form	f.	limits a view of data to specific records without requiring you to alter the design of the form
7. sorting	g.	built into every view that displays data
8. Form tool	h.	database object that you can use to enter, edit, or display data from a table or a query
9. common filters	i.	helps users review and locate records without having to browse the data
10. filter	j.	quickly creates a new blank form in Layout View

True/False

Circle T if the statement is true or F if the statement is false.

T F **1.** The Forms group is located on the Home tab in the Ribbon.

T F **2.** Forms can be used to control access to data, such as which fields or rows of data are displayed.

T F **3.** After you save your form design, you can run the form as often as you want.

T F **4.** Layout View gives you a more detailed view of the structure of your form than Design View.

T F **5.** Using the Blank Form tool is a very quick way to build a form, especially if you plan to put only a few fields on your form.

T F **6.** To access the Theme options, first switch to Form View.

T F **7.** You cannot remove a sort order from just a single field.

T F **8.** The filters available depend on the field's data type and values.

T F **9.** To filter by form, first switch to Design View.

T F **10.** When using the Form Wizard, you can only include fields from one table.

Competency Assessment

Project 5-1: Form Wizard

As a travel agent at Erin's Travel, you need an easy way to input data about events into the database. You decide to use the Form Wizard to create a datasheet form that has a preformatted style.

GET READY. LAUNCH Access if it is not already running.

@ The *Travel Events* file for this lesson is available on the book companion website or in WileyPLUS.

1. **OPEN** *Travel Events* from the data files for this lesson.
2. **SAVE** the database as *Travel Events XXX* (where *XXX* is your initials).
3. On the Create tab, in the Forms group, click the **Form Wizard** button.
4. Click the **>>** button to move all the fields from the Available Fields box to the Selected Fields box.
5. Click the **Next >** button to move to the next page in the Form Wizard.
6. Click **Datasheet** as the layout for the form.
7. Click the **Next >** button to move to the final page in the Form Wizard.
8. Key **Event Details** as the title of the form.
9. Click the **Finish** button to create a datasheet form.
10. On the Home tab, in the Views group, click the lower half of the **View button**, and click **Form View**.
11. Click the **Close** button on Event Details to close the form.
12. **CLOSE** the database.

LEAVE Access open for the next project.

Project 5-2: Used Games Forms

You are the manager at Southridge Video. To expand the store, you have recently started taking used games in trade. You store information about each title in an Access database. You decide to create some forms to help you use the database more efficiently.

GET READY. LAUNCH Access if it is not already running.

@ The *Games inventory* file for this lesson is available on the book companion website or in WileyPLUS.

1. **OPEN** *Games inventory* from the data files for this lesson.
2. **SAVE** the database as *Games inventory XXX* (where *XXX* is your initials).
3. In the Navigation Pane, double-click **Games: Table** to open the table.
4. On the Create tab, in the Forms group, click the **Form** button to create a simple form and display it in Layout View.

5. Click the **File** tab and click **Save**.

6. In the Save As dialog box, click **OK** to accept the Games form name suggested by Access.

7. Click the **Close** button for Games to close the form.

8. On the Create tab, in the Forms group, click the **Form Design** button to create a new blank form in Design View.

9. On the Form Design Tools Design contextual tab, in the Tools group, click the **Add Existing Fields** button to display the Field List pane.

10. Click the **Show all tables link** in the Field List pane.

11. Click the **+** next to Games to list the available fields.

12. Double-click **Title** to add it to the form.

13. Double-click **Rating** to add it to the form.

14. Double-click **Platform** to add it to the form.

15. Click the **File** tab and click **Save**.

16. In the Save As dialog box, key **Game Rating**, and click **OK**.

17. Click the **Close** button to close the Field List.

18. On the Design contextual tab, in the Views group, click the lower half of the **View** button and click **Form View** to display form in Form View.

19. Click the **Close** button for Game Rating to close the form.

20. **LEAVE** the database open for the next project.

LEAVE Access open for the next project.

Proficiency Assessment

Project 5-3: Sort and Filter Games

A customer comes into Southridge Video and asks about game publishers and the availability of a particular game. Sort and filter data in the forms you created to get the information that you need.

USE the database that is open from the previous project.

1. In the Navigation Pane, double-click the **Games** form to open it.

2. Right-click the **Publisher** field to display the shortcut menu.

3. Click **Sort A to Z** to sort the form by publisher name in alphabetic order.

4. Navigate to **record 3**, titled Marvel: Ultimate Alliance.

5. Right-click the **Title** field and click **Contains "Marvel: Ultimate Alliance."**

6. Click the **Next record** button on the record navigator at the bottom of the form to see all the versions of the game with that name.

7. On the Home tab, in the Sort & Filter group, click the **Remove Sort** button.

8. **CLOSE** the database.

LEAVE Access open for the next project.

Project 5-4: Toy Inventory

Your brother owns Wingtip Toys and recently started keeping a list of the store inventory in an Access database. He wants to add a form to the database and asks for your help. Add a simple form and then show him how to sort and apply filters.

GET READY. LAUNCH Access if it is not already running.

1. **OPEN** *Toy inventory* from the data files for this lesson.

2. Save the database as *Toy inventory XXX* (where *XXX* is your initials).

3. Open **Inventory: Table**.

@ The *Toy Inventory* file for this lesson is available on the book companion website or in WileyPLUS.

4. Use the Form tool to create a simple form.

5. Format it using the Trek theme option (last row, first column).

6. Save the form as **Inventory**.

7. Sort the form's *In Stock* field from **Largest to Smallest**.

8. Sort the *Description* field from **A to Z.**

9. Run a filter that finds all the records where the *Price* field is between $50 and $100.

10. Clear all sorts and filters.

11. Create a filter by form to find all the records that have two items in stock.

12. Close the form and **CLOSE** the database.

LEAVE Access open for the next project.

Mastery Assessment

Project 5-5: Red Wines

The Coho Vineyard has started a monthly wine club. Each month features a red wine hand picked for its unique label and diverse style. Information about the monthly club selections is stored in an Access database; you will create forms so that you can retrieve the data in a useful way.

GET READY. LAUNCH Access if it is not already running.

@ The *Red Wine* file for this lesson is available on the book companion website or in WileyPLUS.

1. **OPEN** the *Red Wine* database from the data files for this lesson.

2. Save the database as *Red Wine XXX* (where *XXX* is your initials).

3. Create a simple form that contains all the fields in the Club Selections table and name it **Club Wines**.

4. Use the Form Design button to create a form named **Wine Details** that looks like the one shown in Figure 5-30 when displayed in Form View.

Figure 5-30

Wine Details form

5. **CLOSE** the database.

LEAVE Access open for the next project.

Project 5-6: Personal Contacts

Your address book is becoming outdated, and you decide to transfer all the current information about friends and family to an Access database. Input the data and then create forms to manage it efficiently.

GET READY. LAUNCH Access if it is not already running.

1. **OPEN** *Personal Contacts* from the data files for this lesson.

2. **SAVE** the database as *Personal Contacts XXX* (where *XXX* is your initials).

3. Input as much contact information as you have about at least five friends or family members.

4. Create a simple form named Friends/Family using the Form tool. Apply the Black Tie theme.

5. Create a form named Birthday Contacts using the Form Wizard. Include the following fields: First Name, Last Name, E-mail Address, Home Phone, Mobile Phone, and Birthday. Use the Columnar layout. Keep all other default settings.

6. **CLOSE** the database.

STOP. CLOSE Access.

The *Personal Contacts* file for this lesson is available on the book companion website or in WileyPLUS.

INTERNET READY

Microsoft has numerous online resources available to provide solutions, services, and support for whatever business needs you may have. If you are a small or midsized business, a helpful site is the Microsoft Business for Small & Midsize Companies. Here, you can find advice, products, tools, and information tailored to small and midsized businesses. Search the Microsoft site for Small & Midsize Companies, shown in Figure 5-31. Explore the resources offered on the site. In the Latest Editions section, choose a topic about which you would like to know more, and read an article that interests you.

Figure 5-31

Microsoft Business for Small & Midsize Companies

Circling Back 1

You are a real estate agent and have recently opened your own office—Woodgrove Real Estate—with several other licensed agents. Because you are the one who is most knowledgeable about computers, you will be responsible for keeping track of the listings and other relevant information. You will use Access to begin developing the database that will be used by everyone in the office.

Project 1: Create a Database and Tables

After sketching out a plan on paper, you are ready to begin creating the database and tables.

GET READY. LAUNCH Access if it is not already running.

1. In the Available Templates section, click the blank database icon if it's not already selected.
2. In the File Name box, key **Woodgrove XXX** (where *XXX* is your initials).
3. Click the folder icon and browse to the location where you want to store the file.
4. Click the **Create** button to create a new blank database.
5. Click **Click to Add** and click **Text** on the shortcut menu.
6. Key **Address** as the column name and press **Enter**.
7. Add new Text columns named **Bedrooms**, **Bathrooms**, **Square Feet**, and **Price**.
8. Click the **File** tab and click **Save**.
9. In the Save As dialog box, key **Listings** as the table name and click **OK**.
10. On the Create tab, in the Templates group, click the **Application Parts** button, and click **Contacts** to create a new table. Click **OK**, if necessary, to close and save the Listings table, then click **Cancel** in the Create Relationship dialog box that appears.
11. Open the **Contacts** table.
12. Right-click the **Company** field header and click **Delete Field** on the shortcut menu. Click **OK** if you receive a dialog box warning you about the deletion.
13. Delete the Job Title, Business Phone, Fax Number, Address, City, State/Province, ZIP/Postal Code, Country/Region, Web Page, Notes, and Attachment columns. (If you get a message asking if you want to delete all indexes for the ZIP column, click **Yes**.)
14. Save the table as **Agents**.
15. Delete all the objects in your database except the Agents and Listings tables.

PAUSE. LEAVE the database open to use in the next project.

Project 2: Modify Tables and Fields

Now that you have created the tables for your database, you need to modify them to suit your needs.

USE the database that is open from the previous project. The Agents table should be displayed.

1. On the Home tab, in the Views group, click **Design** View.
2. On the Table Tools Design contextual tab, in the Show/Hide group, click **Property Sheet**.
3. In the Property Sheet's Description property box, key **Agent contact information**.
4. Click **Close** to close the property sheet.

5. In the upper portion of the table design grid, click the **E-mail Address field**. In the field properties on the bottom, click in the Required property box and set it to **Yes**.

6. Save the table and switch back to Datasheet View.

7. Open the **Listings** table. Place the insertion point in the Price column.

8. On the Table Tools Fields contextual tab, in the Formatting group, click the **down arrow** in the Data Type box and click **Number**.

9. In the Format box, click the **down arrow** and choose **Currency**.

10. Change the data type/format on the Bedrooms, Bathrooms, and Square Feet fields to **Number/General Number**.

11. Click the **Click to Add** column. Choose **Attachment** as the data type to create an attachment column.

12. Save the table.

PAUSE. LEAVE the database open for the next project.

Project 3: Create Forms and Enter Data

Now it is time to enter data into your database. First you create a form to make this task easier.

USE the database that is open from the previous project. The Listings table should be displayed.

1. On the Create tab, in the Forms group, click the **More Forms** button.

2. Click **Datasheet** to create a datasheet form.

3. Click the **File** tab and click **Save**.

4. In the Save As dialog box, key **Listings** as the form name and click **OK**.

5. Use the form to enter data into the Listings table, as shown in Figure 1.

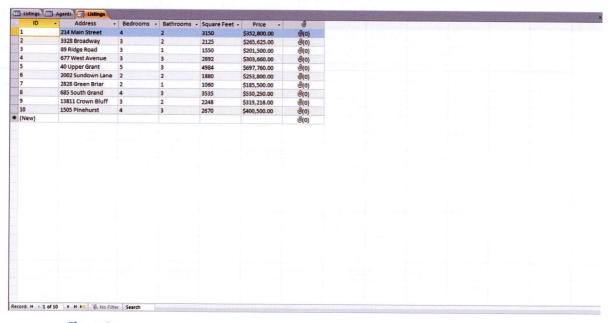

Figure 1

Listings data

6. Display the **Agents** table.
7. On the Create tab, in the Forms group, click the **Form** button.
8. Save the form as **Agents**.
9. Switch to Form View and use the form to enter the data shown in Figure 2.

Figure 2

Agents data, record 1

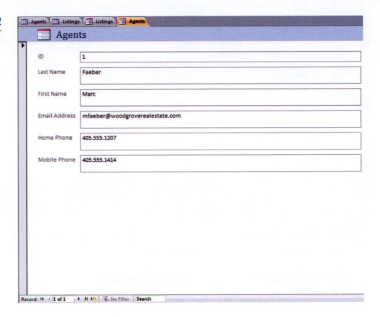

10. Click the **Next record** button on the record navigator.
11. Enter the data shown in Figure 3 as the second record.

Figure 3

Agents data, record 2

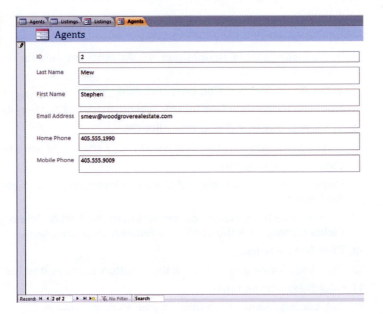

12. Enter the data shown in Figure 4 as the third record.

Figure 4

Agents data, record 3

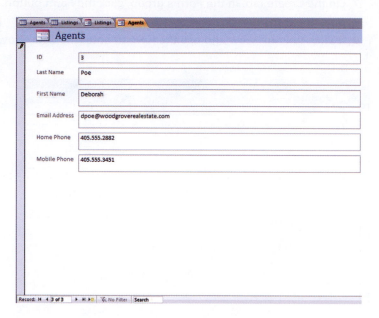

13. Close the Agents form and the Listings form.

PAUSE. LEAVE the database open for the next project.

Project 4: Add Attachments and Create a Lookup Field

You have begun to use the database and realize it would be helpful for the Listings table to include the listing agent. Create a lookup field with this information and attach photos for some of the houses.

USE the database that is open from the previous project.

1. In the Listings table, double-click the **Attachment** field for the fourth record (677 West Avenue).

2. In the Attachments dialog box, click **Add**.

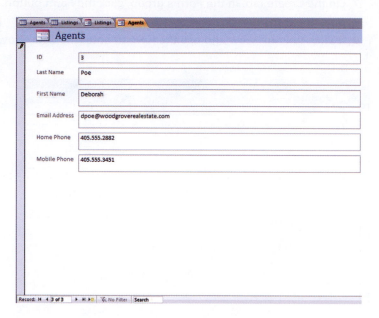 The **677_West_Avenue** file is available for download on the companion website.

3. Navigate to the data files for this lesson, select **677_West_Avenue**, and click **Open**.

4. In the Attachments dialog box, click **OK**.

5. Attach the photo named **2002_Sundown_Lane** to the sixth record.

6. Close the Listings form.

7. Display the Listings table and place the insertion point in the cell under the Click to Add column.

The **2002_Sundown_Lane** file is available for download on the companion website.

8. On the Table Tools Fields contextual tab in the Add & Delete group, click the **More Fields** button. Click the **Lookup & Relationship** command.

9. Click **Next >** twice.

10. Click **Last Name** and then click the **>** button to move it to the Selected Fields box.

11. Click **Next >** three times.

12. Key **Listing Agent** as the title for your lookup column.

13. Click **Finish**.

14. Save the Listings table.

PAUSE. LEAVE the database open for the next project.

Project 5: Modify a Form

Now that you have a lookup field, you want to add it to your form and use it to enter additional information.

USE the database that is open from the previous project.

1. Display the Listings form and switch to Design View.
2. Click the **Field1** field on the design grid and press **Delete**.
3. On the Form Design Tools contextual tab, in the Tools group, click **Add Existing Fields**.
4. In the Fields available for this view box, click **Listing Agent** and drag it to the form below the Price field.
5. Close the Field List and switch to Datasheet View.
6. In the Listing Agent column click the **down arrow** and select the last name for each record, as shown in Figure 5.

Figure 5

Listing agents

ID	Address	Bedrooms	Bathrooms	Square Feet	Price	Listing Agent
1	214 Main Street	4	2	3150	$352,800.00	Faeber
2	3328 Broadway	3	2	2125	$265,625.00	Faeber
3	89 Ridge Road	3	1	1550	$201,500.00	Poe
4	677 West Avenue	3	3	2892	$303,660.00	Mew
5	40 Upper Grant	5	3	4984	$697,760.00	Faeber
6	2002 Sundown Lane	2	2	1880	$253,800.00	Poe
7	2828 Green Briar	2	1	1060	$185,500.00	Poe
8	685 South Grand	4	3	3535	$530,250.00	Faeber
9	13811 Crown Bluff	3	2	2248	$319,216.00	Mew
10	1505 Pinehurst	4	3	2670	$400,500.00	Faeber
* (New)						

7. Close the form.

STOP. CLOSE the database.

6 Create Reports

LESSON SKILL MATRIX

Skill	Exam Objective	Objective Number
Creating Reports	Use the Report Wizard.	5.1.3
	Use Report Design Tools.	5.1.2
Applying a Theme	Apply a Theme.	5.2.1
Working with Reports	Use the Sort command.	5.6.2
	Use Filter commands.	5.6.3
	Use view types.	5.6.4
	Use the Find command.	5.6.1

KEY TERMS

- record source
- report

Alpine Ski House is a small mountain lodge that features cross-country skiing in the winter and hiking in the summer. As an administrative assistant for Alpine Ski House, you take care of many of the administrative duties for the innkeepers, including reservations, billing, and recordkeeping. You have recently started using Access to keep track of customers and reservations at the lodge. In this lesson, you learn three different ways to create reports for the lodge, how to apply auto formats to reports, and how to sort and filter report data.

SOFTWARE ORIENTATION

Reports Group

The Reports group (Figure 6-1) is located on the Create tab in the Ribbon. Use the Reports group of commands to create reports.

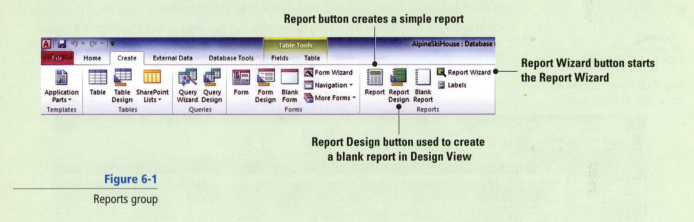

Figure 6-1

Reports group

CREATING REPORTS

The Bottom Line

A **report** is a database object that is used to organize and display data pulled from tables and queries. You can create a report using the Report button, the Report Wizard, or Design View, depending on the amount of customization desired. After creating a report, you can instantly apply a Theme to create a professional look. You can also sort and filter data in a report to display the records to suit your needs.

Creating a Simple Report

You can use Access 2010 to create simple or complex reports. When creating a complex report, you might spend quite a bit of time choosing which fields you want to include from various tables or queries. That is fine when you need such a report, but when you need a simple display of all the fields in a table or query, you can use the Report button to create a simple report. In this exercise, you use the Report button to create a simple report.

Reports are commonly used as formatted hard copies of table or query data. You can modify a report's design, but you cannot add or edit data in a report. The purpose of a report is to allow users to view data, not edit it. For example, a supervisor might ask you to create a sales report that is filtered to show only one region's sales. The supervisor does not need to edit the data, just view it.

A report's **record source** is the table or query that provides the data used to generate a report. Before you can create a report, you need to define the record source by clicking in the Navigation Pane on the table or query on which you want to base the report. Then, click the Report button and a report is generated based on the table or query you selected.

You can modify a report's design, print, or save and close a report. You should save a report's design if you are likely to use it again. To save a report, click the Save button on the File tab or in the Quick Access Toolbar. If you click the Close button without saving, Access will display a dialog box asking if you want to save it. Once it is saved, the report is listed in the Navigation Pane. You can open it and modify it in the future or create a new report based on the original. The next time you run the report, the design will be the same, but the data will be different if the data in the table or query has been updated.

STEP BY STEP   **Create a Report**

 The *Alpine Ski House* file for this lesson is available on the book companion website or in WileyPLUS.

WILEY PLUS **EXTRA**

WileyPLUS Extra! features an online tutorial of this task.

GET READY. Before you begin these steps, be sure to turn on and/or log on to your computer and start Access.

1. **OPEN** *Alpine Ski House* from the data files for this lesson.
2. Save the database as *Alpine Ski House XXX* (where *XXX* is your initials).
3. In the Navigation Pane, click the **Rooms** table to select it. This is your record source.
4. On the Create tab, in the Reports group, click the **Report** button. The report appears in Layout View, as shown in Figure 6-2. Notice the Report Layout tools that appear in the Ribbon.

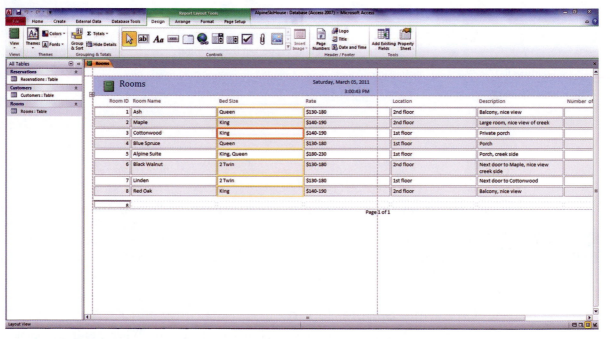

Figure 6-2

Simple report

5. Click the **Room ID** header to select it. Position the pointer over the right border until you see a double-sided arrow. Click and drag to the left, resizing the column to remove excess white space.

6. Resize the other columns until your screen looks similar to Figure 6-3.

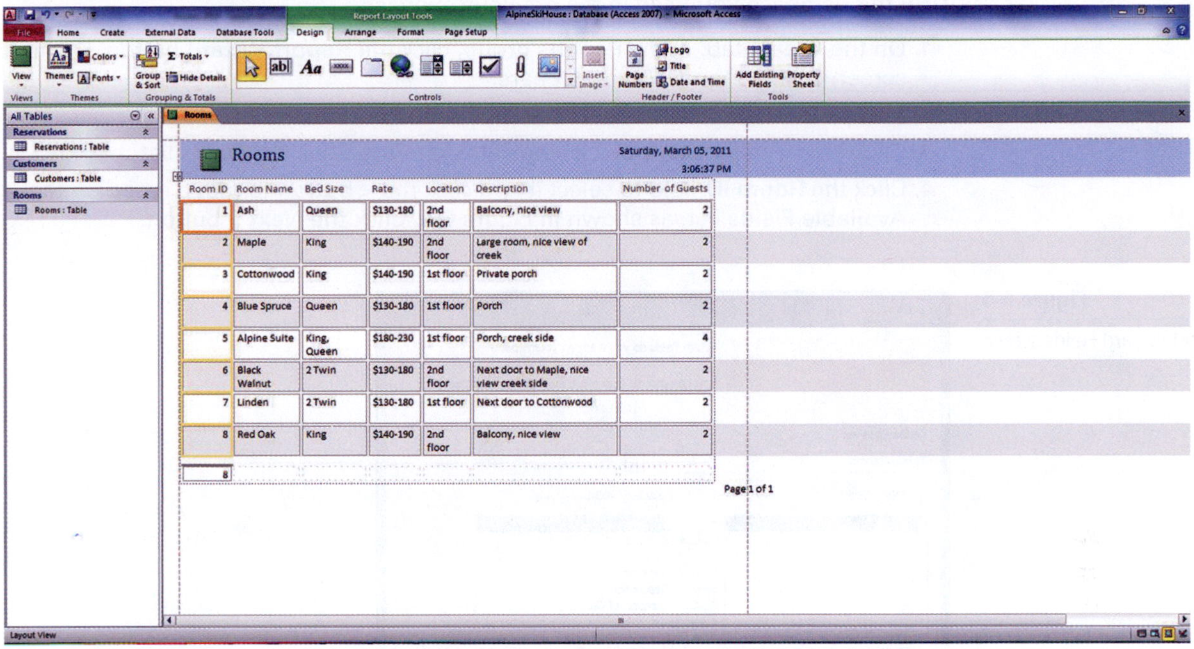

Figure 6-3

Report with resized columns

7. Click the **Save** button on the Quick Access Toolbar. The Save As dialog box appears with Rooms in the Report Name box. Click **OK**. Notice that the Rooms report is listed in the Navigation Pane.

8. Click the **Close** button to close the Rooms report.

PAUSE. LEAVE the database open to use in the next exercise.

Using the Report Wizard

You are probably already familiar with the way a "wizard" works. The Report Wizard displays a series of questions about the report you want and then it creates the report for you based on your answers. The Report Wizard knows what makes a good report, so the questions are designed to help you create a professional report with little effort. The Report Wizard is usually the easiest way to create a report when you want to choose which fields to include. It guides you through a series of questions and then generates a report based on your answers. If you want to skip steps such as Sorting or Grouping in the Report Wizard, click the Next button to go to the next screen. You can click the Finish button anytime it is available to create the report with the choices you have specified. In this exercise, you use the Report Wizard to create a report based on the Rooms table.

The Report Wizard allows you to include fields from more than one table or query. You can click the double right arrow button (>>) to include all the fields in the report or click the single right arrow button (>) to move them one at a time. Likewise, you can click the double left arrow button (<<) to move all the fields out of the report or the single left arrow button (<) to move them one at a time.

You can specify group levels, such as grouping all of the first-floor rooms together and all of the second-floor rooms together if creating a room report. You can also choose up to four fields on which to sort data in ascending or descending order. On the layout screen, you can choose from various layouts such as stepped, block, or outline, all of which indent fields and records in different ways to make the report clearer to read. You can also choose to display the report in portrait or landscape orientation. Access provides a wide variety of design styles from which to choose. On the last screen, you can key a name for the report and choose to preview or modify the report.

X **Ref** You learn more about grouping in Lesson 11.

STEP BY STEP	Use the Report Wizard

USE the database you used in the previous exercise.

1. On the Create tab, in the Reports group, click the **Report Wizard** button. The first screen of the Report Wizard appears.
2. Make sure the Rooms table is selected in the Tables/Queries menu.
3. Click the **>>** button to move all the fields into the Selected Fields list.
4. Click the **Room ID** field to select it and click the **<** button to move it back to the Available Fields list, as shown in Figure 6-4. Click the **Next >** button.

Figure 6-4

The Report Wizard Fields screen

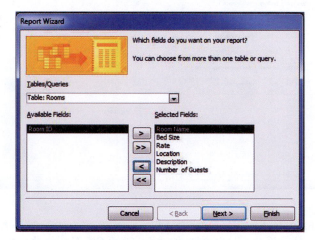

5. Click the **Location** field to select it and click the **>** button to add it as a grouping level, as shown in Figure 6-5.

Figure 6-5

The Report Wizard Grouping screen

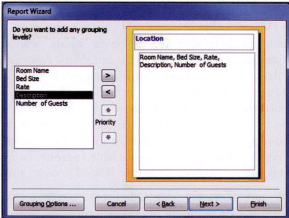

6. Click the **Next >** button.
7. Select **Room Name** from the fields menu to sort in ascending order, as shown in Figure 6-6, and click the **Next >** button.

Figure 6-6

The Report Wizard Sort screen

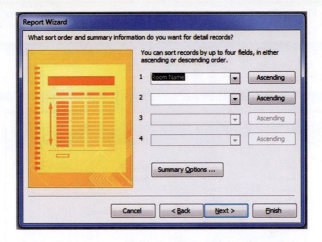

8. In the Layout section, click the **Outline** button. In the Orientation section, click the **Landscape** button, as shown in Figure 6-7. Click **Next >**.

Figure 6-7

The Report Wizard Layout screen

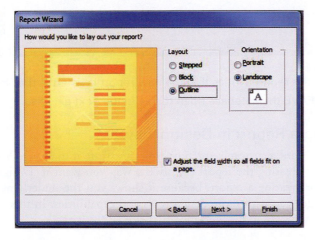

9. Key **Rooms Wizard** as the title of the report, as shown in Figure 6-8.

Figure 6-8

The Report Wizard Title screen

10. Click **Finish**. The Rooms Wizard report appears on the screen, as shown in Figure 6-9.

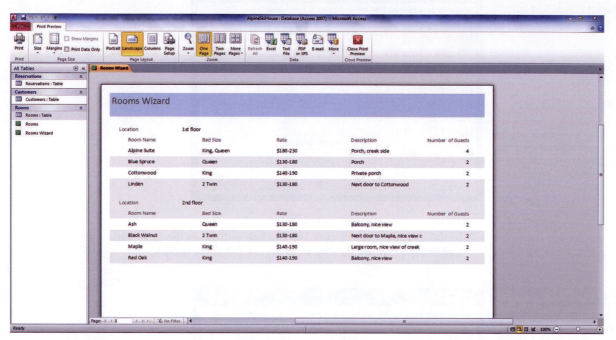

Figure 6-9

The Report Wizard report

11. Close the report. Notice that the new report is listed in the Navigation Pane.

PAUSE. LEAVE the database open to use in the next exercise.

Creating a Report in Design View

When you want a customized report, you can create it in Design View, which offers you many options for creating the report exactly the way you want it. Design View gives you the most options for creating a report, because it shows you the underlying structure of the report. It also provides you with more design tools and capabilities. In this exercise, you create a report in Design View by adding and moving fields.

In the previous exercise, you created a very basic report in Design View. In Lesson 8, you will learn how to add more functionality to a report.

In Design View, a report is displayed on a design grid with sections. Table 6-1 lists the sections.

CERTIFICATION READY 5.1.3

How do you use the Report Wizard to create a report?

Table 6-1

Design View Sections

Section Name	Description
Report header	This section is printed once at the beginning of every report. This is a good place to include a logo, a date, or information that might normally appear on a cover page.
Page header	This section is printed at the top of every page of a report, so it would be good place to include the report title.
Group header	This section is printed at the beginning of a group. It is a good place to include the group name.
Detail	This section includes the body of the report. It is printed once for every row in a record source.
Group footer	This section is printed at the end of a group. It may include summary information for the group.
Page footer	This section is printed at the bottom of every page of a report, so it would be a good place to include information such as a page number.
Report footer	This section is printed once at the end of every report. This is a good place for report totals.

To add fields to the report design, you can display the Field List pane by clicking the Add Existing Fields button. Double-click a field in the Field List to add it to the design grid, or you can drag the field to a location on the grid. If you need to move a field on the grid, click the field to select it and then position the pointer on the border until you see a four-sided arrow. Then, drag to the new location. To change the size of a field, click and drag a selection handle.

To see what your report will look like, click the View button on the Views group and select Report from the menu.

| STEP BY STEP | Create a Report in Design View |

USE the database you used in the previous exercise.

1. If necessary, click the **Rooms** table in the Navigation Pane to select it.

2. On the Create tab, in the Reports group, click the **Report Design** button. A new blank report is displayed in Design View, as shown in Figure 6-10.

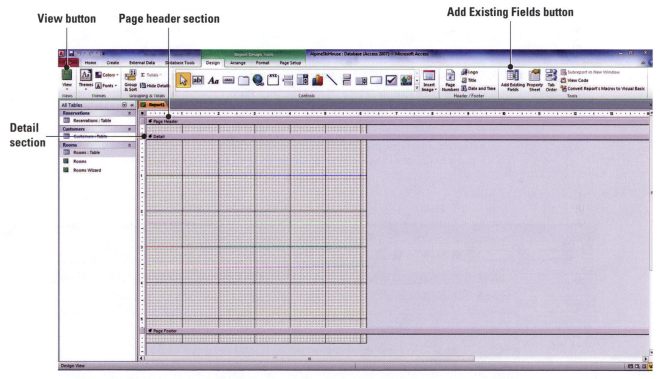

Figure 6-10

New blank report in Design View

3. If the Fields List is not already displayed, on the Design tab, in the Tools group, click the **Add Existing Fields** button. The Show all tables link appears.

4. Click the **Show all tables link** then the **plus (+)** box beside Rooms to display the fields in the table, as shown in Figure 6-11.

Figure 6-11

Fields List pane

5. Double-click **Room ID**. The field is inserted onto the design grid.

6. Double-click **Room Name**, **Bed Size**, and **Rate**.

7. Click the **Close** button on the Field List pane.

8. Click the **Bed Size** label. The border around the label changes to orange, indicating it is selected. Position the insertion point over the top of the border, as shown in Figure 6-12, until the pointer changes to a four-sided arrow.

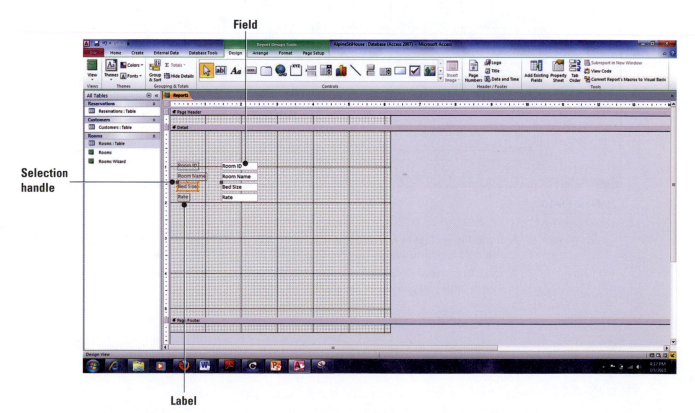

Figure 6-12

Bed Size label selected

9. Click and drag the label to position it about one-half inch to the right of the *Room ID* field and release the mouse button. The field is moved along with the label.

10. In the same manner, move the Rate label and field to position it below the *Bed Size* field, as shown in Figure 6-13.

Figure 6-13

Moved fields

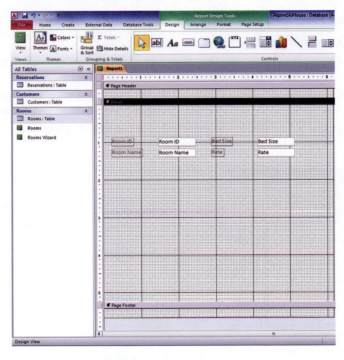

11. Click the **Room ID** field to select it. Position the mouse pointer on the square handle in the middle of the right-side border. Click and drag the field to the left to decrease the size by about one-quarter inch.

12. On the Ribbon, in the Views group, click the bottom-half of the **View** button and select **Report View** from the menu. The report is shown in Report View. Scroll down to see all the records.

13. Click the **Save** button on the Quick Access Toolbar.

14. Key **Report Design** in the Report Name box and click **OK**.

15. Close the report.

PAUSE. LEAVE the table open to use in the next exercise.

CERTIFICATION READY 5.1.2

How do you create a report in Design View?

Take Note

You can add more than one field to a report design at once. Hold down the Ctrl key and click the fields you want, and then drag the selected fields onto the report.

 Ref

In Lesson 8, you learn how to add controls to reports in Design View.

APPLYING A THEME

The Bottom Line

A theme applies a set of predefined fonts, colors, and design to a report. You can apply a theme to any report in Layout View. The Themes gallery displays a variety of designs. After you click the design you want, it is applied to the report. This instant formatting can quickly give your report the professional look you want.

Applying a Theme

To apply a theme, on the Report Layout Tools Design contextual tab, in the Themes group, click the Themes button to display the Themes gallery. You can select a design from the list displayed, or browse for saved themes. You can also customize and then save a theme based on the current report. You can click the Colors button and choose a color scheme from the menu to update the currently applied theme's colors, and even create new theme colors. You can also click the

Fonts button and choose a font scheme to update the currently applied theme's fonts and create new theme fonts. In this exercise, you apply a theme to the Rooms report, and modify the fonts.

STEP BY STEP   **Apply a Theme**

USE the database open from the previous exercise.

1. Open the **Rooms** report.

2. On the Ribbon, in the Views group, click the bottom-half of the **View** button. Select **Layout View** from the menu.

3. On the Report Layout Tools Design contextual tab, in the Themes group, click the **Themes** button. The Themes gallery of predefined report themes appears.

4. In the sixth row, fourth column, click the **Metro** design, as shown in Figure 6-14. The format is applied to the report.

Figure 6-14

Themes gallery with Metro theme chosen

Metro theme chosen

5. In the Themes group, click the **Fonts** button. Select **Newsprint** from the menu, as shown in Figure 6-15, and click OK. The new Font theme is applied.

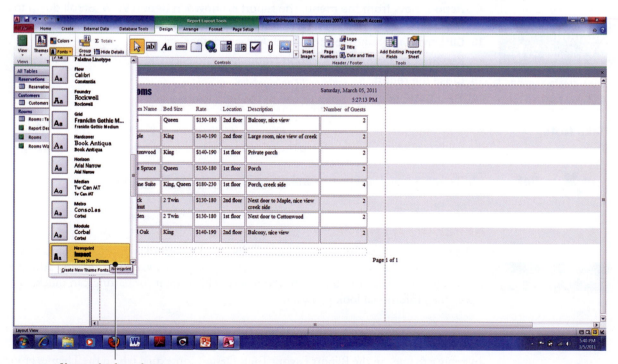

Newsprint font chosen

Figure 6-15

Fonts menu with Newsprint font chosen

6. **SAVE** the report.

PAUSE. LEAVE the report open to use in the next exercise.

WORKING WITH REPORTS

Reports help group and summarize data in different ways. However, after a report is created, you can use Layout View as well as Report View to help locate data. For example, you can use Layout View to easily sort field data one at a time, or perform more complex sorts using the Group, Sort, and Total pane. You can also use Layout View to filter data and view only those records based on the criteria you specify, and use Report or Layout View to find data based on any term you specify.

Sorting Data within a Report

Sorting organizes data into a particular sequence, such as alphabetic order or from smallest to largest numbers. For example, you can sort a customer list in alphabetic order by last name or by customer ID number. You can sort data by clicking the buttons on the Ribbon, right-clicking and choosing commands from the shortcut menu, or by using the Group, Sort, and Total pane. In this exercise, you sort data within a report by using the Ribbon, shortcut menu, and the Group, Sort, and Total pane.

Sorting data in a report is similar to sorting in a table. In Layout View, select the field you want to sort and click the Ascending or Descending button on the Home tab, in the Sort & Filter group. Click the Remove Sort button to remove the sort orders. You can sort as many fields as you like one at a time.

 Ref   Lesson 3 has more information about sorting in a table.

You can also easily sort data by right-clicking in a field and choosing the type of sort you want from the shortcut menu. The sort commands in the shortcut menu vary depending on the type of data in the field. For text, you will choose Sort A to Z or Sort Z to A; for numbers, you will choose Sort Smallest to Largest or Sort Largest to Smallest; and for dates, you will choose Sort Oldest to Newest or Sort Newest to Oldest.

 Ref   Lesson 5 has more information about sorting in a form.

The Group, Sort, and Total pane gives you more sorting options. You can use the pane to specify the sort order or to view the results of sorting using the shortcut menu. To specify a sort, click the Add a Sort button and select a field from the pop-up menu. Click the drop-down menu to specify the type of sort you want. Click the More Options button to display additional commands for creating detailed sorts. Click the Less Options button to return to the basic sorting options.

To delete a sort in the Group, Sort, and Total pane, click the Delete button at the end of the sort line.

 Ref   Lesson 7 has more information about sorting in a query.

STEP BY STEP   **Sort Data within a Report**

USE the report open from the previous exercise.

1. On the Home tab in the Views group, click the bottom-half of the **View** button. Select **Layout View** from the menu.
2. Click the **Room Name** header.
3. On the Home tab, in the Sort & Filter group, click the **Ascending** button. The column is sorted in ascending alphabetic order.
4. On the Home tab, in the Sort & Filter group, click the **Remove Sort** button. The Sort is removed.

5. Right-click the **Room Name** header. The shortcut menu appears.

6. Select **Sort Z to A**, as shown in Figure 6-16. The column is sorted.

Figure 6-16

Shortcut menu

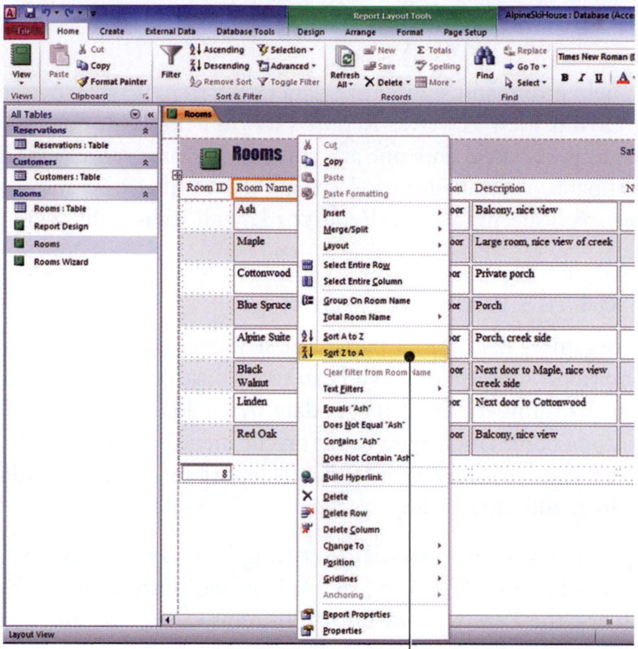

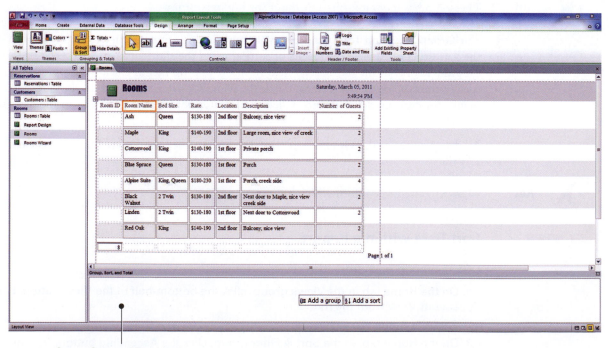

Click Sort Z to A to sort
in descending order

7. On the Home tab, in the Sort & Filter group, click the **Remove Sort** button. The Sort is cleared.

8. On the Report Layout Tools Design contextual tab, in the Grouping & Totals group, click the **Group & Sort** button. The *Group, Sort, and Total* pane appears at the bottom of the screen, as shown in Figure 6-17.

Group, Sort, and Total pane

Figure 6-17

Group, Sort, and Total pane

9. Click the **Add a Sort** button in the *Group, Sort, and Total* pane.

10. Click the **Room Name** field in the fields list. Notice that the field was sorted in ascending order by default and a line was added describing the sort.

11. Click the **down arrow** beside *with A on top* and select **with Z on top** from the menu, as shown in Figure 6-18. The field is sorted in descending order.

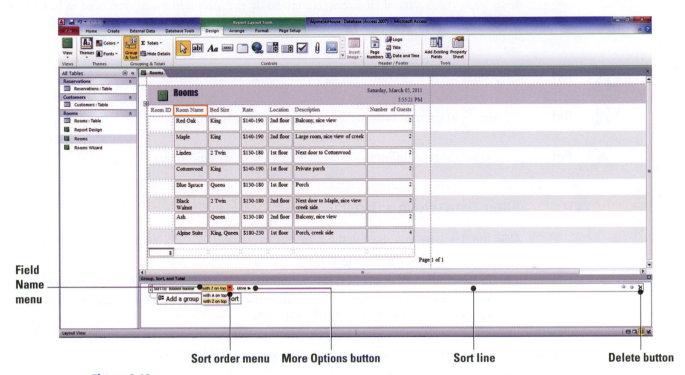

Field Name menu

Sort order menu   More Options button   Sort line   Delete button

Figure 6-18

Sort displayed in the Group, Sort, and Total pane

12. Click the **More Options** button in the Sort line. Notice the options available for customizing a sort.

13. Click the **Delete** button. The sort is cleared.

14. On the Formatting tab, in the Grouping & Totals group, click the **Group & Sort** button. The *Group, Total, and Sort* pane is removed.

15. **SAVE** the report.

PAUSE. LEAVE the database open to use in the next exercise.

CERTIFICATION READY   5.6.2

How do you sort data within a report?

Filtering Data within a Report

A filter displays only data that meet the criteria you have specified and hides the rest. It does not modify the table data or the design of the report. After you remove a filter, all the records are displayed again. Filtering data in Layout View of a report is very similar to filtering data in a table. You can apply common filters using the commands on the Sort & Filter group or by right-clicking a field and choosing a filter from the shortcut menu. The filters available on the shortcut menu vary depending on the type of data in the field. Only one filter can be applied to a field at a time. However, you can specify a different filter for each field. In this exercise, you filter a report using a custom filter, and filter by selection.

You can toggle between filtered and unfiltered views using the Toggle Filter button. To remove a filter from a field, right-click in the field and select the Clear filter from field name command. To remove all filters permanently, select the Clear All Filters command on the Advanced menu in the Sort & Filter group.

Take Note   If you save a report (or other object) while a filter is applied, it will be available the next time you open the report. If you want to open the report and see the filter already applied, set the Filter On Load property setting to Yes.

You can also filter by selection in a report. If you want to view only the reservations for 12/13/11, select that date in the *Check-in* field and click the Selection button. That date will appear in the menu, so that you can choose Equals 12/13/11, Does Not Equal 12/13/11, and so on. You can also access these commands on the shortcut menu by right-clicking the value.

Take Note   If you need to apply a filter that is not in the common filters list, you can write an advanced filter using the Advanced Filter/Sort command on the Advanced menu. You need to be familiar with writing expressions, which are similar to formulas, and be familiar with the criteria that you specify when designing a query.

 Ref   Lesson 3 has more information about filtering records in a table.

 Ref   Lesson 5 has more information about filtering data within a form.

 Ref   Lesson 7 has more information about filtering data within a query.

STEP BY STEP   Filter Data within a Report

USE the database you used in the previous exercise.

1. Click the **Location** header to select it.
2. On the Home tab, in the Sort & Filter group, click the **Filter** button. A menu appears.
3. Point to Text Filters. A second menu appears. Select **Begins with . . .** as shown in Figure 6-19. The Custom Filter box appears.

Figure 6-19

Text Filters menu

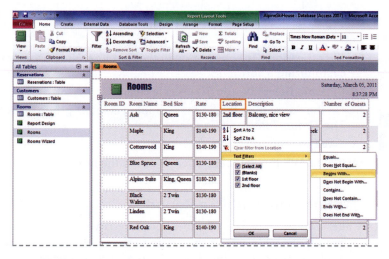

4. Key **1** into the Custom Filter box and click **OK**. The data is filtered to show only the rooms on the first floor.
5. Click the **Remove Filter** button. The report returns to its unfiltered state.
6. In the *Bed Size* field, click **King** in the second row.
7. On the Home tab, in the Sort & Filter group, click the **Selection** button. Select **Equals "King"** from the menu. The data is filtered to show only the rooms with King-sized beds.

8. Right-click the **Bed Size** header. A shortcut menu appears. Notice that the Equals "King" filter and the other filters from the Selection menu are also available in the shortcut menu, shown in Figure 6-20.

Figure 6-20

Shortcut menu

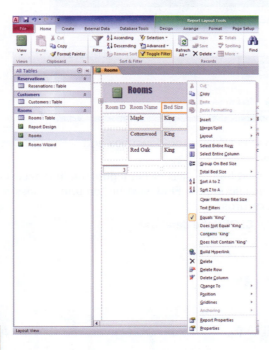

CERTIFICATION
READY   5.6.3

How do you filter data within a report?

9. Select **Clear filter from Bed Size** from the menu. The filter is cleared.

10. **SAVE** and close the table.

PAUSE. LEAVE the database open to use in the next exercise.

Finding Data within a Report

CERTIFICATION
READY   5.6.4

How do you apply and remove filters?

When you want to quickly locate records in a report, you can use the Find command, which searches all the records of the report for any term you specify. Sometimes you may need to quickly find records within a report while in Report View or Report Layout View. To accomplish this, you can use the Find command in the Find group on the Home tab. In this exercise, you locate data in Report View by using the Find command.

 Ref   Lesson 3 has more information about the Find command.

The Find command was overviewed for tables in Lesson 3, Like the Find command in table Datasheet View, once clicked, the Find dialog box appears where you can enter search criteria, set options for where you'd like Access to look for the data, and set data matching and other search options. You can quickly locate records that match your search term and view multiple occurrences; however, remember that you cannot modify record data from within a report, so you cannot replace the record data that is found.

Another Way
You can also access the Find command by pressing Ctrl+F on the keyboard.

Take Note   You cannot use the Find command when you're in Report Design View.

Take Note   You can also use the Find command in tables, forms, and queries.

STEP BY STEP   **Find Data within a Report**

USE the database open from the previous exercise.

1. Open the **Rooms** report.

2. On the Ribbon, in the Views group, click the bottom-half of the **View** button. Select **Report View** from the menu.

3. On the Home tab, in the Find group, click the **Find** button. The Find dialog box appears, as shown in Figure 6-21.

Figure 6-21

Find dialog box

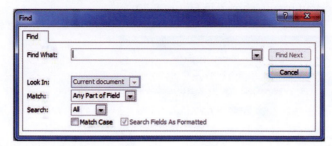

4. Key **King** in the Find What drop-down box and select **Current document** in the Look In drop-down box.

CERTIFICATION READY   **5.6.1**

How do you use the Find command?

5. Click the **Find Next** button. Access highlights the first occurrence of 'King' in the report. Continue clicking the **Find Next** button until Access reports that it has finished searching the records.

6. Close the table. **CLOSE** the database.

STOP. CLOSE Access.

SKILL SUMMARY

In This Lesson You Learned How To:	Exam Objective	Objective Number
Create Reports	Use the Report Wizard.	**5.1.3**
	Use Report Design Tools.	**5.1.2**
Apply a Theme	Apply a Theme.	**5.2.1**
Work with Reports	Use the Sort command.	**5.6.2**
	Use Filter commands.	**5.6.3**
	Use view types.	**5.6.4**
	Use the Find command.	**5.6.1**

Knowledge Assessment

Matching

Match the term in Column 1 to its description in Column 2.

Column 1

1. report

2. record source

3. Report Wizard

4. Field List pane

5. Detail

6. theme

7. Sort

8. Filter

9. design grid

10. Find command

Column 2

a. organizes data in a particular order

b. displays data that meets the criteria you have specified and hides the rest

c. a list of available fields for adding to a report

d. a database object that is used to organize and display data from tables and queries

e. locates data in an open object like a table, query, or report

f. the table or query that provides the data used to generate a report

g. the way a report is displayed in Design View

h. guides you through a series of questions and then generates a report based on your answers

i. the section of a report that includes the body of the report

j. a predefined format that you can apply to any report in Layout View

True/False

Circle T if the statement is true or F if the statement is false.

T   F   1. A simple report contains all the records in a table or query.

T   F   2. You can edit the data in a report.

T   F   3. Click the Report button to define a record source.

T   F   4. In the Report Wizard, you can skip steps such as Sorting or Grouping by clicking the Next button.

T   F   5. You can drag a field from the Field List pane to the design grid to add it to the report.

T   F   6. Layout View gives you the most options for creating a report, because it shows you the underlying structure of the report.

T   F   7. Templates resize column widths for you.

T   F   8. You can save a filter with a report.

T   F   9. You can use the Group, Sort, and Total pane to specify sort order or view the results of sorting using the shortcut menu.

T   F   10. The Toggle Filter button removes a filter permanently.

Competency Assessment

Project 6-1: Soccer Team Report

You need a copy of the soccer team's roster that you can print and take with you to work. Create a simple report and apply a theme.

GET READY. LAUNCH Access if it is not already running.

@ The *SoccerTeam* file for this lesson is available on the book companion website or in WileyPLUS.

1. **OPEN** the *SoccerTeam* database.

2. Save the database as *SoccerTeamXXX* (where *XXX* is your initials).

3. Click the **Roster** table to select it.

4. On the Create tab, in the Reports group, click the **Report** button. A new report is created.

5. Resize each field so that all fields fit on one page.

6. On the Report Layout Tools Design contextual tab, in the Themes group, click the **Themes** button.

7. Select the purple format in the seventh row, third column named **Opulent**.

8. Click the **Save** button on the Quick Access Toolbar. The Save As dialog box appears with the name Roster in it. Click **OK** to accept that name for the report.

9. Close the report.

10. **CLOSE** the database.

LEAVE Access open for the next project.

Project 6-2: Fourth Coffee Inventory Report

In your job at Fourth Coffee, you are responsible for maintaining the coffee inventory. Create a report to view the inventory and prepare for the next order.

GET READY. LAUNCH Access if it is not already running.

@ The *Coffee* file for this lesson is available on the book companion website or in WileyPLUS.

1. **OPEN** *Coffee* from the data files for this lesson.

2. **SAVE** the database as *CoffeeXXX* (where *XXX* is your initials).

3. Click the **Coffee Inventory Table** in the Navigation Pane to select it.

4. On the Create tab, in the Reports group, click the **Report Wizard** button. The first Report Wizard screen appears.

5. Click the double arrow **>>** to move all the fields to the Selected Fields list and click **Next**.

6. On the grouping screen, click the **Scheduled Order Date** field, click the **>**, and click **Next**.

7. On the sorting screen, click the active **down arrow** on the menu, select **Pounds**, and click **Next**.

8. Keep the defaults as is on the layout screen and click **Next**.

9. Click **Finish**. The report is created.

10. Close the report.

11. **CLOSE** the database.

LEAVE Access open for the next project.

Proficiency Assessment

Project 6-3: Alpine Ski House Reservations Report

Every week is different at the Alpine Ski House. Sometimes the lodge is full of guests, and sometimes only a few rooms are occupied. Create a report to show the innkeepers what to expect in the coming weeks.

GET READY. LAUNCH Access if it is not already running.

The *Alpine House* file for this lesson is available on the book companion website or in WileyPLUS.

1. **OPEN** the *Alpine House* database.

2. **SAVE** it as *Alpine House XXX* (where *XXX* is your initials).

3. Use the Report Wizard to create a report using the *Room, Check-in Date,* and *Check-out Date* fields.

4. Group the report by Room and sort it in ascending order by Check-in Date.

5. Use stepped layout and portrait orientation.

6. Name the report **December Reservations** and finish the wizard.

7. Switch to Layout View and increase the width of the *Room* field.

8. Apply the **Foundry** theme.

9. Save and close the table.

10. **CLOSE** the database.

LEAVE Access open for the next project.

Project 6-4: Wingtip Toys Design View Report

The manufacturing department at Wingtip Toys needs summary information about each toy in inventory. Create a report in Design View that will display the requested information.

GET READY. LAUNCH Access if it is not already running.

The *Wingtip Toys* file for this lesson is available on the book companion website or in WileyPLUS.

1. **OPEN** *Wingtip Toys* and save it as *Wingtip Toys XXX* (where *XXX* is your initials).

2. Click the **Inventory** table in the Navigation Pane to select it.

3. On the Create tab, in the Reports group, click the **Report Design** button.

4. On the Design tab, in the Tools group, click the **Add Existing Fields** button. The Field List pane appears.

5. Position the fields from the Inventory table onto the design grid, as shown in Figure 6-22. Adjust field widths as shown.

Figure 6-22

Wingtip Toys report in Design View

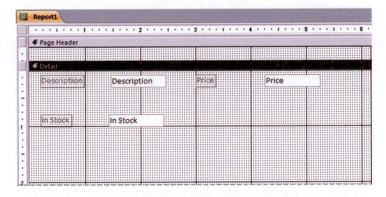

6. Save the report as **Toy Summary**.

7. Close the report.

LEAVE the database open for the next project.

Mastery Assessment

Project 6-5: Filter, Sort, and Find Records in a Wingtip Toys Report

A large order was recently filled, and now the inventory at Wingtip Toys is quite low on some items. Create a report that displays this information.

The **Wingtip Toys XXX** database should be open.

GET READY. LAUNCH Access if it is not already running.

1. Define the **Inventory** table as the record source for a new report.
2. Create a simple report.
3. Apply the **Equity** theme to the new report.
4. Sort the report in ascending order by the *Description* field.
5. Click the first row of the **In Stock** field, which contains the number 10.
6. Filter by selection to display the toys with 10 or fewer items in stock.
7. Click the **In Stock** field header and sort the field in ascending order.
8. Clear all sorts.
9. Clear all filters.
10. Find and cycle through all occurrences of the word **Car**.
11. Save the report as **Inventory**.
12. Close the report.
13. **CLOSE** the database.

LEAVE Access open for the next project.

Project 6-6: Angel Project Report

The school Angel Project has begun. Information for the boy angels needs to be distributed to the boys in the kindergarten classes, and the girl angels' information needs to be distributed to the girls. Create a report with filters that displays the boy and girl information separately.

GET READY. LAUNCH Access if it is not already running.

@ The *Angel Project* file for this lesson is available on the book companion website or in WileyPLUS.

1. **OPEN** the *Angel Project* database.
2. Save the database as *Angel Project XXX* (where *XXX* is your initials).
3. Define the List table as the record source for a new report.
4. Use the Report Wizard to create a report with all the fields.
5. Skip the grouping and sorting screens, and choose a tabular, portrait layout.
6. Name the report *Angel Needs and Wants*.
7. Switch to Layout View and adjust field widths as necessary so that all data fits on the screen and on one page, and apply the **Trek** theme.
8. Display the *Group, Sort, and Total* pane.
9. Sort the report in ascending order by Age.
10. Create a filter to show only the information for the males.
11. Toggle the filter and create a new filter to show only the information for the females.
12. Save and close the report.
13. **CLOSE** the database.

CLOSE Access.

INTERNET READY

Search the Internet for at least five dream vacation packages and create a database table that lists each hotel's location, name, cost, and favorite amenities or activities. After creating the table, use the Report Wizard to create a professional-looking report that displays your data.

Create and Modify Queries 7

LESSON SKILL MATRIX

Skill	Exam Objective	Objective Number
Creating a Query	Create a Select query.	4.1.1
Modifying a Query	Use the Show Table command. Use the Remove Table command. Use Sort and Show options.	4.2.1 4.2.2 4.3.4
Sorting and Filtering Data within a Query	Use Sort and Show options.	4.3.4

KEY TERMS

- field list
- parameter query
- query criterion
- select query

You work for Northwind Traders, a mountain-climbing apparel company dedicated to producing high-quality and technically innovative products. The company has a program called industry friends that offers discount purchasing privileges for employees and other outdoor professionals and friends who qualify. As operations coordinator, you are responsible for approving applications for the program and entering related information into the database. You often need to pull specific data from the database. In this lesson, you learn how to create queries from a single table—including a simple query and a find duplicates query—and how to create queries from multiple tables, including a find un-matched query; how to modify a query by adding a table, removing a table, and adding criteria to a query; and how to sort and filter data within a query.

SOFTWARE ORIENTATION

Queries Group

The Queries group (Figure 7-1) on the Create tab contains the commands used to create queries. The Query Wizard button launches the Query Wizard, which helps you create a simple query, a crosstab query, a find duplicates query, or a find unmatched query. The Query Design button creates a new, blank query in Design View. Use this figure as a reference throughout this lesson as well as the rest of this book.

Figure 7-1

Queries group

Launches the Query Wizard

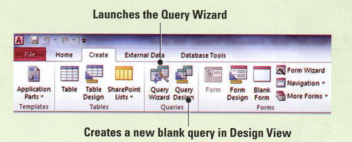

Creates a new blank query in Design View

CREATING A QUERY

The Bottom Line

A query is a set of instructions used for working with data. Creating a query is like asking the database a question. Running a query performs these instructions and provides the answers. The results that a query returns can be sorted, grouped, or filtered. A query can also create, copy, delete, or change data. A **select query** is the most basic type of Access query. It creates subsets of data that you can use to answer specific questions or to supply data to other database objects. The data is displayed in Datasheet View without being changed. A query is a powerful and versatile database tool. Queries differ from sort or filter commands because they can be saved for future use and can extract data from multiple tables or other queries.

Creating a Query from a Table

A query can get its data from one or more tables, from existing queries, or from a combination of the two. The tables or queries from which a query gets its data are referred to as its record source. When one table provides the information that you need, you can create a simple select query using the Query Wizard. You can also use a query to find records with duplicate field values in a single table. In this exercise, you create a simple select query that searches the data in a single table.

To create a simple select query, on the Create tab, in the Queries group, click the Query Wizard button. Click Simple Query Wizard and then click OK. Specify the table you want to use as the record source and the fields that you want to show. Name the query and click Finish. When you close the query, it is automatically saved.

To run a query after it has been created, simply double-click it in the Navigation pane to open it in Datasheet View and see the results.

STEP BY STEP   **Create a Simple Query**

The *Northwind* file for this lesson is available on the book companion website or in WileyPLUS.

GET READY. Before you begin these steps, be sure to **LAUNCH** Microsoft Access.

1. **OPEN** the *Northwind* file from the data files for this lesson.
2. **SAVE** the database as *Northwind XXX* (where *XXX* is your initials).
3. On the Create tab, in the Other group, click the **Query Wizard** button. The New Query dialog box appears, as shown in Figure 7-2.

Figure 7-2

New Query dialog box

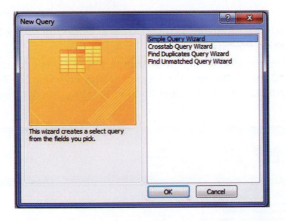

WileyPLUS Extra! features an online tutorial of this task.

4. Click **Simple Query Wizard** and then click **OK**. The Simple Query Wizard appears, as shown in Figure 7-3.

Figure 7-3

Simple Query Wizard, screen 1

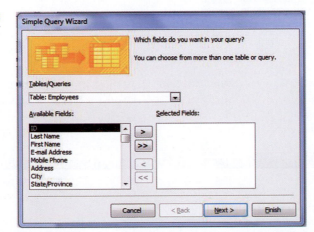

5. In the Tables/Queries drop-down list, Table: Employees should be selected by default. If it is not, select it.
6. Under Available Fields, double-click **Last Name**, **First Name**, **E-mail Address**, **Mobile Phone**, and **Position** to move them to the Selected Fields box.

Take Note   To remove a field from the Selected Fields box, double-click the field. This moves it back to the Available Fields box.

7. Click the **Next >** button. The second screen in the Simple Query Wizard appears, as shown in Figure 7-4.

Figure 7-4

Simple Query Wizard, screen 2

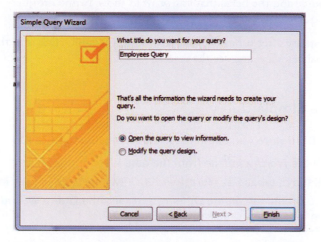

8. Name the query **Employees Contact Query**. *Open the query to view information* should be selected.

9. Click the **Finish** button to accept the default selections and complete the query. The Employees Contact Query is displayed, as shown in Figure 7-5. The results show all of the records, but show only the five fields that you specified in the query wizard.

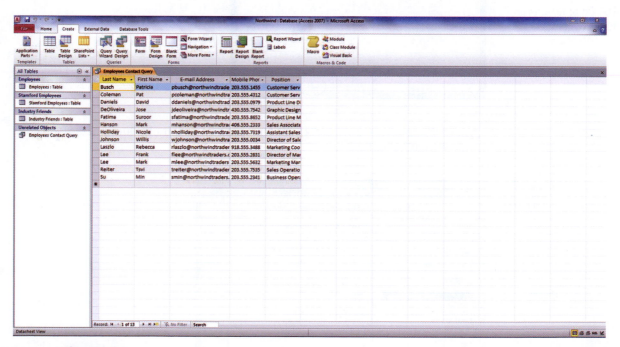

Figure 7-5

Simple select query

10. Click the **Close** button on the Employees Contact Query window to close the query.
PAUSE. LEAVE Access open to use in the next exercise.

CERTIFICATION READY 4.1.1

How do you create select queries?

Creating a Find Duplicates Query

As a general rule, duplicate data should be eliminated from a database whenever possible to reduce costs and increase accuracy. The first step in this process is finding duplicate data. Two or more records are considered duplicates only when all the fields in your query results contain the same values. If the values in even a single field differ, each record is unique. In this exercise, you use the Find Duplicates Query Wizard to find duplicate records.

You can also use the Find Duplicates Wizard to find records that contain *some* matching field values. You should include the field or fields that identify each record uniquely, typically the primary key. The query returns matching records where the values in the specified fields match character for character.

STEP BY STEP   **Create a Find Duplicates Query**

USE the database that is open from the previous exercise.

1. On the Create tab, in the Other group, click the **Query Wizard** button. The New Query dialog box appears.

2. Click **Find Duplicates Query Wizard** and then click **OK**. The *Find Duplicates Query Wizard* appears, as shown in Figure 7-6.

Figure 7-6

Find Duplicates Query Wizard, screen 1

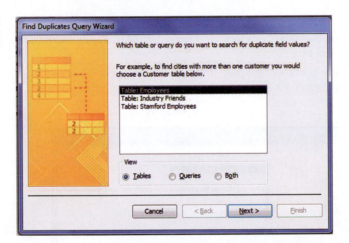

3. Click **Table: Industry Friends** and then click **Next >**. The next screen in the Find Duplicates Query Wizard appears, as shown in Figure 7-7.

Figure 7-7

Find Duplicates Query Wizard, screen 2

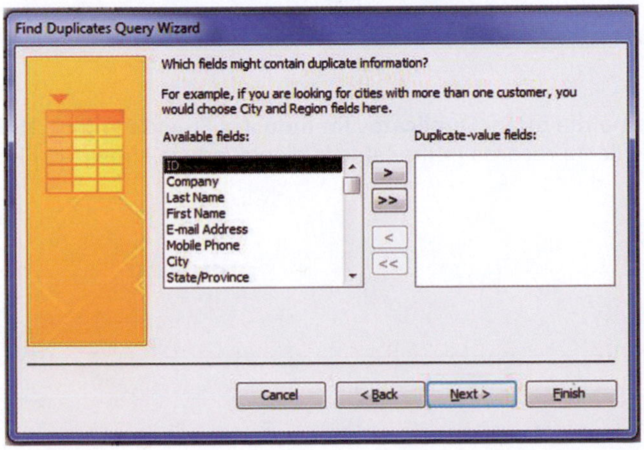

4. Double-click **Last Name**, **First Name**, and **E-mail Address** to move them to the Duplicate-value fields box. These are the fields that you think may include duplicate information.

5. Click **Next >** to display the next screen in the Find Duplicates Query Wizard, shown in Figure 7-8. This screen asks you if you want to show the other fields of the duplicate record besides just the ones with the duplicate data.

Figure 7-8

Find Duplicates Query Wizard, screen 3

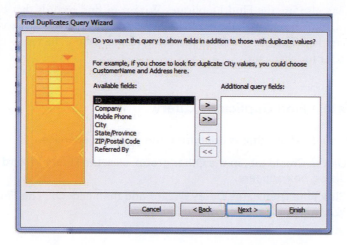

6. Double-click **Company** and **Referred By** to move them to the Additional query fields box.

7. Click **Next >** to display the final screen in the Find Duplicates Query Wizard, shown in Figure 7-9.

Figure 7-9

Find Duplicates Query Wizard, final screen

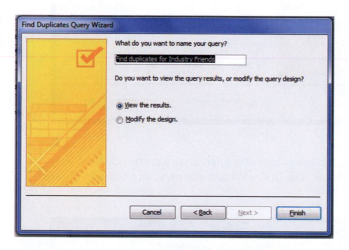

8. Name the query **Duplicates for Industry Friends** and click **Finish**. The query showing duplicate records in the table is displayed, as shown in Figure 7-10.

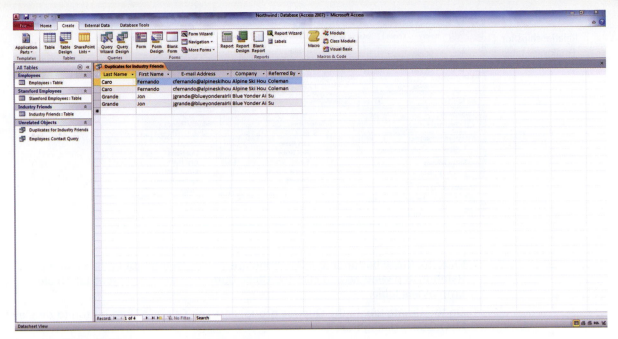

Figure 7-10

Duplicates for Industry
Friends query

9. Click the **Close** button in the Duplicates for Industry Friends tab to close the query.

PAUSE. LEAVE Access open to use in the next exercise.

Creating a Query from Multiple Tables

If the data you need is spread out in more than one table, you can build a query that combines information from multiple sources. You can also create a query that finds records in one table that have no related records in another table. When you need to include multiple tables in your query, you can use the Simple Query Wizard to build a query from a primary table and a related table. The process is similar to creating a query from a single table, except that you include fields from additional tables. In this exercise, you create a simple query to display related data from two tables.

Sometimes using data from a related table would help make the query results clearer and more useful. For example, in this activity, you could pull the name of the industry friends and the employee who referred them from one table. But to get additional information about the referring employees, you need to pull data from the related Employee table.

Before creating a query from multiple tables, you must first ensure that the tables have a defined relationship in the Relationships window. A relationship appears as a line connecting the two tables on a common field. You can double-click a relationship line to see which fields in the tables are connected by the relationship.

STEP BY STEP **Create a Query from Multiple Tables**

USE the database that is open from the previous exercise.

1. In the Navigation pane, double-click **Employees: Table** to open the table.
2. On the Database Tools tab, in the Relationships group, click the **Relationships** button to display the table relationship, as shown in Figure 7-11. The Employees table has a defined relationship with the Industry Friends table as indicated by the relationship line connecting the two tables.

Figure 7-11

Relationships for
Employees table

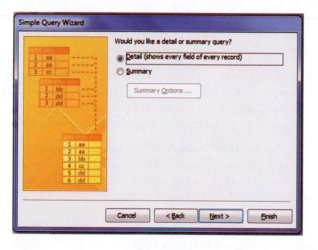

3. Click the **Close** button in the Relationships group on the Ribbon to close the Relationship window and click the **Close** button on the Employees tab to close the Employees table.

4. On the Create tab, in the Queries group, click the **Query Wizard** button to display the New Query dialog box.

5. Click **Simple Query Wizard** and then click **OK** to display the Simple Query Wizard.

6. In the Tables/Queries drop-down list, click **Table: Industry Friends**.

7. Under Available Fields, double-click **Last Name**, **First Name**, and **Referred By** to move them to the Selected Fields box.

8. In the Tables/Queries drop-down list, click **Table: Employees**.

9. Under Available Fields, double-click **Position** and then **E-mail Address** to move them to the Selected Fields box.

10. Click the **Next >** button to display the next screen, shown in Figure 7-12. The Detail option should be selected by default.

Figure 7-12

Simple Query Wizard for
multiple tables

 Ref

If you want your query to perform aggregate functions, you would choose a summary query. You learn about aggregated functions in Lesson 12.

11. Click the **Next >** button to display the final screen, shown in Figure 7-13.

Figure 7-13

Simple Query Wizard for
multiple tables, final screen

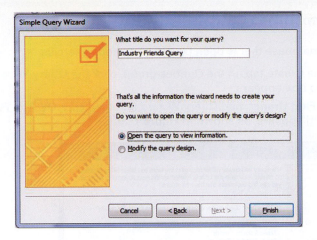

12. Click the **Finish** button to accept the default settings in this screen and display the
query, shown in Figure 7-14. This query shows the last name, first name, position, and
e-mail address of the employee, and who referred each industry friend.

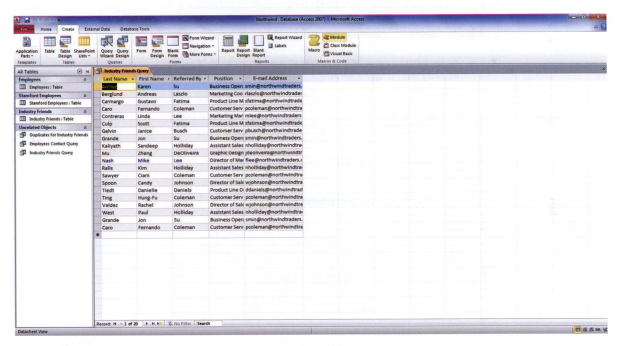

Figure 7-14

Industry Friends query

13. Click the **Close** button on the Industry Friends Query tab to close the query.

PAUSE. LEAVE the database open to use in the next exercise.

 Ref   You learned about defining and modifying table relationships in Lesson 3.

Finding Unmatched Records

To view only the records in one table that do not have a matching record in another table, you
can create a Find Unmatched query. On the Create tab, in the Queries group, click Query
Wizard, and then click Find Unmatched Query Wizard to start the wizard. In this exercise, you
run a Find Unmatched query to display the employees who do not live in Stamford.

Find Unmatched Records

USE the database that is open from the previous exercise.

1. On the Create tab, in the Queries group, click the **Query Wizard** button. The New Query dialog box appears.

2. Click **Find Unmatched Query Wizard** and then click **OK**. The Find Unmatched Query Wizard appears, as shown in Figure 7-15.

Figure 7-15

Find Unmatched Query Wizard, screen 1

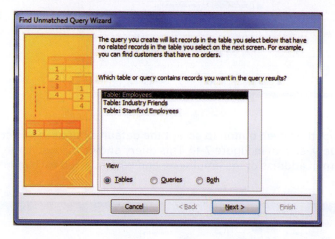

3. Table: Employees is the default selection in this screen. This table will contain the records you'll want to display. Click the **Next >** button to display the next screen in the Find Unmatched Query Wizard, shown in Figure 7-16.

Figure 7-16

Find Unmatched Query Wizard, screen 2

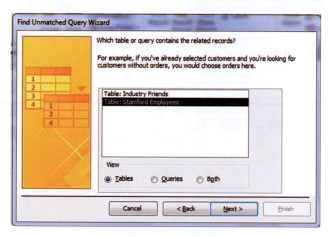

4. Select **Table: Stamford Employees** to select the table that is related to the Employees table and contains the records you *don't* want to display. Click the **Next >** button to display the next screen in the Find Unmatched Query Wizard, shown in Figure 7-17.

Figure 7-17

Find Unmatched Query Wizard, screen 3

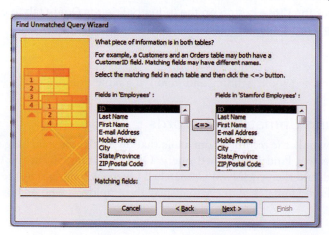

5. Click **E-mail Address** in the *Fields in 'Employees'* list. Click **E-mail Address** in the *Fields in 'Stamford Employees'* list. Click the **<=>** button to display them in the Matching fields box. These fields contain data that's in both tables.

6. Click the **Next >** button to display the next screen in the Find Unmatched Query Wizard, shown in Figure 7-18.

Figure 7-18

Find Unmatched Query Wizard, screen 4

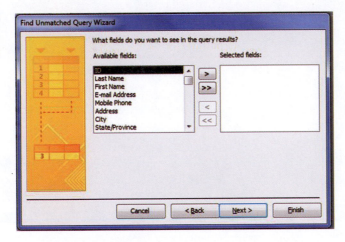

7. In the Available fields box, double-click **Last Name**, **First Name**, **Position**, and **City** to move them to the Selected fields box.

8. Click the **Next >** button to display the final screen in the Find Unmatched Query Wizard, shown in Figure 7-19.

Figure 7-19

Find Unmatched Query Wizard, final screen

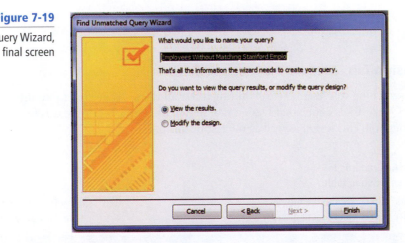

9. Click in the text box at the top of this screen and key **Non-Stamford Employees** to name your query, then click the **Finish** button. The query is displayed, as shown in Figure 7-20.

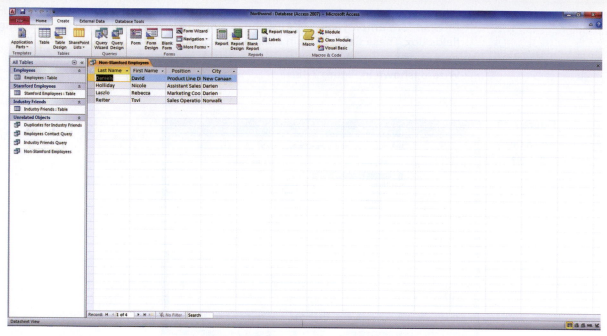

Figure 7-20

Non-Stamford Employees query

10. Click the **Close** button on the Non-Stamford Employees tab to close the query.

PAUSE. LEAVE the database open to use in the next exercise.

SOFTWARE ORIENTATION

Design Tab

By switching to Design View, you can access all the tools needed to modify your query on the Query Tools contextual Design tab, shown in Figure 7-21. Use this figure as a reference throughout this lesson as well as the rest of this book.

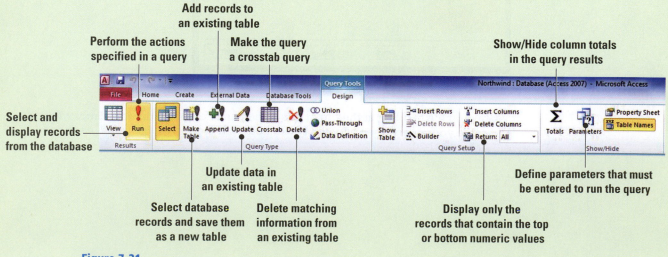

Figure 7-21

Design tab

MODIFYING A QUERY

The Bottom Line

A query can be modified in Design View, regardless of how it was created. You can add or remove a table, add or remove fields, or add criteria to refine query results.

Adding a Table to a Query

To add a table to a query, you must be in Design View. On the Query Tools Design contextual tab, in the Query Setup group, click the Show Table button to display the Show Table dialog box. There is a tab that contains the tables in the database, a tab with the queries, and a tab that displays both. Select the object you want to add to the query, and click the Add button. If you add a second copy of a table to the query, it is indicated by a "1" in the title. In this exercise, you add additional tables to a query using the Show Table dialog box.

STEP BY STEP   **Add a Table to a Query**

USE the database that is open from the previous exercise.

1. Double-click the **Industry Friends Query** in the Navigation pane to open it.
2. On the Home tab, in the Views menu, click the lower half of the **View** button and then click **Design View**. The query appears in Design View, as shown in Figure 7-22.

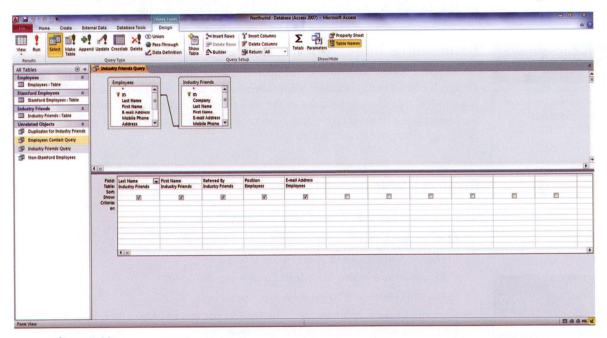

Figure 7-22

Query in Design View

3. On the Query Tools Design contextual tab, in the Query Setup group, click the **Show Table** button to display the Show Table dialog box, shown in Figure 7-23.

Figure 7-23

Show Table dialog box

4. Click **Industry Friends** and click the **Add** button. A second copy of the Industry Friends table is added to the query, as indicated by the "1" in the title, as shown in Figure 7-24.

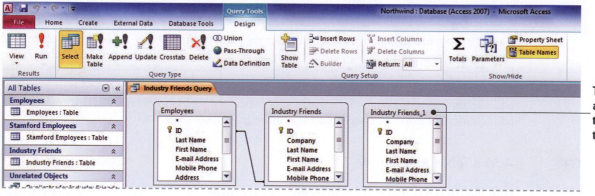

The "1" indicates a second copy of the table added to the query

Figure 7-24

Second copy of table in a query

5. Click **Stamford Employees** and click the **Add** button. The table is added to the query.

6. Click the **Close** button on the Show Table dialog box.

PAUSE. LEAVE the database open to use in the next exercise.

Removing a Table from a Query

To remove a table from a query, first open the query in Design View. In the upper part of query Design View, select the table you want to remove by clicking anywhere in its field list—a **field list** is a window that lists all the fields in the underlying record source or database object—then press the Delete key. The table is removed from the query, but it is not deleted from the database. In this exercise, you remove a table from a query.

STEP BY STEP	**Remove a Table from a Query**

USE the database that is open from the previous exercise.

1. Click anywhere in the **Industry Friends_1** field list.

2. Press the **Delete** key to remove the table.

3. Click anywhere in the **Stamford Employees** field list.

4. Press the **Delete** key to remove the table.

5. Click the **Close** button on the Industry Friends tab to close the query. If a message asks you if you want to save the changes, click **Yes**.

PAUSE. LEAVE the database open to use in the next exercise.

Adding Criteria to a Query

Not all queries must include criteria, but if you are not interested in seeing all the records that are stored in the underlying record source, you can add criteria to a query when designing it. A **query criterion** is a rule that identifies the records that you want to include in the query result. A criterion is similar to a formula. Some criteria are simple and use basic operators and constants. Others are complex and use functions, special operators, and include field references. Criteria can look very different from each other, depending on the data type of the field to which they apply and your specific requirements. You can also run a **parameter query**, in which the user interactively specifies one or more criteria values. This is not a separate query; it extends the flexibility of another type of query, such as a select query, by prompting the user for a value when it is run. In this exercise, you add criteria to queries to display certain records, use the Show check box, and create and run a parameter query that will prompt the user for a city name and display matching records.

To specify one or more criteria to restrict in the records returned in the query results, open the query in Design View. Select the field and type the condition that you want to specify in the Criteria row. To see the results, switch to Datasheet View. The results will show each field, including the one where the criterion was specified.

Sometimes, you may want to show only certain fields from the records that match the criterion to get a more concise view of the resulting data. In this case, deselect the Show row check box above the Criteria row for those fields you don't want to display in the results. The fields that you choose not to show, except the field with the criterion, will be removed from Design View after you switch to Datasheet View.

STEP BY STEP   **Add Criteria to a Query**

USE the database that is open from the previous exercise.

1. In the Navigation pane, double-click the **Employees Contact Query** to open it.
2. On the Home tab, in the Views group, click the lower half of the **View** button and click **Design View**.
3. In the Criteria row of the Position field, key **Like "*Manager*"** as shown in Figure 7-25.

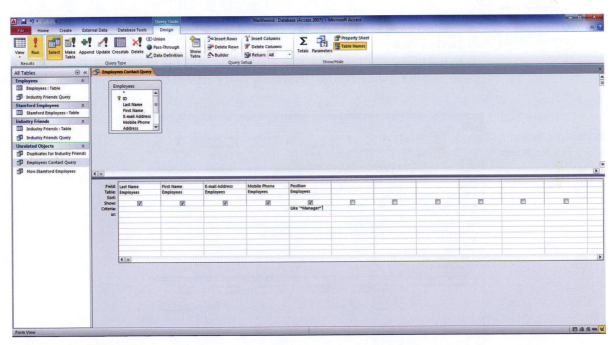

Figure 7-25

Query criterion

4. On the Query Tools Design contextual tab, in the Results group, click the lower half of the **View** button and click **Datasheet View**. The query results display all records with "Manager" in the position field, as shown in Figure 7-26.

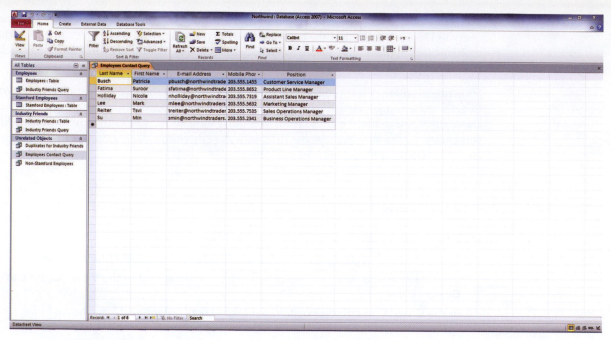

Figure 7-26

Results with query criteria applied

5. On the Home tab, in the Views group, click the lower half of the **View** button, and click **Design View**.

6. In the Show row, under the First Name field, click the **Show** check box to deselect it, as shown in Figure 7-27. The First Name field data will not appear in the query results.

Figure 7-27

Show check box deselected for First Name field

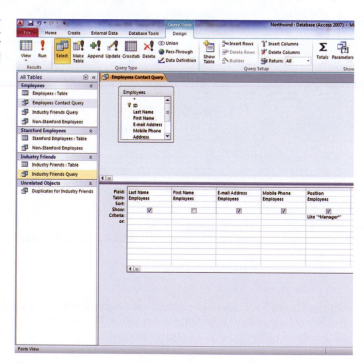

7. On the Home tab, in the Views group, click the lower half of the **View** button and click **Datasheet View**. Notice that the First Name field doesn't appear.

8. Click the **Close** button on the Employees Contact Query tab to close the query. When prompted to save, click **Yes**.

9. In the Navigation pane, double-click the **Non-Stamford Employees Query** to open it.

10. On the Home tab, in the Views group, click the lower half of the **View** button and click **Design View**.

11. In the Criteria row of the City field, key [City?] as shown in Figure 7-28.

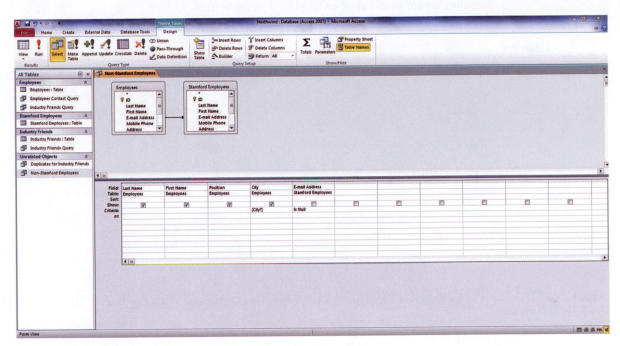

Figure 7-28

Parameter query criteria

12. On the Home tab, in the Views group, click the lower half of the **View** button and click **Datasheet View**. The prompt appears in the Enter Parameter Value dialog box, as shown in Figure 7-29.

Figure 7-29

Parameter query prompt dialog box

13. Key **Darien** in the City? box.

14. Click **OK**. The records for non-Stamford employees who live in Darien are displayed in the results, as shown in Figure 7-30.

Figure 7-30

Parameter query result

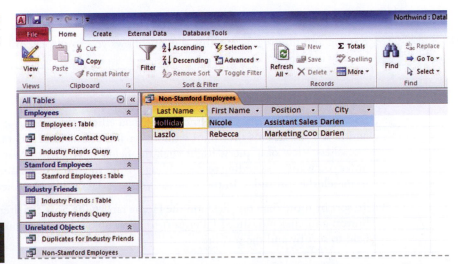

CERTIFICATION READY   4.3.4

How do you use Show options?

PAUSE. LEAVE the database open to use in the next exercise.

Table 7-1 shows some sample criteria and explains how they work. Table 7-2 shows the query results that are returned when specific criterion is used.

Table 7-1

Criteria Examples

Criteria	Description
>25 and <50	This criterion applies to a *Number* field, such as Inventory. It includes only those records where the *Inventory* field contains a value greater than 25 and less than 50.
DateDiff ("yyyy", [BirthDate], Date()) > 21	This criterion applies to a *Date/Time* field, such as BirthDate Only records where the number of years between a person's birth date and today's date is greater than 21 are included in the query result.
Is Null	This criterion can be applied to any type of field to show records where the field value is null.

Table 7-2

Query Result Examples

To Include Records That . . .	Use This Criterion	Query Result
Exactly match a value, such as Manager	"Manager"	Returns records where the given field is set to Manager.
Do not match a value, such as Chicago	Not "Chicago"	Returns records where the given field is set to a value other than Chicago.
Begin with the specified string such as B	Like B*	Returns records for the given field where the value starts with "B," such as Boston, Bakersfield, and so on.
Do not begin with the specified string, such as B	Not Like B*	Returns records for the given field where the value starts with a character other than "B."
Contain the specified string, such as Sales	Like "*Sales*"	Returns records for the given field that contain the string "Sales."
Do not contain the specified string, such as Sales	Not Like "*Sales*"	Returns records for the given field that do not contain the string "Sales."

SORTING AND FILTERING DATA WITHIN A QUERY

The Bottom Line

Sorting and filtering data within a query allows you to display only the records you want and/or only in a particular order.

Sorting Data within a Query

Sorting data in a query can help organize data efficiently and make it easier for users to review and locate the records they want without having to browse the data. Data can be sorted in the Datasheet View of a query. Right-click the field on which you want to sort and click the sort order you want—ascending or descending—from the shortcut menu. The records are rearranged to match the sort order. In this exercise, you sort data using Datasheet View of a query.

To sort by more than one field, on the Home tab, in the Sort & Filter group, click the Advanced button and click Advanced Filter/Sort to open up a tab where you can specify more than one field to sort by and the sort order.

 Ref

You learned about sorting data within a table in Lesson 3, sorting data within a form in Lesson 5, and sorting data within a report in Lesson 6.

STEP BY STEP   **Sort Data within a Query**

USE the database that is open from the previous exercise.

1. In the Navigation pane, double-click the **Industry Friends Query** to open it.
2. Right-click the **Referred By** field to display the shortcut menu shown in Figure 7-31.

Figure 7-31

Shortcut menu

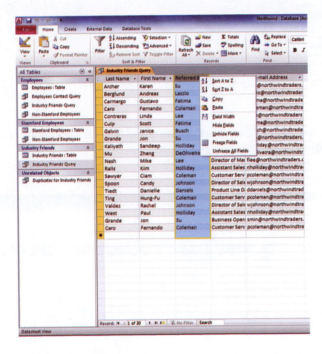

3. Click **Sort A to Z.** The field is sorted in alphabetic order from A to Z, as shown in Figure 7-32.

Figure 7-32

Sorted query

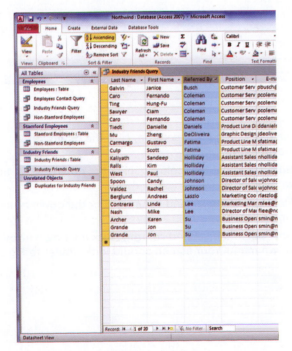

4. On the Home tab, in the Sort & Filter group, click the **Remove Sort** button.

5. On the Home tab, in the Sort & Filter group, click the **Advanced** button to display the menu shown in Figure 7-33.

Figure 7-33

Advanced menu

6. Click **Advanced Filter/Sort**. An Industry Friends QueryFilter1 tab appears, as shown in Figure 7-34.

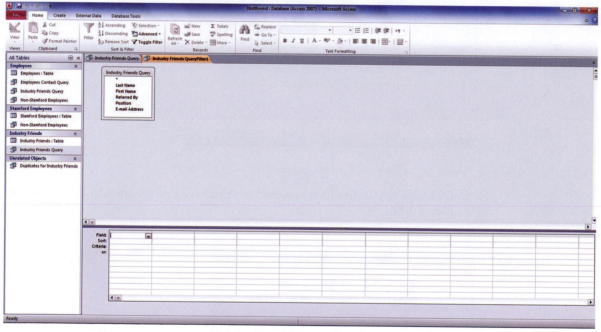

Figure 7-34

Industry Friends QueryFilter1 tab

7. Click the **Field cell** in the first column, click the **down arrow**, and click **Referred By** on the drop-down menu.

8. Click the **Sort cell** in the first column, click the **down arrow**, and click **Ascending** on the drop-down menu.

9. Click the **Field cell** in the second column, click the **down arrow**, and click **Last Name** on the drop-down menu.

10. Click the **Sort cell** in the second column, click the **down arrow**, and click **Ascending** on the drop-down menu. Your screen should look similar to Figure 7-35.

Figure 7-35

Advanced sort criteria

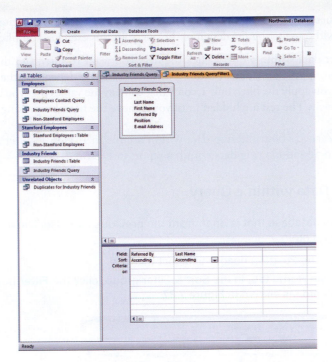

11. On the Home tab, in the Sort & Filter group, click the **Advanced** button and click **Apply Filter/Sort**. The query is sorted by the *Referred By* field in ascending order and then by the *Last Name* field in ascending order, as shown in Figure 7-36.

Figure 7-36

Sorted query

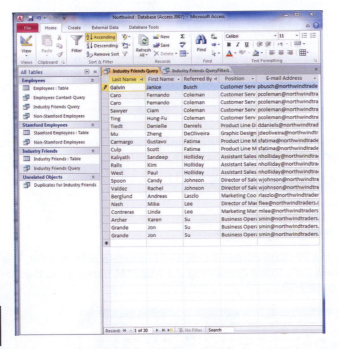

How do you use Sort options?

12. On the Home tab, in the Sort & Filter group, click the **Remove Sort** button.

PAUSE. LEAVE the database open to use in the next exercise.

Take Note   The same tab is used to perform an advanced filter for the query.

Take Note   You can also sort using the sort cell in Query Design View.

Filtering Data within a Query

A filter limits a view of data to specific records without requiring you to alter the design of the underlying query. If the criteria are temporary or change often, you can filter the query result instead of frequently modifying the query criteria. A filter is a temporary criterion that changes the query result without altering the design of the query. In this exercise, you filter data within a query.

To filter data within a query, click the field you want to filter. On the Home tab, in the Sort & Filter group, click the Filter button. The filters available depend on the type and values of the field. When you apply the filter, only records that contain the values that you are interested in are included in the view. The rest are hidden until you remove the filter by clicking the Toggle Filter button.

 Ref

> You learned about filtering data within a table in Lesson 3, filtering data within a form in Lesson 5, and filtering data within a report in Lesson 6.

STEP BY STEP   **Filter Data within a Query**

USE the database that is open from the previous exercise. The Industry Friends Query should be open.

1. Click the **Position** header to select the field.

2. On the Home tab, in the Sort & Filter group, click the **Filter** button. A menu appears on the field, as shown in Figure 7-37.

Figure 7-37

Filter menu

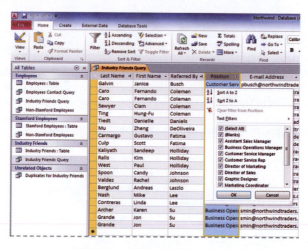

3. Click **Text Filters** and click **Contains** on the submenu. A Custom Filter dialog box appears, as shown in Figure 7-38.

Figure 7-38

Custom Filter dialog box

4. In the Position contains box, key **Marketing** and click **OK**. The records are filtered to show only those containing the word "Marketing" in the *Position* field, as shown in Figure 7-39.

Figure 7-39

Filtered query

5. On the Home tab, in the Sort & Filter group, click the **Toggle Filter** button to remove the filter.

6. Click the **Close** button on Industry Friends Query to close the query and click **Yes** to save changes when prompted.

CLOSE the database.

SKILL SUMMARY

In This Lesson You Learned How To:	Exam Objective	Objective Number
Create a query	Create a Select query.	**4.1.1**
Modify a query	Use the Show Table command.	**4.2.1**
	Use the Remove Table command.	**4.2.2**
	Use Sort and Show options.	**4.3.4**
Sort and Filter data within a query	Use Sort and Show options.	**4.3.4**

Knowledge Assessment

Fill in the Blank

Complete the following sentences by writing the correct word or words in the blanks provided.

1. The Queries group on the _____ tab contains the commands used to create queries.

2. The _____ button creates a new, blank query in Design View.

3. A(n) _____ is the most basic type of Access query.

4. The tables or queries from which a query gets its data are referred to as its _____.

5. To run a query after it has been created, double-click it in the Navigation pane to open it in _____ View and see the results.

6. Two or more records are considered _____ only when all the fields in your query results contain the same values.

7. When you need to include multiple tables in your query, use the _____ Wizard to build a query from a primary table and a related table.

8. To view only the records in one table that don't have a matching record in another table, you can create a _____ query.

9. By switching to _____ View, you can access all the tools needed to modify your query.

10. A(n) _____ is a window that lists all the fields in the underlying record source or database object.

Multiple Choice

Select the best response for the following statements or questions.

1. Creating a query is like
   a. Sorting the data
   b. Asking the database a question
   c. Creating a new table
   d. Opening an existing database

2. The results that a query returns can be
   a. Sorted
   b. Grouped
   c. Filtered
   d. All of the above
   e. None of the above

3. When one table will provide the information that you need, you can create a

  a. Record source

  b. Simple select query

  c. Query criterion

  d. Parameter query

4. Which query cannot be created using the Query Wizard?

  a. Parameter query

  b. Simple query

  c. Find duplicates query

  d. Find unmatched query

5. Queries are different from sort or filter commands because they can be

  a. Applied to multiple fields

  b. Saved

  c. Modified

  d. Used on forms

6. A query can get its data from

  a. One or more tables

  b. Existing queries

  c. A combination of a and b

  d. All of the above

  e. None of the above

7. To find records that contain matching field values, you can create a query using which wizard?

  a. Find Matching

  b. Matching Fields

  c. Duplicate Records

  d. Find Duplicates

8. Before creating a query from multiple tables, you must first ensure that the tables have

  a. Unmatched records

  b. A defined relationship

  c. A filter applied

  d. No related records

9. To add a table to a query, you must be in what view?

  a. SQL

  b. Datasheet

  c. PivotTable

  d. Design

10. A rule that identifies the records that you want to include in the query result is called a

  a. Parameter query

  b. Query criterion

  c. Select query

  d. Field list

Competency Assessment

Project 7-1: Create a Games Select Query

As the manager at Southridge Video, you have stored information in an Access database about each used game that the store has taken in trade. Now that you know how to create queries, you decide to create a select query to list the title, rating, and category, which are the fields that you most often need to view.

GET READY. LAUNCH Access if it is not already running.

@ The *Games* file for this lesson is available on the book companion website or in WileyPLUS.

1. **OPEN** *Games* from the data files for this lesson.
2. **SAVE** the database as *Games XXX* (where *XXX* is your initials).
3. On the Create tab, in the Queries group, click the **Query Wizard** button to display the New Query dialog box.
4. Click **Simple Query Wizard** and then click **OK**.
5. In the Tables/Queries drop-down list, Table: Games should be selected.
6. Under Available Fields, double-click **Title**, **Rating**, and **Category** to move them to the Selected Fields box.
7. Click the **Next >** button. The second screen in the Simple Query Wizard appears.
8. Name the query **Games Query**. *Open the query to view information* should be selected.
9. Click the **Finish** button.
10. Click the **Close** button in the Games Query tab to close the query.
11. **LEAVE** the database open for the next project.

LEAVE Access open for the next project.

Project 7-2: Create a Find Duplicates Query

You have taught the night manager at Southridge Video how to enter used game information into the database, but you have not yet developed a reliable system for determining if the game has already been entered. You are concerned there may be duplicate records. Create a find duplicates query to determine if there are duplicates.

USE the database that is open from the previous project.

1. On the Create tab, in the Queries group, click the **Query Wizard** button.
2. In the New Query dialog box, click **Find Duplicates Query Wizard**, and then click **OK**.
3. Click **Table: Games** and then click **Next >**. The next screen in the Find Duplicates Query Wizard appears.
4. Double-click **Title**, **Platform**, and **Publisher** to move them to the Duplicate-value fields box.
5. Click **Next >** to display the next screen in the Find Duplicates Query Wizard.
6. Double-click **Category** to move it to the Additional query fields box.
7. Click **Next >** to display the final screen in the Find Duplicates Query Wizard.
8. Name the query **Duplicates for Games** and click **Finish** to display the query showing duplicate records in the table.
9. Click the **Close** button on the Duplicates for Games tab to close the query.
10. **CLOSE** the database.

LEAVE Access open for the next project.

Proficiency Assessment

Project 7-3: Create a Query from Multiple Tables

Information about each selection for the Coho Vineyard monthly wine club is stored in an Access database. Information about red wine and white wine is stored in separate tables. In your position as customer service rep, it would be useful to be able to query information from both tables.

GET READY. LAUNCH Access if it is not already running.

@ The *Club Wines* file for this lesson is available on the book companion website or in WileyPLUS.

1. **OPEN** *Club Wines* from the data files for this lesson.
2. **SAVE** the database as *Club Wines XXX* (where *XXX* is your initials).
3. Open the **Red Wines: Table**.
4. Open the Relationships window to ensure there is a relationship between the red and white wine tables. Close the Relationships window.
5. Start the Query Wizard and choose **Simple Query Wizard**.
6. In the Tables/Queries drop-down list, click **Table: Red Wines**.
7. Move the *Bottled, Label,* and *Type* fields to the Selected Fields box.
8. In the Tables/Queries drop-down list, click **Table: White Wines**.
9. Move the *Bottled, Label,* and *Type* fields to the Selected Fields box.
10. Click the **Next >** button.
11. Click the **Next >** button and name the query **Wines Query**.
12. Click the **Finish** button.
13. Review the information in the query and then close it.
14. **LEAVE** the database open for the next project.

LEAVE Access open for the next project.

Project 7-4: Create a Find Unmatched Query

A red wine and a white wine should be selected for each month. To determine if there are any records in the red wine table that don't have a matching record in the white wine table, you decide to create a find unmatched query.

USE the database that is open from the previous project.

1. Start the **Query Wizard** and choose **Find Unmatched Query Wizard**.
2. Table: Red Wines should be selected. Click **Next >**.
3. Select **Table: White Wines** and click the **Next >** button.
4. Click **ID** in the Fields in 'Red Wines' list. Click **ID** in the Fields in 'White Wines' list. Click the **<=>** button to display them in the Matching fields box.
5. Click the **Next >** button.
6. Move the Month?, *Bottled, Label,* and *Type* fields to the Selected Fields box.
7. Click the **Next >** button and name the query.
8. Name the query **Unmatched Month** and click the **Finish** button to display the query.
9. Close the query.
10. **CLOSE** the database.

LEAVE Access open for the next project.

Mastery Assessment

Project 7-5: Create a Query

In your job as a travel agent at Erin's Travel, a client has asked you to provide a list of all the travel packages available to sporting events that start in the month of April or May. You will add criteria to a query to get this information from the database.

GET READY. LAUNCH Access if it is not already running.

@ The *Sports Events* file for this lesson is available on the book companion website or in WileyPLUS.

1. **OPEN** *Sports Events* from the data files for this lesson.
2. Save the database as *Sports Events XXX* (where *XXX* is your initials).
3. Open the **Events** query and switch to Design View.
4. Add criteria that will query the database and display all fields for all events that start between 4/1/2012 and 5/31/2012.
5. Use the Show row to hide the *Start Time* and *End Time* fields.
6. Run the query.
7. Close the query and save the design when prompted.
8. **CLOSE** the database.

LEAVE Access open for the next project.

Project 7-6: Create a Parameter Query

Your brother, who owns Wingtip Toys, wants to be able to pull data from his toy inventory and asks for your help in creating a query. He wants to be able to query the database for toys for specific ages when prompted, so you show him how to create a parameter query.

GET READY. LAUNCH Access if it is not already running.

@ The *Toys* file for this lesson is available on the book companion website or in WileyPLUS.

1. **OPEN** *Toys* from the data files for this lesson.
2. **SAVE** the database as *Toys XXX* (where *XXX* is your initials).
3. Create a simple query named **Inventory Query** that contains all the available fields, except the *ID* field.
4. Create a parameter query on the *For Ages* field that gives you the prompt shown in Figure 7-40 when the query is run.

Figure 7-40

Enter Parameter Value prompt

5. Query the database for all the toys for ages 10–14 years.
6. Close the query and save when prompted.
7. **CLOSE** the database.

CLOSE Access.

INTERNET READY

Blogs can be a fun way to pass time, but they can also be a great source of business information. If you enjoy blogs, check out some of the business-related blogs available, such as The Small Business Blog from Microsoft, shown in Figure 7-41. The URL for this blog is: *http://blogs.technet.com/b/smallbusiness/*. Search for information on mail merges or another topic of interest to you and see what you can find.

Figure 7-41

The Small Business Blog from Microsoft

LESSON SKILL MATRIX

Skill	Exam Objective	Objective Number
Adding Bound and Unbound Controls	Format Header/Footer.	3.2.3
	Header/Footer.	5.2.4
	Add bound controls.	3.2.2
	Add bound/unbound controls.	5.2.3
	Rename label in a report.	5.4.1
	View Property Sheet.	3.2.5
	Add calculated controls.	5.2.2
	Add Existing Fields.	3.2.6
	View Code.	3.2.4
Defining Control Tab Order	Reorder tab function.	5.2.5
Formatting Controls	Add bound/unbound controls.	5.2.3
	Change shape in report.	5.4.3
	Apply background image to a form.	3.4.2
	Apply background image to a report.	5.4.2
	Reformat Font in a form.	3.4.1
	Apply Quick Styles to controls in a form.	3.4.3
	Apply conditional formatting in a form.	3.4.4
	Apply conditional formatting in a report.	5.4.4
Arranging Control Layout	Create a Blank Report.	5.1.1
	Reposition/Format form controls.	3.3.3
	Reposition/Format report records.	5.3.3
	Use the Table functions with forms.	3.3.1
	Use the Move table command with forms.	3.3.2
	Use the Table functions with reports.	5.3.1
	Use the Move table command with reports.	5.3.2
Arranging Control Alignment, Size, and Position	Reposition/Format form controls.	3.3.3
	Align report outputs to grid.	5.3.4

KEY TERMS

- bound control
- calculated control
- conditional formatting
- control
- control layouts
- control tab order
- Control Wizard
- Expression Builder
- stacked layout
- tabular layout
- unbound control

WingtipToys is a mom-and-pop operation with fewer than 25 employees, many of whom craft the heirloom-style wooden toys that the company has sold successfully for more than 20 years. As the newly hired marketing coordinator, you are learning every aspect of the business in order to market its products effectively. In this lesson, you learn to add, format, and arrange controls on forms and reports that you can use to evaluate sales and inventory for the company.

SOFTWARE ORIENTATION

Controls and Header/Footer Groups in Reports and Forms

When you view a report in Design View, the Report Design Tools are displayed in the Ribbon. The Controls and Header/Footer groups are located on the Design tab. When you position the mouse pointer over a tool, Access will display the tool's name in a ScreenTip. Use the Controls and Header/Footer groups on the Design tab (Figure 8-1) to add controls to a report.

Header/Footer group

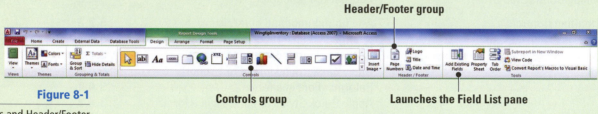

Controls group   **Launches the Field List pane**

Figure 8-1

Controls and Header/Footer groups on the Report Design Tools tab

The Controls group located on the Design tab in the Form Design Tools on the Ribbon, shown in Figure 8-2, is very similar to the one for reports. The procedure for adding controls to a form and a report are similar as well. Use the Controls and Header/Footer groups on a form's Design tab to add controls to a form.

Header/Footer group

Controls group   **Launches the Field List pane**

Figure 8-2

Controls and Header/Footer groups on the Form Design Tools tab

ADDING BOUND AND UNBOUND CONTROLS

The Bottom Line

A **control** is an object that displays data, performs actions, and lets you improve the look and usability of a form or report. Access uses three different types of controls: bound, unbound, and calculated.

Controls add functionality to a report or form. For example, you can add a logo control to a report to enhance the look of the report or a list box control to allow users to choose from a list of items. You can insert bound, unbound, and calculated controls using the tools on the Controls and Header/Footer groups. The Control Wizard, located on the Controls group, is helpful when creating some of the more complicated controls.

Adding Unbound Controls

An **unbound control** does not have a data source; it displays information such as lines, shapes, or pictures. Unbound controls are not connected to a field, but they display information that is important for reports and forms, some of which will appear in report and form header and footer sections, such as titles, dates, and page numbers. You can add both bound and unbound controls using the tools on the Controls group, or add unbound controls to the header and footer sections of reports and forms by using the Header/Footer group. In this exercise, you use the tools on the Header/Footer group to add unbound controls to the Report Header section.

STEP BY STEP   **Add Unbound Controls**

GET READY. Before you begin these steps, be sure to turn on and/or log on to your computer and **LAUNCH** Access.

 The *WingtipInventory* file for this lesson is available on the book companion website or in WileyPLUS.

 *EXTRA*

WileyPLUS Extra! features an online tutorial of this task.

 The *Chrysanthemum* file for this lesson is available on the book companion website or in WileyPLUS.

1. **OPEN** *WingtipInventory* from the data files for this lesson.
2. Save the database as *WingtipInventoryXXX* (where *XXX* is your initials).
3. Double-click the **Toy Summary** report in the Navigation pane.
4. On the Home tab, in the Views group, click the **View** button and select **Design View** from the menu.
5. On the Design tab, in the Header/Footer group, click the **Logo** button. The Insert Picture dialog box appears.
6. Navigate to the student data files for this lesson and select *Chrysanthemum.jpg* and click **OK**. The picture is inserted in the Report Header section.
7. On the Design tab, in the Header/Footer group, click the **Title** button. The title control with the title Toy Summary is inserted in the Report Header section. The text in the title is selected.
8. Key **Inventory Summary by Toy** and press the **Enter** key.
9. On the Design tab, in the Header/Footer group, click the **Date and Time** button. The Date and Time dialog box appears, as shown in Figure 8-3.

Figure 8-3

Date and Time dialog box

10. Click **OK** to accept the default date and time formats. The Date and Time controls are inserted in the Report Header section of the report, as shown in Figure 8-4.

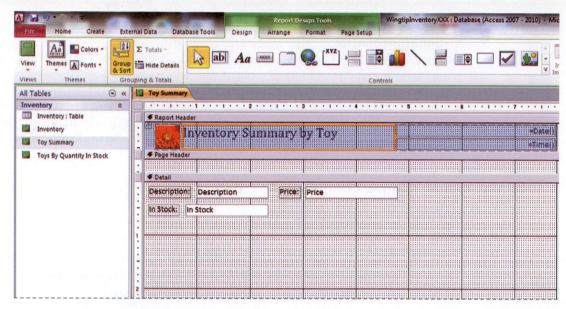

Figure 8-4

Report Header shown in Design View

11. On the Design tab, in the Header/Footer group, click the **Page Numbers** button. The Page Numbers dialog box appears, as shown in Figure 8-5.

Figure 8-5

Page Numbers dialog box

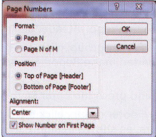

12. In the Position section of the Page Numbers dialog box, select the **Bottom of Page [Footer]** option then click **OK**. If necessary, scroll to the bottom of the report window. The page number is inserted in the Page Footer section near the bottom of the report, as shown in Figure 8-6.

Figure 8-6

Report shown in Design View

CERTIFICATION READY   3.2.3

How do you apply form design options by formatting a header and footer?

CERTIFICATION READY   5.2.4

How do you apply report design options to a header and footer by inserting a page number?

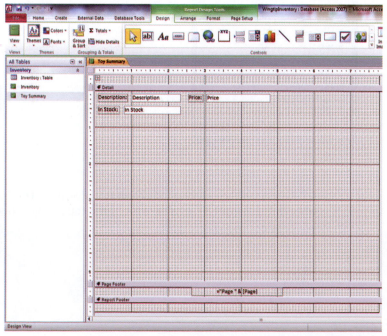

Another Way
You can also display the Field List pane by pressing Alt+F8.

Take Note

Another Way
You can also display the property sheet by clicking control and pressing F4.

13. Click the **Save** button on the Quick Access Toolbar.
PAUSE. LEAVE the report open to use in the next exercise.

Adding Bound Controls

A **bound control** uses a field in a table or query as the data source. Bound controls, such as text boxes, display information such as text, dates, numbers, pictures, or graphs from a field in a table or query.

You can bind a control to a field by moving it from the Field List pane or by using the Property Sheet. In this exercise, you practice adding a bound control to a report by using the Field List pane, and adding a bound control and unbound controls to a report by using the Controls group.

When you bind a control to a field, you connect it to that field. The easiest way to create a bound control is to double-click or drag a field from the Field List pane to the report. Access creates the appropriate control, binds the control to the field, and creates a label for the control.

You can display the Field List pane by clicking the Add Existing Fields button on the Tools group.

Another way to bind a control to a field is to first add an unbound text box to a report or form using the Controls group. Then, open its Property Sheet either by right-clicking and choosing Properties from the shortcut menu or by clicking the Property Sheet button on the Tools group in the Design tab. On the Property Sheet, in the Data tab, click the down arrow beside the Control Source property and select the field you want to display in the control.

The process for adding a control to a form and a report is the same. Once shown how to add a control to a report, you can add a similar control to a form in the same manner.

When you click any button on the Controls group (except the Hyperlink and Insert Image buttons) the pointer changes to the move pointer with a plus sign (+). Click where you want the upper-left portion of the control to start. Remember that a label will also be inserted, so leave enough space for the label. Click once to create a default-sized control, or click the tool and then drag it into the design grid to create the size you want.

When you click the Hyperlink and Insert Image buttons on the Controls group, a dialog box appears requesting additional information before these unbound controls are created. For example, the insert Hyperlink dialog box asks what file or location you'd like to link to, and the corresponding hyperlink text to display on the form or report; the Insert Image button displays a submenu with two selections, one of which allows you to browse your computer for images to add to the report or form, and the other allows you to view a gallery of images you've already included on your report or form so you may easily add them again.

You can use the Controls group to add other unbound controls like lines and page breaks to forms and reports. For example, you may want to use the line control to visually separate controls on a form to help it look more aesthetically pleasing, or the Insert Page Break control to create a report's title page by separating controls in the Report Header from the rest of the report.

To delete a control from the grid, select it, display the shortcut menu, and choose Delete.

STEP BY STEP   **Add a Bound Control to a Report**

USE the database open from the previous exercise.

1. On the Design tab, in the Tools group, click the **Add Existing Fields** button. The Field List pane appears. Click the **Show all tables** link. The fields for the Inventory table appear, as shown in Figure 8-7.

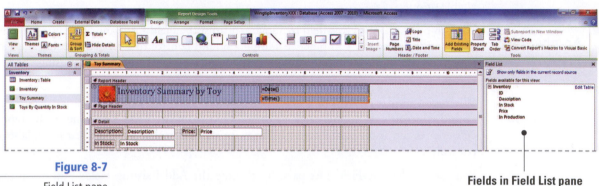

Figure 8-7

Field List pane

Fields in Field List pane

2. Click the **ID** field and drag it to the right of the *Price* field, as shown in Figure 8-8.

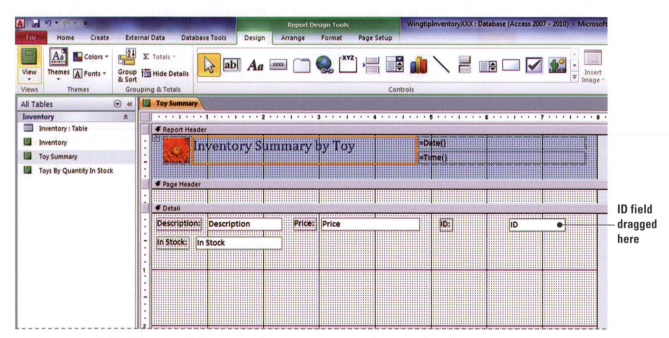

ID field dragged here

Figure 8-8

Bound control dragged from the Field List pane

3. Drag the *In Production* field to the design grid below the *ID* field.
4. Click **Close** on the Field List pane.
5. Click the **ID** field control until you see the orange border with selection handles on the borders and corners.
6. Right-click in the control to display the shortcut menu.

7. Select **Delete** from the menu, as shown in Figure 8-9. The control and label are removed from the design grid.

Figure 8-9

Shortcut menu

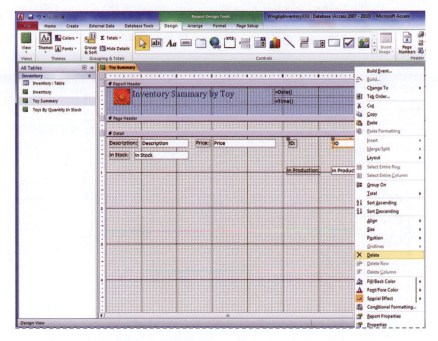

8. Select the **In Production** control, right-click and select **Delete** from the menu. If necessary, right-click the check box control that may still appear and select **Delete** from the menu.

9. On the Design tab, in the Controls group, click the **Text Box** button. The mouse pointer changes to a move pointer.

10. Position the pointer at approximately the same location as the deleted *ID* field control and click to create the text box control as shown in Figure 8-10. Notice that the word Unbound is shown in the control and the word Text and a number (depending on the number of controls you have created in this session) appear in the label.

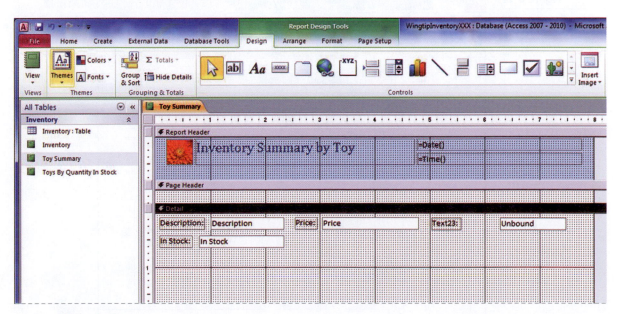

Figure 8-10

Unbound control

11. Select the control if it isn't selected already.

12. On the Design tab, in the Tools group, click the **Property Sheet** button. The Property Sheet appears.

13. In the Data tab, click the **down arrow** on the Control Source row, and click the **ID** field, as shown in Figure 8-11. Notice the control now displays the field name ID, which means that it is now bound to the control.

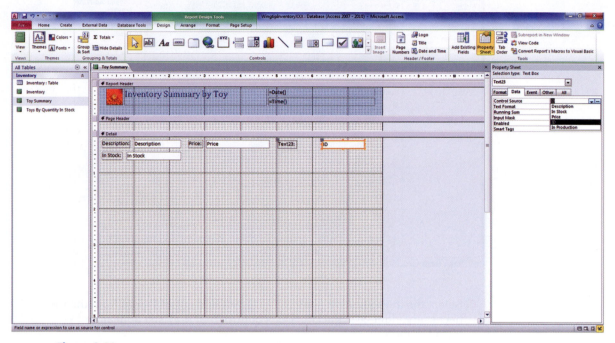

Figure 8-11

Property Sheet

14. Click **Close** on the Property Sheet.

15. Click the **ID** control label on the design grid and select the text in the label.

16. Key **ID** and then press **Enter**. Your screen should look similar to Figure 8-12.

Figure 8-12

Bound control

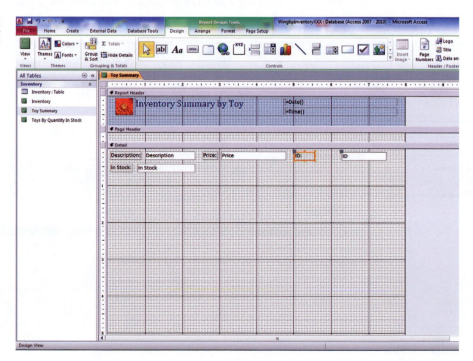

17. On the Design tab, in the Controls group, click the **Hyperlink** button The Insert Hyperlink dialog box appears, as shown in Figure 8-13.

Figure 8-13

Insert Hyperlink dialog box

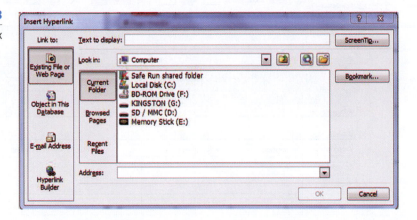

Figure 8-13

Insert Hyperlink dialog box

18. Key **Wingtip Toys Website** in the Text to display box and **www.wingtiptoys.com** in the Address box, then click **OK**. Your screen should look similar to Figure 8-14.

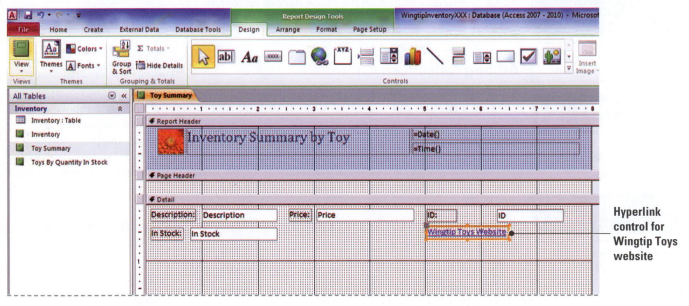

Hyperlink control for Wingtip Toys website

Figure 8-14

Hyperlink control for Wingtip Toys website

CERTIFICATION READY   3.2.2

How do you add a bound text box control to a form?

CERTIFICATION READY   5.2.3

How do you add an unbound hyperlink to a report?

19. Click the Wingtip Toys website control until you see the orange border with selection handles on the borders and corners.

20. Position the pointer on the orange border until you see a four-sided arrow. Then, drag the control to the Report Header section and release it over the lower half of the Inventory Summary by Toy control. The Wingtip Toys website control should appear below the *Inventory Summary by Toy* control, as shown in Figure 8-15. You have just created a hyperlink to the Wingtip Toys website that is active in Report View.

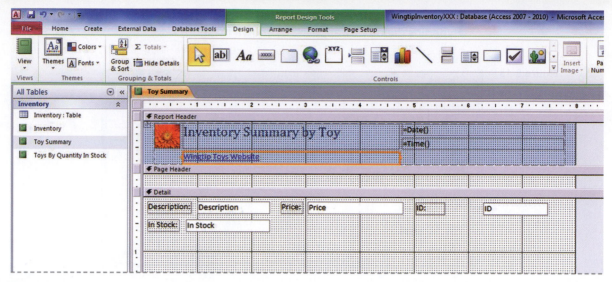

Figure 8-15

Wingtip Toys website control in Report Header section

Figure 8-15

Wingtip Toys website control in Report Header section

CERTIFICATION
R E A D Y   5.2.3

How do you add a bound text box control to a report?

CERTIFICATION
R E A D Y   5.4.1

How do you rename a label in a report?

CERTIFICATION
R E A D Y   3.2.5

How do you view a control's property sheet?

21. Switch to Report View to test the hyperlink. When finished, switch back to Report Design View.

22. Click the **Save** button on the Quick Access Toolbar.

PAUSE. LEAVE the report open to use in the next exercise.

Adding Calculated Controls

A **calculated control** is a control that displays the result of a calculation or expression. Calculated controls can display calculations that are vital to the usefulness of a report or form. For example, when your company needs to know the amount of sales dollars generated by each toy in a product line, you can multiply the number of toys sold by the price and display the value in a report or form. Text boxes are the most popular choice for a calculated control because they can display so many different types of data. However, any control that has a Control Source property can be used as a calculated control. In this exercise, you use the Expression Builder to add a calculated control to a report.

An expression is like a formula in Excel. An expression consists of the following elements used alone or in combination:

- **Identifiers**: The names or properties of fields or controls
- **Operators**: Such as + (plus), – (minus), or * (multiply)
- **Functions**: Such as SUM or AVG
- **Constants**: Values that do not change, such as numbers that are not calculated

NEW
to Office 2010

To create a calculated control, you can either key an expression in the Control Source property box or use the **Expression Builder**, which is a feature that provides names of the fields and controls in a database, lists the operators available, and has built-in functions to help you create an expression. New to Access 2010 is a more intuitive Expression Builder, which reorganizes the layout of its dialog box and includes IntelliSense, which presents you with a drop-down box of potential values as you're typing an identifier or function name to create your expression.

STEP BY STEP   **Add a Calculated Control**

USE the database open from the previous exercise.

1. On the Design tab, in the Controls group, click the **Text Box** button.

2. Position the mouse pointer on the design grid and drag down and to the right to create a control the size of the one shown in Figure 8-16.

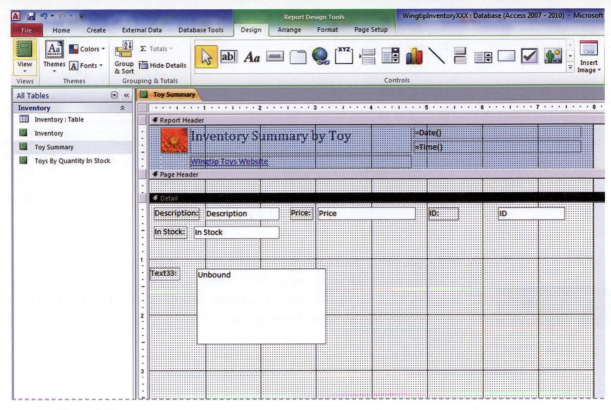

Figure 8-16

Text box control

3. With the control selected, right-click to display the shortcut menu.

4. Select **Properties** from the menu. The Property Sheet appears.

5. On the Data tab, in the Control Source row, click the **Build** button. The Expression Builder dialog box appears.

6. In the Expression Categories list, scroll down and double-click **In Stock**, as shown in Figure 8-17. All the list items in the Expression Categories on your screen may not match exactly to the figure. The *In Stock* field is inserted in the expression box.

Figure 8-17

Expression Builder

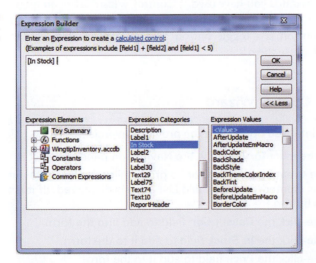

7. In the Expression Elements box, click the **Operators** item then double-click the *** asterisk** item in the Expression Values box to select the multiplication operator.

8. In the Expression Elements box, click the **Toy Summary** item, then find and double-click the **Price** field in the list that appears in the same box below.

9. Click **OK**. The expression appears in the Control Source row of the Property Sheet, as shown in Figure 8-18. Notice that Access added the equal sign (=) that starts an expression.

Expression in Control Source row of Property Sheet

Figure 8-18

Controls group on the Design tab for forms

10. Click **Close** on the Properties Sheet.
11. Select the text in the label and key **Investment**.
12. Switch to Report View and scroll through the records to view the calculated totals.
13. Click the **Save** button on the Quick Access Toolbar.
14. Close the report.

PAUSE. LEAVE the database open to use in the next exercise.

CERTIFICATION READY 5.2.2

How do you add a calculated control to a report?

Take Note It is often easiest to add and arrange all the bound controls first, and then add the unbound and calculated controls to complete the design of the report.

Adding Controls Using a Wizard

It could take quite a bit of time to figure out how to set all the properties necessary to create option groups and combo and list boxes for a report or form. To speed up this task, Access 2010 includes wizards that help you create some of the more complicated controls, such as option groups and combo and list boxes. A **Control Wizard** can help you create controls such as command buttons, list boxes, combo boxes, and option groups. In this exercise, you add a combo box to a form using the Control Wizard.

Like other wizards you have used, a Control Wizard asks you questions about how you want the control to look and operate, and then it creates the control based on your answers. The Control Wizard's button is a toggle button that you can click to activate and deactivate wizards on controls that use them.

STEP BY STEP **Use the Control Wizard**

USE the database open from the previous exercise.

1. Click the **Inventory** table in the Navigation pane to select it.
2. On the Create tab, in the Forms group, click the **Form Design** button. A new, blank form is created, and the Field List pane is displayed. (If it isn't, click the Add Existing Fields button.)
3. Double-click the **Description** field to add it to the form.
4. Double-click the **In Stock** field to add it to the form.
5. Double-click the **Price** field to add it to the form.
6. Double-click the **In Production** field to add it to the form.
7. On the Design tab, in the Controls group, locate the **Use Control Wizards** command and make sure it is turned on. The image next to the command should be displayed in orange.
8. On the Design tab, in the Controls group, click the **Combo box** button.

9. Position the mouse pointer and drag to draw a rectangle, as shown in Figure 8-19.

Figure 8-19

Drag to draw a custom control

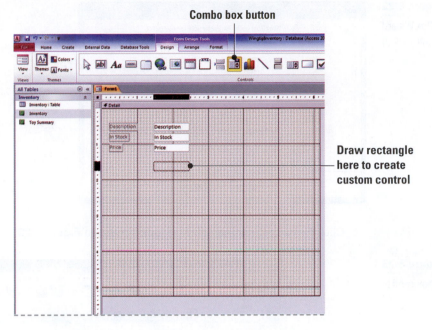

Combo box button

Draw rectangle
here to create
custom control

10. When you release the mouse button, the Combo Box Wizard appears. Click the button beside *I will type in the values that I want* and click **Next**. In the empty cell below the Col1 header, key **Yes**. Continue keying values in the column as shown in Figure 8-20.

Figure 8-20

Combo Box Wizard

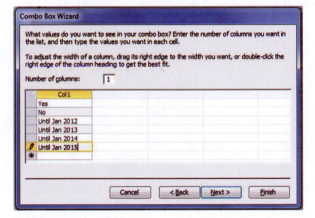

11. Click **Next >**.

12. Click the button beside *Store that value in this field* and click the **down arrow** to display the menu. Select **In Production** from the menu, as shown in Figure 8-21.

Figure 8-21

Combo Box Wizard store values screen

13. Click **Next >**.

14. Key **In Production** in the text box, as shown in Figure 8-22.

Figure 8-22

Combo Box Wizard
caption screen

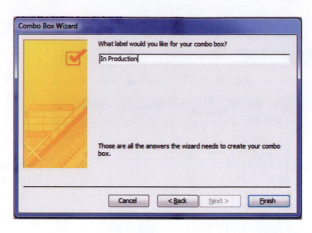

15. Click **Finish**. Your screen should look similar to Figure 8-23.

Figure 8-23

Form with combo box control

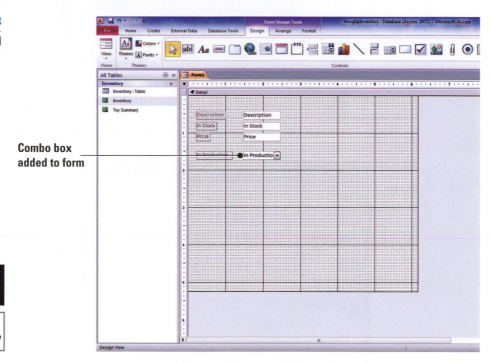

Combo box
added to form

Take Note   A combo box is also known as a drop-down control, because it is a combination of a text box with a list box that is hidden until you select the arrow next to the text box and it *drops down*.

16. Delete the first In Production control and label you added to the form since the combo box you added is a better control format to keep track of inventory.

17. Switch to Form View, scroll through the records, and modify the *In Production* field based on the items in the combo box.

18. Click the **Save** button on the Quick Access Toolbar and save the form as Inventory.

PAUSE. LEAVE the form open to use in the next exercise.

Adding Button Controls Using the Wizard

You can also use Control Wizards to add Button controls to forms. Button controls can be created by using the Command Button wizard and assigned certain tasks created by macros. Macros are useful since they add additional functionality to a database by automating a series of tasks to create an action. For example, Button controls can be created on a form to perform many different actions, including moving to the next or previous record, or even to display the

Print dialog box or close the form. The code that enables this functionality is automatically created as a macro by the Command Button wizard. In this exercise, you create a Button control using the Command Button wizard and use the View Code button to open the Visual Basic for Applications program.

You can further customize the function of database controls and even objects by viewing and modifying their code using a programming language called Visual Basic for Applications (VBA). You can click the View code button in the Tools group of the Form Design Tools contextual tab to open the VBA program. The VBA program is built into Access and provides you with an interface to write and modify code associated with database controls and objects. You can really harness the power of Access 2010 by directly interacting with controls and objects via VBA.

STEP BY STEP   **Use the Control Wizard to Add Button Controls**

USE the form open from the previous exercise.

1. Switch to Design View, if necessary.

2. On the Design tab, in the Controls group, click the **Button** button.

3. Position the mouse pointer on the design grid and drag down and to the right to create a control the size of the one shown in Figure 8-24.

Figure 8-24

Button control

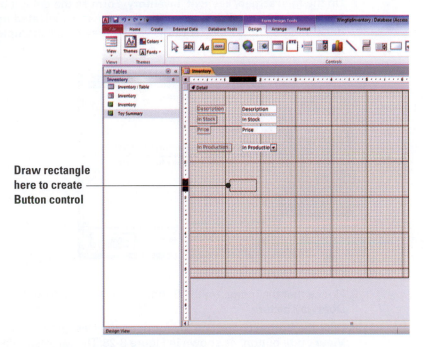

Draw rectangle here to create Button control

4. When you release the mouse button, the Command Button Wizard appears. In the Categories list box, click **Form Operations** and in the Actions list box click **Close Form**, as shown in Figure 8-25.

Figure 8-25

Command Button Wizard, screen 1

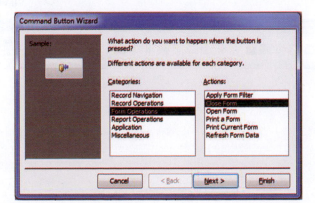

5. Click **Next >**.

6. On the next screen, keep the default settings to have the button contain the Exit Doorway picture displayed in the dialog box, as shown in Figure 8-26.

Figure 8-26

Command Button Wizard, screen 2

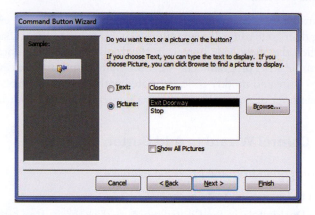

7. Click **Next >**.

8. On the final screen, key **Exit_Inventory_Form** as the default button name, as shown in Figure 8-27, and click **Finish**. (The button name indicated on your screen may differ depending on how many controls you've previously attempted to include.)

Figure 8-27

Command Button Wizard, final screen

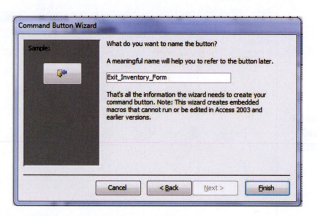

9. Notice that the image on the Button control on the form has changed to the Exit Doorway picture.

10. Click the **Button** control on the form, on the Design tab, in the Tools group, click the **View Code** button, as shown in Figure 8-28. The Microsoft Visual Basic for Applications window appears, as shown in Figure 8-29.

View Code button

Figure 8-28

View Code button in Tools group

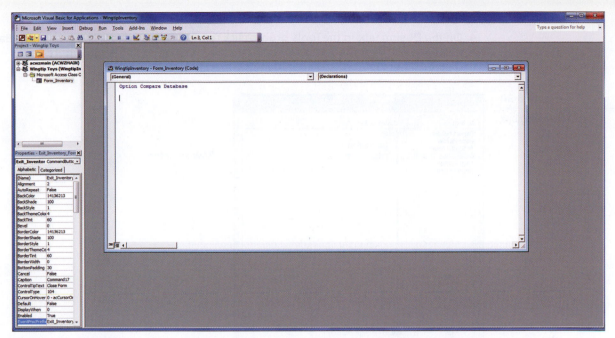

Figure 8-29

Microsoft Visual Basic for Applications window

CERTIFICATION
R E A D Y **3.2.4**

How do you use the View Code button?

The Bottom Line

Another Way
You can also right-click the design grid in Design View to access the Tab Order dialog box.

11. Click the **Close** button on the Visual Basic for Applications window to return to Access.

12. Save and close the form.

PAUSE. LEAVE the database open to use in the next exercise.

DEFINING CONTROL TAB ORDER

When you are in Form or Report View, pressing the Tab key moves the selection, or focus, to the next field. **Control tab order** refers to the order in which the selection, or focus, moves from field to field in a form or report. When entering data in a form, it is helpful to set the control tab order to a sequence that matches the order of the data you are entering. It's also helpful to set the tab order of a report to a logical field sequence when reviewing report records. In this way, you can efficiently concentrate on meaningful data as you use the change of focus as a guide. In this exercise you define report control tab order.

You can change the tab order using the Tab Order dialog box, which is located in the Tools group of the Report Design Tools Design contextual tab. The Tab Order dialog box lists each section of the report or form and the tab order of the fields in each section. Click the selection button to the left of each row in the Custom Order list to select the row. You can drag the rows into the tab order you want, from top to bottom. The AutoOrder button places the fields in the order that they appear on the form or report, from top to bottom, left to right.

STEP BY STEP **Define Control Tab Order**

USE the database you used in the previous exercise.

1. Open the **Toys By Quantity In Stock** report in Report View.

2. Press the **Tab** key several times to see the order in which the controls are selected each time you press it. Notice that the tab order begins in the Report Header section with the Print Report control, and moves to the In Stock control (grouping field) then moves to the ID, Description, and Price controls. The tab order then continues in sequence through the controls in the In Stock grouping level, skipping the *In Stock* field until it reaches the next group.

3. Switch to Design View.

4. On the Design tab, in the Tools group, click the **Tab Order** button. The Tab Order dialog box appears. Click the **Detail** option in the Section list, as shown in Figure 8-30, displaying the tab order in the Custom Order list.

Figure 8-30

Tab Order dialog box

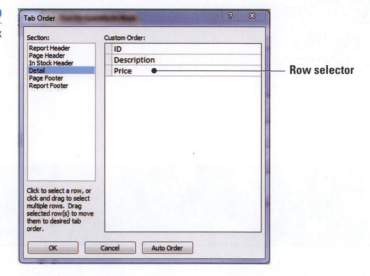

Row selector

5. Click the **Auto Order** button. Nothing changed. The order of the fields already has been automatically set based on the order that they appear on the form or report.

6. Click the **row selector** to the left of the *Price* field to select it.

7. Click and hold the **row selector**. The mouse pointer changes to a move pointer with an empty rectangle. Drag up a row and notice the black horizontal line moves with you. Drag up until the black horizontal line is in place at the bottom of the *ID* field; release the mouse button. The *Price* field should be second, right below the *ID* field, as shown in Figure 8-31.

Figure 8-31

New order on the Tab Order dialog box

8. Click **OK**.

9. Save the report design.

10. Switch to Report View.

11. Press the **Tab** key several times to see the new tab order.

12. Close the report.

PAUSE. LEAVE the database open to use in the next exercise.

SOFTWARE ORIENTATION

Report Design Tools Format Tab

When you are working with reports, the Format tab is located in the Report Design Tools and contains groups of commands used to format reports, as shown in Figure 8-32. Refer to this figure in the following section and throughout the book.

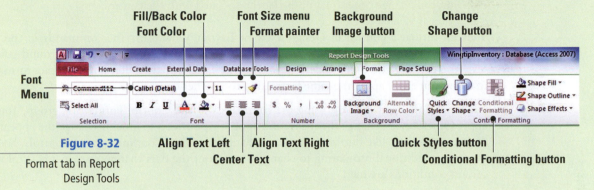

Figure 8-32

Format tab in Report Design Tools

When you are working with forms, the Format tab contains the same groups of commands and is available in the Form Layout Tools. Use these common formatting commands to change the display of controls and their labels in forms and reports.

FORMATTING CONTROLS

Formatting professional-looking reports and forms not only projects a high-quality image, but it also improves the form or report's readability. Display formatting allows you to refine the look of your reports and forms. You can change the font, font size, font color, alignment, and other attributes of text and numbers in controls and their associated labels. You can also change the background images of your reports and forms, as well as change the shapes of certain controls. You can even apply Quick Styles to controls to quickly change their appearance, or use conditional formatting to change the look of data when certain conditions are met.

Formatting Controls

To format the display of a control, you can use many of the formatting tools that you have probably used before to format text, numbers, and objects in other Office programs, such as Word. In this exercise, you format the display of controls on a report and increase the amount of space in the Report Header section to include an Insert Page Break unbound control.

You can resize controls and their labels by clicking the resize handles, which are tiny squares located on the borders and corners of a selected control or label. Position the mouse pointer over a handle to get a two-sided arrow, then drag to increase or decrease the width or height of a label. To move a control and its label, select the control and position the mouse pointer over the selection until you see a four-sided arrow, then drag to the new position.

As you remember from previous lessons, forms and reports are divided into sections, including the Report Header, Page Header, Detail, Page Footer, and Report Footer. You can change the amount of space between sections to eliminate extra space and to accommodate the controls in the report or form. To increase or decrease the height of the section, position the mouse pointer over the top edge of the section border until you see a double-sided resizing arrow and drag up or down.

Take Note   Double-click a section bar or any blank space within a section to display the Property Sheet for that section.

Controls on forms and reports display the format applied to the source table. However, you can change the display formatting for each control and label on a form or report. Your changes will only affect each control and the way the data appears. It does not change how users enter data or how data is stored.

Take Note   You cannot apply visual formats to controls bound to *Attachment* and *OLE Object* fields. However, you can change the format of the label associated with the control.

You can format a control in Design View or Layout View using the commands in the Font group. You can change the font as well as the size, color, alignment, and background color of text. You can also add bold, underline, and italics. The Format Painter button copies formats so that you can easily apply the same formatting to another control.

You can also format controls using the commands in the Control Formatting group. You can apply Quick Styles, change the shape, and apply shape effects to quickly change the appearance of certain controls like button controls, or change the fill and outline color of controls. You can even use conditional formatting to change the look of the data that appears in a control when certain conditions are met.

Take Note   By default, text does not automatically wrap when it reaches the edge of a field or box. It remains on a single line and extends beyond the edges of the control. To enable text wrapping in a form or report, set the height to a nondefault size and change the CanGrow and CanShrink properties for the control to Yes.

STEP BY STEP   **Format Controls on a Report**

USE the database open from the previous exercise.

1. Open the **Toy Summary** report and switch to Design View.
2. Click the **In Stock** control. Position the mouse pointer over the resize handle on the right border. The mouse pointer changes to a double-sided arrow. Drag to the left to resize the control. ↔
3. In the same manner, reduce the size of the Price and ID controls.
4. Click the **Description** control to select it.
5. On the Format tab, in the Font group, click the **Bold** button. The Description control displays bold.
6. Click the **arrow** on the Font Size menu and select **12** from the menu. The point size becomes 12.
7. Click the **In Stock** control to select it.
8. On the Design tab, in the Font group, click the **Left Align** button. The In Stock text aligns to the left of the control box. Your report should look similar to Figure 8-33.

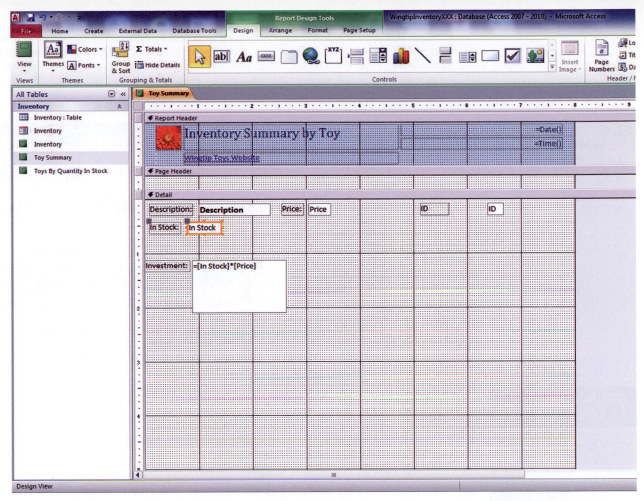

Figure 8-33

Report with display
formatting applied

9. Position the mouse pointer over the top edge of the Page Header section border until you
see a double-sided resizing arrow and drag down to increase the height of the Report
Header section by approximately one-quarter of an inch, as shown in Figure 8-34.

Figure 8-34

Resize Report Header section

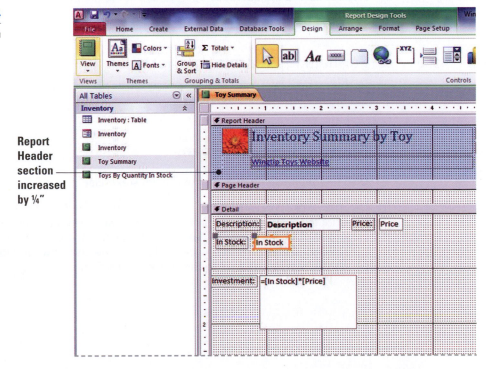

**Report
Header
section
increased
by ¼"**

10. On the Design tab, in the Controls group, click the **Insert Page Break** button.

11. Position the mouse pointer on the design grid and under the Wingtip Toys Website Hyperlink control, drag down and to the right to create an Insert Page Break control, as shown in Figure 8-35. This will divide the Report Header section from the rest of the Report when printed, essentially creating a title page.

Figure 8-35

Insert Page Break control added to Report Header section

Insert Page Break control in Report Header section

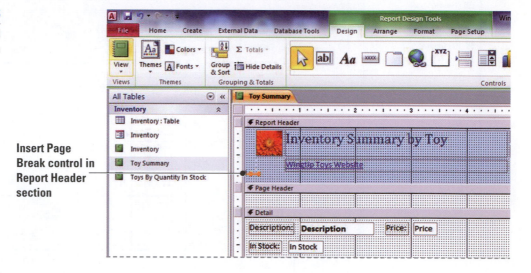

How do you insert a page break into a report?

How do you change the shape of a control in a report?

12. Save the report.

13. Switch to Print Preview to see the changes you've made. Notice the Report Header section is on the first page by itself.

14. Open the **Toys By Quantity In Stock** report in Design View.

15. In the Report Header section, click the **Print Report** Button control to select it.

16. On the Format tab, in the Control Formatting group, click the **Change Shape** button to display the menu. Click the **Oval** option. The Button control's style changes to an oval.

17. Save and close the report.

PAUSE. LEAVE the database open to use in the next exercise.

Formatting Controls on a Form

In this exercise, you learn how to format the display of controls on a form and include a background image.

STEP BY STEP   **Format Controls on a Form**

USE the database open from the previous exercise.

1. Open the **Inventory Form** if it's not open already, and switch to Design View.

2. Click the **Button** control on the form. On the Format tab, in the Control Formatting group, click the **Quick Styles** button to display the Quick Styles gallery. Click the **Colored Outline – Aqua, Accent 5** Quick Style, as shown in Figure 8-36. The Button control's style changes to the chosen Quick Style.

Figure 8-36

Quick Styles gallery

Quick Styles button and gallery

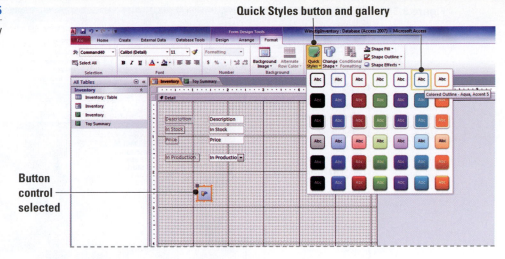

Button control selected

3. Click the **Description** label to select it.
4. On the Format tab, in the Font group, click the **Font Color** button and click **Black** from the Font Color menu. The Description label displays in black. Change the font color to black for the In Stock, Price, and In Production labels. Your screen should resemble Figure 8-37.

Figure 8-37

Color of labels changed to black

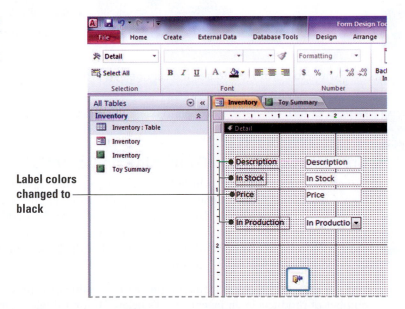

Label colors changed to black

5. On the Format tab, in the Background group, click the **Background Image** button and select the **Chrysanthemum** thumbnail that displays in the gallery. (If the Chrysanthemum image doesn't appear, then use the Browse command under the gallery to access the data files for this lesson.) Notice the form's background image is now that of the chrysanthemum, as shown in Figure 8-38.

Figure 8-38

Form background image

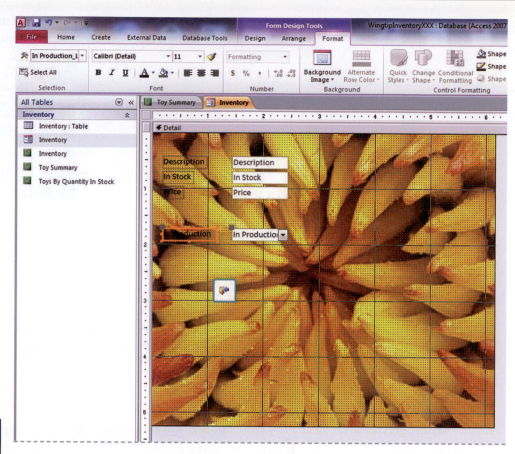

CERTIFICATION
READY   3.4.2

How do you apply a
background image to a form?

6. Switch to Form View to see the changes you made.

7. Save and close the form.

PAUSE. LEAVE the database open to use in the next exercise.

CERTIFICATION
READY   5.4.2

How do you apply a
background image to a report?

Creating Conditional Formatting on Controls

Sometimes employees need a little help recognizing when inventory is low or when sales are high. Conditional formatting in forms and reports helps alert users to text or numbers that need attention so that important data is not overlooked. **Conditional formatting** changes the appearance of a control or the value in a control when certain conditions are met. You can change the color of text or numbers in the control or the background color. In this exercise, you create conditional formatting for a report field.

CERTIFICATION
READY   3.4.1

How do you reformat a font
in a form?

You can create conditional formatting based on a value or expression. For example, when the number of products in an inventory falls below 10 for a single product, you can set the conditional formatting so that Access will display that number in red or with a red background so that you and others will notice the low inventory number.

The easiest way to add conditional formatting to a form or report is by using the Conditional Formatting Rules Manager dialog box, which displays a list of the existing formatting rules, if any. Here you can add new rules, and edit or delete existing rules.

CERTIFICATION
READY   3.4.3

How do you apply Quick Styles
to controls in forms?

STEP BY STEP   **Create Conditional Formatting**

USE the database you used in the previous exercise.

1. Open the **Toy Summary** report, if necessary, and switch to Design View.

2. Click the **In Stock** control to select it.

3. On the Format tab, in the Control Formatting group, click the **Conditional Formatting** button. The Conditional Formatting Rules Manager dialog box appears.

4. Click the **New Rule** button. The New Formatting Rule dialog box appears. You will create a new rule based on criteria you will enter.

5. In the *Edit the rule description* section, keep the Field Value Is in the first menu. Click the **drop-down arrow** next to *between* and scroll to the bottom of the list to select **less than or equal to**. Click in the empty text box and key **10**.

6. Click the **Bold** button in the Preview section.

7. Click the **down arrow** on the **Background Color** button. A menu of colors appears. Click **Red**, as shown in Figure 8-39.

Figure 8-39

Fill Color menu on New Formatting Rule dialog box

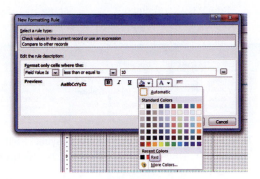

8. Click the **OK** button. A formatting rule for the *In Stock* field is added to the dialog box, as shown in Figure 8-40. Now, when the report is viewed in Report View, the value for the *In Stock* field will appear bold and the control background color will appear red if the formatting rule applies.

Figure 8-40

Formatting rule for the In Stock field

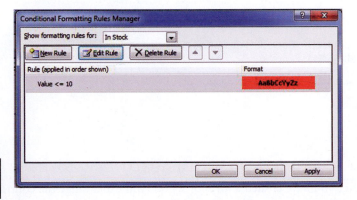

CERTIFICATION
READY   **3.4.4**

How do you apply conditional formatting to form controls?

9. Click **OK**.

10. Save the report.

11. Switch to Report View and scroll through the records to see the conditional formatting at work.

12. Close the report.

PAUSE. LEAVE the database open to use in the next exercise.

CERTIFICATION
READY   **5.4.4**

How do you apply conditional formatting to report controls?

SOFTWARE ORIENTATION

Arrange Tab

The Arrange tab, shown in Figure 8-41, is located in the Report Layout Tools as well as the Report Design Tools area of the Ribbon. It contains groups of commands for arranging the layout, alignment, size, and position of controls on a report. Use the commands in the Arrange tab to arrange controls on a report.

Figure 8-41

Arrange tab in the Report Design Tools Ribbon in Layout View

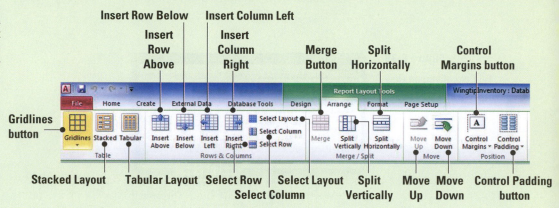

Similar to a report, the Arrange tab is displayed in both the Form Layout Tools and Form Design Tools area of the Ribbon. The buttons and commands on the Arrange tab are the same as the Arrange tab for reports, except for the Anchoring button located in the Position group. The Position group, shown in Figure 8-42, contains an Anchoring button that helps position controls on a form when the containing window is resized. Use the commands in the Arrange tab to arrange controls on a form.

Figure 8-42

Position group on Arrange tab in the Form Design Tools Ribbon in Layout View

ARRANGING CONTROL LAYOUT

The Bottom Line

After you have created a form or report, you can arrange the controls on it to fit the data or to best display the data. Access provides commands for arranging the layout, alignment, position, and size of controls. **Control layouts** align your controls horizontally and vertically to give your report or form a uniform appearance. The two types of control layouts are tabular and stacked. Controls are arranged vertically in a **stacked layout**, with a label on the left and the control on the right. Stacked layouts are contained in one report or form section. In a **tabular layout**, the controls are arranged in rows and columns like a spreadsheet, with labels across the top. Tabular layouts use two sections of a report or form. The labels are displayed in one section and the fields are arranged in the section below. In this exercise, you arrange controls on a form using control layouts.

You can have more than one layout on a report. For example, you could have a tabular layout to create a row of data for each record, then a stacked layout underneath with more information about the same record.

Access automatically creates tabular control layouts when you create a new report using the Report button or the Blank Report button in the Create tab. When you create a new form using the Form button or the Blank Form button, Access creates stacked control layouts.

On an existing blank report, you can create a new control layout by holding down the Shift key and selecting the fields you want to include in the form or report from the Field List pane. On the Arrange tab, in the Table group, click the Tabular button or the Stacked button.

You can switch the entire layout of a report or form to the other by selecting all the cells in the layout and then clicking the layout button you want, either Stacked or Tabular.

You can split a control layout into two different layouts. Hold down the Shift key and click the controls you want to move to the new control layout and click the Tabular or Stacked button.

STEP BY STEP   **Arrange Control Layout**

USE the database open from the previous exercise.

1. Click the **Inventory** table in the Navigation pane to select it.

2. On the Create tab, in the Reports group, click the **Blank Report** button. A new, blank report is created and the Field List pane is displayed.

3. Close the Field List pane, and close the Blank Report. Notice Access didn't ask us if we wanted to save the report since we didn't add any fields to it. We want to create an interface to interact with the Inventory table to input, modify, and delete records, so a form would be necessary.

4. On the Create tab, in the Forms group, click the **Form Design** button. A new, blank form is created, and the Field List pane is displayed. (If it isn't, click the **Add Existing Fields** button.)

5. Double-click the **Description** field to add it to the form.

6. Double-click the **In Stock** field to add it to the form.

7. Double-click the **Price** field to add it to the form.

8. Press and hold the **Shift** key and click each of the three controls to select them all.

9. On the Arrange tab, in the Table group, click the **Stacked** button. The controls and labels are arranged in a stacked layout, as shown in Figure 8-43.

Figure 8-43

Stacked control layout

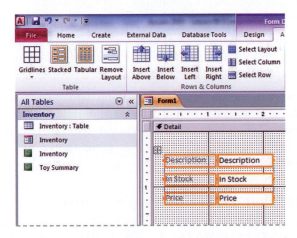

10. On the Arrange tab, in the Table group, click the **Tabular** button. The controls and labels are arranged in a tabular layout, as shown in Figure 8-44.

Figure 8-44

Tabular control layout

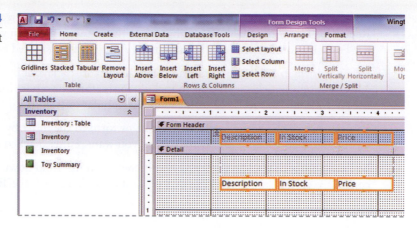

11. On the Arrange tab, in the Table group, click the **Stacked** button to switch it back to a stacked layout.

12. Save the form as **Stacked Form** and leave it open for use in the next exercise.

PAUSE. LEAVE the database open to use in the next exercise.

You can adjust the location of information displayed in a control with the Control Margins button in the Position group. You can choose None, Narrow, Medium, or Wide settings in the Control Margins menu.

The Control Padding button adjusts the amount of space between a control and the gridlines of a layout. The Control Padding menu contains choices for None, Narrow, Medium, or Wide padding.

The Position group also contains the Anchoring button and menu, which ties a control to other controls so that they resize with the parent. The Anchoring button only appears in the Form Design Tools Arrange contextual tab in the Position group since the anchoring option is only available for forms and not reports. Anchoring is helpful when you want to control the position of the controls on a form when the form window is resized. For example, you can anchor the *Description* field control (the parent) to stretch down and to the right so you can see more text within the field control as the form becomes larger. The anchoring of the surrounding controls is set automatically based on the parent. You can only anchor one control in each control layout. You have nine anchoring options to choose from.

By using the new tools in the Rows & Columns group, Merge/Split group, and Move group on the Arrange tab, Access 2010 gives you even greater flexibility over arranging and controlling the cells in control layouts.

By using the tools in the Rows & Columns group, you can add new rows and columns of cells above and below existing cell rows and to the left and right of existing cell columns. By using the tools in the Merge/Split group, you can merge two cells into one, as well as split them vertically and horizontally. Finally, the tools in the Move group can be used to reorganize cells by moving them up or down.

Adding, Moving, and Removing a Control

When you want to add a new field from the Field List to an existing control layout, just drag the field from the Field List pane to the grid. To add it to the layout, select all the controls in the layout and the new control, and click the Stacked or Tabular button. Removing a control from a control layout allows you to place it anywhere on the report or form without affecting the positioning of any other controls. Click the control you want to remove and click Remove Layout from the Table group. The Remove Layout button is only available in the Table group in report or form Design View. In this exercise, you add and move controls within a layout and remove a control from a layout.

STEP BY STEP   **Add, Move, and Remove a Control from a Layout**

USE the database open from the previous exercise.

1. Select all three controls, if they aren't selected already.

2. Click on the selection and move the group of fields down about half an inch.

3. Click the **In Production** field from the Field List pane. Drag it to the grid and place it to the right of the *Description* field.

4. Drag the *ID* field to the grid and place it above the *Description* field.

5. Press and hold the **Shift** key and select the **ID** field control, if necessary. Still holding the **Shift** key, select the **Description**, **In Stock**, and **Price** field controls so that all four are selected.

6. On the Arrange tab, in the Table group, click the **Stacked** button. The ID control is added to the bottom of the stacked layout.

7. On the Arrange tab, in the Position group, click the **Control Margins** button and select **Narrow** from the menu, as shown in Figure 8-45. The margins within the field control and label are formatted using the Narrow option.

Figure 8-45

Control Margins button and menu

Narrow option selected

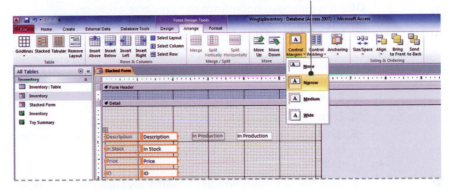

8. On the Arrange tab, in the Position group, click the **Control Padding** button and select **Wide** from the menu, as shown in Figure 8-46.

Figure 8-46

Control Padding button and menu

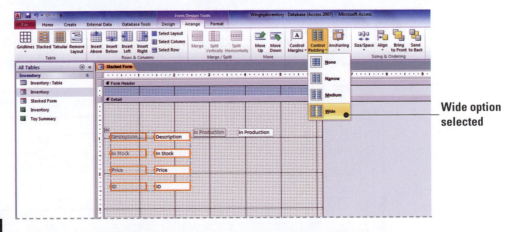

Wide option selected

CERTIFICATION READY   3.3.3

How do you apply form arrange options by repositioning and formatting controls and records?

9. Select the **ID** field control and click **Select Row** in the Rows & Columns group. Notice the ID label and field control are both outlined in orange. Click the **Move Up** button three times to move it to the top of the layout.

10. Move the In Stock label and field control to the bottom of the layout.

11. Try to move the Price control into place under the *In Production* field. It won't move out of the layout.

CERTIFICATION
READY 5.3.3

How do you apply report arrange options by repositioning and formatting controls and records?

12. Select the **Price** label and field control if they aren't selected already.

13. On the Arrange tab, in the Table group, click the **Remove Layout** button. Notice the In Stock label and field control automatically move up to occupy the area where the Price label and field control were when they were part of the layout.

14. Drag the Price control into place under the In Production control.

15. Save and close the form.

PAUSE. LEAVE the form open to use in the next exercise.

Take Note   To select multiple controls, hold down the Shift key and then click the controls.

Arranging and Anchoring Controls

In this exercise you practice arranging controls within a layout using a variety of arrangement tools.

STEP BY STEP   **Arrange and Anchor Controls within a Layout**

USE the database open from the previous exercise.

1. Click the **Inventory** table in the Navigation pane to select it.

2. On the Create tab, in the Forms group, click the **Form** button. A new form containing all the fields from the Inventory table is created in Layout View. Notice the stacked control layout is the default.

3. Switch to Design View.

4. Click the **ID** control to select it.

5. On the Arrange tab, in the Merge/Split group, click the **Split Horizontally** button. Notice the *ID* field control splits into two columns with the right-most column outlined by dashed lines.

6. Click the **In Production** field control and drag it to the right of the *ID* field control to place it next to it. Your screen should resemble Figure 8-47.

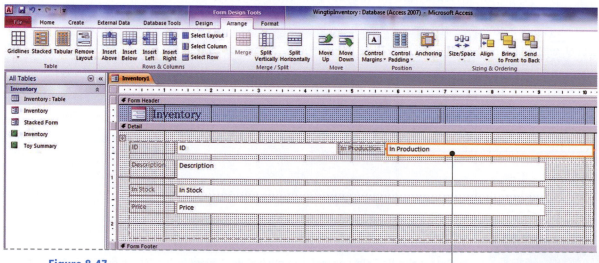

Figure 8-47

In Production control next to ID control

In Production control dragged to this location

7. Click the **In Stock** field control to select it. Press and hold the **Shift** key and select the **In Stock** control label. On the Arrange tab, in the Move group, click the **Move Down** button once. The *In Stock* field control and label move to the bottom of the layout.

8. Click the **Description** field control to select it. Press and hold the **Shift** key and select the cell below the *Description* field control you just selected. Both the *Description* field control and cell below should be outlined in orange. On the Arrange tab, in the Merge/Split group, click the **Merge** button. The *Description* field control and cell have now merged into one, as shown in Figure 8-48.

Figure 8-48

Description field control
merged with cell

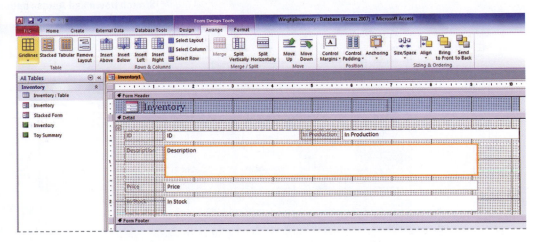

9. Click the **In Stock** field control to select it. On the Arrange tab, in the Rows & Columns group, click the **Insert Below** button twice. Two empty cells are added under the In Stock control.

10. Click the **In Stock** field control to select it. On the Arrange tab in the Rows & Columns group, click the **Select Row** button. Both the In Stock label and field control should be selected.

11. On the Arrange tab, in the Move group, click the **Move Down** twice to move the In Stock control to the last cell row at the bottom of the layout, as shown in Figure 8-49.

Figure 8-49

In Stock control moved to
bottom of layout

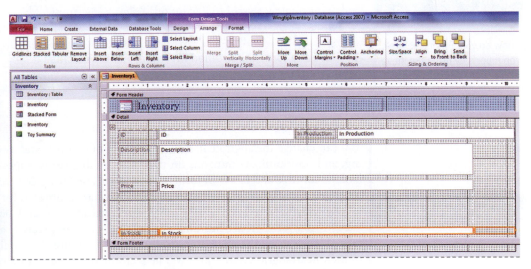

Take Note   In Layout View, you can also use the tools on the Arrange tab to arrange controls within a layout for both forms and reports.

12. Click the **Description** field control to select it. On the Arrange tab in the Position group, click the **Anchoring** button. The Anchoring menu appears. Click the **Stretch Down and Across** option, as shown in Figure 8-50. The *Description* field control will now automatically resize to display all the containing text if the form window is resized in Form View.

Stretch Down and Across option selected

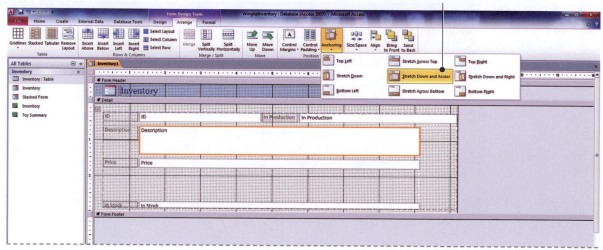

Figure 8-50

Anchoring menu

13. Switch to Form View to display the new arrangement of the controls and resize the form window to see the *Description* field control stretch and shrink in conjunction with the window size.

Take Note

As you learned in a previous exercise, you could resize the field controls to make them more consistent with the data they display. For example, in this exercise, some of the data in the *In Stock* field control is not completely shown within the field control. The control can be easily and appropriately resized in Layout or Design View. You will have the opportunity to do this in an exercise at the end of this lesson.

14. Save the form as Modified Inventory Form and close it.
PAUSE. LEAVE the database open to use in the next exercise.

ARRANGING CONTROL ALIGNMENT, SIZE, AND POSITION

The Bottom Line

You can change the alignment, size, or position of controls and associated labels. Aligning, sizing, and positioning commands on the Arrange tab gives you more options for improving the look of controls and labels in forms and reports. The Sizing & Ordering group, present on the Arrange tab only in report or form Design View has commands for aligning labels and controls to the grid (the intersecting horizontal and vertical lines, and points that appear in Design View) to allow for precise position. For example, you can precisely align a group of controls and related labels using the align To Grid command to ensure all the labels' upper-left corners align to their nearest grid points. This will help ensure the organization of your controls is consistent throughout. In this exercise, you arrange the alignment, size, and position of controls and labels.

You can also align multiple controls and labels at one time so their left, right, top, and bottom borders are perfectly aligned to each other using the align left, right, top, and bottom commands.

Also in the Sizing & Ordering group, you can use the commands to adjust the size of controls and labels to Size to Fit, Size to Grid, Size to Tallest, Size to Widest, Size to Shortest, or Size to Narrowest.

Additionally you can use the Bring to Front and Send to Back commands to move objects in front or to the back of other objects. Also in the Sizing & Ordering group, you can use the commands to increase or decrease horizontal or vertical spacing using the Equal Horizontal,

Equal Vertical, Increase Horizontal, Decrease Horizontal, Increase Vertical, and Decrease Vertical commands.

Finally, the Sizing & Ordering group contains toggle commands for showing or hiding the Grid, the Ruler, and enabling or disabling Snap to Grid—allowing you to precisely arrange a label when you move the associated control by enabling Access to automatically align the upper-left corner of a label to its closest grid point—as well as Group and Ungroup commands that allow you to group several controls together so you can move or modify them all at once.

STEP BY STEP   Arrange Alignment, Size, and Position

USE the database open from the previous exercise.

1. Open the **Stacked Form** form in Design View.

2. Select the **Price** label and control.

3. On the Arrange tab, in the Sizing & Ordering group, click the **Size/Space** button. In the Size category on the menu that appears, click the **To Fit** button.

4. Select all the controls in the stacked layout, (the labels and controls for the ID, Description, and In Stock controls).

5. On the Arrange tab, in the Table group, click the **Remove Layout** button.

6. All the controls and labels should be still selected. On the Arrange tab, in the Sizing & Ordering group, click the **Size/Space** button. In the Size category on the menu that appears, click the **To Fit** button.

7. With the controls and labels still selected, on the Arrange tab, in the Sizing & Ordering group, click the **Align** button. In the menu that appears, click the **Right** button. The labels are right-aligned to the controls. Click on a blank space on the design grid to deselect all the highlighted controls and labels.

8. Press and hold the **Shift** key and click on both the labels and controls for the In Production and ID controls.

9. With the controls and labels still selected, on the Arrange tab, in the Sizing & Ordering group, click the **Align** button. In the menu that appears, click the **Bottom** button. The In Production control is bottom-aligned with the ID control.

10. With the controls and labels still selected, press and hold the **Shift** key and select the **Price** label and control.

11. On the Arrange tab, in the Sizing & Ordering group, click the **Size/Space** button. In the Spacing category on the menu that appears, click the **Decrease Horizontal Spacing** button until your screen looks similar to Figure 8-51.

Figure 8-51

Form with decreased horizontal spacing between controls

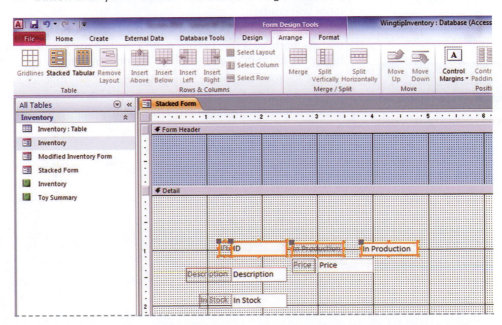

12. Click on a blank space on the design grid to deselect all highlighted controls and labels. Press and hold the **Shift** key and click on both the labels and controls for the **Description** and **Price** controls.

13. With the controls and labels still selected, on the Arrange tab, in the Sizing & Ordering group, click the **Align** button. In the menu that appears, click the **Bottom** button. The Price control is bottom-aligned with the Description control. Your screen should resemble Figure 8-52.

Figure 8-52

Form with bottom aligned controls

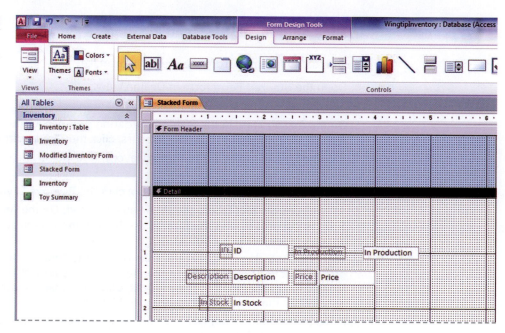

14. Click on a blank space on the design grid.

15. On the Arrange tab, in the Sizing & Ordering group, click the **Size/Space** button. In the Grid category on the menu that appears, click the **Grid** button. The design grid disappears.

16. Click the **Grid** button again. The design grid appears.

17. Click on a blank space on the design grid and drag to draw a box around the labels and controls so they are all selected, or press and hold the **Shift** key and select each label and control.

18. On the Arrange tab, in the Sizing & Ordering group, click the **Align** button. In the menu that appears, click the **To Grid** button. Notice the control and labels slightly move. The upper-left corners of all the labels are now aligned to their nearest grid points.

19. On the Arrange tab, in the Sizing & Ordering group, click the **Size/Space** button. In the Grid category on the menu that appears, click the **Ruler** button. The rulers disappear.

20. Click the **Ruler** button again. The rulers reappear.

21. Save and close the form.

PAUSE. CLOSE the database.

CERTIFICATION READY   3.3.3

How do you arrange controls on forms by repositioning and formatting?

CERTIFICATION READY   5.3.4

How do you arrange controls on reports by aligning to the grid?

SKILL SUMMARY

In This Lesson, You Learned How To:	Exam Objective	Objective Number
Add Bound and Unbound Controls	Format Header/Footer.	3.2.3
	Header/Footer.	5.2.4
	Add bound controls.	3.2.2
	Add bound/unbound controls.	5.2.3
	Rename label in a report.	5.4.1
	View Property Sheet.	3.2.5
	Add calculated controls.	5.2.2
	Add Existing Fields.	3.2.6
	View Code.	3.2.4
Define Control Tab Order	Reorder tab function.	5.2.5
Format Controls	Add bound/unbound controls.	5.2.3
	Change shape in report.	5.4.3
	Apply background image to a form.	3.4.2
	Apply background image to a report.	5.4.2
	Reformat Font in a form.	3.4.1
	Apply Quick Styles to controls in a form.	3.4.3
	Apply conditional formatting in a form.	3.4.4
	Apply conditional formatting in a report.	5.4.4
Arrange Control Layout	Create a Blank Report.	5.1.1
	Reposition/Format form controls.	3.3.3
	Reposition/Format report records.	5.3.3
	Use the Table functions with forms.	3.3.1
	Use the Move table command with forms.	3.3.2
	Use the Table functions with reports.	5.3.1
	Use the Move table command with reports.	5.3.2
Arrange Control Alignment, Size, and Position	Reposition/Format form controls.	3.3.3
	Align report outputs to grid.	5.3.4

Knowledge Assessment

Matching

Match the term in Column 1 to its description in Column 2.

Column 1	Column 2
1. control	a. a control that displays the result of a calculation or expression
2. unbound control	b. help you create controls such as command buttons, list boxes, combo boxes, and option groups
3. bound control	c. a layout in which the controls are arranged in rows and columns, with labels across the top
4. calculated control	d. a control that doesn't have a source; it displays information such as lines, shapes, or pictures
5. Expression Builder	e. controls that are arranged vertically with a label on the left and the control on the right
6. Control Wizards	f. layouts that align controls horizontally and vertically to give your report or form a unique appearance
7. conditional formatting	g. an object that displays data, performs actions, and lets you improve the look and usability of a form or report
8. control layouts	h. a control that uses a field in a table or query as the data source
9. tabular layout	i. means to change the appearance of a control or the value in a control when certain conditions are met
10. stacked layout	j. provides the names of the fields and controls in a database, lists the operators available, and has built-in functions to help you create an expression

True/False

Circle T if the statement is true or F if the statement is false.

T F **1.** The easiest way to create a bound control is to double-click or drag a field from the Property Sheet to the report.

T F **2.** You can bind a control to a field using the Property Sheet.

T F **3.** You can turn off Control Wizards.

T F **4.** Display formatting can be applied to controls and labels in a form or report.

T F **5.** You can specify only one condition for conditional formatting.

T F **6.** You can switch an entire control layout of a report or form from one type to the other.

T F **7.** Control padding adjusts the amount of space between a control and the gridlines of a layout.

T F **8.** The Remove Layout command in the Table group removes a control from a form or report.

T F **9.** You can set a tab order for each section of a form or report.

T F **10.** Tab order refers to the order of tabs displayed in a dialog box.

Competency Assessment

Project 8-1: Refine the Alpine Ski House Report

You have learned a great deal about reports and forms while working as an administrative assistant at the Alpine Ski House. Refine the basic report you created previously so you can display it proudly at the front desk.

GET READY. LAUNCH Access if it is not already running.

@ The *Alpine* file for this lesson is available on the book companion website or in WileyPLUS.

1. **OPEN** the *Alpine* database.
2. **SAVE** the database as *AlpineXXX* (where *XXX* is your initials).
3. Open the **Report Design** report.
4. Switch to Design View.
5. Select all four controls in the report.
6. On the Arrange tab, in the Table group, click the **Tabular** button.
7. On the Arrange tab, in the Position group, click the **Control Margins** button, and select **Narrow** from the menu.
8. On the Arrange tab, in the Position group, click the **Control Padding** button, and select **Medium** from the menu.
9. On the Design tab, in the Header/Footer group, click the **Title** button. A title is inserted in the report header.
10. Key **Alpine Ski House Rooms Report** and press **Enter**.

@ The *Winter* file for this lesson is available on the book companion website or in WileyPLUS.

11. On the Design tab, in the Header/Footer group, click the **Logo** button. Navigate to the student data files for this lesson and select *Winter*. Click **OK**.
12. On the Format tab, in the Background group, click the **Background Image** button. Open the folder that contains the data files for this lesson and select *winterbackground*. Click **OK**.

@ The *winterbackground.jpg* file for this lesson is available on the book companion website or in WileyPLUS.

13. Press and hold the **Shift** key and click on all four labels and controls to select them.
14. On the Format tab in the Font group, click the **Font Color** menu button. Select the dark blue color called **Dark Blue, Text 2** in the first row and fourth column of the Access Theme Colors section.
15. Make sure all the controls are still selected. On the Arrange tab, in the Table group, click **Remove Layout**.
16. With the controls still selected, click and drag them together up to position just below the Detail section bar.
17. Scroll down and position the mouse pointer over the Page Footer section bar. Drag the section bar up to position just below the controls. Your screen should look similar to Figure 8-53.

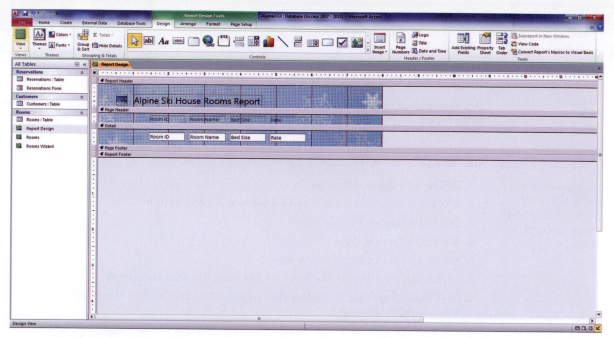

Figure 8-53

Report design

18. Save and close the report.

CLOSE the database.

Project 8-2: Format the Soccer Roster

Since you have increased your Access skills, you decide to improve on the soccer roster you created at the beginning of the season. There have been a few changes anyway, so you need an updated version.

GET READY. LAUNCH Access if it is not already running.

@ The *SoccerData* file for this lesson is available on the book companion website or in WileyPLUS.

1. OPEN *SoccerData* from the data files for this lesson.

2. SAVE the database as *SoccerDataXXX* (where *XXX* is your initials).

3. Open the Roster report.

4. Switch to Design View.

5. Press and hold the **Shift** key and click on all the labels in the Page Header section to select them.

6. On the Format tab, in the Font group, click the **Bold** button.

7. Select the title, Roster, and key **Soccer Roster**.

8. On the Format tab, in the Font group, click the **Font** menu and select **Arial Black**.

9. On the Format tab, in the Font group, click the **Font Size** menu and select **22**.

10. On the Arrange tab, on the Size/Space menu in the Sizing & Ordering group, click the **To Fit** button.

11. Press and hold the **Shift** key and click on all the controls in the Detail section. On the Arrange tab, on the Align menu in the Sizing & Ordering group, click **To Grid**.

12. Delete the report image.

13. On the Design tab, in the Header/Footer group, click the **Logo** button.

@ The *soccer* file for this lesson is available on the book companion website or in WileyPLUS.

14. Navigate to the student data files for this lesson and select *Soccer.jpg*.

15. Save the report and view it in Report View.

CLOSE the database.

Proficiency Assessment

Project 8-3: Create the Fourth Coffee Order Summary Form

In your part-time job at Fourth Coffee, you are often involved in taking and filling orders. Create a summary table to help make your job easier.

GET READY. LAUNCH Access if it is not already running.

@ The *Coffee Data* file for this lesson is available on the book companion website or in WileyPLUS.

1. **OPEN** *Coffee Data* from the data files for this lesson.
2. **SAVE** the database as *CoffeeDataXXX* (where *XXX* is your initials).
3. Select the Order Summary table in the Navigation pane.
4. Create a simple form using the Form button.
5. Insert a Date and Time control with the format **00/00/0000**.
6. Delete the Paid control and create a Yes/No option group control using check boxes with **Paid** as the caption. Set the value for Yes as **−1** and the value for No as **0**.
7. Delete the Attachment field.
8. Resize and arrange the controls to look similar to the form in Figure 8-54. Remember to remove the control layout formatting so that you can move individual controls.

Figure 8-54

Order Summary form

9. Save the form as Order Summary.
10. Check your work in Form View.
11. Close the form.

CLOSE the database.

Project 8-4: Create the Alpine Ski House Reservations Form

Entering data in the table is becoming cumbersome, so you decide to create a form you can use to enter reservation data.

USE *AlpineXXX* database, which you saved in a previous exercise.

1. Click the Reservations table in the Navigation pane to select it.
2. Create a new form using Design View.

3. Insert a title control. Change the title to **Alpine Ski House Reservations Form**.

4. Insert a logo control using the ***Penguins.jpg*** image from the student data files from this lesson.

@ The ***Penguins*** file for this lesson is available on the book companion website or in WileyPLUS.

5. Add the following bound controls to the design grid: **Customer ID**, **Room**, **Rate**, **Check-In Date**, **Check-Out Date**, and **Notes**.

6. Select all the controls and apply the **Stacked** control layout.

7. Position the controls in the upper-left corner of the Details section, remove the stacked layout and resize the Notes control, as shown in Figure 8-55.

Figure 8-55

Reservations form

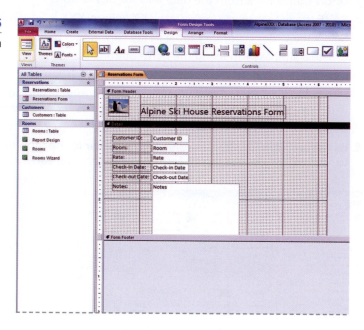

8. Save the form as **Reservations Form** and leave it open for use in the next exercise.

LEAVE the database open for the next project.

Mastery Assessment

Project 8-5: Refine the Alpine Ski House Reservations Form

The reservations form you created is very helpful; however, you need to add more functionality to the form using calculated controls and Control Wizards.

USE the form open from the previous exercise.

1. Add an Option group control on the right side of the form. Use the Control Wizard to create the option box for the *Credit Card on File* field. Using the Option Group Wizard, add two Labels, one for Yes and the other for No. Set the value for Yes to **−1** and the value for No to **0**. Use option buttons, and label the control **Credit Card on File**.

2. Add an unbound text box control below the *Credit Card on File* field.

3. Open the Property Sheet and click the **Build** button in the Control Source property.

4. Create an expression to subtract the Check-In Date from the Check-Out date.

5. Key **Number of Nights** as the label. (Note the default label number, such as Text##.)

6. Add an unbound text box control beside the Notes control.

7. Open the Property Sheet and click the **Build** button in the Control Source property.

8. Create an expression to multiply the Number of Nights (or Text##) by the Rate.

9. Key **Rate Subtotal** as the label.

10. Change all the controls and labels you added with black text to the red color.

11. Switch to Layout View. Your screen should look similar to Figure 8-56.

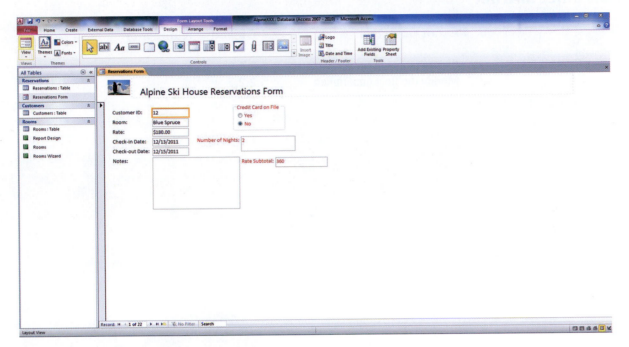

Figure 8-56

Revised Reservations form

12. Save the form and switch to Form View.

CLOSE the database.

Project 8-6: Fix the Angel Project Contact Information Form

A volunteer did some work on the Angel Project database while you were on vacation. The Contact Information form has a few problems that you need to fix.

GET READY. LAUNCH Access if it is not already running.

1. **OPEN** *AngelData* from the data files for this lesson.

2. **SAVE** the database as *AngelDataXXX* (where *XXX* is your initials).

3. Open the Contact Information Form.

4. Change the layout from tabular to stacked.

5. Bind the unbound control to the *City* field.

6. Fix the control tab order.

7. Save and close the form.

CLOSE Access.

INTERNET READY

What are your favorite toys? Maybe you have some favorites from childhood or perhaps you have some favorite grown-up toys, such as electronic gadgets. Search online stores for details about the toys. Create a database table with fields like Name, Description, Store, and Price. Use what you've learned in this lesson to create a form with controls for each field. Enter the data for five toys into your form. For extra practice, create a report that displays a summary of all your data.

9 Advanced Tables

LESSON SKILL MATRIX

Skill	Exam Objective	Objective Number
Creating a Custom Table	Create tables in Design View.	2.1.1
	Modify the field description.	2.2.7
Using the Table Analyzer		
Summarizing Table Data		

KEY TERMS
- aggregate functions
- Table Analyzer
- Totals row

Lucerne Publishing is a large publisher with a variety of products. You have just been hired as sales manager for the business books division. You will be responsible for working with the salespeople in your division to increase sales. The previous sales manager used Access 2010 to track sales, so some data is already available. In this lesson, you create a new custom table, use the Table Analyzer to divide one table into two tables, and add a Totals row to a table.

CREATING A CUSTOM TABLE

The Bottom Line

When a table template doesn't suit your needs, you can create a custom table in Design View. In Design View, you can insert fields, set data types, and perform other advanced table design tasks.

Creating a Custom Table

Creating a table from scratch in Design View gives you maximum flexibility. You can do everything you need to do to create the table in Design View, including adding fields, setting data types, defining field properties, and defining a primary key. As you create a table, you can also easily insert and delete rows in your table design. In this exercise, you create a new blank table and then add fields for the new table in Design View.

Creating a new field for a table in Design View includes keying the name in the Field Name column; choosing a data type from the menu in the Data Type column; and keying a description, if you want, in the Description column. Additionally, you can modify field properties in the Field Properties section of the design grid.

After you have completed your table design, you'll need to save it. If you haven't already defined a primary key, Access will prompt you to do so when you save the table.

STEP BY STEP   **Create a Custom Table in Design View**

@ The *Lucerne Publishing* file for this lesson is available on the book companion website or in WileyPLUS.

GET READY. Before you begin these steps, be sure to turn on and/or log on to your computer and **LAUNCH** Access.

1. **OPEN** *Lucerne Publishing* from the data files for this lesson.
2. **SAVE** the database as *Lucerne PublishingXXX* (where *XXX* is your initials).
3. On the Create tab, in the Tables group, click the **Table Design** button. A new blank table is created in Design View, as shown in Figure 9-1.

Figure 9-1

Blank table in Design View

WileyPLUS Extra! features an online tutorial of this task.

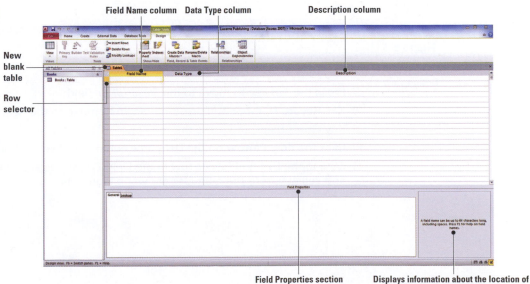

Field Name column   Data Type column   Description column

New blank table

Row selector

Field Properties section   Displays information about the location of the insertion point

4. Key **ID** in the Field Name column, as shown in Figure 9-2.

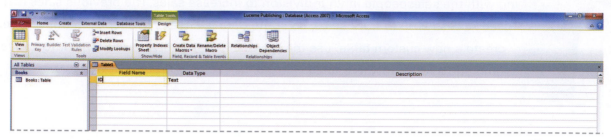

Figure 9-2

Field Name in Design View

5. Press the **Tab** key to move to the Data Type column.

6. Click the **down arrow** in the Data Type column and select **AutoNumber** from the menu, as shown in Figure 9-3. The AutoNumber data type will automatically number your records starting at 1.

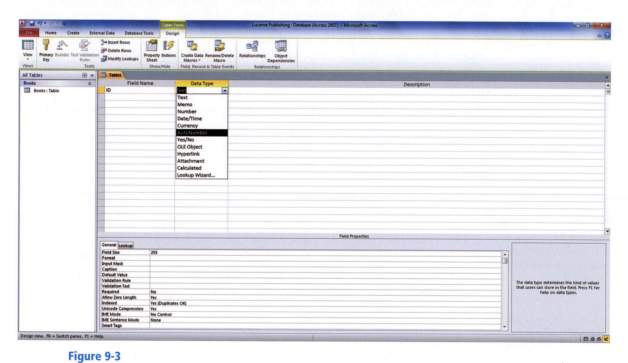

Figure 9-3

Data Types menu in Design View

7. Press the **Tab** key to move to the *Description* field.

8. Key **Record Number** and press **Tab** again to move to the next blank field row.

9. Key **Gross Sales** and press the **Tab** key.

10. Click the **down arrow** on the Data Type column and select **Currency** from the menu.

11. Click in the **Decimal Places** row in the Field Properties section. Click the **down arrow** and select **0** from the menu, as shown in Figure 9-4.

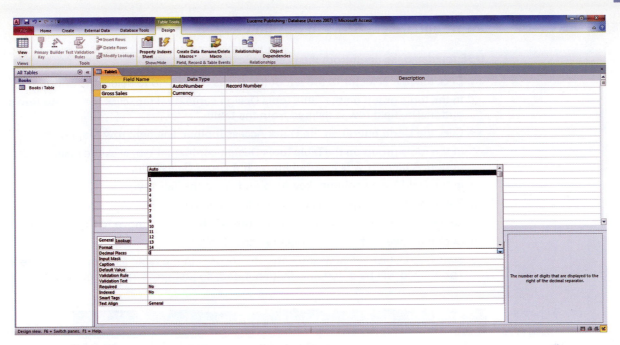

Figure 9-4

Field Properties in Design View

12. Enter the remaining fields, as shown in Figure 9-5, formatting each with the **Currency** data type and **0** decimal places.

Row selector

Figure 9-5

Custom table in Design View

CERTIFICATION
READY   **2.1.1**

How do you create tables in Design View?

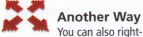

CERTIFICATION
READY   **2.2.7**

How do you modify the field description?

Another Way
You can also right-click a selected row and choose Insert Rows or Delete Rows from the shortcut menu.

13. Click the **row selector** to the left of the **ID** field to select the row.
14. On the Design tab, in the Tools group, click the **Primary Key** button.
15. Click the **Save** button on the Quick Access Toolbar. The Save As dialog box appears.
16. Key **Sales** and click **OK**.
PAUSE. LEAVE the database open to use in the next exercise.

Inserting and Deleting Rows

When creating a custom table in Design View, you can insert and delete rows as needed using the Insert Rows and Delete Rows commands in the Tools group on the Table Tools Design contextual tab. When you click the Insert Rows button, a new row is inserted above the selected row. The field order from top to bottom in Design View will be displayed from left to right in Datasheet View. In this exercise, you insert and delete rows using the new table you created in the previous exercise.

STEP BY STEP

Insert and Delete Rows in Design View

USE the database open from the previous exercise.

1. Click the **row selector** to the left of the *Gross Sales* field to select the entire row.

2. In the Tools group on the Table Tools Design contextual tab, click the **Delete Rows** button. The field row is deleted from the table.

3. Click the **Undo** button on the Quick Access Toolbar. The field row reappears.

4. In the Tools group on the Table Tools Design contextual tab, click the **Insert Rows** button. A blank row is inserted above the *Gross Sales* field.

5. In the Field Name column, key **Area** and press the **Tab** key.

6. Press the **Tab** key again to accept the **Text** data type.

7. Leave the *Description* field blank and press **Tab** again to move to the next field.

8. Click the **Save** button on the Quick Access Toolbar.

9. Switch to Datasheet View and enter the records in the table as shown in Figure 9-6. The *ID* field will be automatically generated, so just press **Tab** to get past it.

Figure 9-6

Sales table

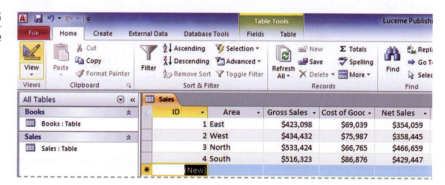

10. Save and close the table.

PAUSE. LEAVE the database open to use in the next exercise.

USING THE TABLE ANALYZER

The Bottom Line

The **Table Analyzer** is a wizard that performs the normalization process for you by examining a table design and suggesting a way to divide the table for maximum efficiency. The Table Analyzer helps you design efficient tables. The Table Analyzer will suggest primary keys for the new tables or will allow you to determine the primary keys. You can also have the wizard insert a unique identifier field. If it determines that a table has duplicate information, it can split a table into two more efficient tables for you, or you can choose to do it yourself. You can create the new tables yourself if you prefer.

Using the Table Analyzer

The Table Analyzer is a wizard that examines a table and asks you a series of questions about the table to determine whether it should be divided into two or more tables. In this exercise, you use the Table Analyzer Wizard to analyze a table in the database.

Well-designed databases do not store data in more than one place. Redundant data storage takes more disk space and increases the likelihood for data entry errors. In Lesson 1, you were introduced to the concept of normalization, which is the process of applying rules to a database design to ensure that you have divided your data into the appropriate tables.

In the Books table, contact information for authors has to be entered for each book the author wrote. The Table Analyzer Wizard will determine that a more efficient database would split the table into two tables—one with author contact information and one with book sales data.

Ref   Lesson 1 contains more information about normalization.

In addition to analyzing the table, the Table Analyzer Wizard will also analyze the redundant data in a table and suggest corrections for records that should match. It will also give you the choice of whether to create a query, which is similar to the original table. Creating the query allows forms and reports that were created with the original table to continue to function properly. The original table may be renamed, but it will not be removed or altered.

 **Troubleshooting** If you run the Table Analyzer before entering records in the table, you may get a message stating that you need to enter at least two records in the table to get a meaningful analysis.

STEP BY STEP   **Use the Table Analyzer**

USE the database open from the previous exercise.

1. Open the **Books** table.

2. Scroll through the table to become familiar with the fields in the table.

3. On the Database Tools tab, in the Analyze group, click the **Analyze Table** button. The first Table Analyzer Wizard screen appears, as shown in Figure 9-7. This first dialog box provides more information about the types of problems the wizard will find.

Figure 9-7

Table Analyzer Wizard, screen 1

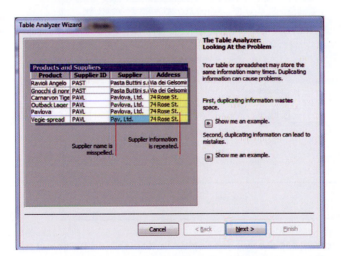

4. Click the **Next >** button. The second Table Analyzer Wizard screen appears, as shown in Figure 9-8. This dialog box provides more information about what the wizard will do.

Figure 9-8

Table Analyzer Wizard, screen 2

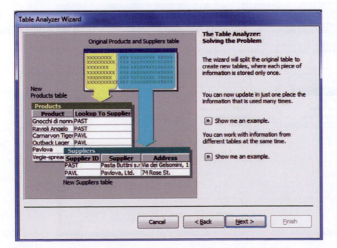

5. Click the **Next >** button. The third Table Analyzer Wizard screen appears, as shown in Figure 9-9.

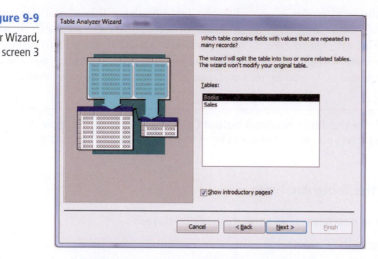

6. The **Books** table should be selected in the list; if it is not, select it. Click the **Next >** button. The fourth Table Analyzer Wizard screen appears, as shown in Figure 9-10.

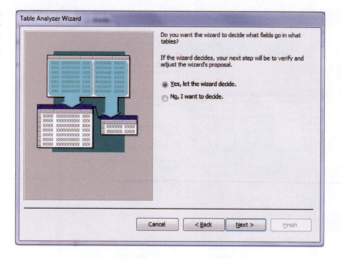

7. The **Yes, let the wizard decide** button should be selected; if it is not, select it. Click the **Next >** button. The fifth Table Analyzer Wizard screen appears, as shown in Figure 9-11.

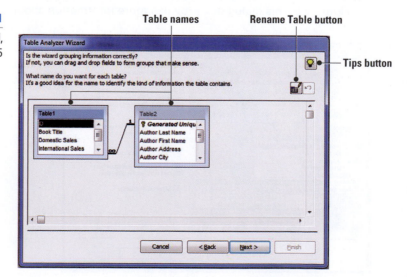

8. Scroll to the bottom of the Table2 box and click the **Year** field to select it. Notice that the wizard has placed it in the wrong table.

9. Drag the selected field to the Table1 box. Position the horizontal black line below the *Book Title* field and release the mouse button to place the *Year* field in its new location.

10. Click the **Table1** name to select it. Click the **Rename Table** button. The Table Analyzer Wizard dialog box appears, as shown in Figure 9-12.

Figure 9-12

Rename Table dialog box

11. Key **Book Sales** and click **OK**.

12. Click the **Table2** name and click the **Rename Table** button. The Table Analyzer Wizard dialog box appears.

13. Key **Author Contact Information** and click **OK**.

14. Scroll down to the bottom of the Book Sales table. Notice that the *Lookup to Author Contact Information* field was added.

15. Scroll through the Author Contact Information table. Notice that the Generated Unique *ID* field was added as a primary key. Click the **Next >** button. The sixth Table Analyzer Wizard screen appears, as shown in Figure 9-13.

Figure 9-13

Table Analyzer Wizard, screen 6

Set Unique Identifier button

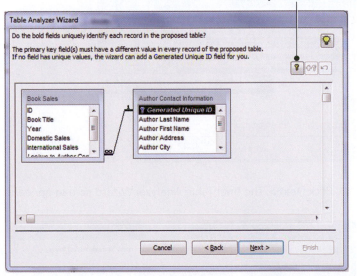

Another Way
You can also double-click a table name to launch the Table Analyzer Wizard Rename Table dialog box.

16. Click the **ID** field in the Book Sales table to select it. Click the **Set Unique Identifier** button. A primary key is inserted.

17. Click **Next >**. The seventh Table Analyzer Wizard screen appears, as shown in Figure 9-14.

Figure 9-14

Table Analyzer Wizard,
screen 7

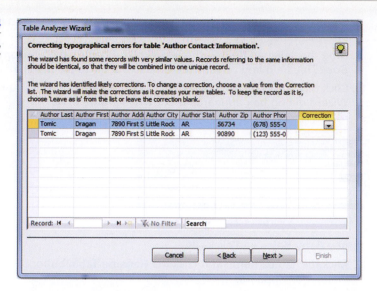

18. Notice that the Table Analyzer Wizard has detected two similar records, one with an incorrect zip code and phone number. Click the **down arrow** in the first row of the *Correction* field and select **Leave as is**. This is the correct record.

19. Click the **down arrow** on the second row of the *Correction* field and select the **Tomic** correction from the menu, as shown in Figure 9-15, to replace the incorrect record.

Figure 9-15

Corrections to the new tables

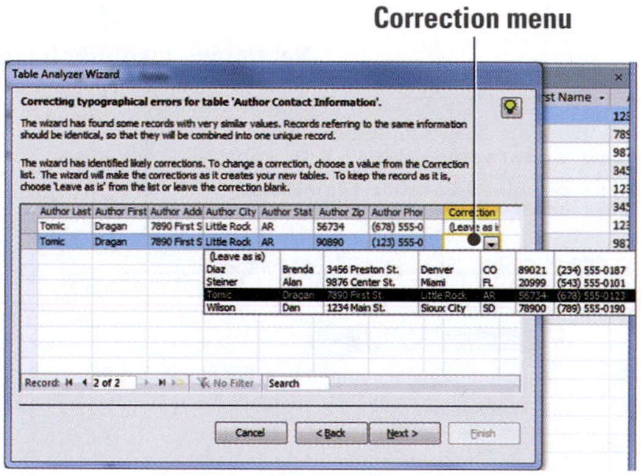

Correction menu

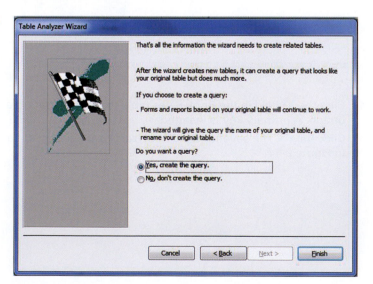

20. Click **Next >**. The final Table Analyzer Wizard screen appears, as shown in Figure 9-16.

Figure 9-16

Table Analyzer Wizard,
final screen

21. The **Yes, create the query** option button should be selected. Click the **Finish** button.
22. A message saying that the new query will be saved as Books_NEW appears. Click **OK**.
23. If Access Help appears on your screen, close it. Your screen should look similar to Figure 9-17.

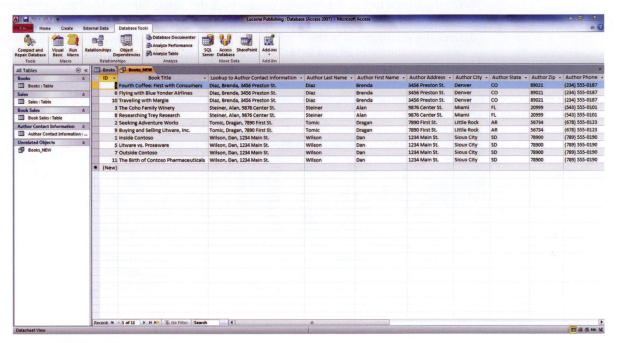

Figure 9-17

New tables and queries created by the Table Analyzer Wizard

24. Close all tables and queries.

PAUSE. LEAVE the database open to use in the next exercise.

SUMMARIZING TABLE DATA

The Bottom Line

It is often necessary to count or summarize data in a table column by column. Tables that contain columns of sales figures or other numbers need to be summed, averaged, or counted to be more useful. The Totals row makes these tasks easy.

Summarizing Table Data

Much like the bottom row of a spreadsheet, the Totals row is a feature in Access 2010 that makes it easy to sum, average, or count the values in a datasheet column. You can also find maximum or minimum values and use statistical functions such as standard deviation and variance. In this exercise, you summarize table data by inserting a Totals row.

Aggregate functions are functions that calculate values across a range of data, such as in a column. You can use these functions in queries or in Visual Basic for Applications (VBA) code. Although you can still use those methods, the Totals row saves you time by allowing you to choose one of these functions from a menu, applying it instantly. The **Totals row** is a row inserted at the bottom of a table that provides a menu of functions for each column in the row.

Take Note

You can also add a Totals row to queries open in Datasheet View and to a split form open in Form View. You cannot add a Totals row to a report, but you can use aggregate functions in reports using other methods.

Insert a Totals Row

USE the database open from the previous exercise.

1. Open the **Book Sales** table.
2. On the Home tab, in the Records group, click the **Totals** button. The Totals row appears below the asterisk (*) row.
3. Click the **down arrow** in the Book Title column of the Totals row. Select **Count** from the menu, as shown in Figure 9-18. The number of records in the column is counted, and the number 11 is displayed.

Figure 9-18

Totals row

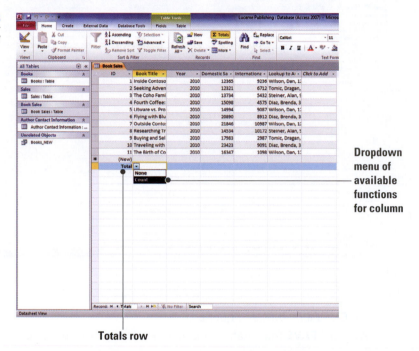

Dropdown menu of available functions for column

Totals row

4. Click the **down arrow** in the Domestic Sales column of the Totals row and select **Sum** from the menu.
5. Click the **down arrow** in the International Sales column of the Totals row and select **Sum** from the menu. Your screen should look similar to Figure 9-19.

Figure 9-19

Totals row in the Book Sales table

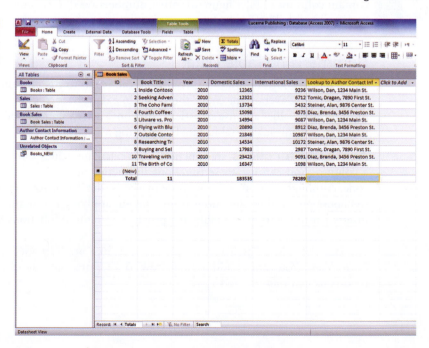

6. Save the table.

7. On the Home tab, in the Records group, click the **Totals** button. The Totals row is hidden.

8. On the Home tab, in the Records group, click the **Totals** button again. The Totals row reappears.

9. Save and close the table.

CLOSE Access.

Table 9-1 describes the aggregate functions available in the Totals row and the data types that they work with.

Table 9-1

Aggregate Functions in the Totals Row

Aggregate Function	Description	Data Types
Average	Calculates the average value for a column	Number, Decimal, Currency, Date/Time
Count	Counts the number of items in a column	All (except multivalued list)
Maximum	Returns the item with the highest value	Number, Decimal, Currency, Date/Time
Minimum	Returns the item with the lowest value	Number, Decimal, Currency, Date/Time
Standard Deviation	Measures how widely values are dispersed from an average value	Number, Decimal, Currency
Sum	Adds items in a column	Number, Decimal, Currency
Variance	Measures the statistical variance of all values in the column	Number, Decimal, Currency

As shown in the table, some functions only work with certain data types. For example, you cannot sum a column of text, so that function would not be available for a column with the data type of text.

Take Note   If you want to sort or filter data, Access will exclude the Totals row by default.

SKILL SUMMARY

In This Lesson You Learned How To:	Exam Objective	Objective Number
Create a Custom Table	Create tables in Design View. Modify the field description.	2.1.1 2.2.7
Use the Table Analyzer		
Summarize Table Data		

Knowledge Assessment

Matching

Match the term in Column 1 to its description in Column 2.

Column 1	Column 2
1. aggregate function	**a.** square to the left of a field in Design View
2. Table Analyzer	**b.** inserts a blank row above a selected row in Design View
3. Totals row	**c.** the process of applying rules to a database design to ensure that you have divided your information into the appropriate tables
4. row selector	**d.** a wizard that performs the normalization process by examining a table design and suggesting a way to divide the table for maximum efficiency
5. Insert Rows button	**e.** an aggregate function that counts the records in a column
6. Delete Rows button	**f.** an optional part of Design View where you can enter a field description
7. normalization	**g.** a data type
8. count	**h.** function that calculates values across a range of data
9. currency	**i.** a row inserted at the bottom of a table that provides a menu of functions for each column in the row
10. description	**j.** deletes a selected field row in Design View

True/False

Circle T if the statement is true or F if the statement is false.

T   F   1. If you haven't already defined a primary key, Access will prompt you to do so when you save the table in Design View.

T   F   2. Well-designed databases store data in more than one place.

T   F   3. The row selector is located at the bottom of the table.

T   F   4. The Table Analyzer does not remove the original table.

T   F   5. The Table Analyzer gives you the choice of whether to create a query.

T   F   6. The Table Analyzer does not add new fields.

T   F   7. Average is an example of an aggregate function.

T   F   8. The Totals row is inserted above the asterisk row.

T   F   9. Certain functions only work with certain data types.

T   F   10. You cannot delete a Totals row, but you can hide it.

Competency Assessment

Project 9-1: Summarize the Sales Table

The Sales table you created at Lucerne Publishing seems incomplete. Add a Totals row to summarize the data.

USE *Lucerne Publishing XXX* that you saved in a previous exercise.

1. Open the Sales table.

2. On the Home tab, in the Records group, click the **Totals** button. The Totals row appears.

3. Click the **down arrow** in the Totals row of the Gross Sales column. Select **Sum** from the menu.

4. Click the **down arrow** in the Totals row of the Cost of Goods column. Select **Sum** from the menu.

5. Click the **down arrow** in the Totals row of the Net Sales column. Select **Sum** from the menu.

6. Save and close the table.

CLOSE the database.

Project 9-2: Analyze the Fourth Coffee Customers Table

In your part-time job as an office assistant at Fourth Coffee, you have been taking on most of the database responsibilities. As you learn more and more about Access, you decide to use the Table Analyzer to check a table you created previously to make sure it is efficient.

GET READY. LAUNCH Access if it is not already running.

@ The *Fourth Coffee Inventory* file for this lesson is available on the book companion website or in WileyPLUS.

1. **OPEN** *Fourth Coffee Inventory* from the data files for this lesson.

2. **SAVE** the database as *Fourth Coffee Inventory XXX* (where *XXX* is your initials).

3. Open the **Customers** table.

4. On the Database Tools tab, in the Analyze group, click the **Analyze Table** button. The Analyze Table Wizard dialog box appears.

5. Click **Next >** to display the next Analyze Table Wizard dialog box.

6. Click **Next >** to display the next Analyze Table Wizard dialog box.

7. The Customers table should be selected. Click **Next**.

8. The **Yes, let the Wizard decide** option button should be selected. Click **Next**.

9. A message is displayed that says the wizard does not recommend dividing the table. Click **OK**.

10. Click **Cancel** to close the Table Analyzer Wizard.

11. Close the table.

LEAVE the database open for use in the next project.

Proficiency Assessment

Project 9-3: Design the Fourth Coffee Sales Table

Sales data for Fourth Coffee has just come in for the first quarter. The manager asks you to create a table that displays the sales for each of the five stores in your division. Note: Each store is known by a three-digit number, such as 656.

USE the *Fourth Coffee Inventory XXX* database that you saved in a previous exercise.

1. Create a new table in Design View.

2. Key **ID** as the first field name and press the **Tab** key. Set the data type to **AutoNumber**.

3. Key **Month** as the second field name and press the **Tab** key. A message appears stating that the word month is a reserved word. Click **OK**. Change the field name to **Mon** and set its data type to **Text**.

4. Enter the remaining field names and data types, as shown in Figure 9-20. Set the primary key as shown.

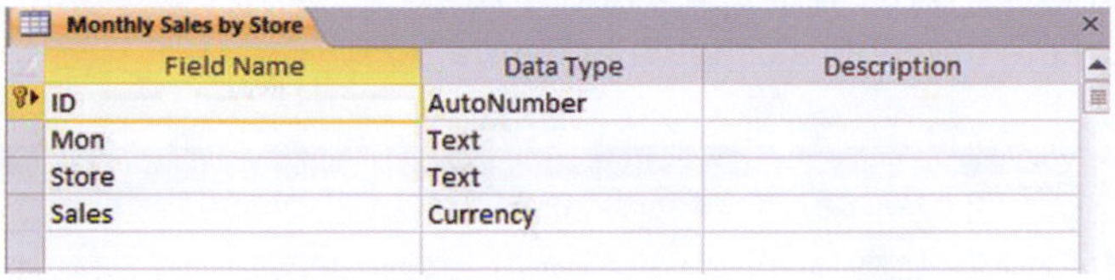

Figure 9-20

Monthly Sales by Store in Design view

Field Name	Data Type	Description
ID	AutoNumber	
Mon	Text	
Store	Text	
Sales	Currency	

5. Save the table as **Monthly Sales by Store**.

6. Switch to Datasheet View.

7. Enter the data in the table as shown in Figure 9-21.

Figure 9-21

Monthly Sales by Store table

ID	Mon	Store	Sales	Click to Add
1	January	651	$88,432.00	
2	February	651	$97,798.00	
3	March	651	$67,890.00	
4	April	651	$59,098.00	
5	January	656	$105,890.00	
6	February	656	$96,789.00	
7	March	656	$96,789.00	
8	April	656	$87,890.00	
9	January	660	$106,098.00	
10	February	660	$77,998.00	
11	March	660	$94,927.00	
12	April	660	$84,123.00	
13	January	662	$90,890.00	
14	February	662	$67,223.00	
15	March	662	$87,010.00	
16	April	662	$74,280.00	
*	(New)			

8. Insert a **Totals** row.

9. Count the *Mon* field and sum the *Sales* field.

10. Save and close the table.

CLOSE the database.

Project 9-4: Summarize the Wingtip Toys Table

As marketing coordinator at Wingtip Toys, you are constantly examining sales data and trying to think of ways to increase sales. Total the inventory table to get a clear picture of the current inventory.

GET READY. LAUNCH Access if it is not already running.

@ The *Wingtip Toys Inventory* file for this lesson is available on the book companion website or in WileyPLUS.

1. **OPEN** *Wingtip Toys Inventory* from the data files for this lesson.

2. **SAVE** the database as *Wingtip Toys Inventory XXX* (where *XXX* is your initials).

3. Open the **Inventory** table.

4. Insert a Totals row.

5. Count the *Description* field, sum the *In Stock* field, and sum the *Price* field.

6. Save and close the table.

LEAVE the database open for use in the next project.

Mastery Assessment

Project 9-5: Design the Wingtip Toys Yearly Sales Table

The owner of Wingtip Toys has given you yearly sales data for each of the company's sales channels. Create a table in which to store and total the data.

USE the *Wingtip Toys Inventory XXX* that you saved in a previous exercise.

1. Create a new table in Design View.

2. Create the table as shown in Figure 9-22.

Figure 9-22

Yearly Sales table in Design View

Field Name	Data Type	Description
ID	AutoNumber	
Catalog	Currency	
Internet	Currency	
Stores	Currency	
Other	Currency	

3. Save the table as **Yearly Sales** and switch to Datasheet View and review the table you just created.

4. Switch back to Design View.

5. Insert a blank row above the *Catalog* field.

6. Key **Yr** as a new field with the Text data type.

7. Select the **Yr** field and click the **Primary Key** button to designate the *Yr* field as the new primary key.

8. Delete the *ID* field.

9. Save the table and switch to Datasheet View.

10. Enter data in the table as shown in Figure 9-23.

Figure 9-23

Yearly Sales table

Yr	Catalog	Internet	Stores	Other	Click to Add
2011	$87,987.00	$109,897.00	$208,767.00	$23,987.00	
2012	$57,984.00	$98,789.00	$197,098.00	$10,761.00	
2013	$61,089.00	$78,907.00	$168,234.00	$9,125.00	

11. Save the table.

12. Insert a **Totals** row.

13. Sum the Catalog, Internet, Stores, and Other columns.

14. Save and close the table.

CLOSE the database.

Project 9-6: Analyze the Alpine Reservations Table

As administrative assistant for Alpine Ski House, you have noticed that one of the tables you use on a regular basis seems large and cumbersome and you have to enter some of the same data again and again. You decide to run the Table Analyzer to see if the table needs to be split.

GET READY. LAUNCH Access if it is not already running.

@ The *Alpine Reservations* file for this lesson is available on the book companion website or in WileyPLUS.

1. **OPEN** *Alpine Reservations* from the data files for this lesson.

2. **SAVE** the database as *Alpine Reservations XXX* (where *XXX* is your initials).

3. Select the **Reservations** table in the Navigation pane.

4. Run the Table Analyzer, letting the wizard decide how to split the table.

5. Rename Table1 to **Reservation Details** and rename Table2 to **Room Details**.

6. Select the **ID** field in the Reservation Details table and designate it as the primary key.

7. Create the query and finish the wizard.

8. Save and close the database.

CLOSE Access.

INTERNET READY

Readers, writers, and publishers around the world closely watch the *New York Times* best-sellers list. Categories of best sellers include fiction, nonfiction, advice, and children's books. Search the www.nytimes.com website for the *New York Times* best-sellers list of your choice. Create a new table in Design View that includes information about the top five best sellers in your favorite category. Include relevant fields such as the title, author, description, and price.

10 Advanced Forms

LESSON SKILL MATRIX

Skill	Exam Objective	Objective Number
Creating Advanced Forms		
Using Application Parts to Create Blank Forms	Use Blank Forms.	1.3.1
Creating a Navigation Form	Create Navigation forms.	3.1.4

KEY TERMS

- Blank Forms
- hierarchical form
- main form
- Multiple Items tool
- Navigation form
- split form
- subform

240

As a regional manager for Contoso Pharmaceuticals, you are in charge of overseeing the sales reps in your division. The salespeople you supervise call on doctors to promote Contoso medications and to leave samples. You use Access to put the sales information together and pull data from a variety of sources. In this lesson, you learn how to create a multi-item form, a split form, and a subform.

SOFTWARE ORIENTATION

The Templates Group and the Forms Group

The Application Parts button in the Templates group and the Navigation and More Forms buttons in the Forms group, all located on the Create tab, contain menus with commands for creating all types of forms—some of which you have already learned about. Figures 10-1, 10-2, and 10-3 show the menus and commands you use to create advanced forms. Use these figures as references throughout this lesson as well as the rest of this book.

Figure 10-1

Application Parts button and menu

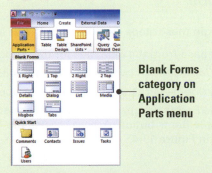

Blank Forms category on Application Parts menu

Figure 10-2

Navigation button and menu

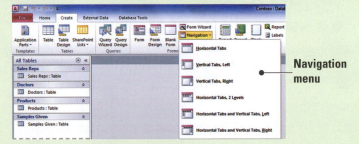

Navigation menu

Figure 10-3

More Forms button and menu

More Forms menu

Ref

In Lesson 5, you learned how to use some of the commands in the Forms group to create several basic forms.

CREATING ADVANCED FORMS

The Bottom Line

Access provides tools to help you create forms quickly—including advanced forms with features that can improve the usability of your database. The **Multiple Items tool** creates a customizable form that displays multiple records. A **split form** gives you two views of your data at the same time—in both Form View and Datasheet View. A **subform** is a form that is inserted into another form.

Creating a Multi-Item Form

When you create a simple form by using the Form tool, Access creates a form that displays a single record at a time. To create a form that displays multiple records but that is more customizable than a datasheet, you can use the Multiple Items tool. In this exercise, you create a Multi-Item form using the Multiple Items tool.

When you use the Multiple Items tool, the form that Access creates resembles a datasheet. The data is arranged in rows and columns, and you see more than one record at a time. However, a Multiple Items form gives you more customization options than a datasheet, such as the ability to add graphical elements, buttons, and other controls.

STEP BY STEP | **Create a Multi-Item Form**

 The *Contoso* file for this lesson is available on the book companion website or in WileyPLUS.

WileyPLUS Extra! features an online tutorial of this task.

GET READY. Before you begin these steps, be sure to **LAUNCH** Microsoft Access.

1. **OPEN** the *Contoso* database from the data files for this lesson.
2. **SAVE** the database as *Contoso XXX* (where *XXX* is your initials).
3. In the Navigation pane, double-click the **Doctors** table to open it.
4. On the Create tab, in the Forms group, click the **More Forms** button. On the menu that appears, click the **Multiple Items** button. Access creates the form and displays it in Layout View, as shown in Figure 10-4.

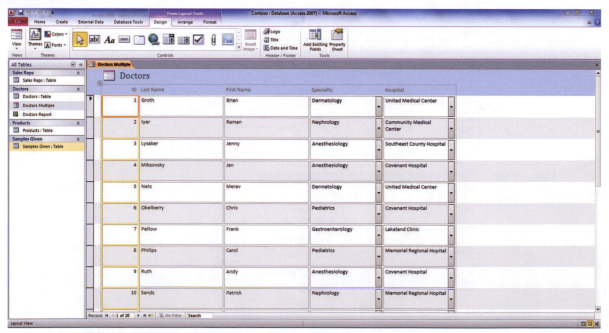

Figure 10-4

Multiple Items form in Layout View

5. Scroll down and to the right to view the multiple records on the form.

6. Click the **File** tab and click **Save**.

7. In the Save As dialog box, key **Doctors Multiple** and click **OK**.

8. Click the **Close** button on Doctors Multiple to close the form.

9. Click the **Close** button on Doctors to close the table.

10. **LEAVE** the database open.

PAUSE. LEAVE Access open to use in the next exercise.

 Ref   You learned about using controls to format your forms in Lesson 7.

Creating a Split Form

Creating a split form allows you to see two views of your data at the same time—in Form View and in Datasheet View. The two views are connected to the same data source and are completely synchronized with each other. In this exercise, you create a split form.

Working with split forms gives you the benefits of both types of forms in a single form. Selecting a field in the datasheet part of the form selects the same field in the form part of the form. When you add, edit, or delete data in the datasheet part, the change is reflected in the form part.

STEP BY STEP   **Create a Split Form**

USE the database that is open from the previous exercise.

1. In the Navigation pane, double-click the **Sales Reps** table to open it.

2. On the Create tab, in the Forms group, click the **More Forms** button. On the menu that appears, click the **Split Form** button. Access creates the form and displays it in Form View and Datasheet View at the same time, as shown in Figure 10-5.

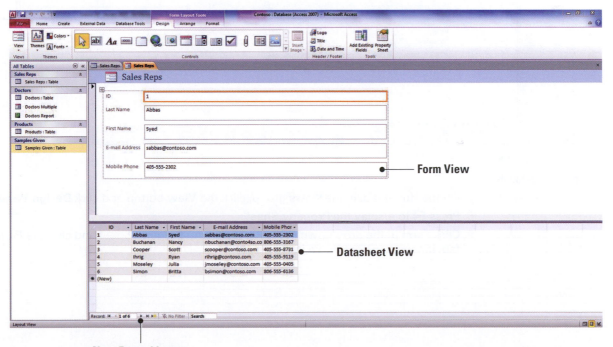

Figure 10-5

Split form

3. Click the **Next Record** navigation button to display the next record in Form View.

4. In the datasheet part on the bottom, place the insertion point in the *Mobile Phone* field for Nancy Buchanan. Notice that the same field is selected in the form part at the top.

5. Change the number for Nancy Buchanan in the *Mobile Phone* field to **806-555-4489**.

6. Click anywhere on the form part above the datasheet and notice that the mobile phone number has been changed there as well, as shown in Figure 10-6.

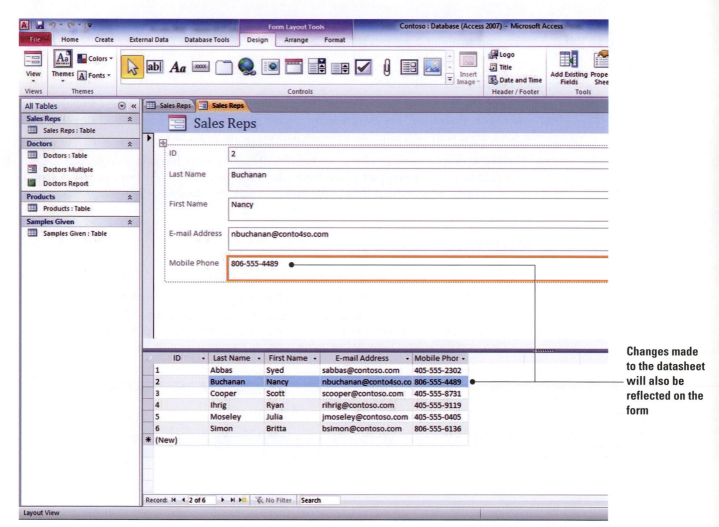

Changes made to the datasheet will also be reflected on the form

Figure 10-6

Editing a split form

7. On the Home tab, in the Views group, click the **View** button and click **Design View**.

8. Press **F4** to display the Property Sheet.

9. Click **Form** in the drop-down list at the top of the Property Sheet and click the **Format** tab, if necessary, as shown in Figure 10-7.

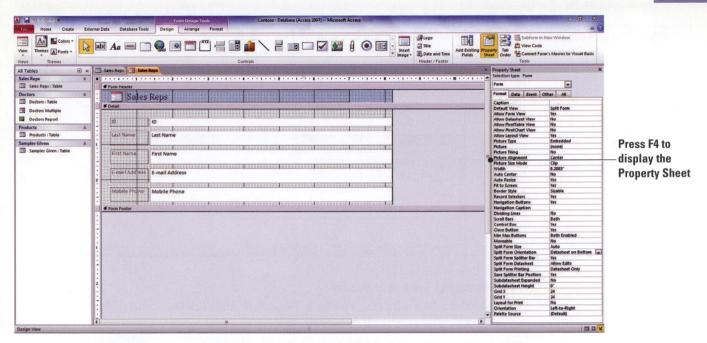

Press F4 to display the Property Sheet

Figure 10-7

Property Sheet

10. Scroll down to the Split Form Orientation property, click the **down arrow**, and click **Datasheet on Top**, as shown in Figure 10-8.

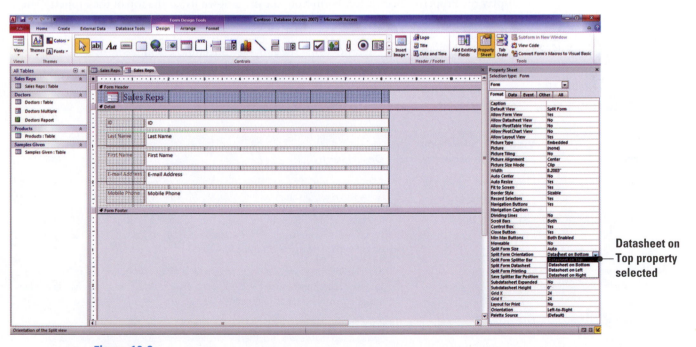

Datasheet on Top property selected

Figure 10-8

Changing a property

Take Note   If all text for the properties is not visible, click the left border of the Property Sheet and drag to widen it.

11. Click the **Close** button to close the Property Sheet.

12. On the Home tab, in the Views group, click the **View** button and click **Layout View**. The split form is displayed with the datasheet on top, as shown in Figure 10-9.

Figure 10-9

Split form with datasheet
on top

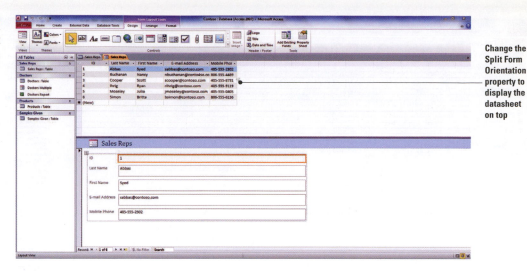

Change the
Split Form
Orientation
property to
display the
datasheet
on top

13. Click the **File** tab and click **Save**.

14. In the Save As dialog box, key **Sales Reps Split** and click **OK**.

15. Click the **Close** button on Sales Reps Split to close the form.

16. Click the **Close** button on Sales Reps to close the table.

17. **LEAVE** the database open.

PAUSE. LEAVE the database open to use in the next exercise.

Table 10-1 lists some of the properties related to split forms that you can set on the Property Sheet to fine-tune your form. To change form properties, switch to Design View, press F4 to display the Property Sheet, select Form from the drop-down list at the top of the Property Sheet, and click the Format tab.

  Ref   You learned how to set properties using the Property Sheet in Lesson 4.

Table 10-1

Properties Related to Split Forms

Property	View(s) in which you can set the property	Description
Split Form Orientation	Design View	Allows you to define whether the datasheet appears above, below, to the left, or to the right of the form.
Split Form Datasheet	Design View or Layout View	If set to Allow Edits (and the form's record source is updateable), Access allows edits to be made on the datasheet. If set to Read Only, Access prevents edits from being made on the datasheet.
Split Form Splitter Bar	Design View	If set to Yes, Access allows you to resize the form and datasheet by moving the splitter bar that separates the two parts. If set to No, the splitter bar is hidden, and the form and datasheet cannot be resized.
Save Splitter Bar Position	Design View	If set to Yes, the form opens with the splitter bar in the same position in which you last left it. If set to No, the form and datasheet cannot be resized, and the splitter bar is hidden.
Split Form Size	Design View or Layout View	Allows you to specify an exact height or width (depending on whether the form is split vertically or horizontally) for the form part of the split form. For example, key 1" to set the form to a height or width of 1 inch. Key Auto to set the dimension by other means, such as dragging the splitter bar in Layout View.
Split Form Printing	Design View or Layout View	Allows you to define which portion of the form is printed when you print the form. If set to Form Only, only the form portion is printed. If set to Datasheet Only, only the datasheet portion is printed.

Creating a Subform

A subform is a convenient tool that allows you to view data from more than one table or query on the same form. A subform is a form that is inserted into another form. The primary form is called the **main form**, and the form within the form is called the subform. A form/subform combination is sometimes referred to as a **hierarchical form**, a *master/detail form,* or a *parent/ child form.* You can use the Form Wizard to help you create subforms quickly. For best results, all relationships should be established first. This enables Access to automatically create the links between subforms and main forms. In this exercise, you create a subform.

When working with a relational database, you often need to view data from more than one table or query on the same form. For example, you want to see customer data, but you also want to see information about the customer's orders at the same time. Subforms are a convenient tool for doing this.

Subforms are especially effective when you want to show data from tables or queries that have a one-to-many relationship—the main form shows data from the "one" side of the relationship and the subform shows the data from the "many" side of the relationship.

STEP BY STEP   **Create a Subform**

USE the database that is open from the previous exercise.

1. On the Create tab, in the Forms group, click **Form Wizard**.
2. In the first screen on the Form Wizard, click the **down arrow** in the Tables/Queries box and click **Table: Samples Given**.
3. In the Available Fields box, double-click the **Week Name**, **Sales Rep**, **Product**, and **Quantity** fields to move them to the Selected Fields box.
4. Click the **down arrow** in the Tables/Queries box and click **Table: Doctors**.
5. In the Available Fields box, double-click the **Last Name**, **First Name**, **Specialty**, and **Hospital** fields to move them to the Selected Fields box. The screen should look like Figure 10-10.

Figure 10-10

Form Wizard, screen 1

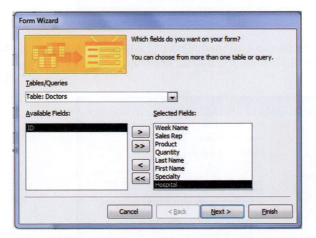

6. Click the **Next >** button.
7. In the *How do you want to view your data?* box, click **by Doctors**. The *Form with subform(s)* radio button should be selected, and the Form Wizard should look like Figure 10-11.

Figure 10-11

Form Wizard, screen 2

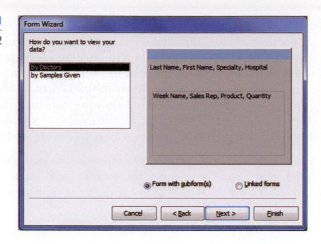

8. Click the **Next >** button.

9. Click the **Tabular** radio button to select that as the layout for your subform, as shown in Figure 10-12.

Figure 10-12

Form Wizard, screen 3

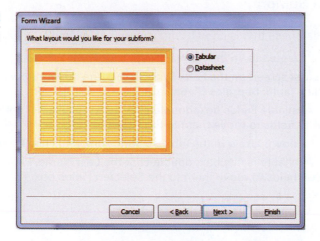

10. Click the **Next >** button. Access has suggested titles for the forms, as shown in Figure 10-13. Keep the default selection to open the form.

Figure 10-13

Form Wizard, screen 4

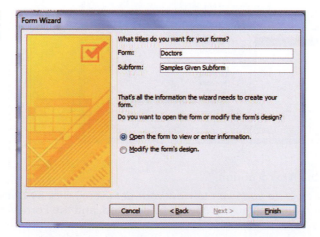

11. Click the **Finish** button to create the forms. The Doctors form appears with the Samples Given subform, as shown in Figure 10-14.

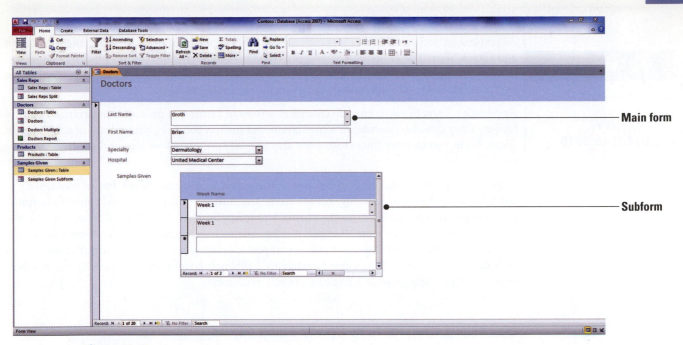

Figure 10-14

Doctors form with subform

12. In the Navigation pane, double-click the **Samples Given subform** to open it, as shown in Figure 10-15.

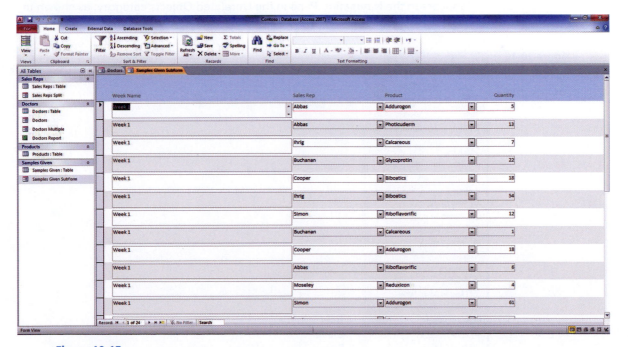

Figure 10-15

Samples Given subform

13. Scroll down and to the right, if necessary, to see the data contained in the records and then click the **Close** button on the Samples Given subform to close the subform.

14. Click the **Close** button on the Doctors form to close the form.

15. **LEAVE** the database open.

PAUSE. LEAVE the database open to use in the next exercise.

USING APPLICATION PARTS TO CREATE BLANK FORMS

As you learned in Lesson 2, the Application Parts gallery consists of two categories, **Blank Forms** and Quick Start. The Blank Forms category contains a collection of 10 form parts that allow you to add predefined forms to a database. In this exercise, you create an Application Parts Blank Form and populate the form with bound controls using the Field List.

Application Parts Blank Forms are created as unbound forms and provide a prearranged control layout. They can also provide unbound command button controls, depending on what type of Blank Form you choose. These forms can also be easily populated with bound controls by using the Field List.

Application Parts Blank Forms differ from adding a form using the Blank Forms tool since you can add forms that automatically include command buttons that provide additional functionality such as saving a record or closing a form. Using Application Parts Blank Forms, you can also easily add forms that do more than just display data from a record source. Unbound forms can be created to display messages to a user, or to provide dialog boxes that prompt the user for an action. These unbound forms can be referenced through code using Visual Basic for Applications (VBA) to help provide a more functional database.

Use Application Parts to Create Blank Forms

USE the database that is open from the previous exercise.

1. On the Create tab, in the Templates group, click the **Application Parts** button and in the Blank Forms category, hover your mouse over the 1 Right button. A Tooltip appears informing you of the form's layout.

2. Click the **1 Right** button and a new form object named SingleOneColumnRightLabels appears in the Navigation Pane in the Unrelated Objects category, as shown in Figure 10-16.

Figure 10-16

New Blank Form object in Navigation pane

3. Open the **SingleOneColumnRightLabels** form. The form displays in Form View, as shown in Figure 10-17.

Figure 10-17

Blank Form in Form View

4. Switch to Layout View and shift-click each label control placeholder titled **Field1**, **Field2**, **Field3**, and **Field4** to select them all. Press the **Delete** key on the keyboard to delete the label controls. Also delete the label control placeholder that contains the red asterisk, which could be used to denote an important field, like a key field.

5. Click the **Add Existing Fields** button in the Tools group. The Field List pane appears. If necessary, click the **Show all tables** link. Your screen should resemble Figure 10-18.

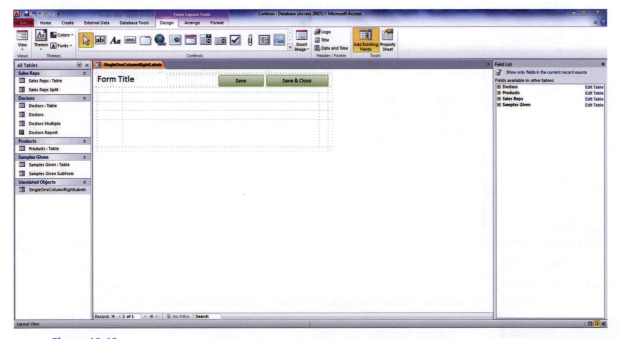

Figure 10-18

Blank Form in Layout View and Field List pane

6. In the Field List pane, expand the Doctors table.

7. In the Field List pane, click and drag each **Last Name**, **First Name**, **Specialty**, and **Hospital** field to the form and to the right placeholder of the original locations of the Field1, Field2, Field3, and Field4 label controls that you just deleted. You screen should resemble Figure 10-19.

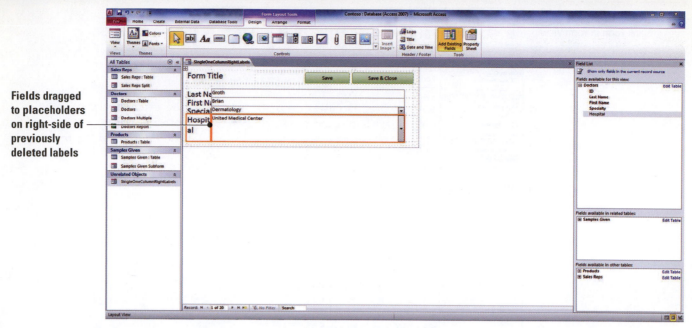

Fields dragged to placeholders on right-side of previously deleted labels

Figure 10-19

Form with fields from Field List pane

8. Resize the label and field controls that you just added until your screen resembles Figure 10-20.

Figure 10-20

Form with resized label and field control

9. Click the **Form Title** label, and delete Form Title. Key **Doctors**.

10. Switch to Form View and cycle through the records. Click the **Save & Close** button on the form to close the form.

11. Rename the form **Doctors Blank Form**.

12. **LEAVE** the database open.

PAUSE. LEAVE the database open to use in the next exercise.

CERTIFICATION
READY   1.3.1

How do you use Application Parts to create Blank Forms?

CREATING A NAVIGATION FORM

The ability to create **Navigation forms** is a new feature in Access 2010. A Navigation form includes a set of navigation tabs that you can click to display forms and reports. In this exercise you create a Navigation form.

As you learned in Lesson 2, you can create databases based on templates. When a database is created using a web database template, a navigation form is used as the main interface within the database since the Navigation pane cannot be viewed from within a web browser. However, Navigation forms can also be used from within the Access application window to simplify your interaction with database objects. For example, you can easily click a tab on a Navigation form to view a form to add, view, or edit data. Similarly, you can simply click a button on the Navigation form to work with reports. Navigation forms are created by clicking the Navigation button in the Forms group on the Create tab. There are six Navigation form layouts to choose from. Each layout includes a specific arrangement of tabs that can then be modified in Layout or Design View to access forms and reports. In Layout View, form and report objects can be clicked and dragged from the Navigation pane to tabs to quickly add functionality to the Navigation form. You can also type a form or report's name as the tab's label and Access will automatically bind the associated form or report to that label. You can also work with Navigation forms using Design View to have the most control over design options, but you lose the ability to quickly add form and report objects just by clicking and dragging them to the tabs, or modifying the labels.

NEW to Office 2010

Take Note   You can also add fields from multiple tables using the Field List pane to your Navigation form in both Design and Layout Views to allow for even greater customization.

Create a Navigation Form

USE the database that is open from the previous exercise.

1. On the Create tab, in the Forms group, click the **Navigation** button to display a menu that contains six form layouts.
2. Click the **Horizontal Tabs** button and a new Navigation form appears in Layout View, as shown in Figure 10-21.

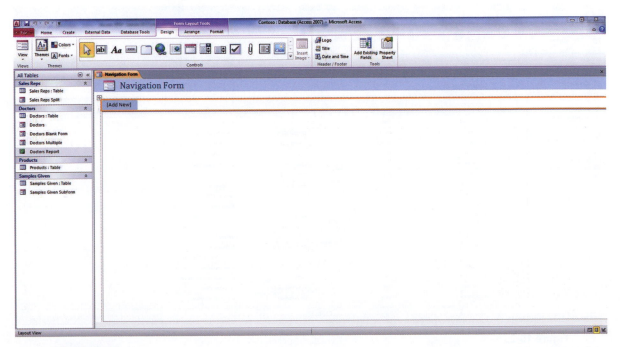

Figure 10-21

Navigation form in Layout View

3. Click and drag the **Doctors** form object from the Navigation pane to the [Add New] tab near the top of the form. The form tab has been renamed Doctors and all the Doctors form's controls appear. A new [Add New] tab appears next to the Doctors tab. Your screen should resemble Figure 10-22.

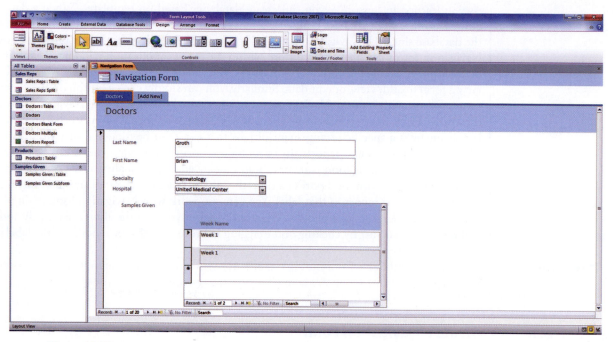

Figure 10-22

Navigation form displaying Doctors form

4. Click and drag the **Doctors** report object from the Navigation pane to the [Add New] tab near the top of the form. The form tab has been renamed **Doctors Report** and all the Doctors report controls appear. A new [Add New] tab appears next to the Doctors tab. Your screen should resemble Figure 10-23.

Figure 10-23

Navigation form displaying Doctors report

5. Double-click the **Doctors** tab and key **Doctors Form** to rename the tab.
6. Switch to Form View and use the form's tabs to switch between the form and report.
7. Click the **File** tab and click **Save**.
8. In the Save As dialog box, key **Doctors Navigation Form** and click **OK**.
9. Click the **Close** button to close the Doctors Navigation Form.

STOP. CLOSE the database.

<table>
<tr><td>CERTIFICATION READY 3.1.4</td></tr>
<tr><td>How do you create Navigation forms?</td></tr>
</table>

SKILL SUMMARY

In This Lesson You Learned How To:	Exam Objective	Objective Number
Create Advanced Forms		
Use Application Parts to Create Blank Forms	Use Blank forms.	1.3.1
Create a Navigation Form	Create Navigation forms.	3.1.4

Knowledge Assessment

Fill in the Blank

Complete the following sentences by writing the correct word or words in the blanks provided.

1. The Forms group, located on the _____ tab, contains commands for creating all types of forms.
2. When Access creates a Multiple Items form, it is displayed in _____ View.
3. Creating a(n) _____ form allows you to see two views of your data at the same time.
4. To set properties for a split form, first switch to _____ View.
5. For best results, all _____ should be established before creating a subform.
6. When creating a subform, the primary form is called the _____ form.
7. To create a Navigation form, first select the Navigation button in the _____ group.
8. A(n) _____ form resembles a datasheet, but it gives you more customization options.
9. The views in a split form are connected to the same data _____ and are completely synchronized with each other.
10. Subforms are especially effective when you want to show data from tables or queries that have a(n) _____ relationship.

Multiple Choice

Select the best response for the following statements or questions.

1. Which tool creates a customizable form that displays multiple records?
   a. PivotTable
   b. Subform
   c. Split Form
   d. Multiple Items

2. When you use the Multiple Items tool, the form that Access creates resembles a
   a. Control
   b. Datasheet
   c. Filter
   d. Query

3. A split form shows your data in which views?
   a. Form View and Datasheet View
   b. Layout View and Design View
   c. Form View and Design View
   d. Layout View and Datasheet View

4. Which split form property allows you to define whether the datasheet appears above, below, to the left, or to the right of the form?
   a. Split Form Orientation
   b. Split Form Datasheet
   c. Split Form Splitter Bar
   d. Split Form Size

5. Which type of form allows you to view data from more than one table or query on the same form?
   a. Multi-item form
   b. Split form
   c. Subform
   d. Navigation form

6. Which tool would you use to create a subform?
   a. Form Design
   b. Blank Form
   c. Form
   d. Form Wizard

7. A form/subform combination is sometimes referred to as a
   a. Hierarchical form
   b. Master/detail form
   c. Parent/child form
   d. All of the above

8. Which type of form already has a predefined layout and can automatically contain command buttons?
   a. Multi-item form
   b. Split form
   c. Subform
   d. Application Parts Blank form

9. What type of form can be added to a database to simplify your interaction with objects preventing the need to use the Navigation pane?
   a. Subform
   b. Blank form
   c. Split form
   d. Navigation form

10. Unbound forms can be easily created that display messages to users using
   a. Application Parts Blank forms
   b. Navigation forms
   c. Split forms
   d. None of the above

Competency Assessment

Project 10-1: Create a Multi-Item Form

In your job as a travel agent at Margie's Travel, you want to create a form that displays multiple database records but that is more customizable than a datasheet. You use the Multiple Items tool to create the form.

GET READY. LAUNCH Access if it is not already running.

@ The *Margie's Events* file for this lesson is available on the book companion website or in WileyPLUS.

1. **OPEN** the *Margie's Events* database from the data files for this lesson.
2. **SAVE** the database as *Margie's Events XXX* (where *XXX* is your initials).
3. In the Navigation pane, double-click the **Events** table to open it.
4. On the Create tab, in the Forms group, click the **More Forms** button and then click the **Multiple Items** button on the menu that appears.
5. Scroll down and to the right to view the multiple records on the form.
6. Click the **File** tab and click **Save**.
7. In the Save As dialog box, key **Events Multiple** and click **OK**.
8. Click the **Close** button to close the Events Multiple form.
9. Click the **Close** button to close the Events table.
10. **CLOSE** the database.

LEAVE Access open for the next project.

Project 10-2: Create a Split Form

Your brother, who owns Wingtip Toys, wants to be able to see two views of his inventory data at the same time—in Form View and in Datasheet View. He asks you to help him create a split form and to modify it so that the datasheet is on top.

GET READY. LAUNCH Access if it is not already running.

@ The *Toy Stock* file for this lesson is available on the book companion website or in WileyPLUS.

1. **OPEN** *Toy Stock* from the data files for this lesson.
2. **SAVE** the database as *Toy Stock XXX* (where *XXX* is your initials).
3. In the Navigation pane, double-click the **Inventory** table to open it.
4. On the Create tab, in the Forms group, click the **More Forms** button and then click the **Split Form** button on the menu that appears to create the form and display it in Form View and Datasheet View at the same time.
5. On the Home tab, in the Views group, click the **View** button and click **Design View**.
6. Press **F4** to display the Property Sheet.
7. Click **Form** in the drop-down list at the top and click the **Format** tab, if necessary.
8. Scroll down to the Split Form Orientation property, click the **down arrow**, and click **Datasheet on Top**.
9. Click the **Close** button to close the Property Sheet.
10. On the Home tab, in the Views group, click the **View** button and click **Layout View** to display the split form with the datasheet on top.
11. Click the **File** tab and click **Save**.
12. In the Save As dialog box, key **Inventory Split** and click **OK**.
13. Click the **Close** button to close the Inventory Split form.
14. Click the **Close** button to close the Inventory table.
15. **CLOSE** the database.

LEAVE Access open for the next project.

Proficiency Assessment

Project 10-3: Create Forms for the Wine Club Database

Information about each selection for the Coho Vineyard monthly wine club is stored in an Access database. As purchasing manager, you use the database frequently and need to have several types of forms available to work with the data. Create a multi-item form and a split form.

GET READY. LAUNCH Access if it is not already running.

@ The *Wines* file for this lesson is available on the book companion website or in WileyPLUS.

1. **OPEN** *Wines* from the data files for this lesson.
2. **SAVE** the database as *Wines XXX* (where *XXX* is your initials).
3. Create a multi-item form for the red wine table.
4. Name the form **Red Wines Multi** and close it.
5. Create a multi-item form for the white wine table.
6. Name the form **White Wines Multi** and close it.
7. Create a split form for the red wine table.
8. Name the form **Red Wines Split** and close it.
9. Create a split form for the white wine table.
10. Name the form **White Wines Split** and close it.
11. **LEAVE** the database open for the next project.

LEAVE Access open for the next project.

Project 10-4: Create a Subform

As purchasing manager for Coho Winery, it would be helpful to view data about wines by distributor. Create a subform that shows the red wines in the monthly club by distributor.

GET READY. LAUNCH Access if it is not already running.

1. On the Create tab, in the Forms group, click **Form Wizard**.
2. In the first screen on the Form Wizard, select **Table: Red Wines** in the Tables/Queries box.
3. Move the *Bottled, Label,* and *Type* fields to the Selected Fields box.
4. Select **Table: Distributors** in the Tables/Queries box.
5. Move the *Company* field to the Selected Fields box.
6. In the second screen of the Form Wizard, choose to view your data by distributors.
7. In the third screen of the Form Wizard, choose to view your data in tabular layout.
8. In the final screen of the Form Wizard, accept the default form names and click **Finish**.
9. Navigate to the third record to see which red wines in your monthly club are distributed by Northwind Traders.
10. Close the form.
11. **CLOSE** the database.

LEAVE Access open for the next project.

Mastery Assessment

Project 10-5: Modify a Split Form

As the manager at Southridge Video, you created a split form to work with the used game information in the Access database. However, when you open the form, it appears that someone has made changes because the datasheet is on the right and the splitter bar is not visible. Change the form properties back to the way you want them.

GET READY. LAUNCH Access if it is not already running.

@ The *Used Games* file for this lesson is available on the book companion website or in WileyPLUS.

1. **OPEN** *Used Games* from the data files for this lesson.
2. **SAVE** the database as *Used Games XXX* (where *XXX* is your initials).
3. Open the split form Games.
4. Switch to Design View and open the form properties.
5. Change the property to make the datasheet appear on the top.
6. Change the property to make the splitter bar visible, thus allowing the form and datasheet to be resized.
7. Change the form property so the form will open with the splitter bar in the same position in which you last left it.
8. Change the property to allow edits to be made on the datasheet.
9. Change the property to print only the datasheet portion of the form.
10. Switch to Layout View.
11. Close the form and save the changes to the design when prompted.
12. **CLOSE** the database.

LEAVE Access open for the next project.

Project 10-6: Create a Navigation Form

Your son plays on a recreational league basketball team, and you have volunteered to manage the team's database of games, players, and statistics by tracking and updating data. In order to be able to quickly and efficiently update data, you decide to create a Navigation form.

GET READY. LAUNCH Access if it is not already running.

@ The *Stats* file for this lesson is available on the book companion website or in WileyPLUS.

1. **OPEN** *Stats* from the data files for this lesson.
2. **SAVE** the database as *Stats XXX* (where *XXX* is your initials).
3. Use the Stats: Table and the skills you have learned in this lesson to create a Navigation form using the Vertical Tabs, Left layout.
4. Save the form as Games, Player, Stats Navigation Form and close it.
5. **CLOSE** the database.

CLOSE Access.

INTERNET READY

Get help learning Access or other Microsoft Office applications with self-paced training courses and more. Using your browser, go to office.microsoft.com and conduct a search for Resources for learning Access 2010. Explore the page that contains several helpful links to Access 2010 resources arranged in categories for different types of Access users. When finished, click the Access training on Office.com link in the Resources for all Access 2010 users category. On the Training courses page, shown in Figure 10-24, you can find links to several articles to help you improve your skills, as well as training courses to help you practice your skills. Online resources don't have to be dull. These training courses also contain audio and slideshows to help you learn visually.

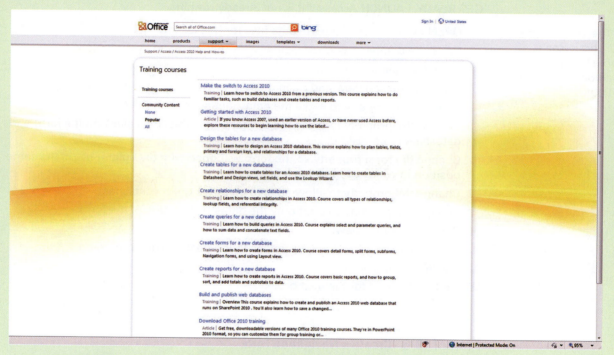

Figure 10-24

Training courses page

Circling Back 2

Woodgrove Real Estate is growing and adding more listings. Your office has added another real estate agent and has begun listing commercial properties as well as residential ones. The database you created has been a great way to keep track of all the listings and other relevant information. As you learn more about Access, you begin using it for a wider variety of tasks.

Project 1: Create and Format a Report

You want to create a report to display data about each agent's listings. Use the Report Wizard and then switch to Design View to make changes to the format and add a control.

GET READY. LAUNCH Access if it is not already running.

 The *Real Estate* file for this lesson is available on the book companion website or in WileyPLUS.

1. **OPEN** the *Real Estate* database from the data files for this lesson.

2. **SAVE** the database as *Real Estate XXX* (where *XXX* is your initials).

3. On the Create tab, in the Reports group, click the **Report Wizard** button.

4. In the Tables/Queries menu, choose **Table: Listings**.

5. Click the **>>** button to move all the fields into the Selected Fields list.

6. Click the **ID** field to select it and click the **<** button to move it back to the Available Fields list.

7. Click the **Next >** button.

8. Click the **Listing Agent** field to select it and click the **>** button to add it as a grouping level.

9. Click the **Next >** button.

10. Select **Price** from the fields menu to sort in ascending order and click the **Next >** button.

11. In the Layout section, click the **Outline** button. In the Orientation section, click the **Landscape** button. Click **Next**.

12. Key **Listings Report** as the title of the report.

13. Click **Finish** to display the Listings Report.

14. On the Print Preview tab, in the Close Preview group, click the **Close** button on Print Preview to display the report in Design View.

15. In the Listing Agent Header section, click and drag the right border of the *Listing Agent* field to make it smaller.

16. Continue clicking and dragging the borders of the remaining report fields to size them so your report looks similar to the report displayed in Report View, as shown in Figure 1.

Figure 1

Listings report

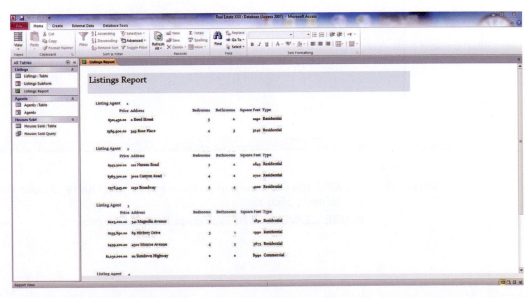

17. Click the **Close** button on the Listings Report to close the report and save the changes when prompted.

PAUSE. LEAVE the database open to use in the next project.

Project 2: Create and Modify Queries

You want to query the database to find all the house sales that closed in June. Create a query using the Query Wizard and then add criteria to get the information you need.

USE the database that is open from the previous project.

1. On the Create tab, in the Other group, click the **Query Wizard** button to display the New Query dialog box.

2. Click **Simple Query Wizard** and then click **OK** to display the Simple Query Wizard.

3. In the Tables/Queries drop-down list, click **Table: Houses Sold**.

4. Under Available Fields, double-click **Listing Agent**, **Address**, **Selling Price**, and **Closing Date** to move them to the Selected Fields box.

5. Click the **Next >** button to display the next screen. Detail query should be selected.

6. Click the **Next >** button to display the final screen.

7. Click the **Finish** button to display the query.

8. On the Home tab, in the Views group, click the **View** button and click **Design View**.

9. In the Criteria row of the *Closing Date* field, key **Between #6/1/2011# And #6/30/2012#**.

10. On the Design tab, in the Results group, click the **View** button and click **Datasheet View** to display the query results of all records for houses that closed in June.

11. Right-click the **Closing Date** field header and choose **Sort Oldest to Newest** on the menu. Your query should look similar to Figure 2.

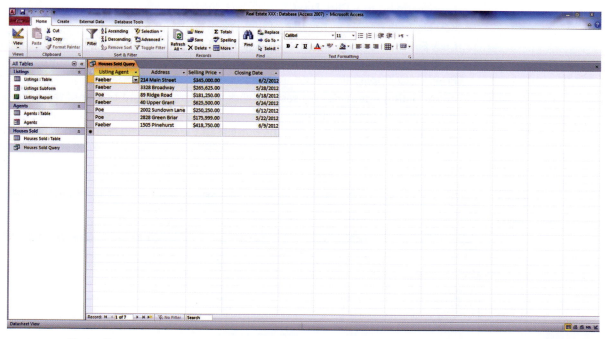

Figure 2

Query results

12. Click the **Close** button on the Houses Sold Query to close the query. When prompted to save, click **Yes**.

PAUSE. LEAVE the database open for the next project.

Project 3: Sum Table Data

You want to know the total value of the current listings. Open the table and add a Totals row to get this information.

USE the database that is open from the previous project.

1. Open the **Listings** table.
2. On the Home tab, in the Records group, click the **Totals** button. The Totals row appears below the asterisk (*) row.
3. Click the **down arrow** in the Price column of the Totals row. Select **Sum** from the menu. Your screen should look similar to Figure 3.

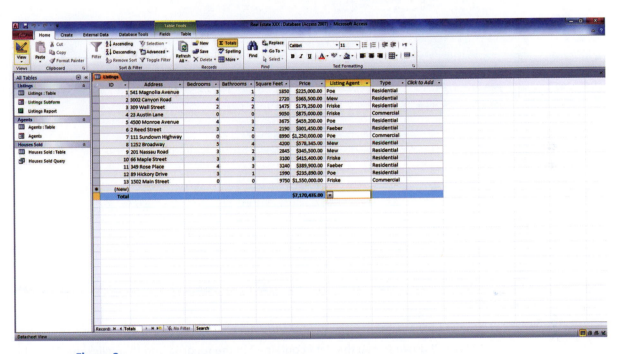

Figure 3

Totals row

4. On the Home tab, in the Records group, click the **Totals** button to hide the Totals row.
5. On the Home tab, in the Records group, click the **Totals** button again. The Totals row reappears.
6. Save and close the table.

PAUSE. LEAVE the database open for the next project.

Project 4: Create a Subform

You want to see the real estate agent's contact information along with the listings. Use the Form Wizard to create a subform that will show all the data in the same place.

USE the database that is open from the previous project.

1. On the Create tab, in the Forms group, click **Form Wizard**.
2. In the first screen on the Form Wizard, click the **Tables/Queries box down arrow** and click **Table: Agents**.
3. In the Available Fields box, double-click the **Last Name**, **First Name**, and **Mobile Phone** fields to move them to the Selected Fields box.
4. Click the **Tables/Queries box down arrow** and click **Table: Listings**.
5. In the Available Fields box, double-click the **Address**, **Square Feet**, and **Price** fields to move them to the Selected Fields box.
6. Click **Next >**.

7. In the How do you want to view your data? box, click **by Agents**. The Form with subform(s) radio button should be selected.

8. Click **Next >**.

9. Click the **Tabular** radio button to select that as the layout for your subform.

10. Click **Next >**.

11. Click the **Finish** button to create the Agents form with the Listings subform. Your form should look similar to Figure 4.

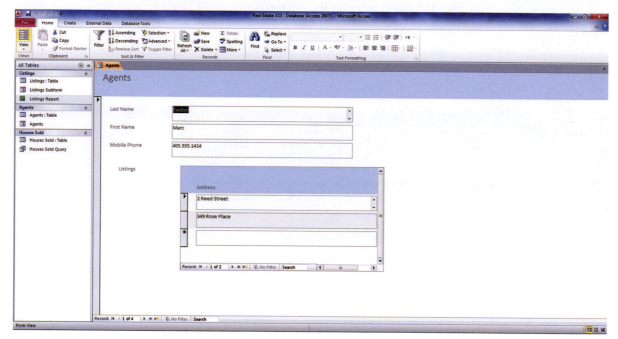

Figure 4

Subform

12. In the Navigation pane, double-click the **Listings subform** to open it.

13. Scroll down to see the data contained in the records and then click the **Close** button on the Listings subform to close the subform.

14. Click the **Close** button on the Agents table to close it.

STOP. CLOSE the database.

Advanced Reports 11

LESSON SKILL MATRIX

Skill	Exam Objective	Objective Number
Defining Groups	Add calculated controls.	5.2.2
Creating Aggregate Fields	Add calculated controls.	5.2.2
Creating the Print Layout	Change page size. Change page orientation.	5.5.1 5.5.2
Using the Label Wizard		

KEY TERMS

- **aggregate fields**
- **group**
- **group footer**
- **group header**
- **grouping fields**
- **grouping intervals**
- **grouping levels**
- **Label Wizard**
- **Print Preview**

Consolidated Messenger is a New York City—based company that provides quick and reliable pickup and delivery services to area businesses. The company provides courier service by foot, bike, or truck. The company has a sales force that negotiates contracts with some of its larger corporate clients. As sales manager, you have created a database with tables and reports to keep track of this data. In this lesson, you generate reports that group data, create aggregate fields to total data in reports, use Print Preview to adjust reports before printing, and use the Label Wizard to create labels for customer mailings.

DEFINING GROUPS

The Bottom Line

A **group** is a collection of records separated visually with any introductory or summary information displayed with it. Reports can be grouped on fields or expressions. A **grouping field** is a field by which data is grouped. **Grouping levels** are the nested arrangement of the groups in a report. Access creates indented levels to show the groups from highest to lowest priority. You can change a group's level in the Report Wizard by using the priority up and down arrows. Access allows you to specify as many as 10 groups in a report. Groups can be nested so that that you can easily see the group structure.

When data is arranged in groups, it is often easier to comprehend and it becomes more meaningful. For example, if you want to see the sales performance for each region, it is easier to review this data if each region's sales are grouped together. You can go a step further and specify another group level, such as salesperson. This allows you to group a report by region and by salesperson within each region.

You can specify grouping intervals by using the Grouping Options button. **Grouping intervals** establish the way that records are grouped together. They can be very useful in arranging a large number of records in a group. You can group on the first character of a text field so that all of the records are visually separated alphabetically. You can specify a group interval of a day, week, month, or quarter on a date field. This is useful if you want to view the sales for each week in a report. You can also specify a custom interval.

Using the Report Wizard

You can easily specify groups with the Report Wizard when creating a new report. This is an easy and fast way to create a report with groups. The Report Wizard lets you specify how you would like data to be grouped as you create the report. You can also add grouping to an existing report using the Group, Sort, and Total pane. Grouping options let you further specify how you want the groups to appear in your report. In this exercise, you use the Report Wizard to specify grouping levels and create a report.

STEP BY STEP   **Use the Report Wizard**

The *Messenger* file for this lesson is available on the book companion website or in WileyPLUS.

WileyPLUS Extra! features an online tutorial of this task.

GET READY. Before you begin these steps, be sure to turn on and/or log on to your computer and start Access.

1. **OPEN** *Messenger* from the data files for this lesson.
2. **SAVE** the database as *Messenger XXX* (where *XXX* is your initials).
3. Open the **Corporate Sales** table.
4. On the Create tab, in the Reports group, click the **Report Wizard** button. The first Report Wizard dialog box appears.
5. Select the **Region (Borough)** field and click the **>** button to move the field to the Selected Fields list.

6. Using the same method, move the *Sales Person Last Name, Company Name,* and *Contract Amount* fields from the Available Fields list to the Selected Fields list, as shown in Figure 11-1.

Figure 11-1

Report Wizard, screen 1

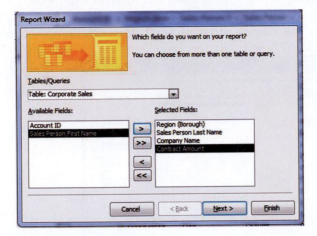

7. Click the **Next >** button. The second Report Wizard screen appears.

8. Select the **Region (Borough)** field and click the **>** button to move it to the grouping levels box.

9. Select the **Contract Amount** field and click the **>** button to move it to the grouping levels box.

10. Select the **Sales Person Last Name** field and click the **>** button to move it to the grouping levels box.

11. Notice that the *Sales Person Last Name* field is the active field in bold type. Click the **Priority up arrow** to move the *Sales Person Last Name* field to the second level of grouping. Your screen should look similar to Figure 11-2.

Figure 11-2

Report Wizard, screen 2

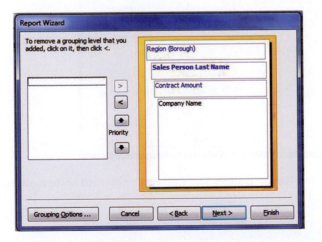

12. Click the **Grouping Options** button at the bottom of the dialog box. The Grouping Intervals dialog box appears, as shown in Figure 11-3.

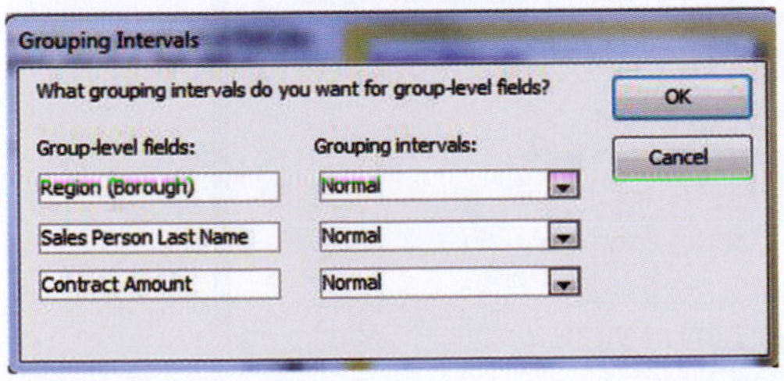

Figure 11-3

Grouping Intervals dialog box

13. Click the **down arrow** on the first Grouping intervals menu to see the choices available. Select **Normal** from the menu and click **OK**.

14. Click the **Next >** button. The third Report Wizard screen appears. You can sort in either ascending or descending order, and by up to four fields.

15. Click the **down arrow** on the Sort menu and select **Company Name**, as shown in Figure 11-4. You will sort in ascending order by Company Name.

Figure 11-4

Report Wizard, screen 3

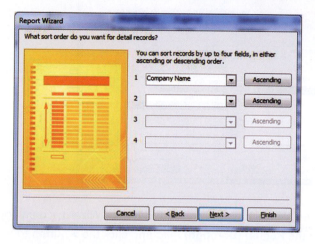

16. Click the **Next >** button. The fourth Report Wizard screen appears. You can choose from three different layouts for your report as well as two different orientations.

17. In the Layout section, click the **Block** radio button, as shown in Figure 11-5. Keep the default orientation as Portrait and keep the selection so all fields fit on one page.

Figure 11-5

Report Wizard, screen 4

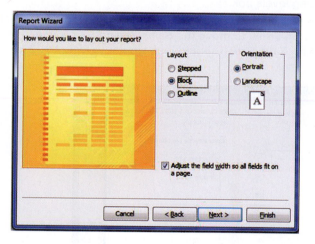

18. Click the **Next >** button. The fifth Report Wizard screen appears, as shown in Figure 11-6.

Figure 11-6

Report Wizard, screen 5

19. Click the **Finish** button to accept the settings. The Report Wizard creates the report, shown in Figure 11-7, with the groups you specified.

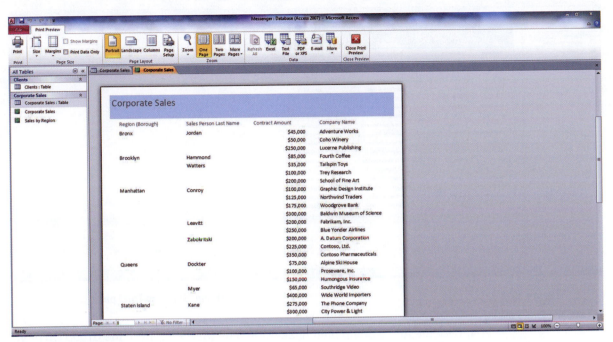

Figure 11-7

Corporate Sales report

20. Close the report and close the table.

PAUSE. LEAVE the database open to use in the next exercise.

Adding Group Headers and Footers

You can add group headers and footers to a report using the Group, Sort, and Total pane. When you select a field from the Group On menu, the group header is added to the report. In this exercise, you add group headers using the Group, Sort, and Total pane.

As you may remember from Lesson 6, a report is organized into sections. You can view sections of a report in Design View. The **group header** is the section of a report where the name of a grouped field is displayed and printed. Group headers take on the name of the group, so instead of seeing a group header named *Group Header* you will see *[Fieldname] Header*.

A **group footer** is the section of the report where the data in the group is summarized. It is optional. If you do not have any summary data, such as a total, you don't need a group footer.

STEP BY STEP   **Use the Group, Sort, and Total Pane**

USE the database open from the previous exercise.

1. Open the **Sales by Region** report. Notice that the report is not arranged by groups.
2. Switch to Layout View and close the Field List pane if it opens.
3. On the Design tab, in the Grouping & Totals group, click the **Group & Sort** button. The Group, Sort, and Total pane appears at the bottom of the screen, as shown in Figure 11-8.

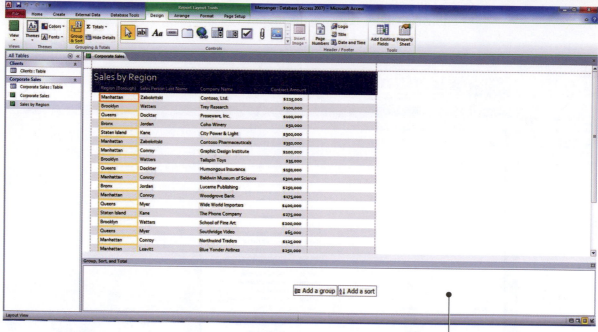

Figure 11-8

Group, Sort, and Total Pane

Group, Sort, and Total pane

4. Click the **Add a group** button. Select **Region (Borough)** from the Group On menu, as shown in Figure 11-9. The report is now grouped on the **Region (Borough)** field.

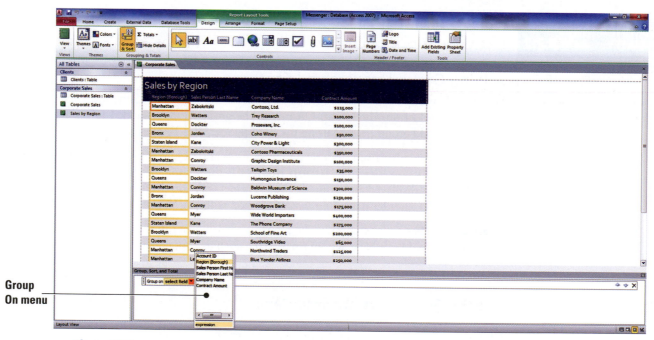

Group On menu

Figure 11-9

Group On menu

5. Click the **Add a group** button on the Group, Sort, and Total pane. Select **Sales Person Last Name** from the Group On menu. The report is now also grouped on the *Sales Person Last Name* field.

6. Switch to Design View. Your screen should look similar to Figure 11-10. Notice that there is a Region (Borough) Header for that group and a Sales Person Last Name header for that group. The *Company Name* and *Contract Amount* fields are arranged in the Detail section.

Another Way

You can also right-click a field header in Layout View and select Group on Field name from the shortcut menu to define a group header.

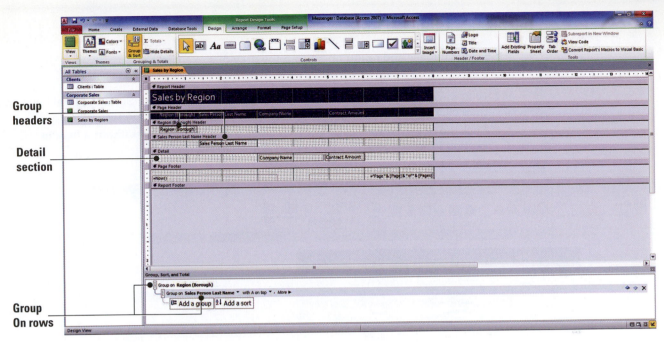

Group headers

Detail section

Group On rows

Figure 11-10

Group headers in Design View

7. Save the report.

PAUSE. LEAVE the database open to use in the next exercise.

Changing Grouping Options

After grouping data, Access gives you options for displaying grouped data. To display the grouping options in the Group, Sort, and Total pane, click More on the group level that you want to change. If you want to hide the grouping options, click Less. In this exercise, you use the Group, Sort, and Total Pane to change group options.

Grouping options include:

- **Sort order:** Choose ascending or descending
- **Group interval:** Change the way records are grouped together
- **Totals:** Add totals to fields
- **Title:** Change the label of a column heading or summary field
- **With/without header:** Add or remove the header section
- **With/without footer:** Add or remove footer section
- **Keep group together:** Decide how or if you want to keep grouped data together on the same page
- **Do not keep group together on one page:** Groups can be broken up by page breaks
- **Keep whole group together on one page:** Minimizes the number of page breaks in a group
- **Keep header and first record together on one page:** Makes sure a group header is not printed by itself at the bottom of a page

You can also click the Move up and Move down arrows at the end of the Group On row to change the priority of grouping levels. To delete a grouping level, click the Delete button at the end of its Group On row and Access will move the data to the Detail section of the report. However, if other controls are in the header, Access will warn you that these could be deleted.

The Hide Details command is a toggle button that hides data in the Details section of the report. Click it again to display the data.

STEP BY STEP   **Change Grouping Options**

USE the database and report open from the previous exercise.

1. Switch to Layout View.

2. Click the **Group On Sales Person Last Name** row in the Group, Sort, and Total Pane and then click the **More** button to view the available grouping options.

3. Click the **down arrow** beside *with a header section* and select **without a header section** from the drop-down menu, as shown in Figure 11-11.

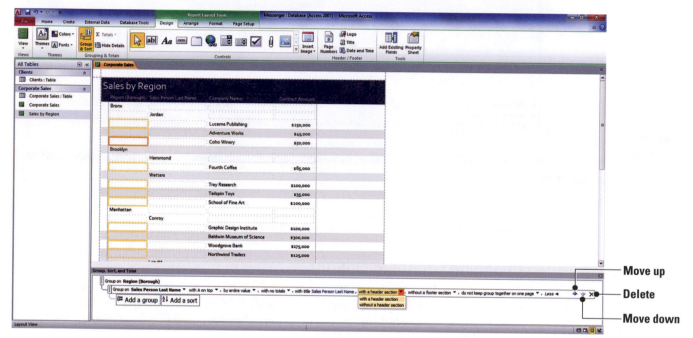

Figure 11-11

Group On *Sales Person Last Name* row

4. Switch to Design View. Note that the Sales Person Last Name Header has been deleted.

5. Switch to Layout View.

6. Click the **down arrow** beside the *without a header section* (if the *without a header section* option doesn't appear, click the **More** button) and select **with a header section** from the drop-down menu.

7. Click the **Move up arrow** at the end of the Group On Sales Person Last Name row. Notice that the Sales Person Last Name group is now the top level group in the report.

8. Click the **Add a group** button and select **Company Name** from the menu. A new group level is added to the report.

9. On the Design tab, in the Grouping & Totals group, click the **Hide Details** button. The data in the *Contract Amount* field is hidden.

10. On the Design tab, in the Grouping & Totals group, click the **Hide Details** button. The data in the *Contract Amount* field is displayed.

11. Click the **More** button in the Group, Sort, and Total pane.

12. Click the *with A on top* **down arrow** on the Group On Company Name row in the Group, Sort, and Total Pane and select **with Z on top** from the drop-down menu. The sort order is changed from ascending to descending order.

13. Click the *with Z on top* **down arrow** and select **with A on top**.

14. Click the **Delete** button on the right side of the Group On Company Name row in the Group, Sort, and Total pane. The row is deleted, as is the Company Name header section.

15. Switch to Report View to see the report. Your screen should resemble Figure 11-12.

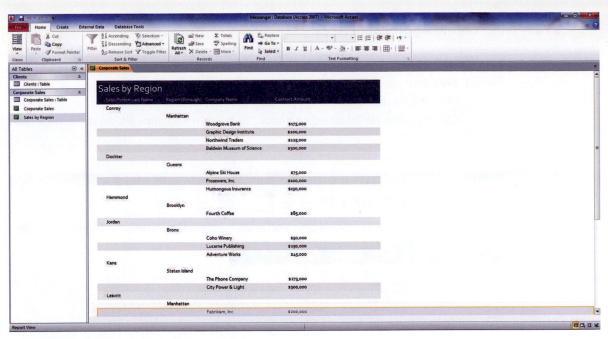

Figure 11-12

Sales by Region report

16. Save the report.

PAUSE. LEAVE the database open to use in the next exercise.

CREATING AGGREGATE FIELDS

The Bottom Line

Report data often contains numbers, such as sales figures, that need to be totaled. A report that lists sales for each month in a quarter but does not total all the sales for the quarter is incomplete. **Aggregate fields** use functions to provide summary information of such data. You can create an aggregate field by using aggregate functions to calculate data in a field. The aggregate functions you can use are Sum, Average, Count Records, Count Values, Max, Min, Standard Deviation, or Variance.

Access 2010 provides a Totals command that lets you create an aggregate field that provides not only grand totals, but totals for groups in a report as well. You can also use the Group, Sort, and Total pane to add aggregate functions to fields.

The Totals command is located on the Format tab, in the Grouping & Totals group, but you can also access it on the shortcut menu. In Layout View, just right-click the field you want to total and select Totals from the shortcut menu. The Totals command adds a calculated control in the report footer where it displays the grand total. If you don't already have group footers in your report, the Totals command adds group footers and calculated controls to calculate the totals for each group.

Ⓧ Ref   For more information about aggregate functions, see Lesson 9.

Creating Aggregate Fields

You have a few more options when using the Group, Sort, and Total pane to create an aggregate field in a report. The Totals menu gives you options for choosing the field and type of function as well as options on how you want to display totals. You can display a grand total or a group total as a percentage of the grand total. You can also choose to show the totals in the group header or footer. In this exercise, you use the Group, Sort, and Total pane to create aggregate fields.

Create Aggregate Fields

USE the database and report open from the previous exercise.

1. Switch to Layout View.
2. Click the **Group On Sales Person Last Name** row and click **More**.
3. Click the **With No Totals down arrow**. The Totals menu appears, as shown in Figure 11-13.

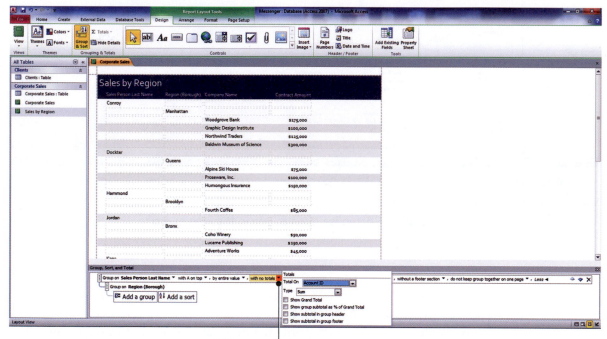

With no totals down arrow

Figure 11-13

Totals menu

4. Click the **Total On menu down arrow** and select **Contract Amount**.
5. Click the **Type menu down arrow** and select **Sum** if it isn't selected already.
6. Click the **Show Grand Total** box. The menu disappears and the grand total appears in the Contract Amount column at the bottom of the report.
7. Click the **Group On Sales Person Last Name** row again and click **More**, then click the *with Contract Amount totaled* **down arrow**.
8. Click the **Total On menu down arrow** and select **Contract Amount**, then click the **Show subtotal in Group Footer** box. The settings are applied, and the subtotals are now shown in each group's footer.
9. Select the **Sales Person Last Name** field header on the report.
10. On the Design tab, in the Grouping & Totals group, click the **Totals** button and select **Count Records** from the menu.
11. Switch to Report View. The total number of records appears at the bottom of the report.
12. Save the report and close it.

PAUSE. LEAVE the database open to use in the next exercise.

Another Way
You can also right-click a field in Layout View and select Total from the shortcut menu to apply an aggregate function to a field.

CERTIFICATION READY 5.2.2

How do you total report records?

SOFTWARE ORIENTATION

Print Preview Tab

The Print Preview tab (Figure 11-14) has commands for viewing a report in a variety of ways and for adjusting its layout. You can display the Print Preview tab by choosing the Print Preview option on the File tab's Print menu. Use the Print Preview tab to view and adjust page layout before printing.

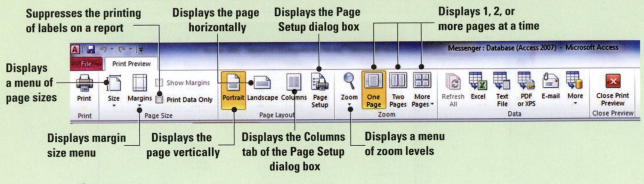

Figure 11-14

Print Preview tab

CREATING THE PRINT LAYOUT

The Bottom Line

Reports are often created so that they can be printed and displayed or shared with colleagues. You can print a report from any view: Report, Layout, Design, or Print Preview. **Print Preview** displays a report as it will look when printed. It is helpful to preview a report before printing it. This allows you to make adjustments to the layout before clicking the Print button so that you can make sure the report prints the way that you want. The settings that you choose will be saved with the report, so you won't have to select the same settings each time you print.

When you are confident your report will print correctly, you can click the Print button. The Print dialog box lets you select the printer, choose the number of copies you want to print, and specify which pages you want to print. If you don't need to preview a report, you can skip Print Preview and select Print or Quick Print on the File tab's Print menu. The Print command displays the Print dialog box, but the Quick Print command sends the report directly to the printer.

Take Note

You can even print a report from the Navigation pane. But before you print a report, you should check settings such as margins and page orientation to make sure the report will print correctly.

Using Print Preview to Create a Print Layout

The Print Preview tab has commands for printing, changing the page layout, and zooming in or out to view the pages. When you are finished previewing a report, you can click the Close Print Preview button to leave the view. In this exercise you use Print Preview to create the print layout of a report.

STEP BY STEP **Create the Print Layout**

USE the database open from the previous exercise.

1. Right-click the **Sales by Region** report in the Navigation pane and select **Rename** from the menu.

2. Key **Sales by Sales Person**.

3. Open the report in Design View and click the **Report title**. Select **Region** and key **Sales Person**, because the report no longer shows sales by region, but sales by salesperson.

4. On the Home tab, in the Views group, click the **View** button and select **Print Preview** from the menu. The report is displayed in Print Preview, as shown in Figure 11-15.

Figure 11-15

Report in Print Preview

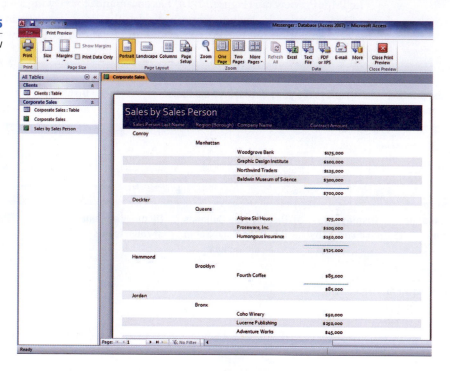

5. On the Print Preview tab, in the Zoom group, click the **Two Pages** button. Both pages of the report are displayed on the screen.

6. On the Print Preview tab, in the Page Layout group, click the **Landscape** button. The report is displayed in landscape orientation.

7. On the Print Preview tab, in the Page Layout group, click the **Portrait** button. The report is displayed in portrait orientation again. The margins need adjustment.

8. Click the **Margins** button and select **Narrow** from the menu.

9. On the Print Preview tab, in the Page Layout group, click the **Page Setup** button. The Page Setup dialog box appears, as shown in Figure 11-16. Notice it has many of the same options that are available in the Page Layout group, but more options and details to choose from.

Figure 11-16

Page Setup dialog box

10. Click the **Page** tab. Click the **Size box down arrow** and select **Legal** from the menu to see if all data will fit on one page.

11. Click **OK**.

12. On the Print Preview tab, in the Zoom group, click the **Zoom** button and select **50%** from the menu. Notice that all data does not fit on one page.

13. On the Print Preview tab, in the Page Layout group, click the **Size** button and select **Letter (8 1/2 × 11 in)** from the menu. Notice that the group at the bottom of the first page is split and continues on the second page.

14. Click the **Close** button on Print Preview.

15. Switch to Layout View.

16. On the Group, Sort, and Total pane, on the *Group On Sales Person Last Name* row, click the **More** button. Click the *Do Not Keep Group Together On One Page* **down arrow** and select **Keep whole group together on one page** from the menu.

17. Save the report design.

18. Right-click in a blank area of the report and select **Print Preview** from the shortcut menu, as shown in Figure 11-17. Notice that the group is no longer split across two pages.

Figure 11-17

Shortcut menu

CERTIFICATION READY 5.5.1

How do you change the page size of a report?

CERTIFICATION READY 5.5.2

How do you change the page orientation of a report?

19. Click the **Print** button. The Print dialog box appears. Click **OK** to print or click **Cancel** to close the dialog box.

20. Close Print Preview and close the report.

PAUSE. LEAVE the database open to use in the next exercise.

Take Note

Another Way
Right-click the report you want to preview in the Navigation pane and select Print Preview from the shortcut menu.

The Bottom Line

You can add the Print Preview and/or the Quick Print command to the Quick Access Toolbar by clicking the Customize Quick Access Toolbar down arrow at the end of the toolbar and selecting Print Preview or Quick Print from the menu.

USING THE LABEL WIZARD

You can create labels for mailing, or other purposes, using the data in your Access databases. The **Label Wizard** helps you create a label-sized report that you can use to print labels. The Label Wizard asks you a series of questions about the labels you want and then creates the labels based on your answers. You can choose from a wide variety of sizes, including sizes to fit label sheets that you purchase at the office supply store or custom-created labels.

Creating Labels Using the Label Wizard

You can create mailing labels or other types of labels from an Access table or query. Access allows you to choose the font name, font size, font weight, and text color for your labels. You can also choose to underline or italicize text in the label. The Sample box displays the choices you make. In this exercise, you use the label wizard to create labels.

You can select predefined label sizes that match popular manufacturer's label sheets. These are listed by Product Number in the first Label Wizard screen. If you don't know the manufacturer of your label sheets, you can choose a sheet with similar dimensions and with the correct number of labels across the sheet. If you don't see the size you need, you can customize the size and create a new label using the Customize button.

As you add fields to the Prototype label, remember to use the Spacebar to add a space between fields and press Enter to move to the next line. You can also key text directly in the Prototype label that you want to appear on each label.

You can sort the labels by one or more fields, such as zip code for bulk mailings. On the last Label Wizard screen, you can choose to See the labels as they will look when printed and they will be displayed in Print Preview. Choose Modify the label design to view the label report in Design View.

STEP BY STEP   **Use the Label Wizard**

USE the database open from the previous exercise.

1. Select the **Clients** table in the Navigation pane.

2. On the Create tab, in the Reports group, click the **Labels** button. The first Label Wizard screen appears, as shown in Figure 11-18.

Figure 11-18

Label Wizard, screen 1

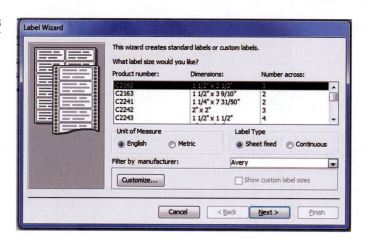

3. Scroll down in the Product number box and select **Avery USA 5160** and click the **Next >** button. The second Label Wizard screen appears, as shown in Figure 11-19.

Figure 11-19

Label Wizard, screen 2

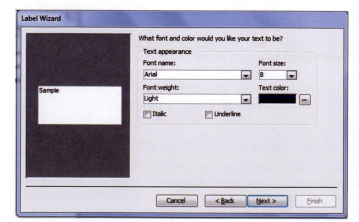

4. Click the **Font name drop-down arrow** and scroll down to select **Times New Roman**. Notice the preview sample displays the new font.

5. Click the **Font size** menu and select **9**.

6. Click the **Font weight** menu and select **Normal**.

7. In the *Text color* section, click the **Ellipses** button to display the Color menu. Notice the options available, then click **Cancel** to close it.

8. Click the **Next >** button. The third Label Wizard screen appears, as shown in Figure 11-20.

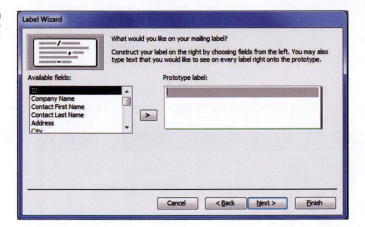

9. Select the **Company Name** field in the Available fields list and click the **>** button to place it on the Prototype label.

10. Press **Enter**.

11. Key **ATTN:** and press the **Spacebar**.

12. Select the **Contact First Name** field and click the **>** button.

13. Press the **Spacebar** to insert a blank space between fields.

14. Select the **Contact Last Name** field and click the **>** button.

15. Press **Enter**.

16. Select the **Address** field and click the **>** button. Press **Enter**.

17. Select the **City** field and click the **>** button. Key a **comma** and press the **Spacebar**.

18. Select the **State** field and click the **>** button. Press the **Spacebar**.

19. Select the **Zip** field and click the **>** button. Your screen should look similar to Figure 11-21.

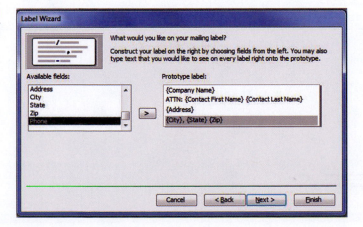

20. Click **Next >**. The fourth Label Wizard screen appears, as shown in Figure 11-22.

Figure 11-22

Label Wizard, screen 4

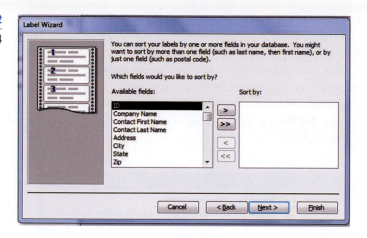

Figure 11-22

Label Wizard, screen 4

21. Select the **Zip** field and click the **>** button.

22. Click **Next >**. The fifth Label Wizard screen appears, as shown in Figure 11-23.

Figure 11-23

Label Wizard, screen 5

23. Click the **Modify the label design** radio button and click **Finish**. Your screen should look similar to Figure 11-24.

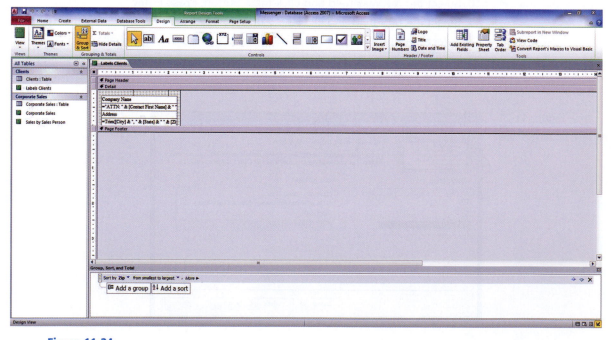

Figure 11-24

Label report

24. On the Home tab, in the Views group, click the **View** menu and select **Print Preview** from the menu. Your screen should look similar to Figure 11-25.

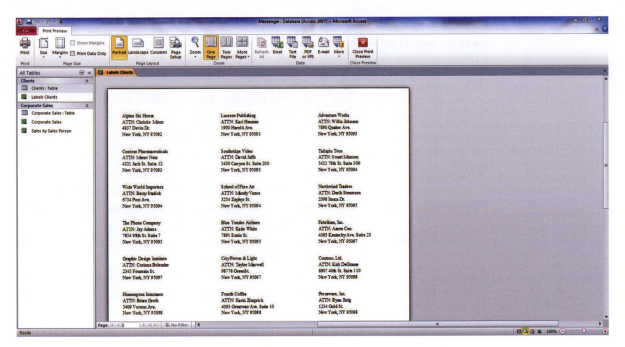

Figure 11-25

Report in Print Preview

25. Click the **Print** button. The Print dialog box appears. Click **OK** to print or click **Cancel** to close the dialog box.

26. Close Print Preview and close the report.

CLOSE the database.

 **Troubleshooting** If Access displays a message warning you that some of your data may not be displayed, this means the controls on the label are too wide for the allotted space. If this happens, try reducing the size of the controls in Design View so that they fit in the space available for a single label or try reducing the page margins using Page Setup.

Take Note As an alternative to printing labels, you can print addresses directly on envelopes. To do this, you will need to create a custom label instead of a predefined label and set the Label Type setting to Sheet Feed.

SKILL SUMMARY

In This Lesson You Learned How To:	Exam Objective	Objective Number
Define Groups	Add calculated controls.	**5.2.2**
Create Aggregate Fields	Add calculated controls.	**5.2.2**
Create the Print Layout	Change page size.	**5.5.1**
	Change page orientation.	**5.5.2**
Use the Label Wizard		

Knowledge Assessment

Matching

Match the term in Column 1 to its description in Column 2.

Column 1

1. group
2. group header
3. group footer
4. Hide Details command
5. grouping field
6. aggregate field
7. Print Preview
8. grouping levels
9. Label Wizard
10. Prototype label

Column 2

a. asks you questions about the labels and data you want to display and then creates labels based on your answers

b. field that contains an aggregate function to calculate data

c. a field by which data is grouped

d. the nested arrangement of the groups in a report

e. a collection of records separated visually with any introductory or summary information displayed with it

f. the section of a report where the name of a grouped field is displayed and printed

g. the sample in the Label Wizard where you create the label design

h. hides the data in the Details section of a report

i. the section of a report where the data in a group is summarized

j. displays a report as it will look when printed

True/False

Circle T if the statement is true or F if the statement is false.

T F **1.** Grouping intervals establish the way that records are grouped together.

T F **2.** You cannot group data in the Report Wizard.

T F **3.** Group headers take on the name of the group.

T F **4.** Group footers are optional in a report.

T F **5.** The arrows at the end of a Group On row determine sort order.

T F **6.** Average is an aggregate function.

T F **7.** The Totals command adds group footers and calculated controls for you.

T F **8.** You must preview a report before you can print.

T F **9.** You can modify labels in Design View.

T F **10.** Labels are small reports.

Competency Assessment

Project 11-1: Create Address Labels for Authors

You need to send out confidential contract information to the authors in the Business Books division. Create labels for the authors using the Author Contact Information table.

GET READY. LAUNCH Access if it is not already running.

@ The *Lucerne* file for this lesson is available on the book companion website or in WileyPLUS.

1. **OPEN** the *Lucerne* database.
2. **SAVE** the database as *Lucerne XXX* (where *XXX* is your initials).
3. Select the **Author Contact Information** table in the Navigation pane.
4. On the Create tab, in the Reports group, click the **Labels** button.
5. Select the **C2242** label in the *Product number* box and click **Next**.
6. Select **Arial** from the *Font name* menu and select **9** from the *Font size* menu.

7. Click the **Italic** button and click **Next**.

8. Key **CONFIDENTIAL** in all caps and press **Enter**.

9. Key **For Addressee Only** and press **Enter**.

10. Select the **Author First Name** field and click the **>** button. Press the **Spacebar**.

11. Select the **Author Last Name** field and click the **>** button. Press **Enter**.

12. Select the **Author Address** field and click the **>** button. Press **Enter**.

13. Select the **Author City** field and click the **>** button. Key a **comma** and press the **Spacebar**.

14. Select the **Author State** field and click the **>** button. Press the **Spacebar**.

15. Select the **Author Zip** field and click the **>** button.

16. Click **Finish**.

17. Close the report.

LEAVE the database open for the next project.

Project 11-2: Total and Preview the Book Sales Report

Finish the Book Sales report to show totals for Domestic and International Sales. You also need to make some adjustments in Print Preview before printing.

USE the database open from the previous project.

1. Open the **Book Sales** report.

2. In Layout View, select the **Domestic Sales** field header.

3. On the Design tab, in the Grouping & Totals group, click the **Totals** button and select **Sum** from the menu.

4. Select the **International Sales** field header.

5. On the Design tab, in the Grouping & Totals group, click the **Totals** button and select **Sum** from the menu.

6. Select the **Book Title** field header.

7. On the Design tab, in the Grouping & Totals group, click the **Totals** button and select **Count Records** from the menu.

8. On the Design tab, in the Views group, click the **View** menu and select **Print Preview** from the menu.

9. On the Print Preview tab, in the Page Size group, click the **Margins** button and select **Wide** from the menu.

10. On the Print Preview tab, in the Zoom group, click the **Zoom** button and select **Fit to Window**.

11. Save the report.

12. On the Print Preview tab, in the Print group, click the **Print** button. Click **OK**.

13. Close the report.

CLOSE the database.

Proficiency Assessment

Project 11-3: Create a Grouped Report with Aggregate Fields

Your supervisor asks you to create a report using the Monthly Sales by Store table that shows monthly sales by store.

GET READY. LAUNCH Access if it is not already running.

The *Fourth Coffee* file for this lesson is available on the book companion website or in WileyPLUS.

1. **OPEN** *Fourth Coffee* from the data files for this lesson.

2. **SAVE** the database as *Fourth Coffee XXX* (where *XXX* is your initials).

3. Select the **Monthly Sales by Store** table.

4. Use the Report Wizard to create a report that includes the *Mon, Store, and Sales* fields.

5. Group **by Store** and create a **Stepped** layout.

6. Close Print Preview and switch to Layout View to **decrease the width** of the Mon and Sales columns.

7. Click the **Group & Sort** button to open the Group, Sort, and Total pane.

8. Click the **Add a Sort** button and select **Sales** from the menu. Sort from smallest to largest.

9. Select the **Sales** column.

10. Click the **Totals** button and select **Sum** from the menu.

11. Save the report.

LEAVE the report open for use in the next project.

Project 11-4: Preview and Print the Monthly Sales Report

You need to print the Monthly Sales by Store report. View the report in Print Preview to make sure the report is centered on the page before printing.

USE the *Fourth Coffee XXX* database that you saved in a previous exercise.

1. Switch to Print Preview.

2. Click the **Zoom** button and select **Fit to Window**.

3. Click the **Margins** button and select **Wide** from the menu.

4. Click the **Landscape** button.

5. Click the **Page Setup** button.

6. Click the **Print Options** tab. In the Margins section, key **1** in the Top box and key **1** in the Bottom box.

7. Key **1.5** in the left box and key **1.5** in the right box.

8. Click **OK**.

9. Click the **Print** button and click **OK** to print the report or click **Cancel** to close the dialog box.

10. Save the report.

11. Click the **Close** button on Print Preview.

12. Close the report.

CLOSE the database.

Mastery Assessment

Project 11-5: Group and Total the Inventory Report

As marketing manager at Wingtip Toys, you review Inventory information regularly with other employees. Add groups and totals to the Inventory report before your meeting with the production manager.

GET READY. LAUNCH Access if it is not already running.

@ The *Wingtip* file for this lesson is available on the book companion website or in WileyPLUS.

1. **OPEN** *Wingtip* from the data files for this lesson.

2. **SAVE** the database as *Wingtip XXX* (where *XXX* is your initials).

3. Open the **Inventory** report.

4. Switch to Layout View and open the Group, Sort, and Total pane.

5. Group the report by the *In Stock* field.

6. Sort the Description column from **A to Z**.

7. Sum the *Price* field. Show a grand total and totals in the group footers.

8. Save and close the report.

CLOSE the database.

Project 11-6: Create Labels for Alpine Ski House Customers

In your position as Administrative Assistant for Alpine Ski House, you are involved in a variety of projects. The owners want to send a special thank you letter and promotion to previous customers. Create labels for the mailing.

GET READY. LAUNCH Access if it is not already running.

@ The *Alpine* file for this lesson is available on the book companion website or in WileyPLUS.

1. **OPEN** *Alpine* from the data files for this lesson.
2. **SAVE** the database as *Alpine XXX* (where *XXX* is your initials).
3. Open the **Customers** table.
4. Use the Label Wizard to create address labels for all the customers in the table.
5. Select the **C2160** labels.
6. Arrange the customers' last name, first name, address, city, state, and zip code fields appropriately on the mailing label.
7. Name the labels **Customers Labels**.
8. Save, print and close the report.
9. **CLOSE** the database.

CLOSE Access.

INTERNET READY

Delivery service companies are used extensively in business. As a result, comparing service and prices can be very important for a company to make sure it is using a reliable and economical delivery service. Search the Internet for three companies that pick up and deliver packages. Gather information such as services offered and prices charged for common services such as overnight delivery or two-day service. Create a database table and report that displays the data grouped by company with group totals for like services. Preview your report, make sure it looks attractive on the page, and then print it.

12 Advanced Queries

LESSON SKILL MATRIX

Skill	Exam Objective	Objective Number
Creating Crosstab Queries	Create a Crosstab query.	4.1.4
Creating a Subquery	Add field.	4.3.1
	Remove field.	4.3.2
	Rearrange fields.	4.3.3
	Use the Zoom box.	4.5.2
Saving a Filter as a Query		
Creating Action Queries	Create an Append query.	4.1.3
	Create a Make Table query.	4.1.2
Understanding Advanced Query Modification	Create ad hoc relationships.	4.2.3
	Use Expression Builder.	4.5.3
	Perform calculations.	4.5.1
	Use Group By.	4.4.2
	Use the Total row.	4.4.1

KEY TERMS

- action query
- aggregate function
- append query
- calculated field
- cross join
- crosstab query
- delete query
- inner join
- join
- left outer join
- make table query
- outer join
- right outer join
- SELECT statement
- subquery
- unequal join
- update query

World Wide Importers is a car dealership that specializes in imported luxury cars. The company has recently opened a used car division that sells vehicles acquired in trade and expands the buyer's purchasing options. As the office manager for the new division, you have started using Access to track inventory and sales. In this lesson, you learn how to create an action query, a crosstab query, a subquery, and how to save filters as a query. You also learn how to create joins, include calculated fields in a query, and create aggregated queries.

CREATING CROSSTAB QUERIES

The Bottom Line

Queries are powerful tools that can be used to retrieve exactly the data you need from your database, showing only the relevant records. Depending on the information you want to display, these advanced queries can help refine the results of your search or perform the actions you want. A **crosstab query** calculates a sum, average, count, or other type of total on records and then groups the results by two types of information: one down the left side of the datasheet and the other across the top. When you summarize data using a crosstab query, you select values from specified fields or expressions as column headings so you can view data in a more compact format than with a select query.

 Ref

In Lesson 7, you learned how to create and modify several types of queries.

Creating Crosstab Queries

A crosstab query is a special type of query that displays its results in a grid similar to an Excel worksheet. Crosstab queries summarize your values and then group them by two sets of facts—a set of row headers down the side and a set of column headers across the top. A crosstab query typically includes data from more than one table and always includes three types of data: the data used as row headings, the data used as column headings, and the values that you want to sum or otherwise compute. A crosstab query does not always populate all the fields in the result set because the tables that you use in the query do not always contain values for every possible data point. In this exercise, you create a crosstab query.

The easiest way to create a crosstab query is to use the Crosstab Query Wizard. To run a crosstab query, double-click it in the Navigation pane, or click it and then press Enter. When you run a crosstab query, the results are displayed in Datasheet View.

STEP BY STEP | **Create Crosstab Queries**

GET READY. Before you begin these steps, be sure to launch Microsoft Access.

 The *Importers* file for this lesson is available on the book companion website or in WileyPLUS.

WileyPLUS Extra! features an online tutorial of this task.

1. **OPEN** the *Importers* database from the data files for this lesson.
2. **SAVE** the database as *Importers XXX* (where *XXX* is your initials).
3. On the Create tab, in the Queries group, click the **Query Wizard** button to display the New Query dialog box, shown in Figure 12-1.

Figure 12-1

New Query dialog box

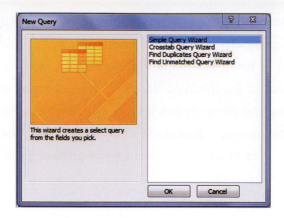

4. Click **Crosstab Query Wizard** and click **OK** to display the Crosstab Query Wizard, shown in Figure 12-2.

Figure 12-2

Crosstab Query Wizard, screen 1

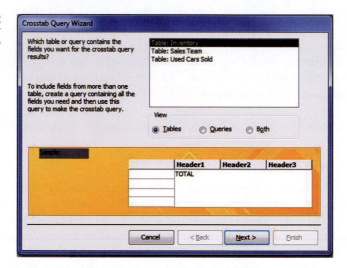

5. Click **Table: Used Cars Sold** and then click **Next >** to display the next screen, shown in Figure 12-3.

Figure 12-3

Crosstab Query Wizard, screen 2

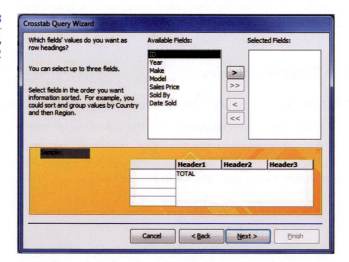

6. In the Available Fields box, double-click **Sold By** to move it to the Selected Fields box and then click **Next >**. The next screen appears, as shown in Figure 12-4.

Figure 12-4

Crosstab Query Wizard, screen 3

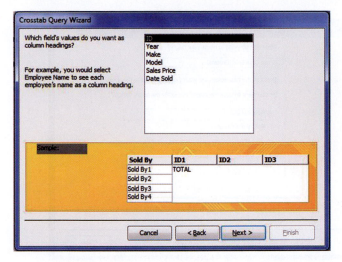

7. Click **Date Sold** and then click **Next >** to display the next screen, shown in Figure 12-5.

Figure 12-5

Crosstab Query Wizard, screen 4

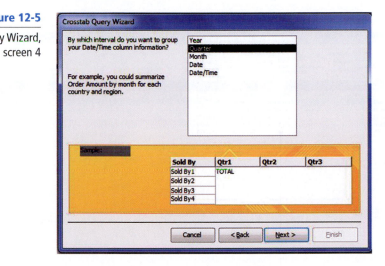

8. Click **Month** and then click **Next >** to display the next screen, shown in Figure 12-6.

Figure 12-6

Crosstab Query Wizard, screen 5

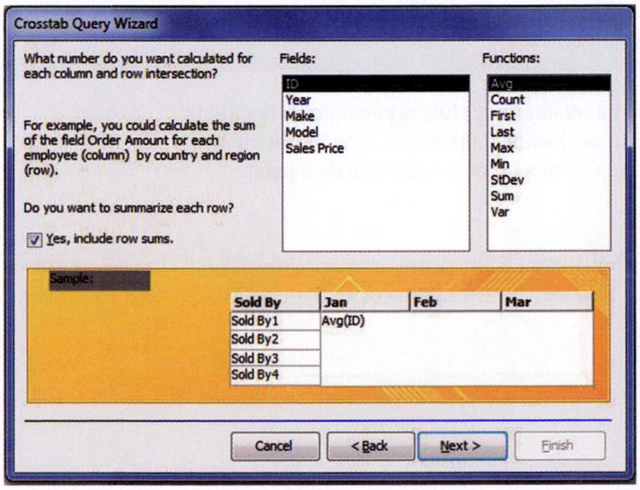

9. In the Fields box, click **Sales Price**, and in the Functions box, click **Sum**. Click **Next >** to display the final screen, as shown in Figure 12-7.

Figure 12-7

Crosstab Query Wizard,
final screen

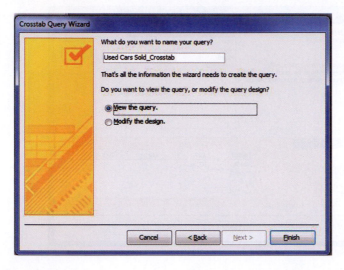

10. Click **Finish** to display the results of the crosstab query, as shown in Figure 12-8.

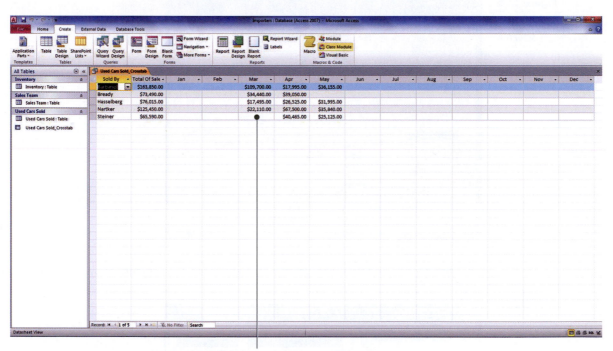

A crosstab query does not always populate all the fields
in the result set because the tables used do not always
contain values for every possible data point.

Figure 12-8

Crosstab query results

11. Click the **Close** button to close the Used Cars Sold Crosstab query.

PAUSE. LEAVE the database open to use in the next exercise.

**CERTIFICATION
READY**   **4.1.4**

How do you create crosstab
queries?

CREATING A SUBQUERY

You can use a subquery to limit the amount of data returned by a query. A **subquery** is a SELECT statement that is inside another select or action query. A **SELECT statement** is a SQL command that instructs the Microsoft Access database engine to return information from the database as a set of records.

At a minimum, the syntax for a SELECT statement is:

SELECT *fields* FROM *table*

An asterisk (*) can be used to select all the fields in a table. The following example selects all the fields in the Inventory table:

SELECT * FROM Inventory

Clauses such as WHERE and ORDER BY can be used in a SELECT statement to restrict and organize your returned data. Table 12-1 shows some SELECT statements and the results that are returned.

Table 12-1

Select Statements with Returned Results

SELECT Statement	Result
SELECT [FirstName], [LastName] FROM [Employees] WHERE [LastName] = "Cooper";	Displays the values in the *FirstName* and *LastName* fields for employees whose last name is Cooper.
SELECT [ProductID], fields [ProductName] FROM [Products] WHERE [CategoryID] = Forms! [New Products]![CategoryID];	Displays the values for ProductID and ProductName in the Products table for records in which the CategoryID value matches the CategoryID value specified in an open New Products form.
SELECT Avg([ExtendedPrice]) AS [Average Extended Price] FROM the [Order Details Extended] WHERE [ExtendedPrice] > 1000;	Displays in a field named Average Extended Price the average extended price of orders for which the value in *ExtendedPrice* field is more than 1,000.
SELECT [CategoryID], Count([ProductID]) AS [CountOfProductID] FROM [Products] GROUP BY [CategoryID] HAVING Count([ProductID]) > 10	Displays in a field named CountOfProductID the total number of products for categories with more than 10 products.

A SELECT statement can be entered in a field or criteria cell in Design View. If you need more space in which to enter the SELECT statement in a field or criteria cell, press Shift+F2 and enter the statement in the Zoom box. You can see the entire SQL statement by switching to SQL View.

In a subquery, you use a SELECT statement to provide a set of one or more specific values to evaluate in the WHERE or HAVING clause expression. A subquery has three parts:

- **Comparison:** An expression and a comparison operator that compares the expression with the results of the subquery
- **Expression:** An expression for which the result set of the subquery is searched
- **Sqlstatement:** A SELECT statement, following the same format and rules as any other SELECT statement. It must be enclosed in parentheses

Creating a Subquery

In this exercise, you create a subquery that returns results that select only the records from the Inventory table whose asking price is equal to or greater than the average asking price. You also add, remove, and reposition fields while working within the query design grid.

Subqueries are created in Design View. You first need to add the table window with the pertinent fields to the query design grid by using the Show Table dialog box. You can easily add fields from the table window either by double-clicking the field name, or by clicking and dragging it to the design grid. You can remove fields from the query design grid by moving the mouse pointer above the field name you want to remove until the pointer changes to a bold down arrow, then press delete on the keyboard, or the Delete Columns button in the Query Setup group on the Design tab. You can rearrange fields on the grid by moving the mouse pointer above the field you want to move until the pointer changes to a bold down arrow, then click and drag the field to any position on the grid using the vertical placeholder bar that appears as a guide.

STEP BY STEP   **Create a Subquery**

USE the database that is open from the previous exercise.

1. On the Create tab, in the Queries group, click **Query Design**. The query designer opens, and the Show Table dialog box appears, as shown in Figure 12-9.

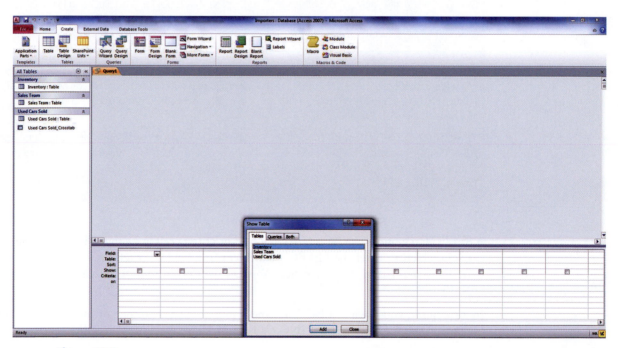

Figure 12-9

Show Table dialog box

2. In the Tables tab, click **Inventory**, click **Add**, and then click **Close**. The table appears as a window in the upper section of the query design grid, as shown in Figure 12-10.

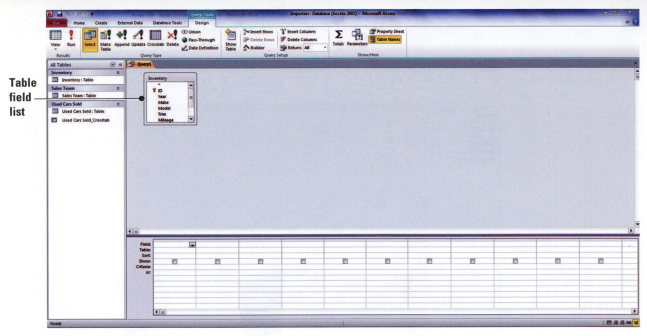

Figure 12-10

Query design grid

Take Note   To quickly add all the fields in a table, double-click the asterisk (*) at the top of the list of table fields.

3. In the list of table fields, double-click **Year**, **Make**, **Model**, **Trim**, and **AskingPrice** to add those fields to the design grid, as shown in Figure 12-11.

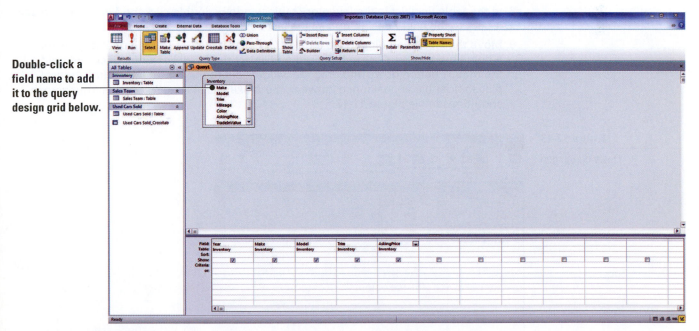

Figure 12-11

Fields added to design grid

4. Move the insertion point above the *Trim* field on the design grid until it turns into a bold down arrow. Click to highlight and select the **Trim column**, as shown in Figure 12-12.

Figure 12-12

Column highlighted on
design grid

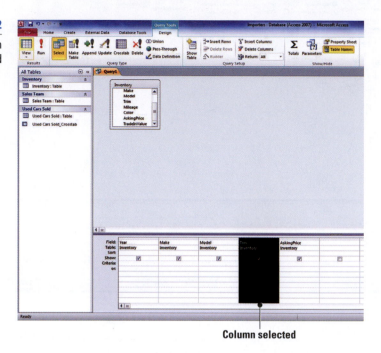

Column selected

5. Press the **Delete** key on the keyboard and the Trim column is deleted. The *AskingPrice* field replaces the Trim column.

6. Move the insertion point above the *Model* field on the design grid until it turns into a bold down arrow. Click to highlight and select the **Model** column.

7. On the Design tab, in the Query Setup group, click the **Delete Columns** button. The Model column is deleted.

8. In the table field list in the Inventory table window, double-click the **Model** field to add it back to the query design grid as the last column.

9. Move the insertion point above the *Model* field on the design grid until it turns into a bold down arrow. Click to highlight and select the **Model** column. Click and hold the mouse button down and drag the *Model* field to the left until the black vertical placeholder bar is positioned between the *Make* and *AskingPrice* fields. Your screen should resemble Figure 12-13.

Figure 12-13

Query design grid

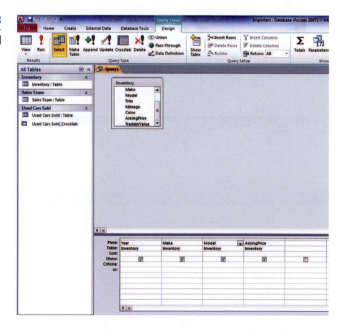

10. Place the insertion point in the Criteria row of the *AskingPrice* field and press **Shift+F2** to display the Zoom dialog box.

11. Key the following expression in the Zoom dialog box, as shown in Figure 12-14:

>=(SELECT Avg(AskingPrice) FROM Inventory WHERE Make = Inventory.Make)

Figure 12-14

Zoom dialog box with expression

12. Click **OK** to insert the expression in the Criteria row of the Asking Price field.

13. On the Design tab, in the Results group, click the **View** tab, and click **SQL View** to see the entire expression, as shown in Figure 12-15.

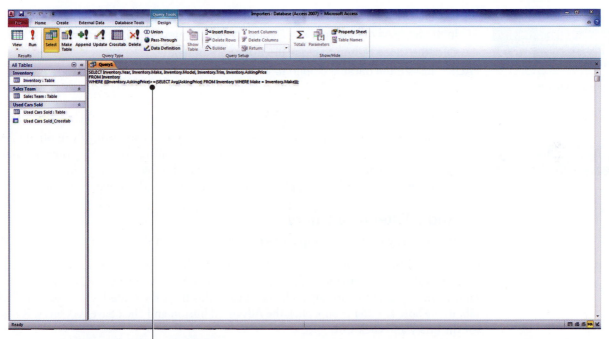

Subquery WHERE clause in SQL View

Figure 12-15

SQL View

14. On the Design tab, in the Results group, click **Run**. The query results are displayed, as shown in Figure 12-16.

Figure 12-16

Subquery results

**CERTIFICATION
READY**   **4.3.1**

How do you add a field to a query?

**CERTIFICATION
READY**   **4.3.2**

How do you remove a field from a query?

**CERTIFICATION
READY**   **4.3.3**

How do you rearrange query fields?

**CERTIFICATION
READY**   **4.5.2**

How do you use the Zoom box?

15. Click the **File** tab and click **Save**.
16. In the Save As dialog box, key **Subquery** as the query name and click **OK**.
17. Click the **Close** button to close the Subquery query.

PAUSE. LEAVE the database open to use in the next exercise.

The Bottom Line

SAVING A FILTER AS A QUERY

A filter can be saved as a query so it can be run again anytime you want. If you often work with certain filters, you might want to save these filters so that you are not wasting time defining them each time. You cannot save more than one filter for each table, query, or form—but, you can save a filter as a query and then apply the query as a filter when and where you want.

Saving a Filter as a Query

In this exercise, you create a simple select query, filter it, and then save it.

Create a filter by form and apply it to the query. On the Home tab, in the Sort & Filter group, click the Advanced button and click Advanced Filter/Sort. The new query appears in the Database window. It automatically includes all the fields from the underlying view. On the Home tab, in the Sort & Filter group, click the Advanced button and click Save As Query. Key a name for the query and click OK.

To apply the query as a filter, click the Advanced button, and click Load from Query to display the Applicable Filter dialog box, shown in Figure 12-17.

Figure 12-17

Applicable Filter dialog box

Only select queries that are based on the same underlying table or query as the form or datasheet will appear in the dialog box. Select the filter, click OK, and then apply the filter.

Save a Filter as a Query

USE the database that is open from the previous exercise.

1. On the Create tab, in the Queries group, click the **Query Wizard** button.
2. In the New Query dialog box, click **Simple Query Wizard** and click **OK**.
3. In the Tables/Queries drop-down list, click **Table: Used Cars Sold**.
4. Click the **>>** button to move all the fields from the Available Fields to the Selected Fields box and then click **Next >**.
5. Click **Next >** again and then click **Finish** to display a simple select query.
6. On the Home tab, in the Sort & Filter group, click the **Advanced** button and then click **Filter by Form**.
7. In the Filter by Form dialog box, click the **Year field down arrow** and click **2010**, as shown in Figure 12-18.

Click the down arrow to select criteria by which to filter a field

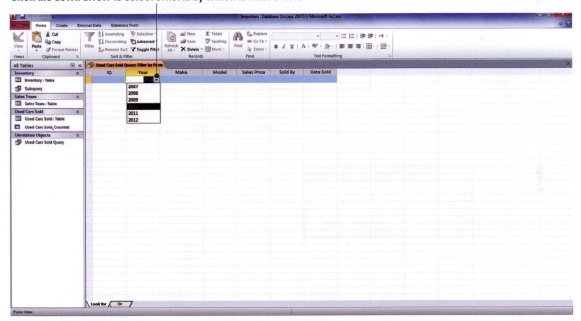

Figure 12-18

Filter by Form

8. On the Home tab, in the Sort & Filter group, click the **Toggle Filter** button to apply the filter. The results are displayed, as shown in Figure 12-19.

Figure 12-19

Filter by Form results

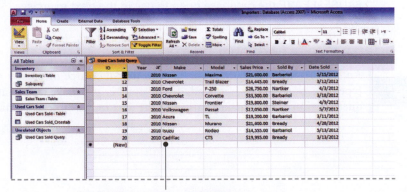

Results filtered to show only 2010 cars

9. On the Home tab, in the Sort & Filter group, click the **Advanced** button and then click **Advanced Filter/Sort** to display the new query design grid, shown in Figure 12-20.

New query filter tab

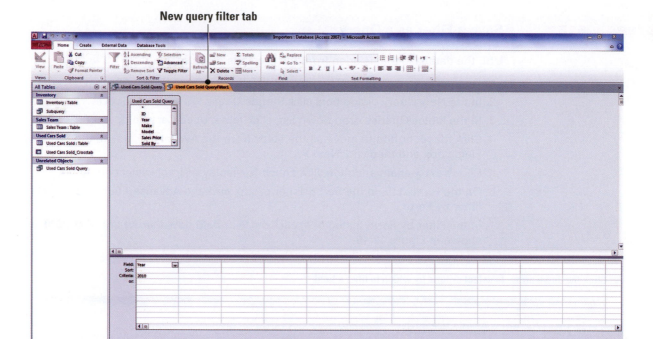

Figure 12-20

New query design grid

10. On the Home tab, in the Sort & Filter group, click the **Advanced** button and then click **Save As Query**. The Save As Query dialog box appears, as shown in Figure 12-21.

Figure 12-21

Design grid

11. Key **Filter Query** in the Query Name box and click **OK**.
12. Click the **Close** button to close the Used Cars Sold Queryfilter1 query.
13. On the Home tab, in the Sort & Filter group, click the **Toggle Filter** button to remove the filter.
14. Click the **Close** button to close the Used Cars Sold Query and save the changes when prompted. If another dialog box appears informing you that another user may have changed the data, click **Yes**.

PAUSE. LEAVE the database open to use in the next exercise.

CREATING ACTION QUERIES

The Bottom Line

An **action query** changes the data in its datasource or creates a new table. There are four types of action queries—append, delete, update, and make table—and except for the make table query, action queries make changes to the data in the tables on which they are based.

As their name suggests, action queries make changes to the data in the tables they are based on (except for make table queries, which creates new tables). There are four types of action queries:

- **Append query:** Adds the records in the query's result set to the end of an existing table
- **Delete query:** Removes rows matching the criteria that you specify from one or more tables
- **Update query:** Changes a set of records according to criteria that you specify
- **Make table query:** Creates a new table and then creates records in it by copying records from an existing table

Changes made by action queries cannot be easily undone, so if you later decide you didn't want to make those changes, usually you will have to restore the data from a backup copy. For this reason, you should always make sure you have a current backup of the underlying data before running an action query.

To minimize the risk involved in running an action query, you can first preview the data that will be acted upon by viewing the action query in Datasheet View before running it. When you are ready to run an action query, double-click it in the Navigation pane or click it and then press Enter. Or, on the Design tab, in the Results group, click Run.

Creating an Append Query

An **append query** adds a set of records from one or more source tables (or queries) to one or more destination tables. Typically, the source and destination tables reside in the same database, but they don't have to. For example, suppose you acquire some new customers and a database that contains a table of information about those customers. To avoid entering that new data manually, you can append it to the appropriate table in your database. In this exercise, you practice creating an append query.

You can also use append queries to append fields that are based on criteria. For example, you might want to append only the names and addresses of customers who have outstanding orders. Or you can use append queries to append records when some of the fields in one table don't exist in the other table. For example, suppose that your Customers table has 10 fields, and the fields in the Clients table in another database match 8 of your 10 fields. You can use an append query to add only the data in the matching fields and ignore the others.

You cannot use append queries to change the data in individual fields in existing records. To do that type of task, you use an update query—you can only use append queries to add rows of data.

STEP BY STEP	**Create an Append Query**

USE the database that is open from the previous exercise.

1. On the Create tab, in the Queries group, click the **Query Design** button.
2. In the Show Table dialog box, double-click **Inventory** to add it to the upper section of the query design grid.
3. Click **Close** to close the Show Table dialog box.
4. In the list of table fields, double-click **Year**, **Make**, **Model**, and **Asking Price** to add those fields to the design grid. Your screen should look similar to Figure 12-22.

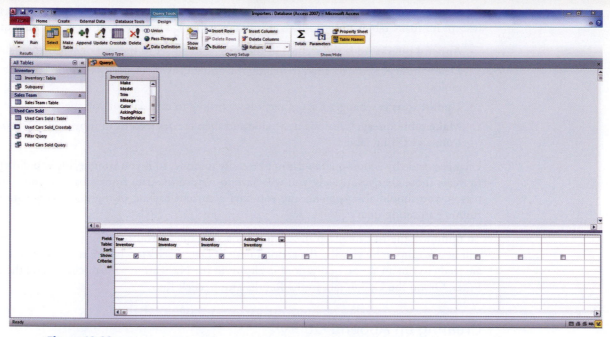

Figure 12-22

Design grid

5. On the Design tab, in the Results group, click **Run**. Verify that the query returned the records that you want to append, as shown in Figure 12-23.

Figure 12-23

Records to be appended

Take Note   If you need to add or remove fields from the query, switch back to Design View and double-click to add fields or select the fields that you don't want and press Delete to remove them from the query.

6. Right-click the document tab for the open query and click **Design View** on the shortcut menu.

7. On the Design tab, in the Query Type group, click **Append**. The Append dialog box appears, as shown in Figure 12-24.

Figure 12-24

Append dialog box

8. In the Table Name box, click the **down arrow** and click **Used Cars Sold**. This is the table you want to append to. The Current Database radio button should be selected.

9. Click **OK**. Access automatically adds the names of the destination fields that match the source field names to the Append To row in the design grid. Because the *Asking Price* field doesn't have a match, Access leaves that field blank.

10. Click the blank field in the Append To row under the Asking Price cell and select **Sales Price** as the destination field, as shown in Figure 12-25.

Figure 12-25

Source and destination fields matched

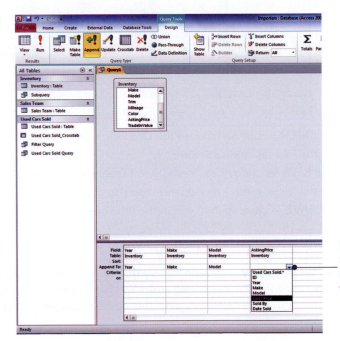

Click the down arrow to manually choose SalesPrice as the destination field for the AskingPrice source field

11. Right-click the document tab for the query, and then click **Datasheet View** to preview your changes.

12. Right-click the document tab for the query, and then click **Design View**.

13. On the Design tab, in the Results group, click **Run**. An alert message appears, as shown in Figure 12-26.

Figure 12-26

Append alert message

14. Click **Yes**.

15. Open the **Used Cars Sold** table and scroll down to see that the records from the Inventory table have been appended to the end, as shown in Figure 12-27.

Figure 12-27

Results of append query

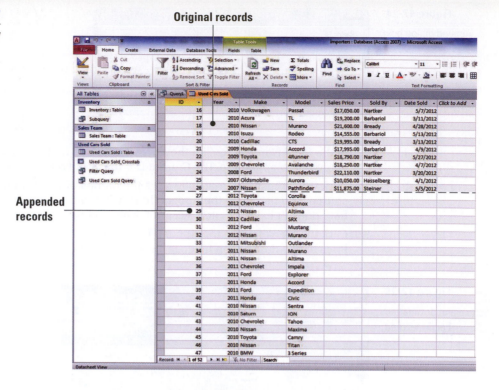

16. Click the **Close** button to close the Used Cars Sold table.
17. Click the **File** tab and click **Save**.
18. In the Save As dialog box, key **Append Query** as the query name and click **OK**.
19. Click the **Close** button on Append Query to close the query.

PAUSE. LEAVE Access open to use in the next exercise.

CERTIFICATION READY   4.1.3

How do you create append queries?

Creating a Make Table Query

A **make table query** is an action query that creates a new table and then creates records in it by copying records from an existing table. You use a make table query when you need to copy the data in a table or to archive data. In this exercise, you practice creating a make table query.

STEP BY STEP   **Create a Make Table Query**

USE the database that is open from the previous exercise.

1. On the Create tab, in the Queries group, click the **Query Wizard** button.
2. In the New Query dialog box, click **Simple Query Wizard** and click **OK**.
3. In the Tables/Queries drop-down list, click **Table: Sales Team**.
4. Click the **>>** button to move all the fields from the Available Fields to the Selected Fields box and then click **Next >**.
5. Click **Finish** to display a simple select query.
6. Right-click the **Sales Team Query** document tab and click **Design View** to display the query in Design View, as shown in Figure 12-28.

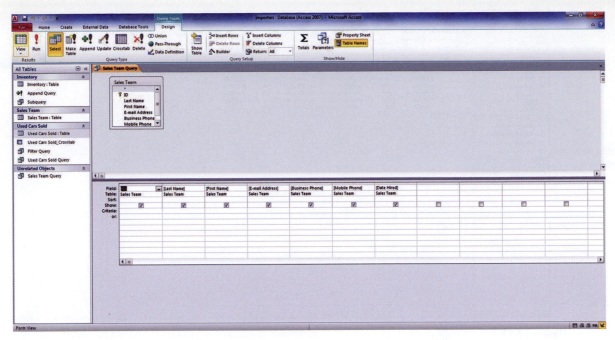

Figure 12-28

Query in Design View

7. On the Design tab, in the Query Type group, click **Make Table**. The Make Table dialog box appears, as shown in Figure 12-29.

Figure 12-29

Make Table dialog box

8. In the Table Name box, key **Sales Team Backup**. If it isn't already selected, click **Current Database**, and then click **OK**.

9. On the Design tab, in the Results group, click **Run**. An alert message appears, as shown in Figure 12-30.

Figure 12-30

Make table alert message

10. Click **Yes**. A new table appears in the Navigation pane.

11. Double-click **Sales Team Backup: Table** in the Navigation pane to open the new table, as shown in Figure 12-31.

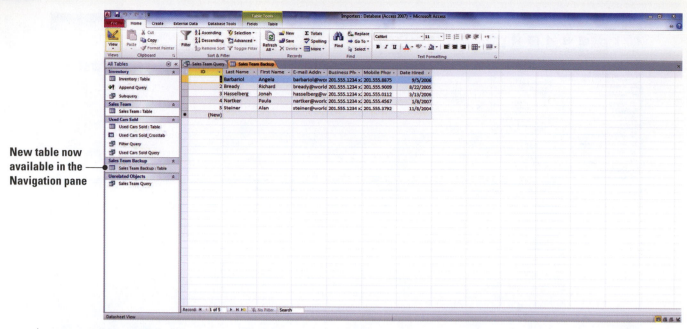

New table now available in the Navigation pane

Figure 12-31

New table

CERTIFICATION READY   4.1.2

How do you create make table queries?

12. Click the **Close** button to close the Sales Team Backup table.

13. Click the **Close** button to close the Sales Team query. Save the changes when prompted.

14. LEAVE the database open.

PAUSE. LEAVE Access open to use in the next exercise.

Creating an Update Query

An **update query** is an action query that changes a set of records according to specified criteria. Use an update query when you need to add, change, or delete the data in one or more existing records. You can think of update queries as a powerful form of the Find and Replace dialog box. In this exercise, you practice making an Update Query.

When making an update query, you enter a select criterion and an update criterion. Unlike the Find and Replace dialog box, update queries can accept multiple criteria. You can use them to update a large number of records in one pass and to change records in more than one table at one time. You can also update the data in one table with data from another—as long as the data types for the source and destination fields match or are compatible.

To create an update query, first create or open a select query. On the Design tab, in the Query Type group, click Update. Access adds the Update to row in the query design grid. Locate the field that contains the data you want to change, and type your change criteria in the Update to row for that field.

You can use any valid expression in the Update to row. Table 12-2 shows some example expressions and explains how they change data.

Table 12-2

Expressions and How They Change Data

Expression	Result
"Chicago"	In a *Text* field, changes a text value to Chicago.
#9/25/11#	In a *Date/Time* field, changes a date value to 25-Sept-11.
Yes	In a Yes/No field, changes a No value to Yes.
"PN" & [PartNumber]	Adds "PN" to the beginning of each specified part number.
[UnitPrice] * [Quantity]	Multiplies the values in fields named *UnitPrice* and *Quantity*.
[Shipping] * 1.5	Increases the values in a field named *Shipping by 50 percent*.
DSum("[Quantity] * [UnitPrice]","Order Details", "[ProductID] ="& [ProductID])	Where the ProductID values in the current table match the ProductID values in table named Order Details, this expression updates sales totals by multiplying the values in a field named *Quantity* by the values in a field named UnitPrice. The expression uses the DSum function because it can operate against more than one table and table field.
Right([PostalCode], 5)	Removes the leftmost characters in a text or numeric string and leaves the 5 rightmost characters.
IIf(IsNull([SalesPrice]), 0, [SalesPrice])	Changes a null (unknown or undefined) value to a zero (0) value in a field named *SalesPrice*.

STEP BY STEP   Create an Update Query

USE the database that is open from the previous exercise.

1. On the Create tab, in the Queries group, click the **Query Wizard** button.
2. In the New Query dialog box, click **Simple Query Wizard** and click **OK**.
3. In the Tables/Queries drop-down list, click **Table: Inventory**.
4. Click the **>>** button to move all the fields from the Available Fields to the Selected Fields box.
5. Click **Trim** and then the **<** button to move it back to the Selected Fields box. Click **Color** and then the **<** button to move it back to the Selected Fields box. Click **Next >**.
6. Click **Next >** again and then click **Finish** to display a simple select query in Datasheet View, as shown in Figure 12-32.

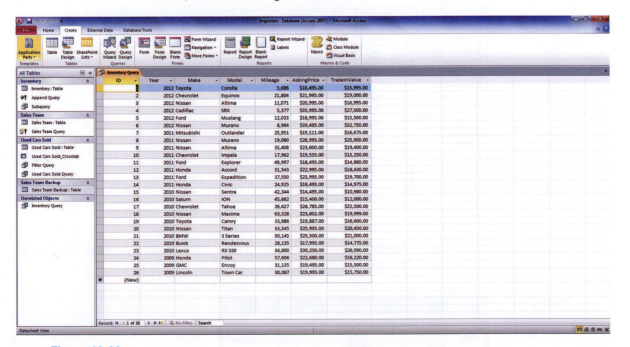

Figure 12-32

Select query in Datasheet View

7. Right-click the **Inventory Query** document tab and click **Design View** to display the query in Design View, as shown in Figure 12-33.

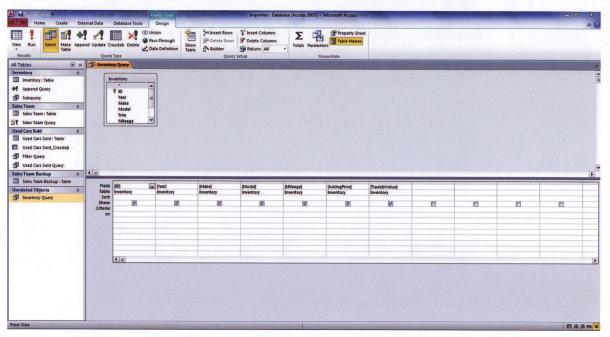

Figure 12-33

Select query in Design View

8. Key **2012** in the Criteria row of the *Year* field.

9. On the Design tab, in the Query Type group, click **Update**. Access adds the Update To row in the query design grid.

10. In the Update To row of the *AskingPrice* field, key **[AskingPrice] + 500**. The design grid should look similar to Figure 12-34.

Figure 12-34

Select and update criterion

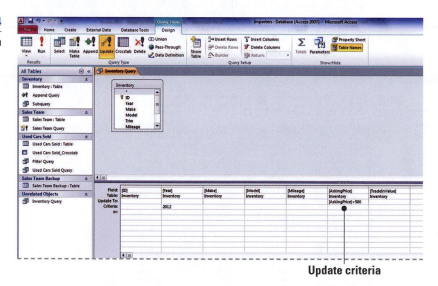

Update criteria

11. On the Design tab, in the Results group, click **Run**. An alert message appears, as shown in Figure 12-35.

Figure 12-35

Update alert message

12. Click **Yes**.

13. Right-click the **Inventory Query** document tab and click **Datasheet View** to display the update query results, as shown in Figure 12-36.

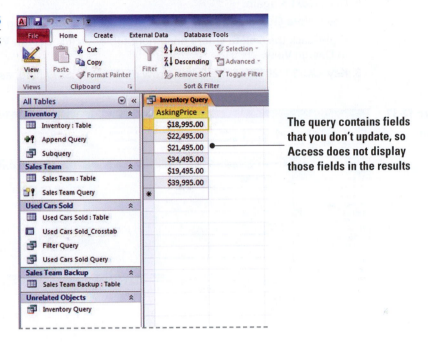

The query contains fields that you don't update, so Access does not display those fields in the results

Take Note   When you run the query, you will notice that some fields are missing from your result set. If the query contains fields that you don't update, Access does not display those fields in the results.

14. Click the **Close** button to close the Inventory query. Save the changes when prompted.

15. Double-click **Inventory: Table** in the Navigation pane to open it. Notice that the asking price for all 2012 cars has been increased by $500.

16. Click the **Close** button to close the Inventory table.

17. **LEAVE** the database open.

PAUSE. LEAVE Access open to use in the next exercise.

Creating a Delete Query

A **delete query** is an action query that removes rows matching the criteria that you specify from one or more tables. A delete query is used to delete entire records from a table, along with the key value that makes a record unique. Typically, delete queries are used only when you need to change or remove large amounts of data quickly. To remove a small number of records, open the table in Datasheet View, select the fields or rows that you want to delete, and press Delete.

To create a delete query, first create or open a select query and add criteria to return the records you want to delete. On the Design tab, in the Query Type group, click Delete. Access changes the select query to a delete query, hides the Show row in the lower section of the design grid, and adds the Delete row. The word Where should appear in any columns that you use for criteria.

When you click Run, Access prompts you to confirm the deletion. Click Yes to delete the data and then open the table to see that the records have been deleted.

STEP BY STEP   **Create a Delete Query**

USE the database that is open from the previous exercise.

1. On the Create tab, in the Queries group, click **Query Wizard**.

2. In the New Query dialog box, click **Simple Query Wizard** and click **OK**.

3. In the Tables/Queries drop-down list, click **Table: Used Cars Sold**.

4. Click the **>>** button to move all the fields from the Available Fields to the Selected Fields box and then click **Next >**.

5. Click **Next >** again.

6. Key **Delete Query** as the title and then click **Finish** displaying a simple select query.

7. Right-click the **Delete Query** document tab and click **Design View** to display the query in Design View.

8. Key **<#3/31/2012#** in the Criteria row of the *Date Sold* field, as shown in Figure 12-37.

Figure 12-37

Date Sold criteria

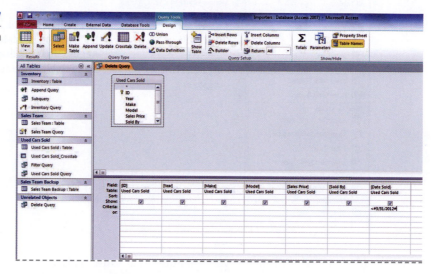

9. On the Design tab, in the Results group, click **Run** to display the records to be deleted, as shown in Figure 12-38.

Figure 12-38

Records to be deleted

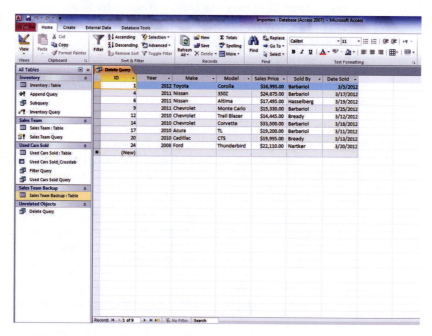

10. Right-click the **Delete Query** document tab and click **Design View** to display the query in Design View.

11. On the Design tab, in the Query Type group, click **Delete**. Access hides the Show row in the lower section of the design grid and adds the Delete row, as shown in Figure 12-39.

Figure 12-39

Delete row in design grid

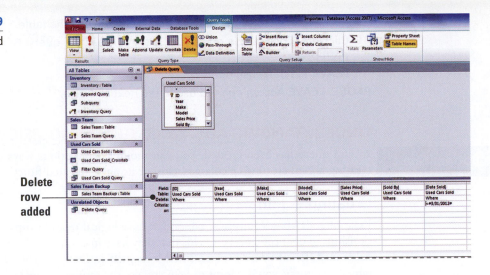

Delete
row
added

12. On the Design tab, in the Results group, click **Run**. An alert message appears, as shown in Figure 12-40.

Figure 12-40

Delete alert message

13. Click **Yes**.

14. Double-click **Used Cars Sold: Table** in the Navigation pane to open it. Notice that all the records for cars sold before March 31, 2012 have been deleted, as shown in Figure 12-41.

Figure 12-41

Table with records deleted

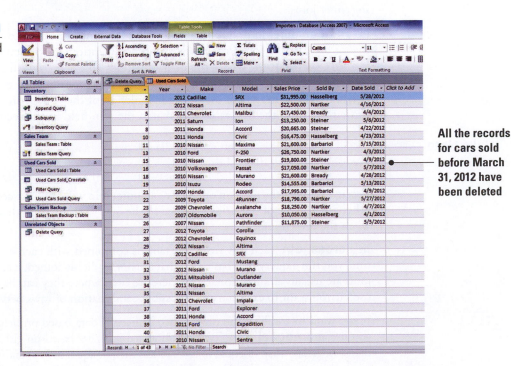

All the records for cars sold before March 31, 2012 have been deleted

15. Click the **Close** button on Used Cars Sold to close the table.

16. Click the **Close** button on Delete Query to close the query. Save the changes when prompted.

17. **LEAVE** the database open.

PAUSE. LEAVE Access open to use in the next exercise.

UNDERSTANDING ADVANCED QUERY MODIFICATION

The Bottom Line

After a query has been created, you can modify it in various ways to suit your purposes—by creating a join, creating calculated fields, or using aggregated functions.

Creating a Join

Relational databases consist of tables that have logical relationships to each other. You use relationships to connect tables on fields that they have in common. A relationship between identical fields in different tables is represented by a **join** in Design View. When you include multiple tables in a query, you use joins to help you get the results you want. A join helps a query return only the records from each table you want to see, based on how those tables are related to other tables in the query. When you add tables to a query, Access creates joins that are based on relationships that have been defined between the tables. You can manually create joins known as ad hoc relationships in queries, even if they do not represent relationships that have already been defined. In this exercise, you create a join between tables.

Take Note

If the relationship is one-to-many, Access displays a "1" above the join line to show which table is on the "one" side and an infinity symbol (∞) to show which table is on the "many" side.

The four basic types of joins are inner joins, outer joins, cross joins, and unequal joins. An **inner join** includes rows in the query only when the joined field matches records in both tables. Inner joins are the most common type of join. Most of the time, you don't need to do anything to use an inner join. Access automatically creates inner joins if you add two tables to a query and those tables each have a field with the same or compatible data type and one of the join fields is a primary key.

An **outer join** includes all of the rows from one table in the query results and only those rows from the other table that match the join field in the first table. You create outer joins by modifying inner joins.

To create an outer join, double-click the line joining the tables to display the Join Properties dialog box. In the Join Properties dialog box, Option 1 represents an inner join. Option 2 is a **left outer join**, where the query includes all of the rows from the first table and only those records from the second table that match the join field in the first table. Option 3 is a **right outer join**, where the query includes all of the rows from the second table and only those rows from the first table that match the join field in the second table.

Take Note

To tell which table is the left table or the right table in a given join, double-click the join to view the Join Properties dialog box.

Because some of the rows on one side of an outer join will not have corresponding rows from the other table, some of the fields returned in the query results from that other table will be empty when the rows do not correspond.

In a **cross join**, each row from one table is combined with each row from another table. Any time you run a query that has tables that are not explicitly joined, a cross join is produced. Cross joins are usually unintentional, but there are cases where they can be useful. A cross join can be used if you want to examine every possible combination of rows between two tables or queries.

If you want to combine the rows of two sources of data based on field values that are not equal, you use an **unequal join**. Typically, unequal joins are based on either the greater than (>), less than (<), greater than or equal to (>=), or less than or equal to (<=) comparison operators. Unequal joins are not supported in Design View. If you wish to use them, you must do so in SQL View.

 **Troubleshooting** If you create a join by mistake, for example, a join between two fields that have dissimilar data types, you can delete it. In the query design grid, click the join you want to remove and press Delete.

STEP BY STEP   **Create a Join**

USE the database that is open from the previous exercise.

1. On the Create tab, in the Queries group, click **Query Design**.
2. In the Show Table dialog box, double-click **Sales Team** and **Used Cars Sold** to add them to the design grid.
3. Click **Close**.
4. In the *Sales Team* field list, double-click **E-mail Address**.
5. In the *Used Cars Sold* field list, double-click **Year**, **Make**, **Model**, and **Sales Price**. Your screen should look similar to Figure 12-42.

Figure 12-42

New query

Double-click join line to open the Join Properties dialog box

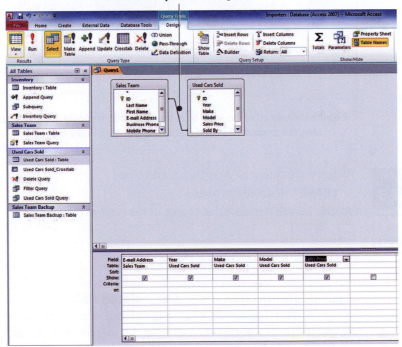

6. Double-click the join line between the tables, indicating which fields are joined. The Join Properties dialog box opens, as shown in Figure 12-43.

Figure 12-43

Join properties dialog box

Inner join option

Left outer join option

Right outer join option

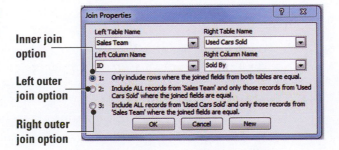

7. Click the radio button for option **2:** and then click **OK** to create a left outer join.

8. On the Design tab, in the Results group, click **Run**.

9. The results of the query are displayed, as shown in Figure 12-44.

Figure 12-44

Left outer join

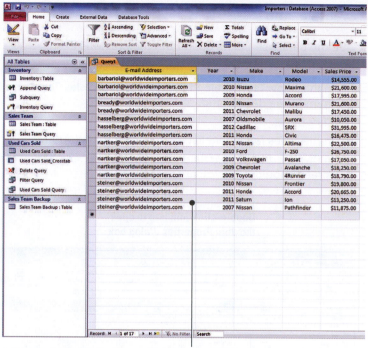

**Results include all of the rows from the first table and only those records
from the second table that match the join field in the first table.**

10. Save the query as **Join Query** and close.

11. **LEAVE** the database open.

PAUSE. LEAVE Access open to use in the next exercise.

Creating a Calculated Query Field

You can create a new field that displays the results of a calculation you define with an expression or that manipulates field values. A **calculated field** is a column in a query that results from an expression. For example, you can calculate a value; combine text values, such as first and last names; or format a portion of a date. In this exercise you use the Expression Builder to create a calculated query by subtracting two fields to determine a markup price.

You can use expressions that perform arithmetic operations in calculated fields to add, subtract, multiply, and divide the values in two or more fields. You can also perform arithmetic operations on dates or use expressions that manipulate text. Table 12-3 shows examples of expressions that can be used in calculated fields.

Expression	Description
PrimeShip: [Ship] * 1.1	Creates a field called *PrimeShip*, and then displays shipping charges plus 10 percent in the field.
OrderAmount: [Quantity] * [Price]	Creates a field called *OrderAmount*, and then displays the product of the values in the *Quantity* and *Price* fields.
LeadTime: [RequiredDate] − [ShippedDate]	Creates a field called *LeadTime*, and then displays the difference between the values in the *RequiredDate* and *ShippedDate* fields.
TotalInventory: [UnitsInStock] + [UnitsOnOrder]	Creates a field called *TotalInventory*, and then displays the sum of the values in the *UnitsInStock* and *UnitsOnOrder* fields.
FullName: [FirstName] & " " & [LastName]	Creates a field called *FullName* that displays the values in the *FirstName* and *LastName* fields, separated by a space.
Address2: [City] & " " & [Region] & " " & [PostalCode]	Creates a field called *Address2* that displays the values in the *City*, *Region*, and *PostalCode* fields, separated by spaces.

A well-designed database does not store simple calculated values in tables. For example, a table might store an employee's hire date, but not how long she has worked for the company. If you know both today's date and the employee's date of hire, you can always calculate her employment length, so there is no need to store that in the table. Instead, you create a query that calculates and displays the pertinent value. The calculations are made every time you run the query, so if the underlying data changes, so do your calculated results.

To create a calculated field, first open or create a query and switch to Design View. In the Field row of the first blank column in the design grid, key the expression. You can use the Zoom box to access a larger screen area to help you enter the expression or, as you learned in Lesson 8, you can use the Expression Builder to easily select the elements of the expression (fields, operators, and built-in functions) from menus. To name the field, key a name followed by a colon before the expression. If you do not supply a name, Access will use a generic name for the field, for example, EXPR1. The string following the colon is the expression that supplies the values for each record. To see the SQL code, you can switch to SQL View.

STEP BY STEP **Create a Calculated Query Field**

USE the database that is open from the previous exercise.

1. On the Create tab, in the Queries group, click **Query Design**.
2. In the Show Table dialog box, double-click **Inventory** to add the table to the design grid.
3. Click **Close**.
4. In the *Inventory* field list, double-click **Year**, **Make**, **Model**, **AskingPrice**, and **TradeInValue**.
5. Click the **Field** cell in the first blank column (to the right of the *TradeInValue* field) and click the **Builder** button in the Query Setup group to open the Expression Builder dialog box.
6. In the blank area of the dialog box, key the following:

   Markup: [AskingPrice]
7. In the Expression Elements category, click **Operators**. The dialog box should resemble Figure 12-45.

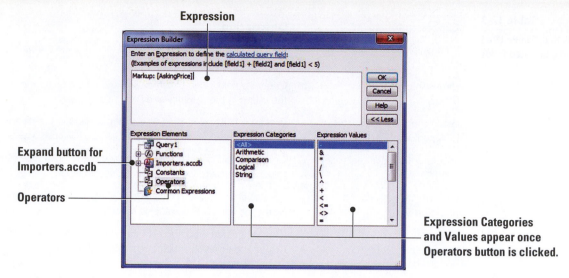

Expression

Expand button for Importers.accdb

Operators

Expression Categories and Values appear once Operators button is clicked.

Figure 12-45

Expression Builder

8. In the Expression Values category, double-click the **minus sign (−)**. The minus sign should appear in the expression and next to the *AskingPrice* field.

9. In the Expression Elements category, click the **expand** button next to Importers.accdb. Tables, Queries, Forms, and Reports should appear under Importers.accdb.

10. In the Expression Elements category, click the **expand** button next to Tables to expand it. The available table names appear. Click **Inventory**. The available field from the Inventory table should appear in the Expression Categories box. Your screen should resemble Figure 12-46.

Figure 12-46

Expression Builder with Expression Elements expanded

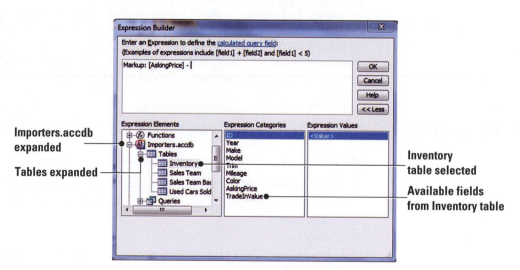

Importers.accdb expanded

Tables expanded

Inventory table selected

Available fields from Inventory table

11. In the Expression Categories box, double-click **TradeInValue**; [Inventory]!TradeInValue should appear in the expression and next to the minus sign (−).

Take Note   The part of the expression that reads *[Inventory]!TradeInValue* specifies that the *TradeInValue* field originates from the Inventory table; however, even though Access automatically formats it this way, this expression format is not required since you're already referencing the Inventory table in the Table row of the design grid.

12. Click **OK**.

13. On the Design tab, in the Results group, click **Run**. The query with the new calculated *Markup* field is displayed, as shown in Figure 12-47.

Figure 12-47

Calculated field query results

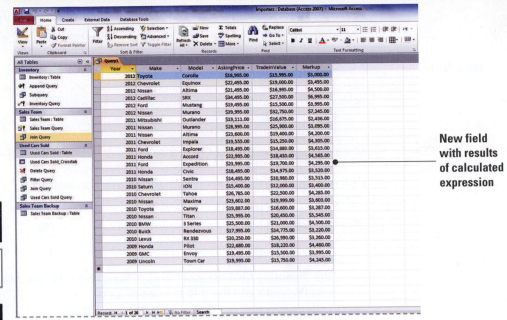

New field
with results
of calculated
expression

14. Save the query as **Calculated Query** and close.

15. **LEAVE** the database open.

PAUSE. LEAVE Access open to use in the next exercise.

Creating Aggregated Queries

An **aggregate function** performs a calculation on a set of values and then returns a single value. You can add, count, or calculate other aggregate values, and display them in a special row, called the Total row, which appears below the asterisk (*) row in Datasheet View. You can use a different aggregate function for each column and you can also choose not to summarize a column. You can use aggregated functions to count the data returned by a query; calculate average values; and find the smallest, largest, earliest, and latest values using a feature called the Total row, which doesn't alter the design of your query. You can work with the Total row in both query Design and query Datasheet Views. In this exercise, you create an aggregated query using the Total row in both query Design and query Datasheet Views.

You can also apply aggregated functions in Design View where you also have the ability to use the Group By function in the Totals row on the design grid. The Group By function can be used in combination with other fields and aggregated functions. For example, if you're managing a human resource database, you can group by employees' gender and display the average salary per group.

The following aggregated functions are available in both Datasheet View and Design View:

- **Count:** Counts the number of items in a field (column of values)
- **Sum:** Sums a column of numbers
- **Average:** Averages a column of numbers
- **Maximum:** Finds the highest value in a field
- **Minimum:** Finds the lowest value in a field
- **Standard Deviation:** Measures how widely values are dispersed from an average value (a mean)
- **Variance:** Measures the statistical variance of all values in the column

The following additional aggregated functions are available in Design View:

- **First:** Finds the first value in a field
- **Last:** Finds the last value in a field

- **Expression:** Groups data based on an expression you can specify
- **Where:** Groups data based on criteria you can specify

Take Note   Many of the aggregated functions work only on data fields set to specific data types. For example, if you are in a column that only displays text values, some functions—such as Sum or Average—are not relevant, and are therefore not available.

STEP BY STEP   **Create an Aggregated Query**

USE the database that is open from the previous exercise.

1. On the Create tab, in the Queries group, click **Query Design**.
2. In the Show Table dialog box, double-click **Inventory** to add the table to the design grid.
3. Click **Close**.
4. In the *Inventory* field list, double-click **Year**, **Make**, **Model**, **Mileage**, **AskingPrice**, and **TradeInValue** to add them to the design grid.
5. On the Design tab, in the Results group, click **Run**.
6. On the Home tab, in the Records group, click the **Totals** button. Scroll down, if necessary, to see the Totals row at the bottom of the result set.
7. In the Totals cell of the *Year* field, click the **down arrow** to display the menu and click **Count**, as shown in Figure 12-48.

Click the down arrow in the Totals row to see aggregate function options.

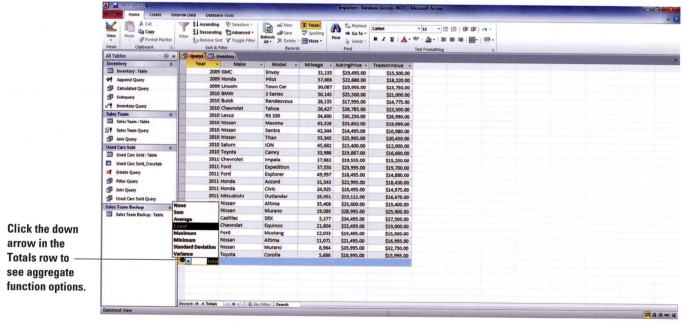

Figure 12-48

Totals row menu options

8. Click the **down arrow** in the Totals cell of the *Mileage* field and click **Average**.
9. Click the **down arrow** in the Totals cell of the *AskingPrice* field and click **Maximum**.
10. Click the **down arrow** in the Totals cell of the *TradeInValue* field and click **Sum**. Your Totals row should appear similar to Figure 12-49.

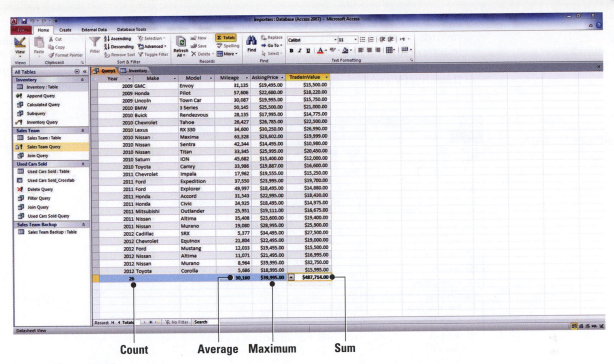

Count   Average Maximum   Sum

Figure 12-49

Aggregate function results

11. Switch to Design View and remove the **Model**, **Mileage**, **AskingPrice**, and **TradeInValue** from the design grid. The *Year* and *Make* fields should be the only ones remaining on the grid.

12. On the Design tab, in the Show/Hide group, click the **Totals** button. A new Totals row should appear below the Table row on the design grid.

13. Click the **Group By** cell below the *Make* field cell and click the **down arrow** to display the aggregate function menu.

14. Click the **Count** aggregate function to select it from the menu, as shown in Figure 12-50.

Figure 12-50

Aggregate function menu in Design View

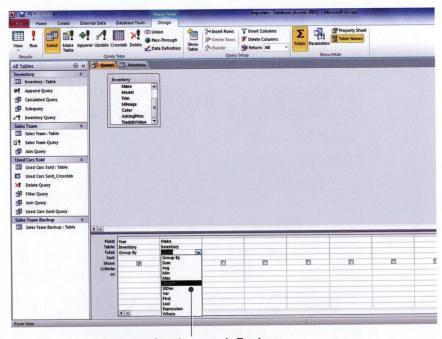

Aggregate function menu in Total row

15. Switch to Datasheet View. Your screen should resemble Figure 12-51. Notice the records in the Make field are grouped by Year and counted with the results appearing in a new column named CountOfMake. Also notice the Year field is grouped and each year remains counted as applied from the aggregate function we created previously in Datasheet View.

Figure 12-51

Aggregate function results

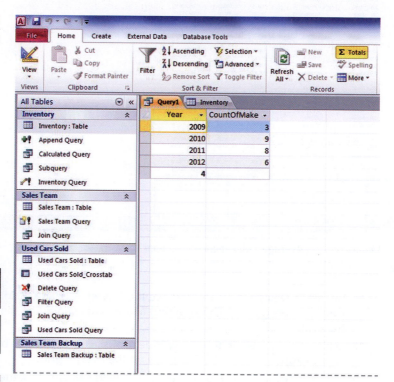

16. Save the query as **Aggregated Query** and close.

17. CLOSE the database.

PAUSE. LEAVE Access running to use in the next exercise.

SKILL SUMMARY

In This Lesson You Learned How To:	Exam Objective	Objective Number
Create Crosstab Queries	Create a Crosstab query.	**4.1.4**
Create a subquery	Add fields.	**4.3.1**
	Remove fields.	**4.3.2**
	Rearrange fields.	**4.3.3**
	Use the Zoom box.	**4.5.2**
Save a Filter as a Query		
Create Action Queries	Create an Append query.	**4.1.3**
	Create a Make Table query.	**4.1.2**
Understand Advanced Query Modification	Create ad hoc relationships.	**4.2.3**
	Use Expression Builder.	**4.5.3**
	Perform calculations.	**4.5.1**
	Use Group By.	**4.4.2**
	Use the Total row.	**4.4.1**

Knowledge Assessment

Fill in the Blank

Complete the following sentences by writing the correct word or words in the blanks provided.

1. A(n) _____ is a SELECT statement that is inside another select or action query.

2. A(n) _____ removes rows matching on the criteria that you specify from one or more tables.

3. To minimize the risk of running an action query, you can first preview the data that will be acted upon by viewing the action query in _____ View before running it.

4. A(n) _____ includes all of the rows from one table in the query results and only those rows from the other table that match the join field in the first table.

5. A(n) _____ is a column in a query that results from an expression.

6. You can use the Group By function in the _____ row on the design grid in query Design View.

7. A(n) _____ performs a calculation on a set of values and then returns a single value.

8. A(n) _____ query always includes three types of data: the data used as row headings, the data used as column headings, and the values that you want to sum or otherwise compute.

9. To quickly add all the fields in a table to the design grid in Design View, double-click the _____ at the top of the list of table fields.

10. To be able to apply a filter when and where you want, save the filter as a(n) _____.

Multiple Choice

Select the best response for the following statements or questions.

1. What type of query displays its results in a grid similar to an Excel worksheet?
   a. Crosstab
   b. Append
   c. Aggregated
   d. Subquery

2. What can you use for a more intuitive interface in which to enter criteria or an expression in a field or criteria cell?
   a. Zoom box
   b. Field list pane
   c. Control label
   d. Expression Builder

3. Which action query does not make changes to the data in the tables that it is based on?
   a. Append
   b. Make table
   c. Update
   d. Delete

4. Which type of query can be thought of as a powerful version of the Search and Replace dialog box?
   a. Filter
   b. Calculated field
   c. Update
   d. Crosstab

5. Which of the following is *not* a type of join?

   a. Inner join

   b. Exterior join

   c. Cross join

   d. Unequal join

6. Which of the following is *not* an aggregated function?

   a. Lowest

   b. Sum

   c. Average

   d. Count

7. Which of the following SELECT statement selects all the fields from the Inventory table?

   a. SELECT all fields FROM Inventory

   b. SELECT [ALL] from [INVENTORY]

   c. SELECT from INVENTORY {all fields}

   d. SELECT * FROM Inventory

8. For more space in which to enter the SELECT statement in a field or criteria cell, what do you press to display the Zoom box?

   a. Shift+F2

   b. Ctrl+2

   c. Shift+Enter

   d. Ctrl+Spacebar

9. To undo the changes made by an action query,

   a. Click the Undo button

   b. Restore the data from a backup copy

   c. Switch to Datasheet View

   d. Run the query again

10. Which type of query adds the records in the query's result set to the end of an existing table?

   a. Append

   b. Make table

   c. Update

   d. Delete

Competency Assessment

Project 12-1: Create a Calculated Query Field

In your job as a travel agent at Margie's Travel, you are frequently asked the length of various trips. So that you don't have to calculate it mentally, create a calculated field that will give you this information.

GET READY. LAUNCH Access if it is not already running.

@ The *M Travel* file for this lesson is available on the book companion website or in WileyPLUS.

1. **OPEN** the *M Travel* database from the data files for this lesson.

2. **SAVE** the database as *M Travel XXX* (where *XXX* is your initials).

3. On the Create tab, in the Queries group, click **Query Design**.

4. In the Show Table dialog box, double-click **Events** to add the table to the design grid.

5. Click **Close**.

6. In the *Inventory* field list, double-click **Event**, **StartTime**, and **EndTime** to add them to the design grid.

7. Click the **Field** cell in the first blank column and press **Shift+F2** to open the Zoom dialog box.

8. In the Zoom dialog box, key the following expression:

   TripLength: [EndTime] − [StartTime]

9. Click **OK**.

10. On the Design tab, in the Results group, click **Run**. The query is displayed, with a new *TripLength* field calculating the number of days of the trip.

11. Save the query as **Calculated Query** and close.

12. **CLOSE** the database.

LEAVE Access running for the next project.

Project 12-2: Save a Filter as a Query

As purchasing manager for the Coho Vineyard monthly wine, you frequently run the same filters on the database. Now that you have learned to save a filter as a query, you can save yourself some time.

GET READY. LAUNCH Access if it is not already running.

@ The **Wine Coho** file for this lesson is available on the book companion website or in WileyPLUS.

1. **OPEN** *Wine Coho* from the data files for this lesson.

2. **SAVE** the database as **Wine Coho XXX** (where *XXX* is your initials).

3. On the Create tab, in the Queries group, click the **Query Wizard** button.

4. In the New Query dialog box, click **Simple Query Wizard** and click **OK**.

5. In the Tables/Queries drop-down list, click **Table: Red Wines**.

6. Click the **>>** button to move all the fields from the Available Fields to the Selected Fields box and then click **Next >**.

7. Click **Next >** again and then click **Finish** to display a simple select query.

8. On the Home tab, in the Sort & Filter group, click the **Advanced** button and then click **Filter by Form**.

9. In the Filter by Form, click the **down arrow** in the *Country* field and click **Italy**.

10. On the Home tab, in the Sort & Filter group, click the **Toggle Filter** button to apply the filter. The results are displayed.

11. On the Home tab, in the Sort & Filter group, click the **Advanced** button and then click **Advanced Filter/Sort** to display the new query design grid.

12. On the Home tab, in the Sort & Filter group, click the **Advanced** button and then click **Save As Query**. The Save As Query dialog box appears.

13. Key **Filter Query** in the Query Name box and click **OK**.

14. Click the **Close** button to close the Red Wines QueryFilter1 query.

15. On the Home tab, in the Sort & Filter group, click the **Toggle Filter** button to remove the filter.

16. Click the **Close** button to close the Red Wines query and save the changes when prompted.

17. **LEAVE** the database open.

LEAVE Access open for the next project.

Proficiency Assessment

Project 12-3: Create a Subquery

You are interested in extracting specific information about the wine prices from the database. Create a subquery to determine which white wines have a purchase price that is above average.

USE the database that is open from the previous project.

1. On the Create tab, in the Queries group, click **Query Design**.
2. Use the Show Table dialog box to add the White Wines table to the upper section of the query design grid and then close it.
3. Add the *Bottled, Label, Type,* and *PurchasePrice* fields to the design grid.
4. Place the insertion point in the Criteria row of *PurchasePrice* field and display the Expression Builder.
5. Key the following expression in the Expression Builder, using the available categories and menus:

   > (SELECT AVG([PurchasePrice]) FROM [White Wines])

6. Click **OK**.
7. On the Design tab, in the Results group, click **Run** to display the query results.
8. Save the query as **Subquery** and close.
9. **CLOSE** the database.

LEAVE Access open for the next project.

Project 12-4: Create a Make Table Query

As the manager at Southridge Video, you want to archive the current table with information about used games. Use the make table action query to create a backup table.

GET READY. LAUNCH Access if it is not already running.

@ The *Games Southridge* file for this lesson is available on the book companion website or in WileyPLUS.

1. **OPEN** *Games Southridge* from the data files for this lesson.
2. **SAVE** the database as *Games Southridge XXX* (where *XXX* is your initials).
3. Create a simple select query named **Games Query** using all the fields in the Games:Table.
4. Display the query in Design View if it is not already.
5. On the Design tab, in the Query Type group, click **Make Table** to display the Make Table dialog box.
6. In the Table Name box, key **Games Backup**. If it is not already selected, click **Current Database**, and then click **OK**.
7. On the Design tab, in the Results group, click **Run**. An alert message appears.
8. Click **Yes**. A new table appears in the Navigation Pane.
9. Close the Games Query and save the changes when prompted.
10. **CLOSE** the database.

LEAVE Access open for the next project.

Mastery Assessment

Project 12-5: Create a Crosstab Query

As a regional manager for Contoso Pharmaceuticals, you are in charge of overseeing the sales reps in your division. To determine the total samples given by each rep in the first two weeks of the quarter, you decide to create a crosstab query.

GET READY. LAUNCH Access if it is not already running.

The *Contoso Data* file for this lesson is available on the book companion website or in WileyPLUS.

1. **OPEN** *Contoso Data* from the data files for this lesson.
2. **SAVE** the database as *Contoso Data XXX* (where *XXX* is initials).
3. Use the Samples Given: Table and the skills you have learned in this lesson to create the crosstab query named Samples Given_Crosstab shown in Figure 12-52.

Figure 12-52

Crosstab query

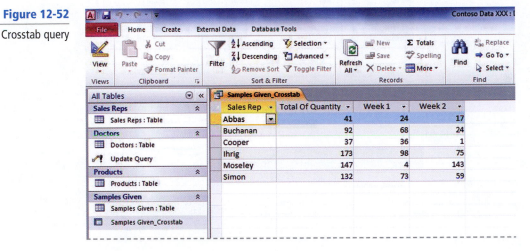

4. **LEAVE** the database open for the next project.

LEAVE Access open for the next project.

Project 12-6: Create an Update Query

The name of one of the hospitals in your region has recently been changed. You need to create an update query to change the name in the database.

USE the database that is open from the previous project.

1. Create a select query named **Update Query** that includes all the fields in the Doctors: Table.
2. Switch to Design View.
3. Use criteria to select only the records that have Community Medical Center in the *Hospital* field.
4. Use the skills you have learned in this lesson to create an update query that will change the name of Community Medical Center to Community Regional Hospital.
5. Open the **Doctors: Table** to verify that the hospital name has been changed. Then, close the table and the query.
6. **CLOSE** the database.

CLOSE Access.

INTERNET READY

At this point in the book, you have learned a lot about using Access. If you want to learn even more about Access from a programming and coding perspective, you can explore the Microsoft Developers Network (MSDN) website. The URL for this site is http://msdn.microsoft.com.

Here you can ask and answer questions in forums related to Access 2010 and all Microsoft applications and technologies, stay connected with the MSDN community to explore new innovations and technologies, and read articles about technical trends. The MSDN home page is shown in Figure 12-53.

Figure 12-53

MSDN home page

Workplace *Ready*

CREATING MAILING LABELS IN ACCESS

Keeping track of sales data and contacts is vital to the success of any business. Access provides the tools you need to not only keep these records available and secure, but also to generate sales and provide customer service. Whether you need to mail a single sales brochure or do a mass mailing of two hundred, you can use Access to create the labels using the records you maintain in your Access databases.

Imagine you are a partner in a start-up software firm named Proseware, Inc., that has developed specialized software for colleges and universities. You have created an Access database with tables that include information for customers as well as sales leads for professors to whom you are marketing the product.

Using the Label Wizard in Access, you can create mailing labels and sort them by zip code for bulk mailing. You can create a parameter query that uses one or more criteria to select only certain records for labels. You can specify a label size that matches a brand of label sheets you can purchase at the office supply store, or you can choose to create a custom-sized sheet of labels. With Access, you can produce professional, high-quality mailings to your targeted audience quickly and efficiently.

Display and Share Data 13

LESSON SKILL MATRIX

Skill	Exam Objective	Objective Number
Creating a Chart Using the Chart Wizard	Add bound/unbound controls.	5.2.3
Formatting a Chart		
Changing Chart Types		
Building a PivotChart		
Saving a Database Object as Another File Type	Use Save Object As. Use Save and Publish.	1.1.1 1.1.3
Printing a Database Object		

KEY TERMS

- chart
- chart body
- Chart Wizard
- legend
- PDF
- PivotChart
- XPS

325

Blue Yonder Airlines is a small but rapidly growing regional airline. In your position as Investor Relations Specialist, you assist in building investor relations programs, creating and distributing analyst reports, maintaining and updating databases, and preparing materials for conference presentations. In this lesson, you create, save, and print charts that will be reproduced and included in a report detailing the growth of Blue Yonder Airlines.

CREATING A CHART USING THE CHART WIZARD

The Bottom Line

Charts are often used in the business world to give a visual representation of numeric data. Because a picture is worth a thousand words, charts play an important role in reports and presentations. In Access 2010, you can insert a chart into a new or existing form or report using the Chart Wizard control.

Creating a Chart Using the Chart Wizard

The Chart Wizard lets you insert a chart into a new or existing report or form using a table or query as your data source. This allows you to insert a pictorial view of the data along with the numbers. The Chart Wizard asks you questions about the chart you want and then creates the chart based on your answers. In this exercise, you insert a chart into the Page Footer section of a report because it is a one-page report and it is helpful to show the data at the bottom of the page after the columnar data.

Take Note
Charts and graphs are terms used synonymously in Microsoft Access. For example, the Chart Wizard inserts a chart control into reports or forms, however, a chart is referred to as a graph in Visual Basic for Applications (VBA) code.

A **chart** is a graphical representation of data. A chart is made up of two basic parts, the body and the legend. The **chart body** is the main area that displays the chart. The **legend** displays a list of the colors, shapes, or patterns used as categories in a chart.

The **Chart Wizard** creates a control that you can insert into forms and reports to quickly create charts. Once you insert a chart, you may need to resize it later; you can do so by clicking and dragging the selection handles to increase or decrease the height or width.

You could also place the chart in the Detail section of the report and, within the Chart Wizard, set the chart to change with each record, so you would have a report displaying the record data and a chart for each record.

You can create 20 different charts using the Chart Wizard, including column, bar, area, line, XY scatter, pie, bubble, and doughnut charts.

To delete a chart, right-click it in Design View and select Delete from the shortcut menu.

STEP BY STEP   **Create a Chart**

GET READY. Before you begin these steps, be sure to turn on and/or log on to your computer and **LAUNCH** Access.

@ The *Blue Yonder Airlines* file for this lesson is available on the book companion website or in WileyPLUS.

1. **OPEN** *Blue Yonder Airlines* from the data files for this lesson.
2. **SAVE** the database as *Blue Yonder Airlines XXX* (where *XXX* is your initials).
3. Open the **Income & Expenses** report.
4. Switch to Design View.

5. On the Design tab, in the Controls group, click the **Chart** button. The pointer changes to a plus sign with a chart icon.

6. Click in the upper-left corner of the Page Footer section and drag to the lower-right corner to create a rectangular placeholder where the chart will be inserted, as shown in Figure 13-1.

Figure 13-1

Report in Design View

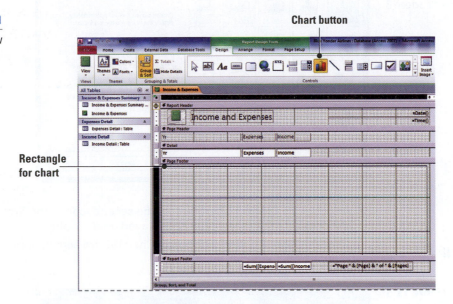

7. Release the mouse button. The first Chart Wizard screen appears, as shown in Figure 13-2.

Figure 13-2

Chart Wizard, screen 1

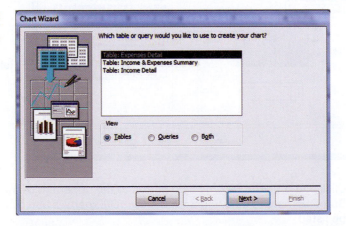

8. Select the **Income & Expenses Summary** table as your data source and click the **Next >** button. The second Chart Wizard screen appears, as shown in Figure 13-3.

Figure 13-3

Chart Wizard, screen 2

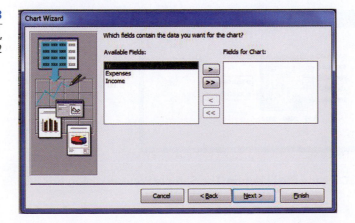

9. Click the **>>** button to move all the fields to the Fields for Chart box and click the **Next >** button. The third Chart Wizard screen appears, as shown in Figure 13-4.

Figure 13-4

Chart Wizard, screen 3

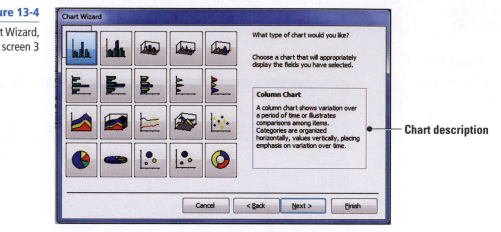

10. Click the **3D Column Chart** button, the second icon in the first row. Notice that the description of the chart type is displayed on the right.

11. Click the **Next >** button. The fourth Chart Wizard screen appears, as shown in Figure 13-5.

Figure 13-5

Chart Wizard, screen 4

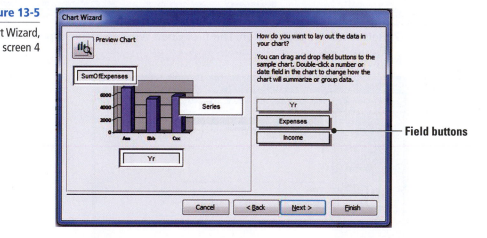

12. Click and drag the *Income* field button to the upper left of the chart and drop on the SumOfExpenses data list. Both the *SumOfExpenses* and *SumOfIncome* fields should be listed.

13. Click the **Preview Chart** button. The Sample Preview dialog box appears, displaying a sample of your chart, as shown in Figure 13-6.

Figure 13-6

Sample Preview dialog box

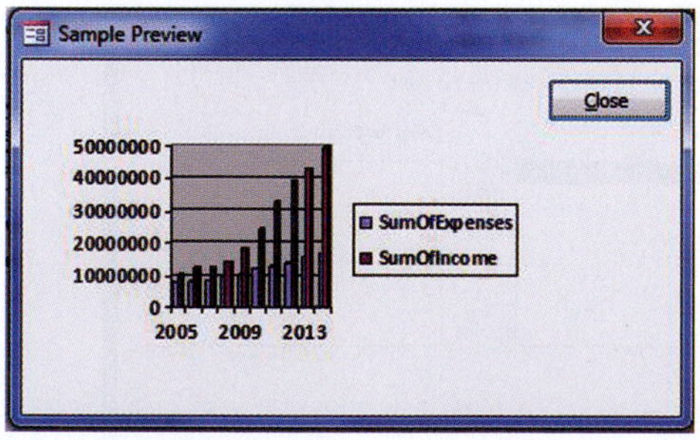

14. Click the **Close** button. The Sample Preview dialog box closes.

15. Click the **Next >** button. The fifth Chart Wizard screen appears, as shown in Figure 13-7.

Figure 13-7

Chart Wizard, screen 5

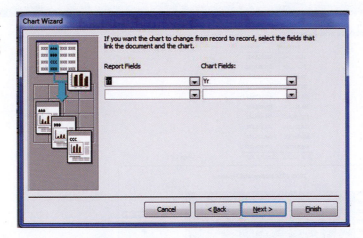

16. Click the **down arrow** in the Report Fields menu and select **<No Field>** since you don't want to display a chart for each record in the data source.

17. Click the **down arrow** in the Chart Fields menu and select **<No Field>** again, since you don't want to display a chart for each record in the data source.

18. Click the **Next >** button. The sixth Chart Wizard screen appears, as shown in Figure 13-8.

Figure 13-8

Chart Wizard, screen 6

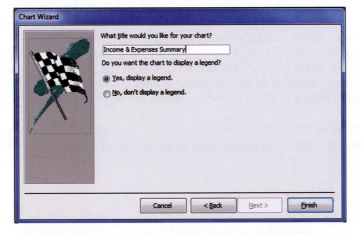

19. Key **2005–2014 Income and Expenses** in the Title box.

20. The **Yes, display a legend** button should be selected. If not, select it and click the **Finish** button. Access inserts your chart. Notice that Design View displays sample data and not the actual data from your chart.

21. Click the chart to select it.

22. On the Design tab, in the Tools group, click the **Property Sheet** button if necessary.

23. Click the **Data** tab of the Property Sheet. Click the **down arrow** at the end of the Enabled line and select **Yes**. This enables the chart data to accurately display the associated table data.

24. Close the Property Sheet.

25. Switch to Report View.

26. On the Home tab, in the Records group, click the **Refresh All** button to ensure the chart displays the latest table data.

27. Scroll to the bottom of the report to view your chart, which should look similar to Figure 13-9.

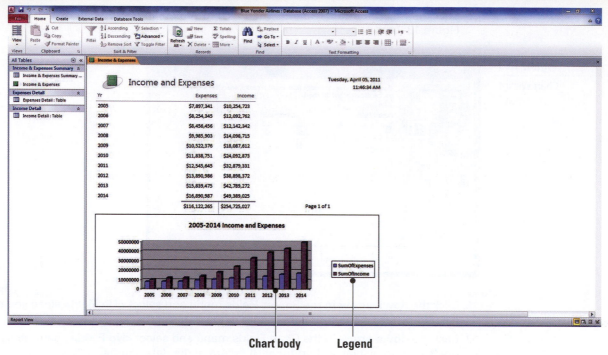

Chart body   Legend

Figure 13-9

Report with 3D bar chart

**Troubleshooting** If your chart is not displaying correctly, you probably need to increase the width and/or height of the placeholder. You do this the same way you resize any control. Switch to Design View and click the resize handles in the center of the vertical borders and drag to increase the size. Drag the resize handles on the horizontal borders to change the height. Then, return to Report View to see the results.

CERTIFICATION
R E A D Y   **5.2.3**

How do you create a graph on a report?

28. Save the report.

PAUSE. LEAVE the report open to use in the next exercise.

FORMATTING A CHART

The Bottom Line

You can use Microsoft Graph to change the formatting of charts created with the Chart Wizard. You can change chart options such as how the title and labels are displayed and where you want the legend located. You can also change formatting options, such as the color or the chart's background and the color and size of the data blocks in the chart.

After you create a chart using the Chart Wizard, you can edit it using Microsoft Graph, which is a component of Office 2010. To launch Microsoft Graph, double-click a chart in Design View. Microsoft Graph displays the chart and the datasheet. You can choose commands from the menu bar or the toolbar.

After you make changes to the chart, it is important to save the changes using the Save command on the File menu. After you save a chart, Microsoft Graph closes and switches you back to Design View.

Changing Chart Options

The Chart Options dialog box has six tabs with options for changing the look and layout of a chart. You can access the Chart Options dialog box from the Chart menu or by right-clicking the white Chart Area and selecting Chart Options from the shortcut menu. In this exercise, you change chart options using Microsoft Graph.

STEP BY STEP   **Change Chart Options**

USE the report open from the previous exercise.

1. Switch to Design View.
2. Double-click the chart. The Microsoft Graph software launches, displaying the chart in a view similar to Design View, as shown in Figure 13-10.

Chart Objects menu   Menu bar   Toolbar

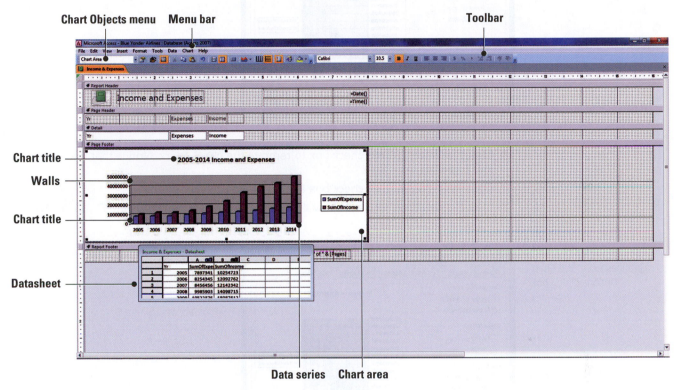

Chart title

Walls

Chart title

Datasheet

Data series   Chart area

Figure 13-10

Chart displayed in Microsoft Graph

3. Click the **Chart** menu and select **Chart Options**. The Chart Options dialog box appears, as shown in Figure 13-11.

Figure 13-11

Titles tab on the Chart Options dialog box

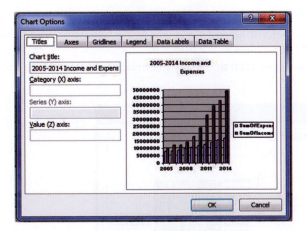

4. Select **2005-2014** in the Chart title box and press the **Delete** key. Notice that the preview on the right adjusts to show the change.

5. Click the **Axes** tab to display the options on the tab, as shown in Figure 13-12.

Figure 13-12

Axes tab of the Chart Options
dialog box

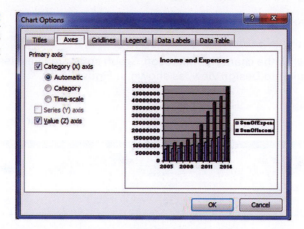

6. Click the **Value (Z) axis** check box to remove the check mark. Notice that the values on the Z axis are removed.

7. Click the **Value (Z) axis** check box again to insert the check mark.

8. Click the **Gridlines** tab to display the options on the tab, as shown in Figure 13-13.

Figure 13-13

Gridlines tab of the Chart
Options dialog box

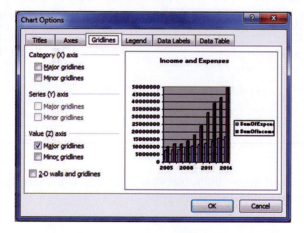

9. Click the **Major gridlines** check box in the Category (X) axis section. Notice that gridlines are added to the preview.

10. Click the **Legend** tab to display the options on the tab, as shown in Figure 13-14.

Figure 13-14

Legend tab of the Chart
Options dialog box

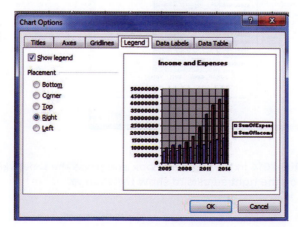

11. Click the **Show legend** check box to remove the check mark. Notice that the legend is removed from the chart.

12. Click the **Show legend** check box again to insert a check mark. The legend is displayed in the preview.

13. Click the **Bottom** radio button to move the legend to the bottom of the chart.

14. Click the **Data Labels** tab to display the options on the tab, as shown in Figure 13-15.

Figure 13-15

Data Labels tab of the Chart Options dialog box

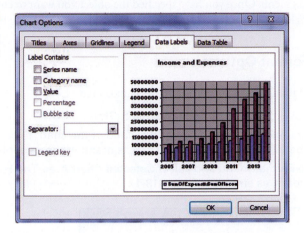

15. Click the **Value** check box to insert a check mark. Notice that values are added to the columns in the chart.

16. Click the **Value** check box again to remove the check mark.

17. Click the **Data Table** tab to display the options on the tab, as shown in Figure 13-16.

Figure 13-16

Data table tab of the Chart Options dialog box

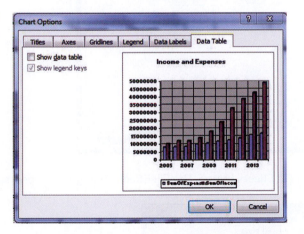

18. Click the **Show data table** check box to insert a check mark. Notice that the datasheet is added to the bottom of the chart.

19. Click the **Show data table** check box again to remove the check mark.

20. Click **OK**.

21. Click the **File** menu and select **Save**. The Microsoft Graph software closes and the report is switched back to Design View.

PAUSE. LEAVE the report open to use in the next exercise.

Troubleshooting Microsoft Graph has its own Help system. To access it, double-click a chart to launch Microsoft Graph and choose Microsoft Graph Help from the Help menu or press F1.

Changing Format Options

Microsoft Graph makes it easy to format a chart. Each part of the chart is an independent object, so you can simply right-click the chart object that you want to change and choose Format [Chart Object] from the shortcut menu. A dialog box appears with the formatting choices available for that object. In this exercise you format the chart you've been working with.

If you prefer to use the menus, you can click on the chart object to select it or choose it from the Chart Objects menu. Once you have specified the object you want to change, click the Format menu and choose Select [Chart Object] from the menu to launch the dialog box of available options.

STEP BY STEP **Change Format Options**

USE the database open from the previous exercise.

1. Double-click the chart to open Microsoft Graph.
2. Click the **Chart Area**, the white background of the chart, to select it. The Chart Area should be displayed in the Chart Objects menu in the upper-left corner of the toolbar.
3. Click the **Format** menu and select **Selected Chart Area**. The Format Chart Area dialog box appears, as shown in Figure 13-17.

Figure 13-17

Format Chart Area dialog box

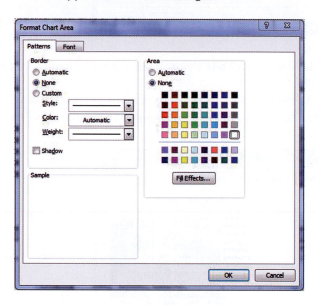

4. Click the **Fill Effects** button. The Fill Effects dialog box appears, as shown in Figure 13-18.

Figure 13-18

Fill Effects dialog box

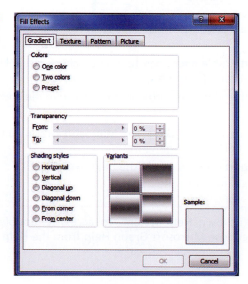

5. Click the **Horizontal** radio button in the Shading styles section and click **OK**.

6. Click **OK** in the Format Chart Area dialog box. Notice the shading style of the chart background changes to your selection.

7. Right-click any of the purple Data Series columns in the chart to display the shortcut menu. Notice that Series SumOfIncome is displayed in the Chart Objects menu.

8. Select **Format Data Series** from the shortcut menu. The Format Data Series dialog box appears.

9. Select the **Green** color (second row, fourth from the left) as shown in Figure 13-19.

Figure 13-19

Format Data Series dialog box

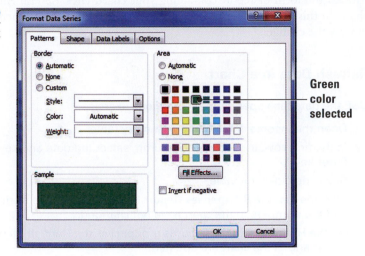

Green color selected

10. Click **OK** in the Format Data Series dialog box.

11. Right-click the gray grid background of the chart, called the Walls, and select **Format Walls** from the shortcut menu.

12. Click the **Fill Effects** button.

13. Click the **From center** button in the Shading styles section and click **OK**.

14. Click **OK** in the Format Walls dialog box.

15. Right-click the **Legend** and select **Format Legend** from the menu. The Format Legend dialog box appears. Select the **Font** tab if it is not already displayed. The Font tab menu now appears, as shown in Figure 13-20.

Figure 13-20

Font tab of the Format Legend dialog box

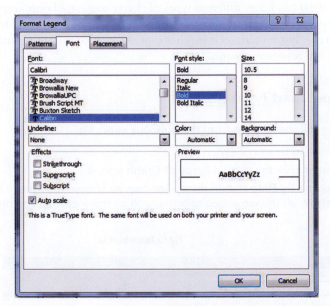

16. Select **10** in the Size menu and click **OK**.

17. Click the **File** menu and select **Save**. Switch to Report View.

18. Save the report.

PAUSE. LEAVE the report open to use in the next exercise.

Refreshing Data in a Chart

The Refresh All button can be a useful tool when working with charts. When you make a change to the data source of a chart, be sure to save the new data in the table or query. When you switch back to the form or report containing your chart, click Refresh All to update the data in the chart. In this exercise, you make a change to a table record and then refresh the data in a chart to view the change.

STEP BY STEP   **Refresh Data in a Chart**

USE the database open from the previous exercise.

1. Open the **Income & Expenses Summary** table.

2. In the first row, in the Income column, select the data and key **9004523** and press the **Enter** key.

3. Save and close the table.

4. Click the **Income & Expenses Report** tab. Notice that the numbers in the report data and the numbers in the chart have not changed.

5. On the Home tab, in the Records group, click the **Refresh All** button. The data in the report and in the chart are updated.

6. Save the report.

PAUSE. LEAVE the report open to use in the next exercise.

CHANGING CHART TYPES

The Bottom Line

Access provides many different chart types and variations of those chart types for you to choose from in the Chart Type dialog box. Access makes it easy to experiment with different configurations before you decide on the chart that best displays the data you want to emphasize. In this exercise, you change the type of chart with which you've been working.

Changing Chart Types

Access 2010 has many different types of charts you can choose from. The key is to choose one that displays your data in a meaningful way. Often, you have a specific chart in mind that you want to use, but sometimes it requires experimentation, choosing and changing chart types until you get the results you want.

STEP BY STEP   **Change Chart Types**

USE the database open from the previous exercise.

1. Switch to Design View.

2. Double-click the chart. Microsoft Graph opens.

3. Click the **By Row** button on the Toolbar, as shown in Figure 13-21. The chart is changed to show all the expenses together and all the income together.

Figure 13-21

Microsoft Graph toolbar

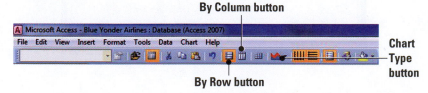

By Column button

By Row button

Chart Type button

4. Click the **By Column** button on the Toolbar to change it back to the original chart.

5. Click the **Chart Type** button and select **3D Area Chart** from the menu, as shown in Figure 13-22. The chart changes to an area chart.

Figure 13-22

Chart Type button and menu

6. Click the **Chart** menu and select **Chart Type**. The Chart Type dialog box appears, as shown in Figure 13-23.

Figure 13-23

Chart Type dialog box

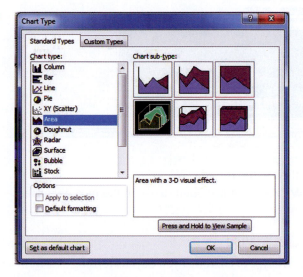

7. On the Standard Types tab, click **Pie** in the Chart type list. In the Chart subtype section, click the **Pie with a 3D visual effect**, the second icon on the first row.

8. Click and hold the **Press and Hold to View Sample** button to see a preview of the chart, as shown in Figure 13-24.

Figure 13-24

Sample pie chart

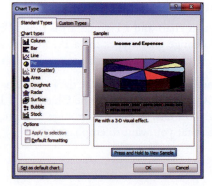

9. Click the **Custom Types** tab.

10. Click **Colored Lines** in the Chart type list and click **OK**.

11. Click the **File** menu and select **Save**.

12. Switch to Report View to see the chart. Your screen should resemble Figure 13-25.

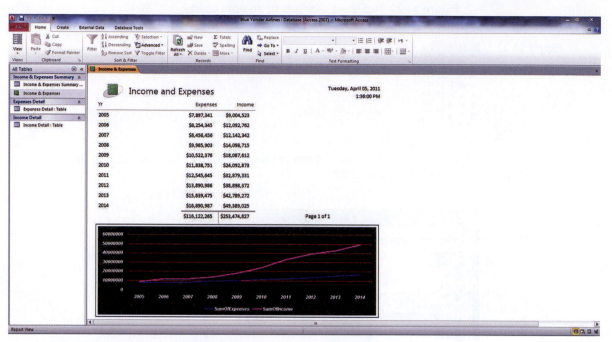

Figure 13-25

Chart in Report View

13. Save and close the report.

PAUSE. LEAVE the database open to use in the next exercise.

BUILDING A PIVOTCHART

The Bottom Line

A PivotChart is a type of chart that you can create using data from a table or PivotTable. A Pivot-Table is a more advanced type of form that you can create that allows you to analyze data from different perspectives by quickly changing the alignment of columns and rows. A **PivotChart** is an interactive chart that shows data totals or summaries. When you view a PivotChart, you can change the chart to view different combinations of data, just as you chose to display only one year of data in the previous exercise.

Creating a Pivot Chart

The difference between a regular chart and a PivotChart is that a PivotChart can be interactive. You can create, format, and change chart types for a PivotChart much like you did with the charts you created with the Chart Wizard. In this exercise you create a PivotChart.

To create a PivotChart, you need to select or open the data source before clicking the PivotChart button. Drag the fields you want to include from the Chart Field List and drop them into the appropriate drop zones. Like most charts, you can arrange the category, series, or data fields in different ways, depending on what you want to emphasize.

STEP BY STEP   **Create a PivotChart**

USE the database open from the previous exercise.

1. Open the **Income Detail** table.

2. On the Create tab, in the Forms group, click the **More Forms** button and then the **PivotChart** button. A blank PivotChart appears and the PivotChart Tools appear in the Ribbon.

3. On the Design tab, in the Show/Hide group, click the **Field List** button to display the Chart Field List if it isn't displayed already. Your screen should look similar to Figure 13-26.

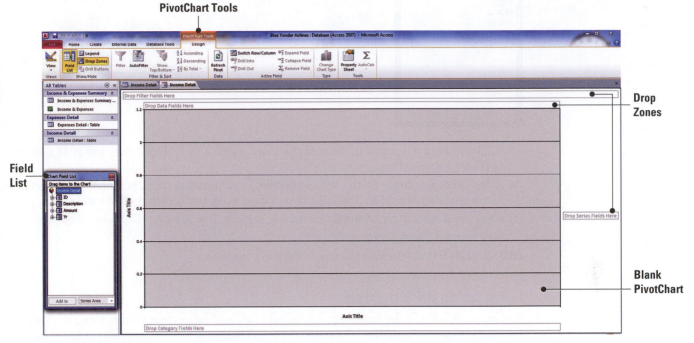

Figure 13-26

Blank PivotChart

4. In the Chart Field List, click the **Amount** field and drag it to the Drop Data Fields Here drop zone box and release the mouse button.

5. Click the **Description** field and drag and drop it in the Drop Series Fields Here drop zone.

6. Click the **Yr** field and drag and drop it in the Drop Category Fields Here drop zone. Your screen should look similar to Figure 13-27.

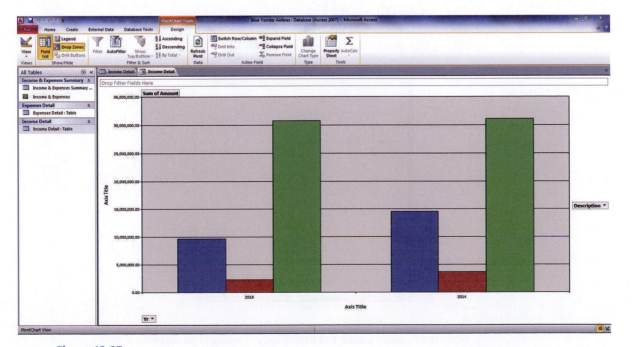

Figure 13-27

PivotChart

7. On the Design tab, in the Show/Hide group, click the **Legend** button. A legend is added to the chart.

8. Click the **down arrow** on the **Yr** field button at the bottom of the chart. A menu of year options appears, as shown in Figure 13-28.

9. Click the **2013** check box to remove the check mark, and click **OK**. Only the 2014 data is displayed in the chart.

10. Click the **down arrow** on the **Yr** field button. Click the **2013** check box again to insert the check mark and click **OK**. The 2013 data is displayed along with the 2014 data.

11. Click the **Save** button on the Quick Access Toolbar. The Save As dialog box appears.

12. Key **Income Chart** and click **OK**.

PAUSE. LEAVE the chart open to use in the next exercise.

Formatting a PivotChart

You can easily change the format of data series, titles, and other chart objects using the Properties dialog box. Just select the object you want to change and click the Property Sheet button to display the Properties dialog box. You can leave the dialog box open while you make all your selections and formatting changes and then close it when you are finished. Remember to save your work. In this exercise, you practice formatting a PivotChart.

STEP BY STEP   **Format a PivotChart**

USE the chart open from the previous exercise.

1. Click the **Axis Title** at the bottom of the chart to select it.

2. On the Design tab, in the Tools group, click the **Property Sheet** button. The Properties dialog box appears, as shown in Figure 13-29.

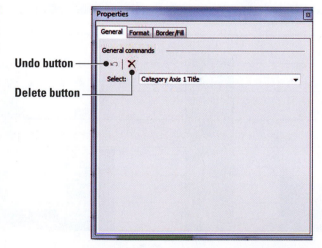

3. Click the **Delete** button in the General commands section. The Axis Title is removed from the screen. Leave the dialog box open on the screen.

4. Click the **Axis Title** on the left side of the chart to select it. The data in the Properties dialog box displays options for the selected title.

5. Click the **Format** tab on the Properties dialog box, as shown in Figure 13-30.

Figure 13-30

Format tab on the Properties dialog box

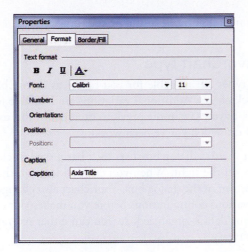

6. Click the **Bold** button.

7. Click the **down arrow** on the Font size menu and select **14**.

8. Select **Axis Title** in the Caption box. Key **Amount** and press the **Enter** key. The changes you made are updated on the chart. Leave the Properties dialog box open on the screen. If you need to move it, click the top blue border and drag it to a new location.

9. Click the green **Passenger** column in the 2013 data to select it.

10. Click the same column again. Both green columns should now be selected.

11. Click the **Border/Fill** tab in the Properties dialog box, as shown in Figure 13-31.

Figure 13-31

Border/Fill tab on the Properties dialog box

12. Click the **down arrow** on the Fill Type menu and select **Gradient**.

13. Click the coral-colored (second) column two times to select both coral columns. Click the **down arrow** on the Fill Type menu and select **Gradient**.

14. Select both blue columns in the chart and select **Gradient** from the Fill Type menu.

15. Click in the gray background, or **Plot Area**, of the chart. Click the **down arrow** on the Fill Type menu and select **Gradient**.

16. Click the **Color** button in the Fill area. A menu of colors appears.

17. Select the **Khaki** color (row seven, seventh from the left) shown in Figure 13-32.

Figure 13-32

Color menu on the Border/Fill tab of the Properties dialog box

18. Click the **Close** box to close the Properties dialog box.

19. Save the chart.

PAUSE. LEAVE the chart open to use in the next exercise.

Changing the PivotChart Type

The same basic chart types are available for you to use as PivotCharts as well as other charts, such as Radar and Stock charts. Additional variations are available for PivotCharts, too, as well as Custom Chart types, as you saw in the previous exercise. In this exercise you change the chart type of the PivotChart on which you've been working.

The Type tab of the Properties dialog box lists each basic type of chart on the left and displays icons of subtype charts on the right. When you click an icon on the right, a description of the chart appears at the bottom of the dialog box. Your chart also changes to that chart type, so you can view your data in various configurations before you make your choice. Some types of charts may not fit the way your data is organized, so you can either rearrange the fields in your chart or try a different chart type.

STEP BY STEP   **Change the Chart Type**

USE the chart open from the previous exercise.

1. Click the white area on the chart, called the **Chartspace**.

2. On the Design tab, in the Type group, click the **Change Chart Type** button. The Properties dialog box appears with the Type tab displayed, as shown in Figure 13-33. Notice that the Clustered Column type is selected, because that is the current chart type.

Figure 13-33

Type tab of the Properties dialog box

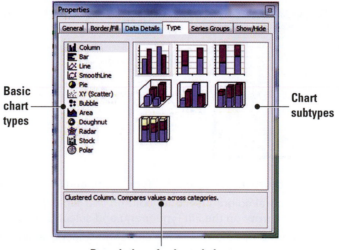

Basic chart types

Chart subtypes

Description of selected chart

Another Way
You can also access the Type tab of the Properties dialog box by right-clicking in the Chartspace and selecting Change Chart Type from the shortcut menu.

3. Click the **3D Stacked Column** type.

4. Close the Properties dialog box.

5. Save and close the chart.

6. Save and close the table.

PAUSE. LEAVE the database open to use in the next exercise.

SAVING A DATABASE OBJECT AS ANOTHER FILE TYPE

The Bottom Line

Microsoft Access 2010 allows you to save database objects, such as tables, reports, and queries as other types of objects. For example, you can save a table as a report. You can also save database objects as PDF or XPS files. Saving a database object as another file type allows you to share data with other users or repurpose the data in other ways.

Another Way
You can also save a database object as another file type by using the Save Object As command in the Backstage view, however, you cannot save database objects as PDF or XPS types by using this method.

You can save objects such as tables, reports, and queries as other types of objects using the Save & Publish tab in the Backstage view. The Save & Publish tab also gives you the option of saving a database object in Portable Document Format (PDF) or XML Paper Specification (XPS) file formats. You might already be familiar with PDF files from documents you view on the Internet or share via emails. The **PDF** file format maintains the exact layout of the original file and can easily be shared. A new alternative to PDF, the **XPS** file format preserves document formatting, can be easily shared, printed, and archived, and is more secure.

Using the Save & Publish Tab

Access includes options on the Publish to Access Services tab to check your database for web compatibility, as well as fields you can complete to specify the remote path to the SharePoint Server. Furthermore, the Save & Publish tab includes options to save a database as different types and versions. In this exercise, you use the Save & Publish tab to save a table object as a report object.

NEW
to Office 2010

The Save & Publish tab also includes the Publish to Access Services command that allows you to share your database with others by publishing it to SharePoint Server 2010 via Access Services. SharePoint Server 2010 allows multiple users to share an Access database remotely using a web browser like Microsoft Internet Explorer as the interface. You must create the database from a new web template before doing so, or already be working with a web compatible database.

STEP BY STEP **Save a Database Object as Another File Type**

USE the database open from the previous exercise.

1. Open the **Income & Expenses Summary** table.
2. Click the **File** tab, and then click the **Save & Publish** tab to display the menu. Click the **Save Object As** tab in the File Types category, as shown in Figure 13-34.

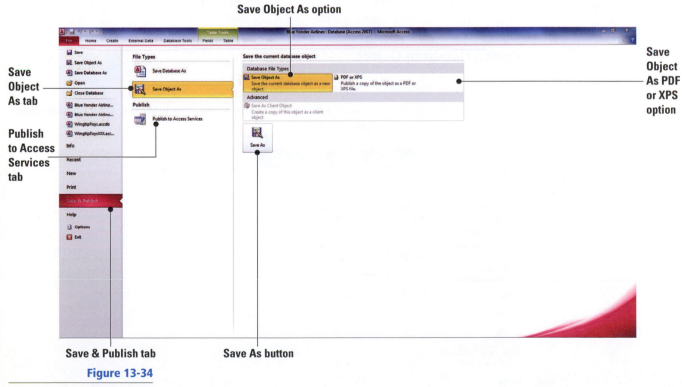

Save Object As option

Save Object As tab

Publish to Access Services tab

Save Object As PDF or XPS option

Save & Publish tab

Save As button

Figure 13-34
Save & Publish menu

3. Click the **Save As** button. The Save As dialog box appears, as shown in Figure 13-35.

Figure 13-35

Save As dialog box

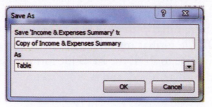

**CERTIFICATION
READY   1.1.1**

How do you save a database
object as another file type?

**CERTIFICATION
READY   1.1.3**

How do you use
Save & Publish?

4. Key **Summary Report** in the Save box.

5. Click the **down arrow** on the As menu and select **Report**.

6. Click **OK**. The table object is saved as a report object and the new Summary Report appears in Layout View.

PAUSE. LEAVE the report open to use in the next exercise.

The Bottom Line

PRINTING A DATABASE OBJECT

You are probably familiar already with printing various kinds of documents from your computer. Printing a database object uses the same print options and settings you use with other types of documents.

You can choose various printing options before sending your document to the printer, such as the number of copies, size of the paper, or the range of pages to print. In this exercise, you learn about some of the options available in the Print dialog box when you print a database object.

You can print tables, queries, forms, reports, or macros just by right-clicking the object in the Navigation pane and selecting Print from the shortcut menu. You can also select the Print tab from the File tab to view available print options before you print an object. To print charts, you must open either the form that contains the chart or the table that is its record source. Changes that you make in the Print dialog box will only be applied to that particular document.

Take Note

When printing lengthy reports, you can choose other options, such as printing a range of pages, collating the pages, or printing multiple pages per sheet.

STEP BY STEP   **Print a Database Object**

USE the report open from the previous exercise.

1. Click the **File** tab and select the **Print** tab on the menu. The Print tab displays available options, as shown in Figure 13-36.

Figure 13-36

Print tab available options

2. Click the **Print** button. The Print dialog box appears, as shown in Figure 13-37.

Figure 13-37

Print dialog box

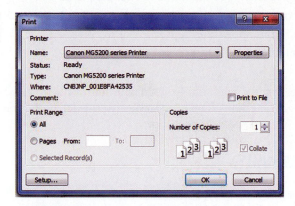

3. Click the **Properties** button. The Properties dialog box appears, as shown in Figure 13-38. Depending on your type of printer, the Properties box could be different. You can change the quality, paper, printing, and orientation options available for your printer. Click the **Cancel** button.

Figure 13-38

Properties dialog box

4. Click the **Setup** button. The Page Setup dialog box appears, as shown in Figure 13-39. Click the **Cancel** button.

Figure 13-39

Page Setup dialog box

5. In the Copies section of the Print dialog box, click the **up arrow** in the Number of Copies menu to change the number of copies to **2**.

6. Click **OK** to print two copies of the report, or click **Cancel**.

7. Close the report and table.

CLOSE the database.

To set a printer as the default, right-click the printer icon and click Set as Default Printer on the shortcut menu. A check mark will appear next to the default printer.

SKILL SUMMARY

In This Lesson You Learned How To:	Exam Objective	Objective Number
Create a Chart Using the Chart Wizard	Add bound/unbound controls.	5.2.3
Format a Chart		
Change Chart Types		
Build a PivotChart		
Save a Database Object as Another File Type	Use Save Object As. Use Save and Publish.	1.1.1 1.1.3
Print a Database Object		

Knowledge Assessment

Matching

Match the term in Column 1 to its description in Column 2.

Column 1	Column 2
1. chart	a. a control that you can insert into forms and reports to quickly create charts
2. chart body	b. an interactive chart that shows data totals or summaries
3. Chart Wizard	c. a file format that maintains the exact layout of the original file and can easily be shared
4. legend	d. a file format that preserves document formatting, can be easily shared, printed, and archived, and is more secure
5. PDF	e. a component of Access 2010 used to make changes to a chart created by the Chart Wizard
6. PivotChart	f. a graphical representation of data
7. XPS	g. includes options to save objects as other file formats like PDF and XPS
8. Refresh All button	h. the main area that displays the chart
9. Microsoft Graph	i. displays a list of the colors, shapes, or patterns used as categories in a chart
10. Save & Publish tab	j. updates the data in a chart

True/False

Circle T if the statement is true or F if the statement is false.

T   F   **1.** You can choose from 20 different chart types in the Chart Wizard.

T   F   **2.** The Chart Wizard is a control.

T   F   **3.** A legend can be displayed only on the right side of a chart.

T   F   **4.** Microsoft Graph displays the chart and the datasheet of the underlying data source.

T   F   **5.** The Refresh All button displays an object's Property Sheet.

T   F   **6.** PivotCharts are a type of report.

T   F   **7.** You can save a table as a report.

T   F   **8.** You can print tables, queries, forms, reports, or macros by right-clicking the object in the Navigation pane and selecting Print from the shortcut menu.

T   F   **9.** An Axis is a type of chart.

T   F   **10.** After you save a chart in Microsoft Graph, Microsoft Graph closes.

Competency Assessment

Project 13-1: City Power & Light Salary Pie Chart

The City Power & Light human resources department is reviewing the salary budgets for the office. Your supervisor asks you to create a pie chart within a report to show the distribution of funds for each employee.

GET READY. LAUNCH Access if it is not already running.

@ The *City Power & Light* file for this lesson is available on the book companion website or in WileyPLUS.

1. OPEN the *City Power & Light* database.

2. Save the database as *City Power & Light XXX* (where *XXX* is your initials).

3. Open the **Salary** report in Design View.

4. Click the **Chart** button and draw a large rectangle in the space provided in the Page Footer section. The Chart Wizard dialog box appears.

5. Click the **Next >** button.

6. Move the *Employee ID* and *Salary* fields to the Fields for Chart list and click **Next >**.

7. Click the **Pie** chart button and click **Next >**.

8. Drag and drop the *Salary* field button to the Data box.

9. Drag and drop the *Employee ID* field button to the Series box.

10. Click the **Preview Chart** button.

11. Click **Close**.

12. Click **Finish**.

13. Click the **Data** tab of the Property Sheet and set the Enabled property to **Yes**.

14. Switch to Report View.

15. Click the **Refresh All** button.

16. Save the Report.

17. Click the **File** tab and select the **Print** tab from the menu.

18. Click the **Print** button and then click **Cancel**.

19. Close the report.

LEAVE the database open for the next project.

Project 13-2: Change the City Power & Light Chart Type

You decide to create a variation of the pie chart that will more clearly show the salary amounts in relationship to each other.

USE the database open from the previous exercise.

1. Open the **Salary** report in Report View.
2. Click the **File** tab, and select **Save Object As**.
3. Key **Salary Line Chart** in the name box and click **OK**.
4. Switch to Design View.
5. Double-click the chart to launch Microsoft Graph.
6. Click the **Chart** menu and select **Chart Type** from the menu.
7. Click **Line** in the Standard types list.
8. In the Chart subtype list, click the **Line with markers displayed at each data value** button.
9. Click **OK**.
10. Click the **Chart** menu and select **Chart Options** from the menu.
11. Click the **Legend** tab and click the **Bottom** check box.
12. Click **OK**.
13. **SAVE** the chart.

CLOSE the database.

Proficiency Assessment

Project 13-3: Create and Format the Expenses PivotChart

You created a chart representing the Income Detail table for Blue Yonder Airlines earlier, now you need to create a chart for the Expenses.

GET READY. LAUNCH Access if it is not already running.

1. **OPEN** *Blue Yonder Airlines XXX* that you saved in an earlier exercise.
2. Create a blank PivotChart using the Expenses Detail table as the data source.
3. Drag the *Yr* field to the Series drop zone, drag the *Amount* field to the Data drop zone, and drag the *Description* field to the Category drop zone.
4. Click the **Legend** button to add a legend to the chart.
5. Click the *Yr* field button and click the **2013** check box to remove the check mark so that only the 2014 data is displayed.
6. Click the **Change Chart Type** button and change it to a *pie* chart.
7. Close the **Properties** dialog box.
8. Save the chart as **Expenses Chart**.
9. Close the chart.

CLOSE the database.

Project 13-4: Create a PivotChart for Lucerne Publishing

As a sales manager for Lucerne Publishing, you are constantly analyzing and sharing sales data in meetings with the sales force as well as other departments in the corporation. Create a chart for your presentation at the next sales meeting.

GET READY. LAUNCH Access if it is not already running.

1. **OPEN** *Lucerne Publishing* from the data files for this lesson.
2. Save the database as *Lucerne Publishing XXX* (where *XXX* is your initials).

@ The *LucernePublishing* file for this lesson is available on the book companion website or in WileyPLUS.

3. Create a new PivotChart using the Sales table.

4. Use the *Gross Sales, Cost of Goods,* and *Net Sales* fields as the *Data* fields. Drag and drop them side by side in the *Data* fields drop zone.

5. Use the *Area* field as the *Category* field.

6. Add a legend to the chart.

7. Save the chart as **Sales Chart**.

LEAVE the chart open for the next project.

Mastery Assessment

Project 13-5: Format the Lucerne Publishing PivotChart

The chart you created worked fine for your presentation; however, you have just been asked to present the information at a meeting with your boss, so you decide to add formatting to make it look more professional.

USE the chart open from the previous exercise.

1. Save the chart object as **Formatted Sales Chart**.

2. Change the Chart to a new Chart Type of your choice.

3. Format the plot area and blocks of data with your choice of colors, patterns, etc.

4. Change the Category Axis Title to **Area** and the Value Axis Title to **Amount**, using the color, size, style, and font of your choice.

5. Save, print, and close the chart.

CLOSE the database.

Project 13-6: Fix the Wingtip Toys Yearly Sales Chart

You asked an assistant to create a chart for the Yearly Sales Report, but it isn't exactly what you wanted. Fix the chart.

GET READY. LAUNCH Access if it is not already running.

@ The *Wingtip Toys* file for this lesson is available on the book companion website or in WileyPLUS.

1. **OPEN** *Wingtip Toys* from the data files for this lesson.

2. **SAVE** the database as *Wingtip Toys XXX* (where *XXX* is your initials).

3. Open the **Yearly Sales Report**.

4. Launch Microsoft Graph and remove the data table at the bottom of the chart.

5. Move the legend to the bottom of the report.

6. Change the background color and pattern of the chart area to a solid **light gray**.

7. Save and close the report.

CLOSE Access.

INTERNET READY

Search the msdn.microsoft.com website for *Creating Web Databases with Access 2010 and Access Services.* Explore the resulting links to learn more about how you can create and publish a Microsoft Access 2010 database to Access Services on Microsoft SharePoint Server 2010. Explore the Visual How-To's that this site includes, and start building a web-friendly database using the skills you've already learned.

14 Import and Export Data

LESSON SKILL MATRIX

Skill	Exam Objective	Objective Number
Importing Data	Import source data into a new table.	2.5.1
	Append records to an existing table.	2.5.2
	Import data as a linked table.	2.5.3
Saving and Running Import Specifications		
Exporting Data		
Saving and Running Export Specifications		

KEY TERMS
- **delimited file**
- **delimiter**
- **fixed-width file**
- **linked table**
- **specification**

You are the human resources coordinator at Humongous Insurance, a private company dedicated to offering products that provide quality protection with value pricing for rural and low-income families, as well as senior citizens on fixed incomes. Your department has just begun to use Access, but you still receive data in different formats that must be merged with your Access databases. At times, you also want to distribute information that your manager prefers to view in a different format. In this lesson, you learn how to import data, link to an external data source, and save and run import specifications. You also learn how to export data from a table and from a query, as well as how to save and run export specifications.

SOFTWARE ORIENTATION

External Data Tab

The External Data tab contains commands that will be used to import and export data in various formats. Use Figure 14-1 as a reference throughout this lesson as well as the rest of this book.

Figure 14-1

External Data tab

View and run the export operations you previously saved

View and run the import operations you previously saved

IMPORTING DATA

The Bottom Line

To store data from an external source in Access, you can import the data into a new or existing database. After you run an import operation, you can save the import settings for reuse. You can also link to data from an external source without actually maintaining a copy of the data in the database.

Importing Data from a Specific Source

You can import data from a variety of sources into an Access database. When you import data, Access creates a copy of the data in a new or existing table without altering the source file. Before you start the import operation, decide whether you want to store the data in a new or existing table. If you choose to store the data in a new table, Access creates a table and adds the imported data to this table. If a table with the specified name already exists, Access overwrites the contents of the table with the imported data. If you choose to add the data to an existing table, the rows in the Excel file are appended to the specified table. In this exercise, you import data from an Excel worksheet into a new Access table.

You can also import data from other specific sources besides Excel, such as a SharePoint list, a Word file, another Access database, or a text file. The same general process is used for importing data, regardless of the source. On the External Data tab, in the Import & Link group, click the More button to see additional formats that you can import from or link to.

Take Note   You can import only one worksheet at a time during an import operation. To import data from multiple worksheets, repeat the import operation for each worksheet.

Before you import, you should always review the source data and make any necessary modifications, as described in Table 14-1.

Table 14-1

Source Data Elements

Element	Description
Number of columns	You cannot import more than 255 source columns, because Access does not support more than 255 fields in a table.
Skipping columns and rows	It is a good practice to include only the rows and columns that you want to import into the source worksheet or named range. Note that you cannot filter or skip rows during the import operation. If you choose to add the data to an existing table, then you cannot skip columns during the operation either.
Tabular format	Ensure that the cells are in tabular format. If the worksheet or named range includes merged cells, the contents of the cell are placed in the field that corresponds to the leftmost column, and the other fields are left blank.
Blank columns, rows, and cells	Delete all unnecessary blank columns and blank rows in the worksheet or range. If the worksheet or range contains blank cells, try to add the missing data. If you are planning to append the records to an existing table, ensure that the corresponding field in the table accepts null (missing or unknown) values. A field will accept null values if its Required field property is set to No and its ValidationRule property setting does not prevent null values.
Error values	If one or more cells in the worksheet or range contain error values, such as #NUM and #DIV, correct them before you start the import operation. If a source worksheet or range contains error values, Access places a null value in the corresponding fields in the table.
Data type	To avoid errors during importing, ensure that each source column contains the same type of data in every row. It is a good practice to format each source column in Excel and assign a specific data format to each column before you start the import operation, especially if a column includes values of different data types.
First row	If the first row in the worksheet or named range contains the names of the columns, you can specify that Access treat the data in the first row as field names during the import operation. If your source worksheet or range does not include the names, it is a good idea to add them to the source before you start the import operation. Note: If you plan to append the data to an existing table, ensure that the name of each column exactly matches the name of the corresponding field. If the name of a column is different from the name of the corresponding field in the table, the import operation will fail. To see the names of the fields, open the table in Design View in Access.

 **Troubleshooting**   The worksheet should be closed before beginning the import operation. Keeping the source file open can result in data conversion errors.

Troubleshooting After an import operation, you should review the contents and structure of the table to ensure that everything looks correct before you start using the table. If you see the message *An error occurred trying to import file*, the import operation failed. If the data imports and you find just a few missing values, you can add them directly to the table. However, if you find that entire columns or a large number of values are either missing or were not imported properly, use Access Help to troubleshoot the results and correct the problem in the source file. After you have corrected all known problems, repeat the import operation.

STEP BY STEP **Import Data from Excel**

GET READY. Before you begin these steps, be sure to **LAUNCH** Microsoft Access.

The *Humongous* file for this lesson is available on the book companion website or in WileyPLUS.

1. **OPEN** the *Humongous* database from the data files for this lesson.
2. **SAVE** the database as *Humongous XXX* (where *XXX* is your initials).
3. On the External Data tab, in the Import & Link group, click **Excel**. The *Get External Data—Excel Spreadsheet* dialog box appears, as shown in Figure 14-2.

Figure 14-2

Get External Data—Excel Spreadsheet dialog box

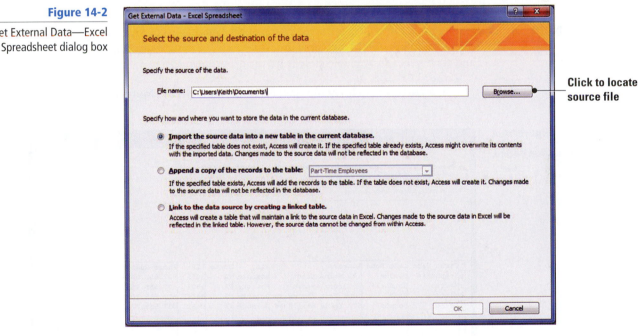

Click to locate source file

The *New_Employees* file for this lesson is available on the book companion website or in WileyPLUS.

4. Click **Browse** to open the File Open dialog box.
5. Use the Look in box to locate the *New_Employees* spreadsheet file and then click **Open**.
6. Notice the three options you have when importing data. Click **Import the source data into a new table in the current database** and click **OK**. The Import Spreadsheet Wizard appears, as shown in Figure 14-3.

Figure 14-3

Import Spreadsheet Wizard, screen 1

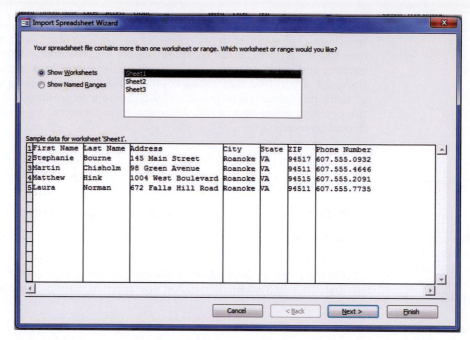

Take Note

On the first screen of the Import Spreadsheet Wizard, Access also allows you to append a copy of the records to an existing table in the database. Choose *Append a copy of the records to the table* and then select an available table from the drop-down list.

7. Click **Next >** to display the next screen, as shown in Figure 14-4.

Figure 14-4

Import Spreadsheet Wizard, screen 2

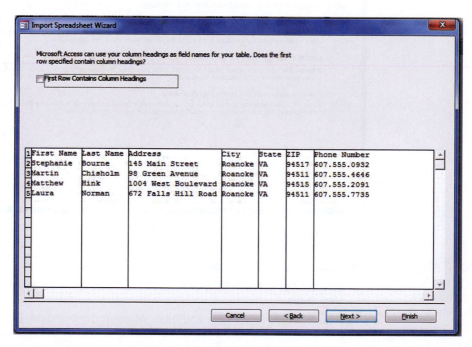

8. Click the **First Row Contains Column Headings** check box. Access uses these column headings to name the fields in the table.

9. Click **Next >** to display the next screen, shown in Figure 14-5, where the wizard prompts you to review the field properties.

Figure 14-5

Import Spreadsheet Wizard, screen 3

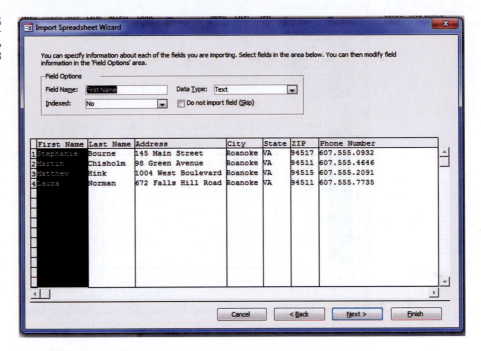

10. Click the **ZIP** column header to display the corresponding field properties.

11. Click the **Data Type down arrow** and click **Text**, as shown in Figure 14-6.

Figure 14-6

Change field properties

Use the menu to change the data type

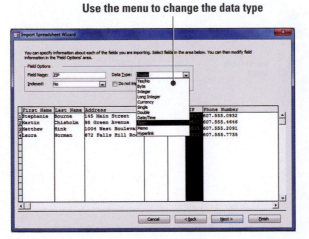

Take Note   Access reviews the first eight rows in each column to suggest the data type for the corresponding field. If the column contains different types of values, the wizard suggests a data type that is compatible with all of the values in the column—usually the text data type. Although you can choose a different data type, values that are not compatible with the chosen data type will be ignored or converted incorrectly during the import process.

12. Click **Next >** to display the next screen, as shown in Figure 14-7.

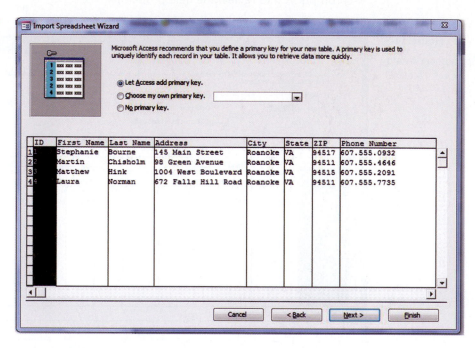

13. Click **Next >** to let Access add the primary key. The final screen appears, as shown in Figure 14-8.

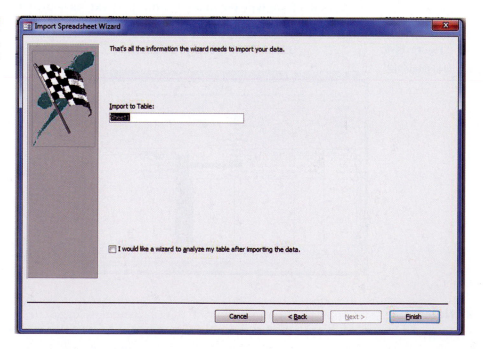

14. In the Import to Table box, key **New Employees** and then click **Finish**. When the Save Import Steps prompt appears, click **Close**.

15. In the Navigation pane, double-click the **New Employees: Table** to open the new table with imported data, as shown in Figure 14-9.

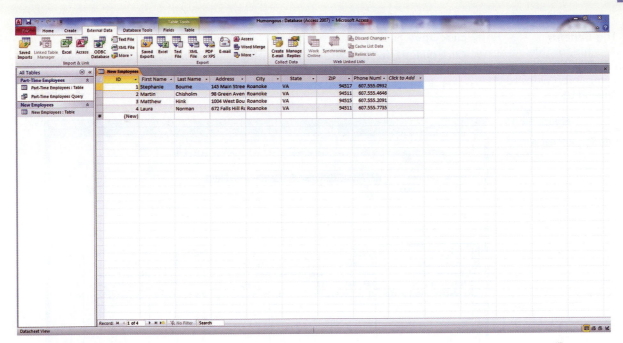

Figure 14-9

New table with imported data

16. Close the New Employees table.

17. LEAVE the database open.

PAUSE. LEAVE Access open to use in the next exercise.

CERTIFICATION
R E A D Y   2.5.1

How do you import source
data into a new table?

CERTIFICATION
R E A D Y   2.5.2

How do you append records
to an existing table?

Linking to an External Data Source

By linking an Access database to data in another program, you can use the querying and reporting tools that Access provides without having to maintain a copy of the external data in your database. You can also link to other external data sources, such as linking tables in another Access database (although you cannot link to queries, forms, or reports), HTML documents, or text files. In this exercise, you link to an Excel spreadsheet.

When you link to an Excel worksheet, Access creates a new table that is linked to the source cells, called a **linked table**. The table shows the data in the source worksheet, but it doesn't actually store the data in the database. Any changes you make to the source cells in Excel appear in the linked table. However, you cannot edit the contents or structure of the corresponding table in Access. If you want to add, edit, or delete data, you must make the changes in the source file.

Take Note   If you don't want to link to the entire worksheet, define a range that includes only the cells you want to link to. To create a named range, select the cells, right-click, and click Name a Range. In the New Name dialog box, key a name for the range and then click OK.

After linking, you should open the linked table and review the fields and data to ensure that you see the correct data in all the fields. If you see error values or incorrect data, use Access Help to troubleshoot the source data and then try linking again.

STEP BY STEP   **Link to an External Data Source**

USE the database that is open from the previous exercise.

1. On the External Data tab, in the Import & Link group, click **Excel** to open the *Get External Data—Excel Spreadsheet* dialog box.

2. Click **Browse** to open the File Open dialog box.

@ The **Benefit_Providers** file for this lesson is available on the book companion website or in WileyPLUS.

3. Use the Look in box to locate the **Benefit_Providers** spreadsheet file and then click **Open**.

4. Click **Link to the data source by creating a linked table** and click **OK**. The Link Spreadsheet Wizard appears, as shown in Figure 14-10.

Figure 14-10

Link Spreadsheet Wizard, screen 1

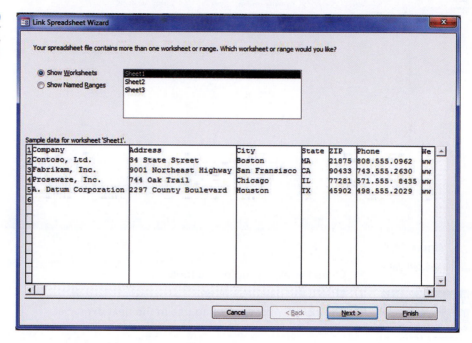

5. Click **Next >** to display the next screen.

6. Click the **First Row Contains Column Headings** check box, shown in Figure 14-11, to use the first row data as field headings in the table.

Figure 14-11

Link Spreadsheet Wizard, screen 2

Click this check box to use the first row as field headers

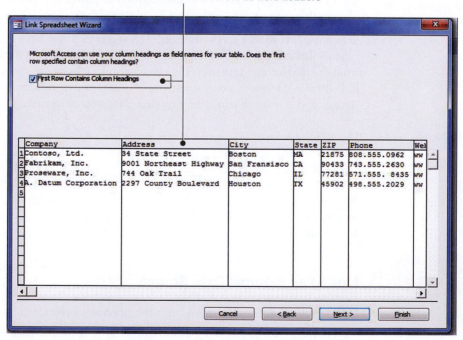

7. Click **Next >** to display the next screen.

8. In the Linked Table Name box, key **Benefit_Providers**, as shown in Figure 14-12.

Figure 14-12

Link Spreadsheet Wizard,
final screen

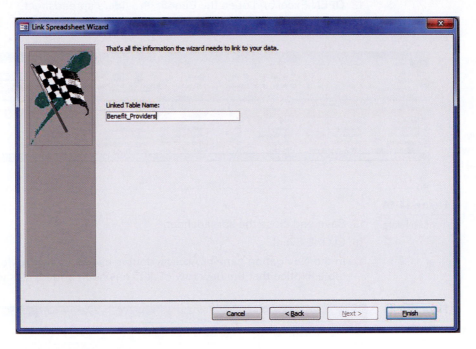

Figure 14-12

Link Spreadsheet Wizard,
final screen

9. Click **Finish**. A Link Spreadsheet Wizard message appears informing you that Access finished linking.
10. Click **OK**.

Troubleshooting If the table with the name you specified already exists, you are asked if you want to overwrite the existing file. Click Yes if you want to overwrite the file; click No to specify a different file name.

11. In the Navigation pane, notice the linked Excel icon next to Benefit_Providers. Double-click **Benefit_Providers** to open the new linked table, shown in Figure 14-13. Notice that there is not an Add New Field column because the structure of a linked table cannot be changed.

Excel icon
next to linked
Benefit_Providers
table object

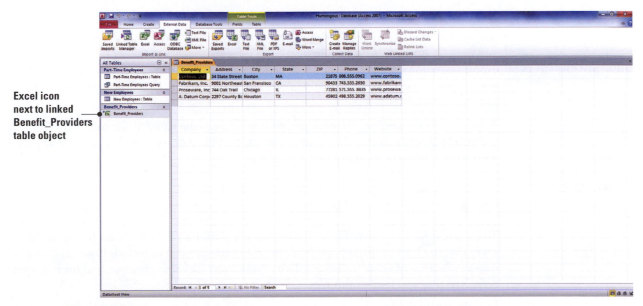

Figure 14-13

New linked table

12. Click the **Close** button on Benefit_Providers to close the table.
13. **OPEN** Excel and open the **Benefit_Providers** spreadsheet.
14. Key the new row of data shown in Figure 14-14.

Key the new data into row 6 of the Excel worksheet

Figure 14-14

New Excel data

15. Save and close the spreadsheet.
16. CLOSE Excel.
17. In the Navigation pane of Access, double-click **Benefit_Providers** to open the linked table. Notice that the new row of data has been added, as shown in Figure 14-15.

Figure 14-15

New Excel data added to linked table

New data appears in a linked Access table

18. Close the Benefit_Providers table.
19. **LEAVE** the database open.

PAUSE. LEAVE Access open to use in the next exercise.

SAVING AND RUNNING IMPORT SPECIFICATIONS

The Bottom Line

Saving the details of an import operation as a specification allows you to repeat the operation at any time. A **specification** contains all the information Access needs to repeat an import or export operation without user input. When you run an import wizard, you can save the settings you used as a specification so that you can repeat the operation at any time without having to provide any additional input.

A specification is flexible. For example, you can change the name of the source file or the destination file before you run the specification again. This way, you can use a single specification with several different source or destination files.

Take Note

If you regularly repeat this saved operation, you can create an Outlook task that reminds you when it is time to perform this operation by clicking the Create Outlook Task check box.

To use a text file as a source file for importing, the contents of the file must be organized in such a way that the Import Wizard can divide the contents into a set of records (rows) and each record into a collection of fields (columns). Two types of text files that are organized for importing are delimited files and fixed-width files.

In a **delimited file**, each record appears on a separate line and the fields are separated by a single character, called the delimiter. The **delimiter** can be any character that does not appear in the field values, such as a tab, semicolon, comma, space, and so on. The following is an example of a comma-delimited file:

Company Name,Employee Name,Position
Fourth Coffee,Dana Burnell,Sales Manager
Woodgrove Bank,Michael Emmanuel,Vice President
Wingtip Toys,Billie Murray,Owner

In a **fixed-width file**, each record appears on a separate line and the width of each field remains consistent across records. For example, the first field of every record is always 9 characters long, the second field of every record is always 14 characters long, and so on. If the actual character length of a field's value varies from record to record, the values that fall short of the required width must be padded with trailing space characters. The following is an example of fixed-width file where the first field is said to be 16 characters, second field is said to be 20 characters and third field is said to be 14 characters:

Company Name   Employee name   Position
Fourth Coffee   Dana Burnell   Sales Manager
Woodgrove Bank Michael Emmanuel   Vice President
Wingtip Toys   Billie Murray   Owner

Saving Specifications

You can save an import or export operation involving any of the file formats supported in Access, but you cannot save the details of a linking operation or an operation where you export only a portion of a datasheet. In this exercise you import a text file and then save the import specifications.

STEP BY STEP   **Save Import Specifications**

USE the database that is open from the previous exercise.

@ The *Applicants* file for this lesson is available on the book companion website or in WileyPLUS.

1. On the External Data tab, in the Import & Link group, click **Text File** to open the *Get External Data—Text File* dialog box.

2. Click **Browse** to open the File Open dialog box.

3. Use the Look in box to locate the *Applicants* text file and then click **Open**.

4. Click **Import the source data into a new table in the current database** and click **OK**. The Import Text Wizard appears, as shown in Figure 14-16.

Figure 14-16

Import Text Wizard, screen 1

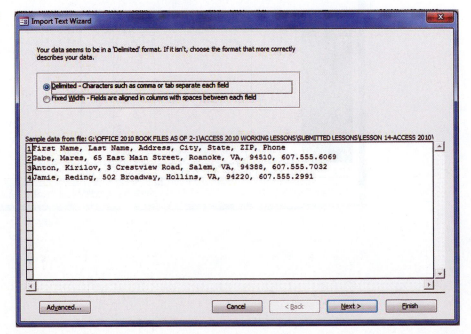

5. Click **Next >** to display the next screen, shown in Figure 14-17.

Figure 14-17

Import Text Wizard,
screen 2

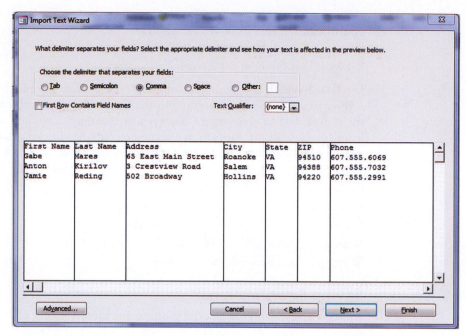

6. Comma should be selected as the delimiter. Click the **First Row Contains Field Names** check box to use the first row data as field headings in the table.

7. Click **Next >** to display the next screen, shown in Figure 14-18, where you can specify field information.

Figure 14-18

Import Text Wizard,
screen 3

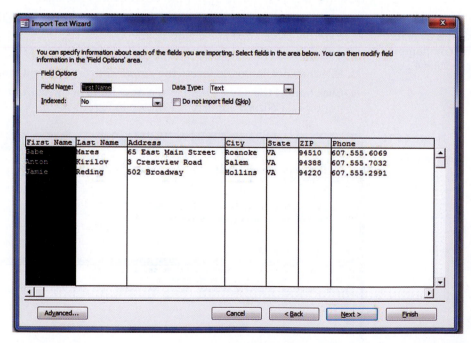

8. Click **Next >** to accept the default settings and display the next screen, shown in Figure 14-19, where you can define a primary key.

Figure 14-19

Import Text Wizard, screen 4

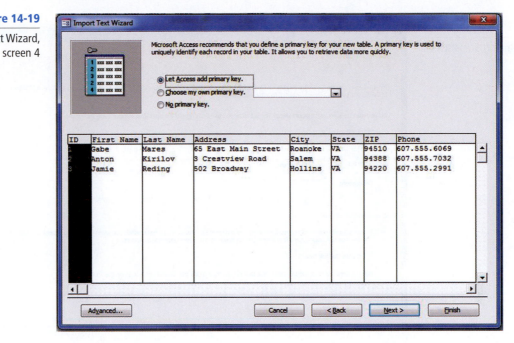

9. Click **Next >** to let Access add the primary key and to display the final screen, shown in Figure 14-20.

Figure 14-20

Import Text Wizard, final screen

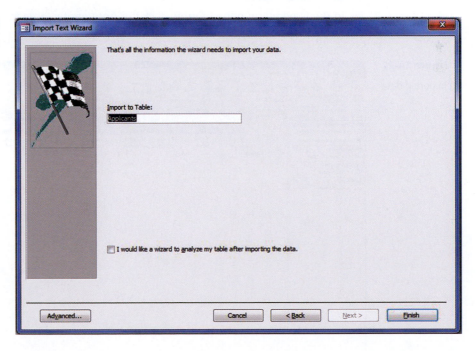

10. Click **Finish** to accept the default table name. A Save Import Steps screen appears.

11. Click the **Save import steps** check box to display the specification details, shown in Figure 14-21.

Figure 14-21

Save Import Steps screen

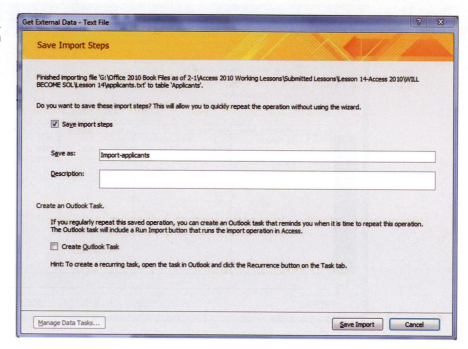

12. In the Description box, key **Import text file with job applicant contact information**.

13. Click **Save Import**.

14. In the Navigation pane, double-click the **Applicants: Table** to open the new table with imported data, as shown in Figure 14-22.

Figure 14-22

New table with imported data

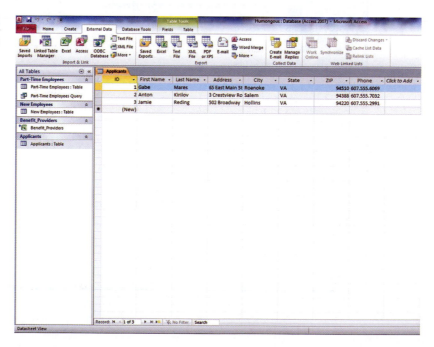

15. Close the Applicants table.

16. **LEAVE** the database open.

PAUSE. LEAVE Access open to use in the next exercise.

Running Import Specifications

To run a saved specification, on the External Data tab, in the Imports group, click Saved Imports. In the Manage Data Tasks dialog box, on the Saved Imports tab, click the specification that you want to run. In this exercise, you run import specifications.

If you want to change the source file, click the path of the file to edit it. The new file you specify must satisfy all the requirements essential for successfully completing the operation.

Before you click Run, make sure that the source and destination files exist, that the source data is ready for importing, and that the operation will not accidentally overwrite any data in your destination file. Do everything that you would do to ensure the success of a wizard-driven operation before running any saved specification and then click Run.

If you no longer need to perform a specific operation, you can delete the specification by selecting it and clicking Delete.

STEP BY STEP **Run Import Specifications**

USE the database that is open from the previous exercise.

1. On the External Data tab, in the Import & Link group, click **Saved Imports** to open the Manage Data Tasks dialog box, shown in Figure 14-23.

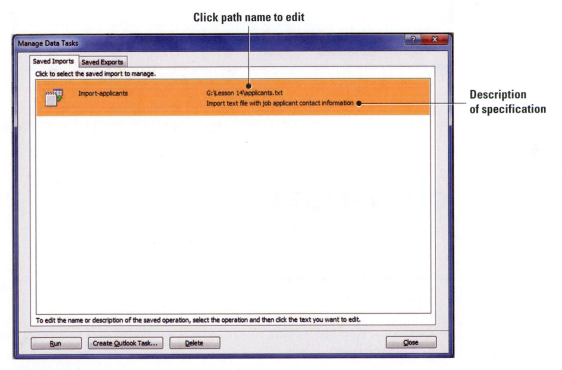

Figure 14-23

Manage Data Tasks dialog box

2. Click the file path and edit it by changing the source file name to **March Applicants.txt**, as shown in Figure 14-24.

Figure 14-24

Changing source file name

Edit file name

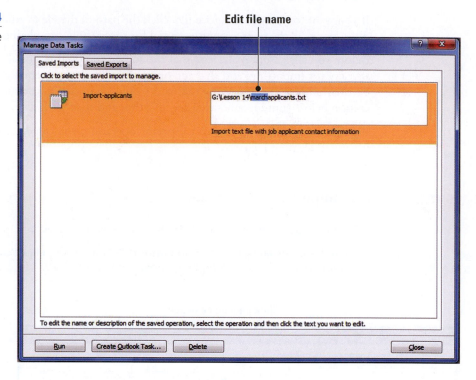

3. Click **Run**. A message appears asking if you want to overwrite the existing table, as shown in Figure 14-25.

Figure 14-25

Overwrite message

4. Click **Yes**. A message appears confirming that all objects were successfully imported, as shown in Figure 14-26.

Figure 14-26

Successful import message

5. Click **OK**.

6. Click **Close** to close the Manage Data Tasks dialog box.

7. In the Navigation pane, double-click the **Applicants: Table** to open the table. The existing data has been replaced with new imported data, as shown in Figure 14-27.

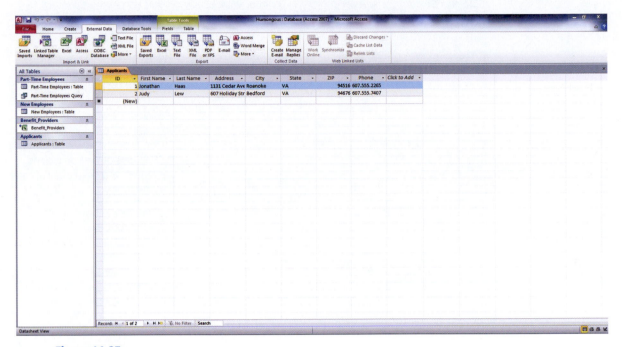

Figure 14-27

Table with new imported data

8. Close the Applicants table.

9. LEAVE the database open.

PAUSE. LEAVE Access open to use in the next exercise.

EXPORTING DATA

The Bottom Line

To use Access data in another program, you can use the various commands in the Export group to export the selected object in the format you want.

Exporting from a Table

When you export data from a table to Excel, Access creates a copy of the data and then stores the copy in an Excel worksheet. In this exercise, you export data from an Access table to an Excel worksheet.

Besides exporting to Excel, you can also export data to other destinations, such as a SharePoint list, a Rich Text Format file, another Access database, or a text file. The process for exporting data is similar, regardless of the destination.

Table 14-2 summarizes the options for creating or overwriting a workbook.

Table 14-2

Destination Workbook Options

Destination		Data	
Workbook	**Source Object**	**Exported**	**Result**
Does not exist	Table, query, or form	With or without formatting	Workbook is created during the export operation.
Already exists	Table or query	Without formatting	The workbook is not overwritten. A new worksheet is added to the workbook and is given the name of the object from which the data is being exported. If a worksheet having that name already exists in the workbook, Access prompts you to either replace the contents of the corresponding worksheet or specify another name for the new sheet.
Already exists	Table, query, or form	With formatting	The workbook is overwritten by the exported data. All existing worksheets are removed, and a new worksheet having the same name as the exported object is created. The data in the Excel worksheet inherits the format settings of the source object.

If the source object is a table or a query, decide whether you want to export the data with or without its formatting. If you choose without formatting, all fields and records in the underlying object are exported and the Format property settings are ignored during the operation. If you choose with formatting, only the fields and records displayed in the current view are exported and the Format property settings are respected.

You can export a table, query, or form to Excel. You can only export one database object in a single export operation. However, you can merge the data in multiple worksheets in Excel after completing the individual export operations. The data is always added in a new worksheet. You cannot append the data to an existing worksheet.

STEP BY STEP **Exporting from a Table**

USE the database that is open from the previous exercise.

1. In the Navigation pane, select the **Part-Time Employees: Table**.
2. On the External Data tab, in the Export group, click **Excel**. The Export—Excel Spreadsheet dialog box appears, as shown in Figure 14-28.

Figure 14-28

Export—Excel Spreadsheet
dialog box

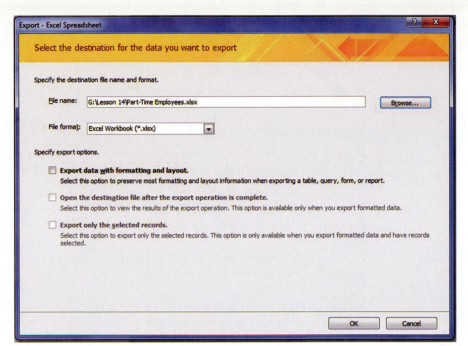

3. If you want to specify a different destination, click **Browse** to open the File Save dialog box, use the Save in box to choose a folder, and then click **Save**.

4. Click the **Export data with formatting and layout** check box and then click the **Open the destination file after the export operation is complete** check box.

5. Click **OK**. Excel opens and the new worksheet with exported data is displayed, as shown in Figure 14-29.

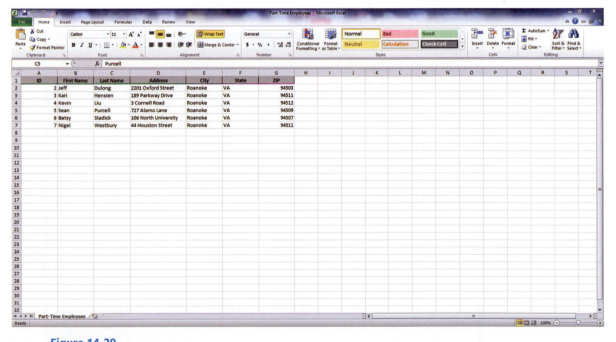

Figure 14-29

Excel worksheet with
exported data

6. Close the worksheet and **CLOSE** Excel.

7. Switch to Access.

8. On the Save Export Steps screen, click **Close**.

9. **LEAVE** the database open.

PAUSE. LEAVE Access open to use in the next exercise.

Exporting from a Query

You can export data from an Access query to a variety of formats, just as you can export data from an Access table. In this exercise, you export a query to Word.

You can export a table, query, form, or report to Word. When you export an object to Word, Access creates a copy of the object's data in a Microsoft Word Rich Text Format file (*.rtf) and the visible fields and records appear as a table, with the field names in the first row.

Take Note   Pictures or attachments that are part of the source data are not exported to Word. Expressions are not exported either, but the results are.

When you export from Access to a Word document, the Export Wizard always exports format-ted data and the data is always exported into a new Word file. You cannot append data to an existing Word document.

STEP BY STEP   **Export from a Query**

USE the database that is open from the previous exercise.

1. In the Navigation pane, select the **Part-Time Employees Query**.

2. On the External Data tab, in the Export group, click the **More** button. On the menu that appears, click **Word**. The Export—RTF File dialog box appears, as shown in Figure 14-30.

Figure 14-30

Export—RTF File dialog box

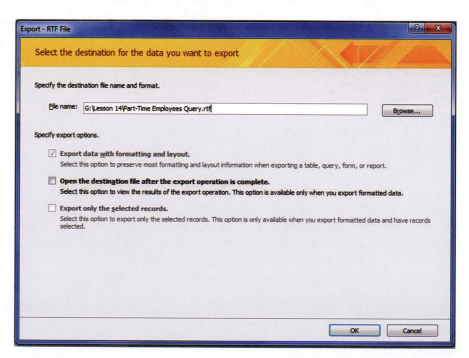

3. If you want to specify a different destination, click **Browse** to open the File Save dialog box, use the Save in box to choose a folder, and then click **Save**.

4. Click the **Open the destination file after the export operation is complete** check box.

5. Click **OK**. Word opens and the new document with exported data is displayed, as shown in Figure 14-31.

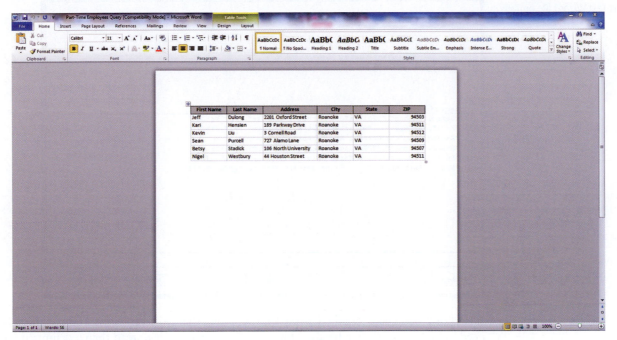

Figure 14-31

Word document with exported data

6. Close the document and **CLOSE** Word.

7. Switch to Access.

8. On the Save Export Steps screen, click **Close**.

9. **LEAVE** the database open.

PAUSE. LEAVE Access open to use in the next exercise.

SAVING AND RUNNING EXPORT SPECIFICATIONS

The Bottom Line

When you perform an export operation, you can save the details for future use so you can repeat the operation at a later time without having to walk through the steps in the wizard each time. You can even schedule the export operation to run automatically at specified intervals by creating an Outlook task.

In the Save as box, type a name for the export specification. Optionally, type a description in the Description box. If you want to perform the operation at fixed intervals, such as weekly or monthly, select the Create Outlook Task check box. Doing this creates an Outlook task that lets you run the specification by clicking a button.

You can change the name of the specification, its description, and the path and file name of the destination file by clicking and making changes in the text box and then pressing Enter. Repeat an operation by clicking the specification and then clicking Run. If you are exporting data with formatting and layout, you are asked to choose the encoding to be used for saving the file. When the operation is complete, you will see a message that communicates the status of the operation.

Although you can export Access data in various formats, sometimes you might need to export data to a program that uses a file format that Access does not support. In that case, if the destination program can use text (*.txt) files, you can export your data in that format and open the resulting file with the second program. When you export the contents of a table or query to a text file with formatting and layout, hyphens (-) and pipe characters (|) are used to organize the content in a grid in the text file. The records appear as rows, fields appear as columns, and field names appear in the first row.

When exporting without formatting or layout, the Export Wizard gives you the option of creating a delimited file or a fixed-width file, as shown in Figure 14-32.

Figure 14-32

Export Text Wizard file options

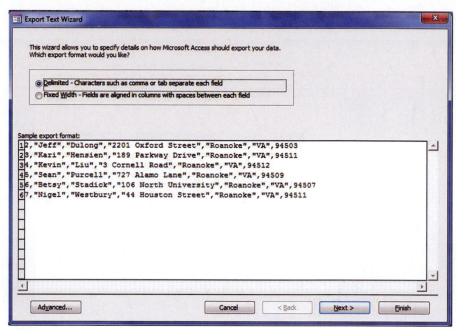

The choice you make usually depends on the system that works with the exported files. If users need to look at the data, a fixed-width file can be much easier to read than a delimited file.

Saving Export Specifications

After you have performed an export operation, you are given the opportunity to save it for future use. Saving the details helps you repeat the same export operation in the future without having to step through the wizard each time. In this exercise, you export data from Access to a text file, and then save the export specification.

STEP BY STEP   **Save Export Specifications**

USE the database that is open from the previous exercise.

1. In the Navigation pane, select the **New Employees: Table**.
2. On the External Data tab, in the Export group, click **Text File**. The Export—Text File dialog box appears, as shown in Figure 14-33.

Figure 14-33

Export—Text File dialog box

3. If you want to specify a different destination, click **Browse** to open the File Save dialog box, use the Save in box to choose a folder, and then click **Save**.

4. Click the **Export data with formatting and layout** check box and then click the **Open the destination file after the export operation is complete** check box.

5. Click **OK**. The Encode 'New Employees' As dialog box is displayed, as shown in Figure 14-34.

Figure 14-34

Encode 'New Employees' As dialog box

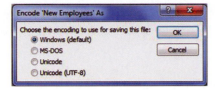

6. Windows (default) should be selected. Click **OK**. Notepad opens and the new file with exported data is displayed, as shown in Figure 14-35.

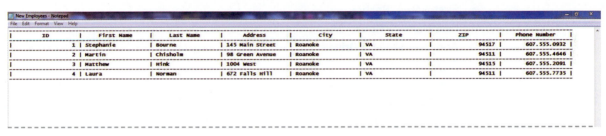

Figure 14-35

Notepad with exported data

7. **CLOSE** Notepad.

8. Switch to Access.

9. On the Save Export Steps screen, click the **Save export steps** check box to display the specification details, as shown in Figure 14-36.

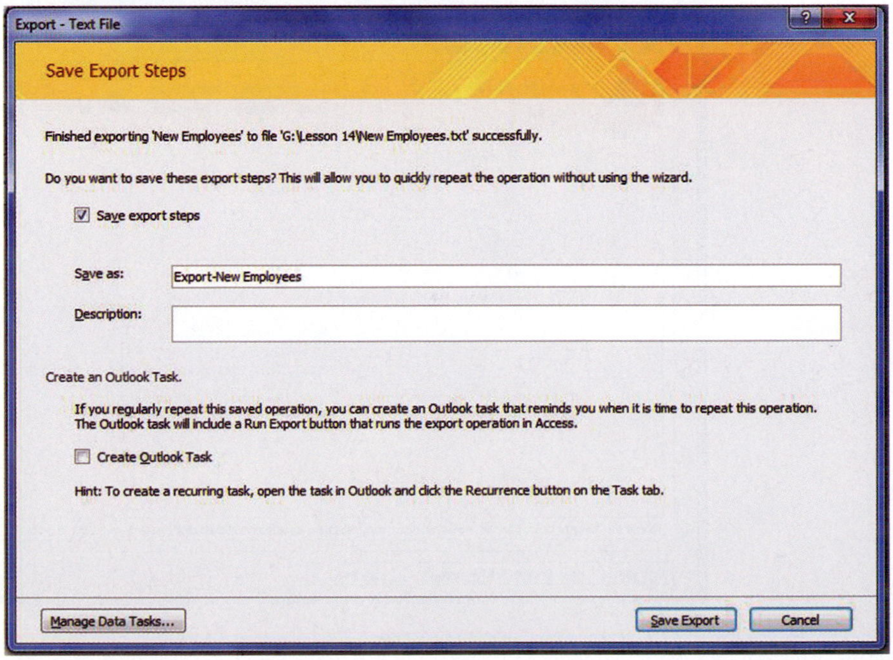

Figure 14-36

Save Export Steps screen

![Export - Text File dialog box showing the Save Export Steps screen. Text reads: "Finished exporting 'New Employees' to file 'G:\Lesson 14\New Employees.txt' successfully. Do you want to save these export steps? This will allow you to quickly repeat the operation without using the wizard." A checked checkbox labeled "Save export steps" is shown. Save as: Export-New Employees. Description: (blank). Create an Outlook Task section with hint text. Buttons: Manage Data Tasks..., Save Export, Cancel.]

10. In the Description box, key **Export new employee information to a text file**.

11. Click **Save Export**.

12. LEAVE the database open.

PAUSE. LEAVE Access open to use in the next exercise.

Running Export Specifications

When you run the Export Wizard, you can save the operation as a specification for future use. In this exercise, you run the export specifications you just saved.

STEP BY STEP   **Run Export Specifications**

USE the database that is open from the previous exercise.

1. In the Navigation pane, double-click the **New Employees: Table** to open it.

2. Add another record with the following information:

First Name: **Rachel**

Last Name: **Valdez**

Address: **39 Vista Drive**

City: **Roanoke**

State: **VA**

ZIP: **94510**

Phone Number: **607.555.1218**

3. Click the **Close 'New Employees'** button to close the table.

4. On the External Data tab, in the Export group, click **Saved Exports** to open the Manage Data Tasks dialog box, shown in Figure 14-37.

Figure 14-37

Manage Data Tasks dialog box

Click path name to edit

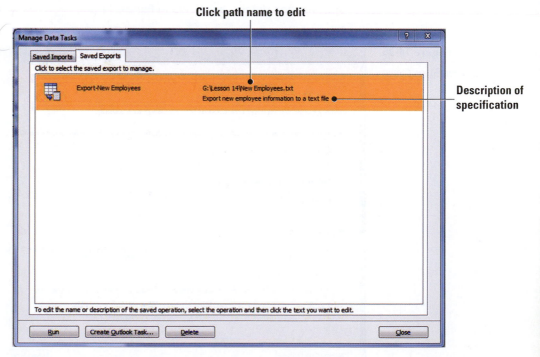

Description of specification

5. Click the file path and edit it by changing the destination file name to **New Employees 2.txt**, as shown in Figure 14-38.

Figure 14-38

Edit destination file

Edit file name

6. Click **Run**. Notepad opens and the new file with exported data is displayed, as shown in Figure 14-39.

Figure 14-39

Notepad with exported data

7. Switch to Access. A message confirms that the export operation was successful, as shown in Figure 14-40.

Figure 14-40

Successful export operation message

8. Click **OK** and then click **Close** to close the Manage Data Tasks dialog box.
9. **CLOSE** Notepad.
10. **CLOSE** the database.

PAUSE. LEAVE Access open to use in the projects.

SKILL SUMMARY

In This Lesson You Learned How To:	Exam Objective	Objective Number
Import Data	Import source data into a new table.	**2.5.1**
	Append records to an existing table.	**2.5.2**
	Import data as a linked table.	**2.5.3**
Save and Run Import Specifications		
Export Data		
Save and Run Export Specifications		

Knowledge Assessment

Fill in the Blank

Complete the following sentences by writing the correct word or words in the blanks provided.

1. When you import data, Access creates a(n) _____ of the data in a new or existing table without altering the source file.

2. When you link to an Excel worksheet, Access creates a new table, called a(n) _____, that is linked to the source cells.

3. A(n) _____ contains all the information Access needs to repeat an import or export operation without user input.

4. In a(n) _____ file, each record appears on a separate line and the fields are separated by a single character.

5. A(n) _____ is any character that separates fields and does not appear in the field values, such as a tab, semicolon, comma, or space.

6. In a(n) _____ file, each record appears on a separate line and the width of each field remains consistent across records.

7. You can schedule an import or export operation to run automatically at specified intervals by creating a(n) _____ task.

8. When you export the content of a table or query to a text file with _____ and _____, hyphens (-) and pipe characters (|) are used to organize the content in a grid.

9. When exporting to Excel, the data is always added in a new _____.

10. To repeat an import or export operation, click the specification and then click _____.

Multiple Choice

Select the best response for the following statements or questions.

1. Which tab contains options for importing or exporting data?

    a. Manage Data

    b. Database Tools

    c. External Data

    d. Create

2. Before beginning an import operation, the source file should be

   a. Open

   b. Closed

   c. Copied

   d. Backed up

3. If you want to add, edit, or delete data in a linked table, you must make the changes in the

   a. First row of data

   b. Access object

   c. Field headers

   d. Source file

4. You can save an import or export operation involving any of the file formats supported in Access, but you cannot save the details of a

   a. Linking operation

   b. Text file import operation

   c. Query export operation

   d. Fixed-width file

5. The following is an example of what kind of text?

1, Fourth Coffee, Dana, Burnell, Sales Manager

   a. HTML

   b. Linked

   c. Fixed-width

   d. Comma-delimited

6. How many database objects can you export in a single export operation?

   a. One

   b. Two

   c. Three

   d. Unlimited

7. When you export an object to Word, Access creates what type of file?

   a. MS-DOS Text

   b. Rich Text Format

   c. HTML

   d. Linked

8. If you choose to store imported data in a new table, Access

   a. Links the new table to an existing table

   b. Overwrites the data in the existing table

   c. Creates a table and adds the imported data to this table

   d. Gives you an error message

9. What is an advantage of linking an Access database to data in another program?

   a. Maintaining a copy of the external data in Access

   b. Being able to use Access querying and reporting tools

   c. Being able to edit the linked table in Access

   d. Easily being able to change the structure of the Access table

10. Which dialog box allows you to manage saved import and export specifications?

   a. External Data

   b. Saved Specifications

   c. Import/Export Tasks

   d. Manage Data Tasks

Competency Assessment

Project 14-1: Import Data from Excel

You are the purchasing manager for Coho Wine Club and an associate has provided some information about champagne and sparkling wines that are being considered for the monthly wine club. The data is in an Excel worksheet and will need to be imported into the database.

GET READY. LAUNCH Access if it is not already running.

@ The *Coho Wine Club* file for this lesson is available on the book companion website or in WileyPLUS.

@ The *Champagne_Sparkling* file for this lesson is available on the book companion website or in WileyPLUS.

1. **OPEN** the *Coho Wine Club* database from the data files for this lesson.
2. **SAVE** the database as *Coho Wine Club XXX* (where *XXX* is your initials).
3. On the External Data tab, in the Import & Link group, click **Excel** to display the *Get External Data—Excel Spreadsheet* dialog box.
4. Click **Browse** to open the File Open dialog box.
5. Use the Look In box to locate the *Champagne_Sparkling* spreadsheet file and then click **Open**.
6. Click **Import the source data into a new table in the current database** and click **OK**. The Import Spreadsheet Wizard appears.
7. Click **Next >** to display the next screen.
8. Click the **First Row Contains Column Headings** check box.
9. Click **Next >** to display the next screen where the wizard prompts you to review the field properties.
10. Click the **Bottled** column heading to display the corresponding field properties.
11. Click the **Data Type down arrow** and click **Text**.
12. Click **Next >** to display the next screen.
13. Click **Next >** to let Access add the primary key. The final screen appears.
14. In the Import to Table box, key **Champagne_Sparkling** and then click **Finish**. When the Save Import Steps prompt appears, click **Close**.
15. In the Navigation pane, double-click the **Champagne_Sparkling: Table** to open the new table with imported data.
16. Close the Champagne_Sparkling table.
17. **LEAVE** the database open for the next project.

LEAVE Access open for the next project.

Project 14-2: Export Data to Word

Your supervisor at Coho Vineyard wants a list of the distributor information in a Word file. Use the Distributor table in the Access database to export the data to a Rich Text Format file.

USE the database that is open from the previous project.

1. In the Navigation pane, select the **Distributors: Table**.
2. On the External Data tab, in the Export group, click **Word** to display the Export—RTF File dialog box.
3. If you want to specify a different destination, click **Browse** to open the File Save dialog box, use the Save in box to choose a folder, and then click **Save**.
4. Click the **Open the destination file after the export operation is complete** check box.
5. Click **OK**. Word opens and the new file with exported data is displayed.
6. Close the file and **CLOSE** Word.
7. Switch to Access.
8. On the Save Export Steps screen, click **Close**.
9. **CLOSE** the database.

LEAVE Access open for the next project.

Proficiency Assessment

Project 14-3: Save Export Specifications

As a travel agent at Margie's Travel, a client asks you to email information about the dates for available travel packages. Because you don't know what program the client will use to open it, you export the data to a text file. Because you do this frequently, you decide to save the export operation as a specification that can be used later.

GET READY. LAUNCH Access if it is not already running.

@ The *Trip Events* file for this lesson is available on the book companion website or in WileyPLUS.

1. **OPEN** the *Trip Events* database from the data files for this lesson.
2. **SAVE** the database as *Trip Events XXX* (where *XXX* is your initials).
3. In the Navigation pane, select the **2011 Events: Table**.
4. On the External Data tab, in the External group, click **Text File** to display the Export—Text File dialog box.
5. Specify the location where you want to store the file.
6. Click the **Export data with formatting and layout** check box and then click the **Open the destination file after the export operation is complete** check box.
7. Click **OK**. The Encode '2011 Events' As dialog box is displayed.
8. Windows (default) should be selected. Click **OK**. Notepad opens and the new file with exported data is displayed.
9. **CLOSE** Notepad.
10. Switch to Access.
11. On the Save Export Steps screen, click the **Save export steps** check box.
12. In the Description box, key **Export event information to a text file**.
13. Click **Save Export**.
14. **LEAVE** the database open.

LEAVE Access open for the next project.

Project 14-4: Run Export Specifications

One of the trip packages is no longer available. Delete the information from the table and run the export specification to create a new text file with the updated information.

USE the database that is open from the previous project.

1. Open the **2011 Events: Table**.
2. Delete the **World Series** record from the table.
3. Close the 2011 Events table.
4. On the External Data tab, in the Export group, click **Saved Exports**.
5. Click the file path and change the destination file name to **2011 Events updated.txt**.
6. Click **Run**. Notepad opens and the new file with exported data is displayed.
7. Switch to Access. A message confirms that the export operation was successful.
8. Click **OK** and then click **Close** to close the Manage Data Tasks dialog box.
9. **CLOSE** the database.

LEAVE Access open for the next project.

Mastery Assessment

Project 14-5: Export Data to a New Database

You are the manager at Southridge Video. You have created a new database to store information about new video games. You want to export the Games table to the new database. You have exported an Access table to other destinations, but not to another Access database. Use Access Help if you need more information.

GET READY. LAUNCH Access if it is not already running.

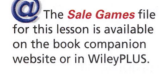 The *Sale Games* file for this lesson is available on the book companion website or in WileyPLUS.

1. Create a new file called **New Games XXX** (where *XXX* is your initials).
2. **CLOSE** the New Games database.
3. **OPEN** *Sale Games* from the data files for this lesson.
4. Save the database as **Sale Games XXX** (where *XXX* is your initials).
5. Use the export skills you have learned in this lesson to export the data and definition of the Games table to the **New Games XXX** database.
6. Do not save the export steps.
7. **OPEN** the **New Games XXX** database to be sure the Games table was successfully exported.
8. **CLOSE** both the databases.

LEAVE Access open for the next project.

Project 14-6: Appending Data to a Table

You are the human resources manager for Contoso, Inc. You have received information about new employees that needs to be imported into the employee database. You already have a table with information about sales reps, so you want to append the information instead of creating a new table. Because you have never appended data before, use Access Help if you need additional information.

GET READY. LAUNCH Access if it is not already running.

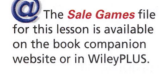 The *Contoso Employees* file for this lesson is available on the book companion website or in WileyPLUS.

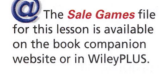 The *New_Contoso* file for this lesson is available on the book companion website or in WileyPLUS.

1. **OPEN** the **Contoso Employees** database from the data files for this lesson.
2. **SAVE** the database as **Contoso Employees XXX** (where *XXX* is your initials).
3. Choose to import from Excel using the **New_Contoso** spreadsheet file.
4. Choose the options necessary to append the spreadsheet data to the Sales Rep table.
5. Do not save the import steps.
6. Open the **Sales Reps: Table**. The data from the Excel spreadsheet should be appended to the table, as shown in Figure 14-41.

Figure 14-41

Appended data

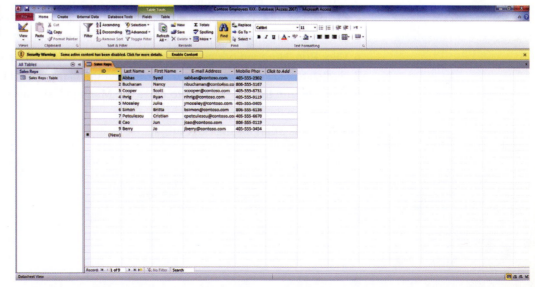

7. Close the Sales Reps table.

8. **CLOSE** the database.

CLOSE Access.

INTERNET READY

To display the contents on the Access Help tab, click the File tab and then click the Help tab. The contents of the Access Help tab, shown in Figure 14-42, is where you can contact Microsoft, find online resources, and the maintain health and reliability of your Office applications. To keep your computer up-to-date, click the Check for Updates button to go to the Microsoft update site. Here you can check to see if you need updates for your programs, hardware, or devices.

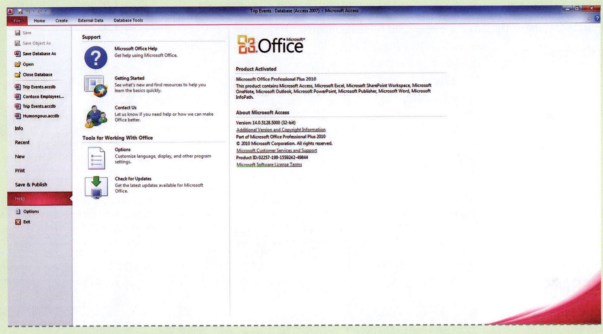

Figure 14-42

Access Help tab

15 Database Tools

LESSON SKILL MATRIX

Skill	Exam Objective	Objective Number
Maintaining a Database	Use Compact & Repair Database.	1.1.4
Setting Database Properties		
Encrypting a Database	Use Encrypt with Password commands.	1.1.5
Configuring Database Options	Set Access options.	1.1.7
Using Database Tools		

KEY TERMS

- **back-end file**
- **backup**
- **Database Documenter**
- **database properties**
- **Database Splitter**
- **decrypting**
- **encrypting**
- **front-end file**
- **object dependencies**

Fabrikam, Inc. Is a furniture manufacturer that supplies new lines, or collections, of furniture to showrooms each season. As an intern in the office, you help maintain the records related to the furniture collections and the showrooms that sell them for your company. Your supervisor is concerned about the maintenance, security, and the overall integrity of the database files, so your assignment is to safeguard these files. In this lesson, you learn to back up a database, compact and repair a database, set database properties, and save databases in previous versions of the software. You also learn to use database tools to configure database options, encrypt a database, identify object dependencies, document a database, refresh linked tables, and split a database.

MAINTAINING A DATABASE

The Bottom Line

You can maintain some important aspects of a database by using the commands on the Info tab and Save & Publish tab on the File tab in Backstage view. Though they might not seem as important as the actual data in your database, the commands on these tabs allow you to provide protection of all the data in the file, and that is important. By using the commands on the Info tab, you can compact and repair your database, set database properties, and protect your database by using encryption. The commands on the Save & Publish tab let you save your database in a previous file format and back up your database.

 Ref   You explored some of the commands on the Save & Publish menu in Lesson 13.

Backing Up a Database

After all the work you have put into a database, you start to depend on being able to access and update the data and the information in it on a regular basis. To protect your work, it is a good idea to back up a database. A **backup** is a copy of a file. It is a good idea to create backup files of all your databases and continue to back them up on a regular basis. Essentially, you are making another copy of the database that you can store on your computer, on a network drive, or in another safe location to prevent the loss of your data. In this exercise, you back up a database.

You can store a backup copy in the same place as your original file, such as on your computer. However, if something happened to your computer, both files would be affected. A better solution is to save a backup copy to a network drive or removable media that is stored in a different physical location. For example, some companies that maintain sensitive client data have elaborate backup processes in place to store backup copies on computers or other media off premises in another part of the city or in another part of the country. If an entire office building is destroyed by fire or a city is involved in a natural disaster, the backup files containing client data are safe in another location. It is a good idea to consider the appropriate precautions needed for even a small company's data.

When backing up a database, Access automatically adds the date to the file name. You can keep this file name as an identifier for the backup file or change the file name to something else. Just keep in mind that you need a new name or location so that you aren't just overwriting your original file. In the Save In box, choose the location where you want to save the file.

STEP BY STEP   **Back Up a Database**

@ The *Fabrikam* file for this lesson is available on the book companion website or in WileyPLUS.

GET READY. Before you begin these steps, be sure to turn on and/or log on to your computer and **LAUNCH** Access.

1. **OPEN** *Fabrikam* from the data files for this lesson.
2. Save the database as *Fabrikam XXX* (where *XXX* is your initials).

3. Click the **File** tab and click **Save & Publish**. The Save & Publish menu appears, as shown in Figure 15-1.

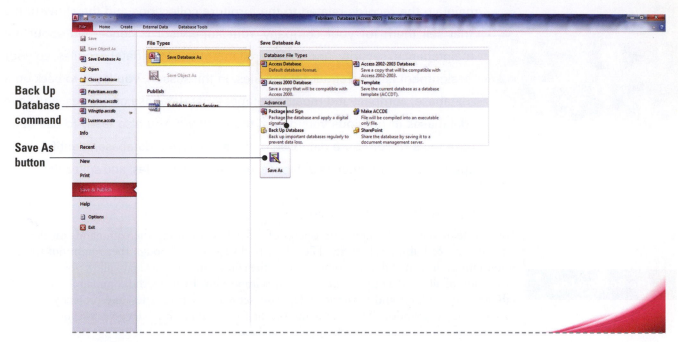

Back Up Database command

Save As button

Figure 15-1

Save & Publish menu

WileyPLUS Extra! features an online tutorial of this task.

4. In the Advanced category, click **Back Up Database** and then click the **Save As** button. The Save As dialog box appears, as shown in Figure 15-2. Notice that Access automatically adds the current date to the end of the file name.

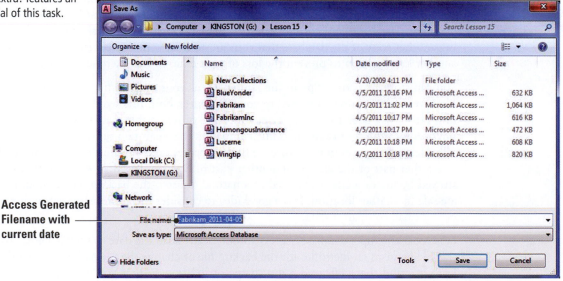

Access Generated Filename with current date

Figure 15-2

Save As dialog box

5. Click the **Save** button to accept the generated file name.

PAUSE. LEAVE the database open to use in the next exercise.

Saving as a Previous Version

Access 2010 allows you to save a database in a previous Access file format so that those using earlier versions of the software can use the database. However, some features of Access 2010 cannot be converted to a file format prior to Access 2007. Access will alert you when this is the case, and you can always remove that feature in order to save the database as a previous version. Before you can save a database in a previous file format, you should open the database, but make sure all objects are closed. In this exercise, you save an Access 2010 database as a previous version so a user who has an earlier version of Access can open your document without any difficulty.

When you save a new, blank database in Microsoft Office Access 2010, you are prompted to give it a file name. Although you may have created the database in Access 2010, it is saved in the Access 2007 format by default, which gives it the .accdb extension. The Office Access 2007 format is not readable by earlier versions of Access. If you need to share a database with others using earlier versions of the software, the Save As command allows you to save the database in the Access 2000 format or the Access 2002–2003 format, both of which have the extension .mdb. When you use the Save As command to save a database in an earlier format, it preserves the original database file in its format and creates a copy in the format you choose.

STEP BY STEP   **Save as a Previous Version**

USE the database open from the previous exercise.

1. Click the **File** tab and then click **Save & Publish**. The Save & Publish menu appears.
2. In the Database File Types category, click **Access 2002–2003 Database** and then click the **Save As** button. The Save As dialog box appears, as shown in Figure 15-3. Notice that Microsoft Access Database (2002–2003) is displayed in the Save as type box.

Figure 15-3

Save As menu

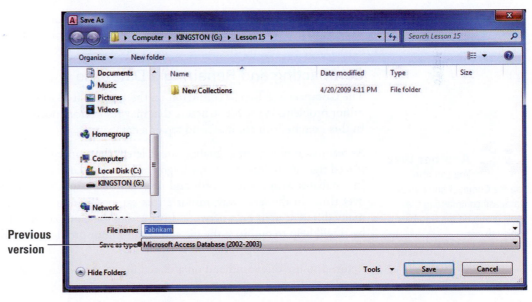

Previous version

3. Key **Fabrikam2002–2003** in the file name box.
4. Click the **Save** button. Notice the file name and format change is displayed in the title bar, as shown in Figure 15-4.

File format displayed in the title bar

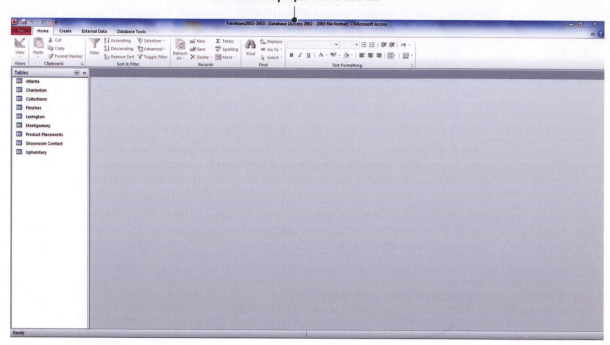

Figure 15-4

Database saved in Access
2002–2003 format

PAUSE. LEAVE the database open to use in the next exercise.

Take Note   If an Access 2010 database file contains complex data, offline data, or attachments created in Access 2010, you will not be able to save it in a format earlier than Access 2007.

Compacting and Repairing a Database

The Compact and Repair command on the Info tab in Backstage view, optimizes files and fixes minor problems in the file structure that may result from normal, everyday use of a database file. In this exercise, you compact and repair a database.

Another Way
You can also use the Compact and Repair Database command in the Tools group on the Database Tools tab.

As records or objects in a database are deleted, the empty space within the file might not be replaced right away, leaving the file fragmented or with large empty spaces within the file structure. In databases with many records and objects, these issues can affect the database's performance over time. In the same way, minor errors can occur in any file, especially when it is shared by many different users on a network drive. Using the Compact and Repair command on a regular basis will help to optimize the file and repair minor problems before they become major ones.

Take Note   Before you use this command on a shared file, make sure no one else has the file open.

STEP BY STEP   **Compact and Repair a Database**

CERTIFICATION READY 1.1.4

How do you compact and repair a database?

USE the database open from the previous exercise.

1. Click the **File** tab and then click the **Info** tab. Select **Compact & Repair** on the Info tab menu that appears, as shown in Figure 15-5. Access compacts and repairs the database.

Compact & Repair command   View and edit database properties link

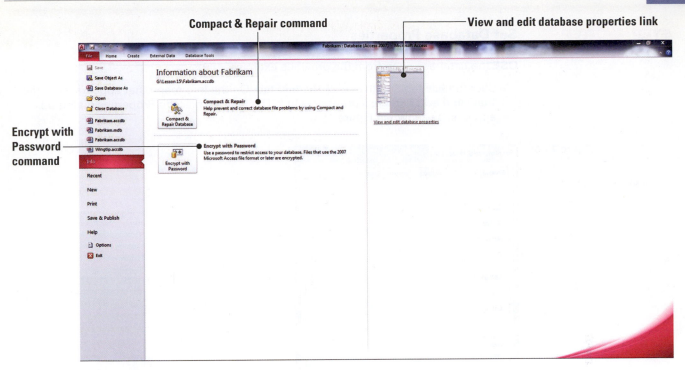

Figure 15-5

Info tab menu   **PAUSE. LEAVE** the database open to use in the next exercise.

SETTING DATABASE PROPERTIES

Database properties are details about a file that describe or identify it. Using database properties makes it easier to organize and identify databases later. Some properties can be specified by you and some are automatically updated by Access. You can search to find files that contain certain properties, such as keywords, file size, or creation date. Standard properties are those such as author, title, and subject that are associated with a document by default. In this exercise, you set database properties that will help you identify and organize it later.

Table 15-1 describes each Standard property in the Summary tab of the Properties dialog box. These properties can all be changed by the user; however, some properties in the General, Statistics, and Contents tabs—such as the file size and date the document was created or updated—are Automatically Updated Properties that are updated by Access and cannot be changed. In the Custom tab, you can define Custom properties by assigning a text, time, numeric values, or yes or no values to custom properties.

The Bottom Line

Another Way
You can set Access to compact a database every time you close it. On the File tab, click the Options button and select Current Database. Click the Compact On Close check box and click OK.

Table 15-1

Standard Database Properties

Property Name	Description
Title	Title of the database
Subject	Topic of the contents of the database
Author	Name of the individual who has authored the database
Manager	Name of the manager who is responsible for the database
Company	Name of the company that owns the database
Category	Category in which the database can be classified
Keywords	A word or set of words that describes the database
Comments	Summary or abstract of the contents of the database
Hyperlink base	Path to the destination of the file; the path may point to a location on your hard drive, a network drive, or the Internet

Encrypt with Password command

Set Database Properties

USE the database open from the previous exercise.

1. Click the **File** tab and then click the **Info** tab. On the Info menu that appears, click the **View and edit database properties** link. The Fabrikam.accdb Properties dialog box appears, as shown in Figure 15-6.

Figure 15-6

Summary Tab of the Fabrikam.accdb Properties dialog box

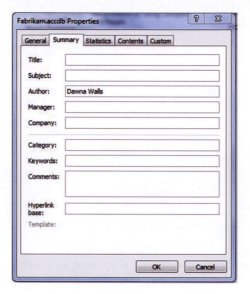

2. Key **Fall Collection** in the Title box.
3. Key **preview** in the Subject box.
4. Select the text in the Author box and key Your Name.
5. Key **Britta Simon** in the Manager box.
6. Key **Fabrikam, Inc**. in the Company box.
7. Click the **General** tab. Notice that this tab displays the file type, location, and size as well as the dates the file was created, modified, and accessed.
8. Click the **Contents** tab to view a list of the types of objects within the database file.
9. Click **OK**.

PAUSE. LEAVE the database open to use in the next exercise.

ENCRYPTING A DATABASE

The Bottom Line

Encrypting a database means to scramble the data in a way that can only be reconverted by an authorized user who has the password. When you use a database password to encrypt a database, you make all data unreadable by other tools and you force users to enter a password to use the database. Encrypting a database can provide security for sensitive data. You can use the decrypt database command to change the password on a regular basis or to remove it.

Take Note

Use strong passwords that combine uppercase and lowercase letters, numbers, and symbols. Weak passwords do not mix these elements. Strong password: W5!dk8. Weak password: CAR381. Passwords should be 8 or more characters in length. A pass phrase that uses 14 or more characters is better.

When you open an encrypted database, the Password Required dialog box appears where you key the password. Passwords are case sensitive, meaning you can use uppercase and lowercase letters as well as numbers and symbols, but you must enter them exactly as they were entered when the password was set in order for there to be a match. It is very important for you to remember your password, because if you forget it Microsoft cannot retrieve it for you. Write down the password and store it in a safe location.

Encrypting and Decrypting a Database

To encrypt a database, you first need to open it in Exclusive mode. **Decrypting** a database is removing the password from a file that has been encrypted. In this exercise you help secure a database by encrypting it, and then decrypting it.

If you want to remove a password, open the database in Exclusive mode, then click the Decrypt Database button from the Database Tools group and key the password in the Unset Database Password dialog box exactly as it was entered to encrypt the database.

STEP BY STEP   **Encrypt and Decrypt a Database**

> **USE** the database open from the previous exercise.
>
> 1. Click the **File** tab and then click the **Info** tab. On the Info menu that appears, click the **Encrypt with Password** button. The Microsoft Office Access message box appears saying you must open the database in Exclusive mode, as shown in Figure 15-7.

Figure 15-7

Microsoft Office Access
Message box

> 2. Click **OK**.
> 3. **CLOSE** the database but don't close Access.
> 4. Click the **Open** command on the File tab. The Open dialog box appears.
> 5. Navigate to the data files for this lesson and select *Fabrikam* (or *Fabrikam XXX*, if you saved it with this name). Make sure you choose the *Fabrikam* database file that has an 'A' as part of the icon, indicating it's an Access 2007 file type.
> 6. Click the **down arrow** on the Open button and select **Open Exclusive** from the menu, as shown in Figure 15-8. The *Fabrikam* database file opens in exclusive mode.

Figure 15-8

Open menu

Fabrikam with 'A'
as part of icon
indicating Access
2007 file type

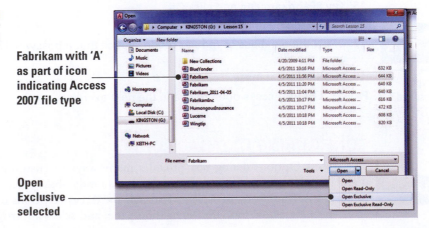

Open
Exclusive
selected

> 7. On the File tab, on the Info tab menu, click the **Encrypt with Password** button. The Set Database Password dialog box appears, as shown in Figure 15-9.

Figure 15-9

Set Database Password
dialog box

8. Key **$Fabrikam09fc** in the Password box.

Troubleshooting Be careful to key the passwords exactly as printed throughout this exercise to avoid error
messages.

9. Key **$Fabrikam09fc** in the Verify box.

10. Click **OK**. If you get another message box informing you that an option will be ignored,
click **OK**. The database is now encrypted with a password.

11. CLOSE the database.

12. OPEN the database in Exclusive mode again. The Password Required dialog box
appears, as shown in Figure 15-10.

Figure 15-10

Password Required dialog box

Take Note   You only need to open the database in Exclusive mode if you are going to set or unset a password. The database will be protected with the password in any mode.

13. Key **$Fabrikam09fc** and click **OK**. The database opens.

14. On the File tab, on the Info tab menu, click the **Decrypt Database** button. (If you hadn't
opened the database in Exclusive mode, you would get a message prompting you to
do so.) The Unset Database Password dialog box appears.

15. Key **$Fabrikam09fc** and click **OK**.

16. CLOSE the database.

17. OPEN the database in regular mode. Notice that a password is no longer required to
open the file.

18. CLOSE the database.

PAUSE. LEAVE Access open to use in the next exercise.

CERTIFICATION
R E A D Y   **1.1.5**

How do you encrypt a
database with a password?

CONFIGURING DATABASE OPTIONS

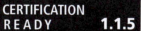

The Bottom Line

The Access Options dialog box provides many ways to customize Access. From changing
popular options to specific or advanced options for databases, Access offers a number of ways
to customize your copy of Access. Through the Access Options dialog box, you can enable
error checking, show/hide the Navigation pane, and select a startup display form.

If you want a form to be displayed automatically when you open a database, the Display Form
menu lets you choose from available forms in the database. You can choose none if you do not
wish to display a form.

The Display Navigation Pane option is turned on by default, but if you don't want the Navigation pane to be displayed when you open your database, click the Display Navigation Pane
check box to remove the check mark. You must close and reopen the current database for these
settings to take effect.

Enable error checking, located in the Object Designers options, is another feature you can change. Error checking is on by default, but you can clear the check box to disable all types of error checking in forms and reports. For example, Access places error indicators in controls that encounter one or more types of errors. The indicators appear as triangles in the upper-left or upper-right corner of the control, depending on text direction. The default indicator color is green, but you can change that to another color if you choose.

Configuring Database Options

The Access Options dialog box lets you customize certain aspects of Access and your databases. The Access Options dialog box has 11 sections of customizable options, including General, Current Database, Datasheet, Object Designers, Proofing, and Language. In this exercise, you use the Access Options dialog box to display a form and hide the Navigation pane.

STEP BY STEP **Configure Database Options**

OPEN *Fabrikam Inc* from the data files for this lesson.

@ The *Fabrikam Inc* file for this lesson is available on the book companion website or in WileyPLUS.

1. Save the database as *Fabrikam Inc XXX* (where *XXX* is your initials).
2. Click the **File** tab and click the **Options** button. The Access Options dialog box appears.
3. Click the **Current Database** button on the left to display the Current Database section of the Access Options dialog box, as shown in Figure 15-11.

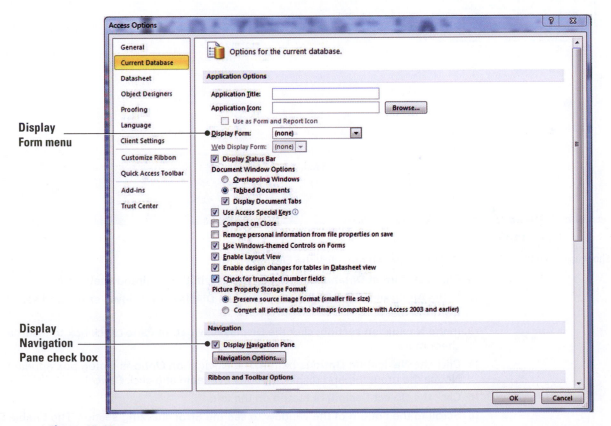

Display Form menu

Display Navigation Pane check box

Figure 15-11

Access Options dialog box

4. In the Application Options section, click the **Display Form down arrow** and select **Showroom Contact Form** from the menu.
5. In the Navigation section, notice that the **Display Navigation Pane** is turned **on** by default.

6. Click the **Display Navigation Pane** check box to remove the check mark and click **OK**. A Microsoft Access dialog box appears, as shown in Figure 15-12, saying you need to close and reopen the database for the changes to take effect.

Figure 15-12

Microsoft Access dialog box

7. Click **OK**.

8. **CLOSE** the database.

9. **OPEN** the *Fabrikam Inc XXX* database. Notice that the Navigation pane is not visible and the Showroom Contact Form is displayed, as shown in Figure 15-13.

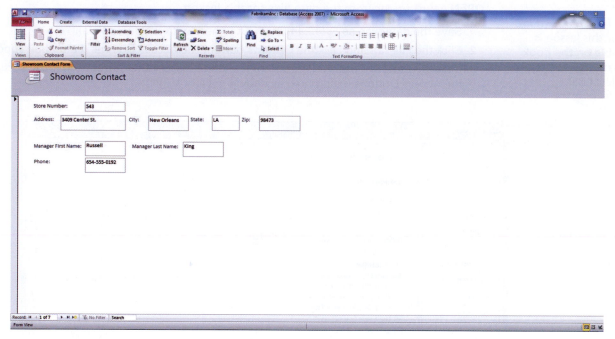

Figure 15-13

Showroom Contact form

10. Click the **File** tab and click the **Options** button.

11. Click the **Current Database** button on the left, if it's not already selected.

12. In the Application Options section, click the **Display Form down arrow** and select **None** from the menu.

13. In the Navigation section, click the **Display Navigation Pane** check box to insert a check mark.

14. Click the **Navigation Options** button. The Navigation Options dialog box appears. Notice the grouping and display options available and click **Cancel**.

15. Click the **Object Designers** button on the left.

16. Scroll to the bottom of the window to see the Error checking section. The Enable Error Checking options are turned on by default.

17. Click **OK**. The Microsoft Access dialog box appears again.

18. Click **OK**.

19. **CLOSE** the database.

20. **OPEN** the *Fabrikam Inc XXX* database. Notice the Navigation pane is displayed and the form is not.

PAUSE. LEAVE the report open to use in the next exercise.

CERTIFICATION READY **1.1.7**

How do you set database options?

SOFTWARE ORIENTATION

Database Tools Tab

The Database Tools tab on the Ribbon contains advanced commands for maintaining documents. Use Figure 15-14 as a reference throughout this lesson as well as the rest of this book.

Figure 15-14

Database Tools tab

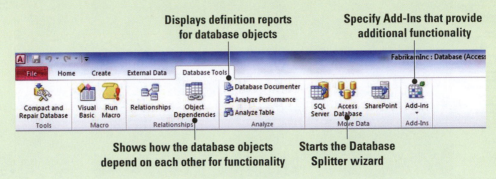

Displays definition reports for database objects

Specify Add-Ins that provide additional functionality

Shows how the database objects depend on each other for functionality

Starts the Database Splitter wizard

USING DATABASE TOOLS

The Bottom Line

The Database Tools tab has advanced commands for maintaining databases. You can do such things as identify object dependencies, create object reports with the Database Documenter, and split a database by using this tab.

Identifying Object Dependencies

Object dependencies describe how objects in a database rely on other components to function properly. The Object Dependencies task pane helps you manage a database by displaying how all its components interact. This can be helpful if you want to delete a table or form. You will be able to see which other objects may also need to be changed so that they will still function without the deleted table. In this exercise, you identify object dependencies.

The Object Dependencies task pane displays how database objects, such as tables or forms, use other objects. This process helps keep databases running smoothly by preventing errors that could result when changes or deletions are made to objects in a database. The Object Dependencies task pane works only for tables, forms, queries, and reports in an Access database.

STEP BY STEP | **Identify Object Dependencies**

USE the database open from the previous exercise.

1. Click the **Product Placements Table** in the Navigation pane to select it.
2. On the Database Tools tab, in the Analyze group, click the **Object Dependencies** button. The Object Dependencies pane displays dependency information for the selected table, as shown in Figure 15-15. Notice that the *Objects that depend on me* radio button is selected.

Figure 15-15

Object Dependencies task pane

3. Click the **Objects that I depend on** radio button. Notice the changes in the Reports section.

4. Click the **Objects that depend on me** radio button. Click the **plus sign (+)** beside the Showroom Contact table to see the tables and forms that depend on the Showroom Contact table.

5. Click the **Showroom Contact** link to display it in Design View where you could make any necessary changes regarding dependencies.

6. Close the Object Dependencies pane.

PAUSE. LEAVE the database open to use in the next exercise.

Using the Database Documenter

The **Database Documenter** provides detailed information about a database and presents it as a report that can be printed. Use the Database Documenter when you need to have a printed record of this information, such as for record-keeping purposes or as insurance in case you have to re-create the database or object. In this exercise, you use the Database Documenter to create a report about the objects included in the database.

The Database Documenter creates a report that shows details, or definitions, about a selected object and opens it in Print Preview. You can view the properties for a form as well as properties for each section of the form and each label, button, or control on the form. The Documenter dialog box contains tabs for each type of object, as well as a tab that displays all objects. Select the object whose definitions you want to view or print. The Options button lets you further specify the features of the object for which you want to view the definitions.

STEP BY STEP   **Use the Database Documenter**

USE the database open from the previous exercise.

1. On the Database Tools tab, in the Relationships group, click the **Database Documenter** button. The Documenter dialog box appears, as shown in Figure 15-16.

Figure 15-16

Documenter dialog box

2. Click the **All Object Types** tab.

3. Click the **Tables** tab.

4. Click the **Showroom Contact** check box in the Tables list.

5. Click the **Options** button. The Print Table Definition dialog box appears, as shown in Figure 15-17.

Figure 15-17

Print Table Definition dialog box

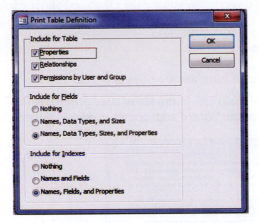

6. Click **OK** to close the Print Table Definition dialog box.

7. Click **OK** to close the Documenter dialog box. If you receive a message box asking you to close the table click **OK**. The Object Definition report appears in Print Preview.

8. Click the **Zoom** button in the Zoom group to view the report, as shown in Figure 15-18. At this point, you could print the report or make any changes to the layout and then print it.

Figure 15-18

Object Definition report

Zoom magnifying glass button

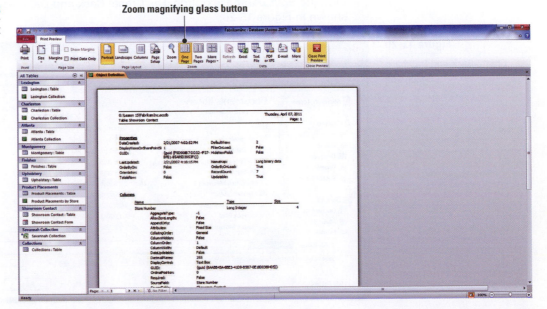

9. Click the Next Page button on the record navigation bar to move to page 4. Notice the relationship diagram included in the report.

10. Click the Close Print Preview button.

PAUSE. LEAVE the database open to use in the next exercise.

Take Note   Some object definitions can be several pages long, so it is a good idea to check the length of the report before printing.

Splitting a Database

It can be difficult for many people to use the data in a database at the same time. Synchronizing data can be difficult and time consuming. To avoid slowing down the network because of constant changes being made to a database, the **Database Splitter** wizard can split the database in two files: one that contains the tables, called the **back-end file**; and one that contains the queries, forms, reports, and other objects created from the tables, called the **front-end file.** Users who need to access the data can customize their own forms, reports, pages, and other objects while maintaining a single source of data on the network. It is a good idea to back up the database before splitting it. In this exercise, you use the Database Splitter wizard to split a database.

STEP BY STEP   **Split a Database**

USE the database open from the previous exercise.

1. On the Database Tools tab, in the Move Data group, click the **Access Database** button. The Database Splitter Wizard appears, as shown in Figure 15-19.

Figure 15-19

Database Splitter Wizard

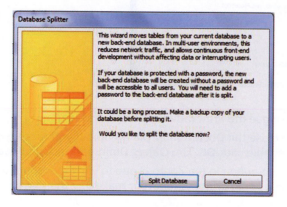

2. Click the **Split Database** button. The Create Back-end Database dialog box appears, as shown in Figure 15-20.

Figure 15-20

Create Back-end Database dialog box

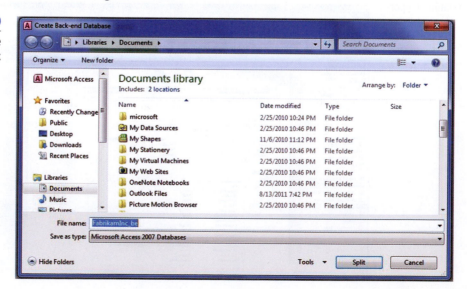

3. Navigate to the location where you want to save the back-end file and click **Split**. After a few moments, the Database Splitter dialog box appears, as shown in Figure 15-21.

Figure 15-21

Database Splitter dialog box

4. Click **OK**.
5. **CLOSE** the database.
6. **OPEN** *Fabrikam XXX_be*. Notice that it contains only the tables for the database.
7. **CLOSE** the database.

CLOSE Access.

SKILL SUMMARY

In This Lesson You Learned How To:	Exam Objective	Objective Number
Maintain a Database	Use Compact & Repair Database.	1.1.4
Set Database Properties		
Encrypt a Database	Use Encrypt with Password commands.	1.1.5
Configure Database Options	Set Access options.	1.1.7
Use Database Tools		

Knowledge Assessment

Matching

Match the term in Column 1 to its description in Column 2.

Column 1

1. backup

2. back-end file

3. front-end file

4. database properties

5. Database Splitter

6. Compact and Repair command

7. encrypting

8. object dependencies

9. Database Documenter

10. decrypting

Column 2

a. in a split database, the file that contains the queries, forms, reports, and other objects created from the tables

b. details about a file that describe or identify it

c. optimizes files and fixes minor problems in the file structure of a database

d. to scramble data in a way that can only be reconverted by an authorized user who has the correct password

e. removing the password from an encrypted file

f. describe how objects in a database are dependent on or rely on other components to function properly

g. creates a report that shows details, or definitions, about a selected object database and opens it in Print Preview

h. a copy of a database file

i. the file that contains the tables in a split database

j. a wizard that splits a database for you

True/False

Circle T if the statement is true or F if the statement is false.

T F **1.** Backing up files on a regular basis is really not necessary.

T F **2.** When you back up a database, Access automatically adds the date to the file name.

T F **3.** Compacting and repairing a database leaves the file fragmented.

T F **4.** Some database properties are updated by Access and cannot be changed.

T F **5.** The .accdb extension is for the Access 2002–2003 file format.

T F **6.** Access Options allow you to customize Access.

T F **7.** If you forget a password for a database, Microsoft can retrieve it for you.

T F **8.** You can print a report from the Database Documenter.

T F **9.** The Compact and Repair command allows you to find missing table links.

T F **10.** It is a good idea to back up a database before splitting it.

Competency Assessment

Project 15-1: Set Database Properties and Compact and Repair the Blue Yonder Database

As an investor relations specialist for Blue Yonder Airlines, you need to maintain and safeguard the databases that you use. Set the database properties and compact and repair the Income and Expenses database.

GET READY. LAUNCH Access if it is not already running.

The *BlueYonder* file for this lesson is available on the book companion website or in WileyPLUS.

1. **OPEN** the *BlueYonder* database from the data files for this lesson.
2. Save the database as *BlueYonder XXX* (where *XXX* is your initials).
3. Click the **File** tab, and then click the **Info** tab, and select the **View and edit database properties** link.
4. Key **Income and Expenses** in the Subject box.
5. Key **your name** in the Author box.
6. Key **Andrew Lan** in the Manager box.
7. Key **BlueYonder Airlines** in the Company box.
8. Click **OK**.
9. Select **Compact and Repair**.

CLOSE the database.

Project 15-2: Back Up and Split the WingTip Database

As part of your maintenance of database files at WingTip Toys, you decide to create a backup of a database and split it so that others in the company can create their own forms and reports using the data in the tables.

GET READY. LAUNCH Access if it is not already running.

The *Wingtip* file for this lesson is available on the book companion website or in WileyPLUS.

1. **OPEN** the *Wingtip* database from the data files for this lesson.
2. **SAVE** the database as *Wingtip XXX* (where *XXX* is your initials).
3. Click the **File** tab, and then click the **Save & Publish** tab, and select **Back Up Database**.
4. Use the generated file name with the date and click **Save**.
5. On the Database Tools tab, in the Move Data group, click the **Access Database** button.

6. Click the **Split database** button.
7. Accept the *Wingtip XXX_be* file name and click **Split**.
8. Click **OK**.

CLOSE the database.

Proficiency Assessment

Project 15-3: Encrypt the Blue Yonder Database

Create a password to protect the data in the Income and Expenses database.

USE the *BlueYonder XXX* database that you saved in a previous exercise.

1. **OPEN** the *BlueYonder XXX* database in Exclusive mode.
2. In Backstage view, on the Info tab click the **Encrypt with Password** button.
3. Key **#1BlueYonder$87** in the Password box.
4. Key **#1BlueYonder$87** in the Verify box.
5. Click **OK**.
6. **CLOSE** the database.
7. **OPEN** the database in regular mode.
8. Key **#1BlueYonder$87** in the Password box.
9. Open the **Database Documenter**.
10. Select the **Income & Expenses Summary** table and click **OK** to view the report.
11. Print the report.
12. Close Print Preview.

CLOSE the database.

Project 15-4: Save the Lucerne Database in a Previous File Format

@ The *Lucerne* file for this lesson is available on the book companion website or in WileyPLUS.

1. **OPEN** the *Lucerne* database from the data files for this lesson.
2. Save the database in the Access 2002–2003 Database file format with the name *Lucerne 2002–2003*.

CLOSE the database.

Mastery Assessment

Project 15-5: Decrypt and Back Up the Blue Yonder Database

Password protection for the Blue Yonder Income and Expenses database is no longer necessary. Remove the encryption.

USE the *BlueYonder XXX* database that you saved in a previous exercise.

1. Remove the encryption with a password from the Blue Yonder database.
2. Create a backup file for the database using the generated file name. Save it in the same location as the original version.

CLOSE the database.

Project 15-6: View Object Dependencies in the Humongous Database

An assistant at Humongous Insurance has moved some files around on the computer you share. Use the Linked Tables Manager to refresh a link to an Excel file that has been imported.

@ The *HumongousInsurance* file for this lesson is available on the book companion website or in WileyPLUS.

OPEN *Humongous Insurance* from the data files for this lesson.

1. Save the database as *Humongous Insurance XXX* (where *XXX* is your initials).
2. View the Object Dependencies Information for the *Part-time Employees* Table.
3. **SAVE** the database.

CLOSE the database.

INTERNET READY

To help you safeguard your computer and files, it's important to understand how security and privacy relates to Access 2010 databases. On the File tab, click the Options button to launch the Access Options dialog box. Click the Trust Center button on the left. The Trust Center contains security and privacy settings and related info for Access 2010. In the Security & More section, click the Microsoft Trustworthy Computing link and read the online article. Browse other links that interest you at the Trust Center.

Circling Back 3

As Woodgrove Real Estate grows, you continue to learn more about Access and use the database for more advanced tasks.

Project 1: Create a Grouped Report

You want to see the houses that have been sold each month. Use the Report Wizard to create a report that groups the data according to the closing date. Then create an aggregate field that will sum the total amount of sales for each month.

GET READY. LAUNCH Access if it is not already running.

 The *Woodgrove Real Estate* database is available for download on the companion website.

1. **OPEN** the *Woodgrove Real Estate* database from the data files for this lesson.
2. **SAVE** the database as *Woodgrove Real Estate XXX* (where *XXX* is your initials).
3. Open the **Houses Sold** table.
4. On the Create tab, in the Reports group, click the **Report Wizard** button to display the first screen in the Report Wizard.
5. Select the **Listing Agent** field and click **>** to move the field to the Selected Fields list.
6. Using the same method, move the *Address, Selling Price,* and *Closing Date* fields from the Available Fields list to the Selected Fields list.
7. Click the **Next >** button to display the second screen in the Report Wizard.
8. Select the **Closing Date** field and click **>** to move it to the grouping levels box.
9. Click the **Next >** button to display the third screen in the Report Wizard.
10. Click the **down arrow** on the Sort menu and select **Closing Date**.
11. Click the **Next >** button to display the fourth screen in the Report Wizard.
12. In the Layout section, the Stepped option button should be selected and in the Orientation section Portrait should be selected.
13. Click the **Next >** button to display the fifth screen in the Report Wizard.
14. Click the **Finish** button to accept the settings and create the report.
15. Close Print Preview.
16. Switch to Layout View.
17. Right-click the first cell under the Selling Price header to display the shortcut menu.
18. Click **Total Selling Price** and then click **Sum**. The totals for each month are displayed. Resize the controls, if necessary, so all the labels and data can be read. Your report should look similar to Figure 1.

Figure 1

Sales report grouped by month

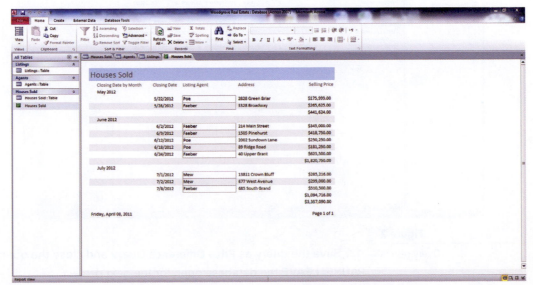

19. Close the report, and close the table.

PAUSE. LEAVE the database open to use in the next project.

Project 2: Create a Calculated Query Field

You are interested in knowing the difference between each house's asking price and selling price. Create a query with a calculated field that will give you this information. Then add a Totals row so you can find the average asking price, selling price, and difference.

USE the database that is open from the previous project.

1. On the Create tab, in the Queries group, click **Query Design**.
2. In the Show Table dialog box, double-click **Houses Sold** to add the table to the design grid.
3. Click **Close**.
4. In the *Houses Sold* field list, double-click **Address**, **Bedrooms**, **Bathrooms**, **Asking Price**, and **Selling Price**.
5. Click the **Field** cell in the first blank column and press **Shift+F2** to open the Zoom dialog box.
6. In the Zoom dialog box, key the following expression:

   Difference: [Asking Price] − [Selling Price]
7. Click **OK**.
8. On the Design tab, in the Results group, click **Run** to create a query with the new calculated *Difference* field.
9. On the Home tab, in the Records group, click the **Totals** button. Scroll down to see the Totals row at the bottom of the result set.
10. In the *Asking Price* field, click the **Totals cell down arrow** to display the menu and click **Average**.
11. In the *Selling Price* field, click the **Totals row down arrow** and click **Average**.
12. In the *Difference* field, click the **Totals row down arrow** and click **Average**. Your query should look similar to Figure 2.

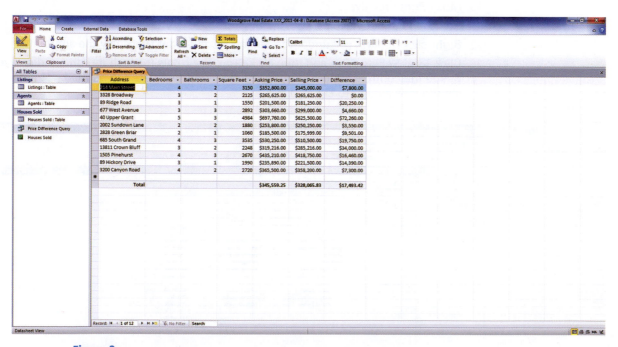

Figure 2

Query results

13. Save the query as **Price Difference Query** and close the query.

PAUSE. LEAVE the database open for the next project.

Project 3: Create a Chart

In the report you created, you want to have a pictorial view of the data along with the numbers. Use the Chart Wizard to insert a 3D column chart into your existing report.

USE the database that is open from the previous project.

1. Open the **Houses Sold** report.
2. Switch to Design View.
3. On the Design tab, in the Controls group, click the **Chart** button. The pointer changes to a plus sign with a chart icon.
4. Click in the upper-left corner of the Page Footer section and drag to the lower-right corner to create a rectangular placeholder where the chart will be inserted.
5. Release the mouse button. The first Chart Wizard screen appears.
6. Select the **Houses Sold** table as your data source and click the **Next >** button. The second Chart Wizard screen appears.
7. Double-click the **Asking Price**, **Selling Price**, and **Closing Date** fields to move them to the Fields for Chart box and click the **Next >** button. The third Chart Wizard screen appears.
8. Click the **3D Column Chart** button, the second icon in the first row.
9. Click the **Next >** button. The fourth Chart Wizard screen appears.
10. Click and drag the **Selling Price** field button to the upper-left of the chart and drop on the **SumofAskingPrice** data list. Both the *SumofSellingPrice* and *SumofAskingPrice* fields should be listed.
11. Click the **Preview Chart** button. The Sample Preview dialog box appears, displaying a sample of your chart.
12. Click the **Close** button. The Sample Preview dialog box closes.
13. Click the **Next >** button. The fifth Chart Wizard screen appears.
14. Click the **Report Fields down arrow** and in the menu select **<No Field>**.
15. Click the **Chart Fields down arrow** and in the menu select **<No Field>**.
16. Click the **Next >** button. The Sixth Chart Wizard screen appears.
17. Key **Summer 2012** in the Title box.
18. The Yes, display a legend button should be selected. If not, select it and click the **Finish** button. Access inserts your chart.
19. Click the chart to select it and resize it appropriately.
20. On the Design tab, in the Tools group, click the **Property Sheet** button.
21. Click the **Data** tab of the Property Sheet. Click the **down arrow** at the end of the **Enabled** line and select **Yes**.
22. Close the Property Sheet.
23. Switch to Report View.
24. On the Home tab, in the Records group, click the **Refresh All** button.
25. Scroll to the bottom of the report to view your chart, which should look similar to Figure 3.

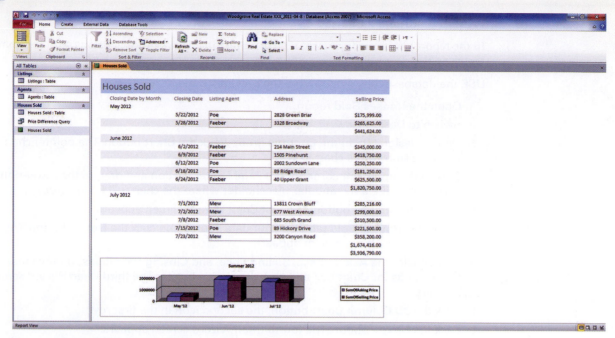

Figure 3

Report with 3D Column Chart

26. Save and close the report.

PAUSE. LEAVE the database open for the next project.

Project 4: Export Data and Save Specification

You need to provide listing information to the agents in your office in another format, so you export the data to Excel. Because you will perform this export operation on a regular basis, you save the specification for future use.

USE the database that is open from the previous project.

1. In the Navigation pane, select the **Listings: Table**.

2. On the External Data tab, in the Export group, click **Excel**. The Export–Excel Spreadsheet dialog box appears.

3. If you want to specify a different destination, click **Browse** to open the File Save dialog box, use the Save in box to choose a folder, and then click **Save**.

4. Click the Export data with formatting and layout check box and then click the Open the destination file after the export operation is complete check box.

5. Click **OK**. Excel opens and the new worksheet with exported data is displayed.

6. Close the worksheet and **CLOSE** Excel.

7. Switch to Access.

8. On the Save Export Steps screen, click the **Save export steps** check box to display the specification details.

9. In the Description box, key **Export listing information to Excel**.

10. Click **Save Export**.

PAUSE. LEAVE the database open for the next project.

Project 5: Maintain, Back Up, and Split a Database

You regularly perform routine maintenance on the database to ensure data integrity. You decide to split the database into two files to reduce network traffic, but after all the work you have put into the database you first want to protect your work by backing it up to prevent data loss.

USE the database that is open from the previous project.

1. Click the **Info** tab in the Backstage view, and click **Compact & Repair Database**. Access compacts and repairs the database.
2. Click the **Save & Publish** tab in the Backstage view, and click **Back Up Database** to display the Save As dialog box. Access automatically adds the current date to the end of the file name.
3. Click the **Save** button to accept the generated file name.
4. On the Database Tools tab, in the Move Data group, click the **Access Database** button to display the Database Splitter Wizard.
5. Click the **Split Database** button to display the Create Back-end Database dialog box.
6. Navigate to the location where you want to save the back-end file and click **Split**. After a few moments, the Database Splitter dialog box appears.
7. Click **OK**.
8. **CLOSE** the database.
9. **OPEN** *Woodgrove Real Estate XXX_be*. Notice that it contains only the tables for the database.
10. **CLOSE** the database.

STOP. CLOSE Access.

Skill Matrix	Objective Number	Lesson Number
Managing the Access Environment		
Create and manage a database.	1.1	
Use Save Object As.	1.1.1	2, 13
Use Open.	1.1.2	1
Use Save and Publish.	1.1.3	13
Use Compact & Repair Database.	1.1.4	15
Use Encrypt with Password commands.	1.1.5	15
Create a database from a template.	1.1.6	2
Set Access options.	1.1.7	15
Configure the Navigation Pane.	1.2	
Rename objects.	1.2.1	4
Delete objects.	1.2.2	4
Set Navigation options.	1.2.3	1
Apply Application Parts.	1.3	
Use Blank Forms.	1.3.1	10
Use Quick Start.	1.3.2	4
Use user templates.	1.3.3	2
Building Tables		
Create tables.	2.1	
Create tables in Design View.	2.1.1	9
Create and modify fields.	2.2	
Insert a field.	2.2.1	4
Delete a field.	2.2.2	4
Rename a field.	2.2.3	4
Hide or Unhide fields.	2.2.4	3
Freeze or Unfreeze fields.	2.2.5	3
Modify data types.	2.2.6	1
Modify the field description.	2.2.7	9
Modify field properties.	2.2.8	4

Skill Matrix	Objective Number	Lesson Number
Sort and filter records.	2.3	
Use Find.	2.3.1	3
Use Sort.	2.3.2	3
Use Filter commands.	2.3.3	3
Set relationships.	2.4	
Define Primary Keys.	2.4.1	3
Use Primary Keys to create Relationships.	2.4.2	3
Edit Relationships.	2.4.3	3
Import data from a single data file.	2.5	
Import source data into a new table.	2.5.1	14
Append records to an existing table.	2.5.2	14
Import data as a linked table.	2.5.3	14
Building Forms		
Create forms.	3.1	
Use the Form Wizard.	3.1.1	5
Create a Blank Form.	3.1.2	5
Use Form Design Tools.	3.1.3	5
Create Navigation forms.	3.1.4	10
Apply Form Design options.	3.2	
Apply a Theme.	3.2.1	5
Add bound controls.	3.2.2	8
Format Header/Footer.	3.2.3	8
View Code.	3.2.4	8
View Property Sheet.	3.2.5	8
Add Existing Fields.	3.2.6	8
Apply Form Arrange options.	3.3	
Use the Table functions.	3.3.1	8
Use the Move table command.	3.3.2	8
Reposition/Format form controls.	3.3.3	8

Skill Matrix	Objective Number	Lesson Number
Apply Form Format options.	3.4	
Reformat Font in form.	3.4.1	8
Apply background image to a form.	3.4.2	8
Apply Quick Styles to controls in a form.	3.4.3	8
Apply conditional formatting in a form.	3.4.4	8
Creating and Managing Queries		
Construct queries.	4.1	
Create a Select query.	4.1.1	7
Create a Make Table query.	4.1.2	12
Create an Append query.	4.1.3	12
Create a Crosstab query.	4.1.4	12
Manage source tables and relationships.	4.2	
Use the Show Table command.	4.2.1	7
Use the Remove Table command.	4.2.2	7
Create ad hoc relationships.	4.2.3	12
Manipulate fields.	4.3	
Add field.	4.3.1	12
Remove field.	4.3.2	12
Rearrange fields.	4.3.3	12
Use Sort and Show options.	4.3.4	7
Calculate totals.	4.4	
Use the Total row.	4.4.1	12
Use Group By.	4.4.2	12
Generate calculated fields.	4.5	
Perform calculations.	4.5.1	12
Use the Zoom box.	4.5.2	12
Use Expression Builder.	4.5.3	12
Designing Reports		
Create reports.	5.1	
Create a Blank Report.	5.1.1	8
Use Report Design Tools.	5.1.2	6
Use the Report Wizard.	5.1.3	6

Skill Matrix	Objective Number	Lesson Number
Apply Report Design options.	5.2	
Apply a Theme.	5.2.1	6
Add calculated controls.	5.2.2	8, 10
Add bound/unbound controls.	5.2.3	8, 13
Header/Footer.	5.2.4	8
Reorder tab function.	5.2.5	8
Apply Report Arrange options.	5.3	
Use the Table functions.	5.3.1	8
Use the Move table command.	5.3.2	8
Reposition/Format report records.	5.3.3	8
Align report outputs to grid.	5.3.4	8
Apply Report Format options.	5.4	
Rename label in a report.	5.4.1	8
Apply background image to a report.	5.4.2	8
Change shape in report.	5.4.3	8
Apply conditional formatting in a report.	5.4.4	8
Apply Report Page Setup options.	5.5	
Change page size.	5.5.1	11
Change page orientation.	5.5.2	11
Sort and filter records for reporting.	5.6	
Use the Find command.	5.6.1	6
Use the Sort command.	5.6.2	6
Use Filter commands.	5.6.3	6
Use view types.	5.6.4	6

Appendix B Microsoft Office Professional 2010

Component	Requirement
Computer and processor	500 MHz or faster processor
Memory	256 MB RAM; 512 MB recommended for graphics features, Outlook Instant Search, and certain advanced functionality.[1,2]
Hard disk	3.0 GB available disk space
Display	1024×576 or higher resolution monitor
Operating system	Windows XP (must have SP3) (32-bit), Windows 7, Windows Vista with Service Pack (SP) 1, Windows Server 2003 R2 with MSXML 6.0 (32-bit Office only), Windows Server 2008, or later 32- or 64-bit OS.
Graphics	Graphics hardware acceleration requires a DirectX 9.0c graphics card with 64 MB or more video memory.
Additional requirements	Certain Microsoft® OneNote® features require Windows® Desktop Search 3.0, Windows Media® Player 9.0, Microsoft® ActiveSync® 4.1, microphone, audio output device, video recording device, TWAIN-compatible digital camera, or scanner; sharing notebooks requires users to be on the same network.
	Certain advanced functionality requires connectivity to Microsoft Exchange Server 2003, Microsoft SharePoint Server 2010, and/or Microsoft SharePoint Foundation 2010.
	Certain features require Windows Search 4.0.
	Send to OneNote Print Driver and Integration with Business Connectivity Services require Microsoft .NET Framework 3.5 and/or Windows XPS features.
	Internet Explorer (IE) 6 or later, 32-bit browser only. IE7 or later required to receive broadcast presentations. Internet functionality requires an Internet connection.
	Multi-Touch features require Windows 7 and a touch-enabled device.
	Certain inking features require Windows XP Tablet PC Edition or later.
	Speech recognition functionality requires a close-talk microphone and audio output device.
	Internet Fax not available on Windows Vista Starter, Windows Vista Home Basic, or Windows Vista Home Premium.
	Information Rights Management features require access to a Windows 2003 Server with SP1 or later running Windows Rights Management Services.
	Certain online functionality requires a Windows LiveTM ID.
Other	Product functionality and graphics may vary based on your system configuration. Some features may require additional or advanced hardware or server connectivity; www.office.com/products.

[1] 512 MB RAM recommended for accessing Outlook data files larger than 1 GB.

[2] GHz processor or faster and 1 GB RAM or more recommended for OneNote Audio Search. Close-talking microphone required. Audio Search is not available in all languages.

Access 2010 Glossary

A

action query   Changes the data in its data source or creates a new table.

aggregate field   A field that uses an aggregate function to calculate data.

aggregate function   Performs a calculation on a set of values and then returns a single value.

append query   An action query that adds the records in a query's result set to the end of an existing table.

Application Parts   A gallery that you can use to insert predefined templates consisting of objects like tables, forms, and reports into a preexisting database.

Ascending   A sort order that sorts data from beginning to end, such as A to Z or 0 to 99. (*See also* Sort.)

B

back-end file   In a split database, the database that contains the tables.

Backstage view   Contains many of the commands that were on the File menu in previous versions of Microsoft Access and allows you to create a new database, create a database from a template, open an existing database, and perform many database maintenance tasks.

backup   A copy of a database file.

badges   Small square labels that contain KeyTips.

Blank Forms   Category in the Application Parts gallery that contains a collection of 10 form parts that allows you to add predefined forms to a database.

Blank Form tool   Creates a new blank form in Layout view.

bound control   Uses a field in a table or query as the data source.

C

calculated control   A control that displays the result of a calculation or expression.

calculated field   A column in a query that results from an expression.

chart   A graphical representation of data.

chart body   The main area that displays the chart.

Chart Wizard   A control that you can insert into forms and reports to quickly create charts.

common filters   Popular filters available as context menu commands, depending on the type and values of the field.

composite key   Two or more primary keys used in a table.

conditional formatting   Changes the appearance of a control or the value in a control when certain conditions are met.

Connection Status menu   A menu that lets you choose between searching help topics online and help topics offline.

control   An object that displays data, performs actions, and lets you improve the look and usability of a form or report.

control layouts   Use to align your controls horizontally and vertically to give your report or form a uniform appearance.

control tab order   The order in which the selection moves from field to field when the Tab key is pressed.

Control Wizard   Helps you create controls such as command buttons, list boxes, combo boxes, and option groups.

cross join   A join in which each row from one table is combined with each row from another table. (*See also* Join.)

crosstab query   A query that calculates a sum, average, count, or other type of total on records and then groups the results by two types of information: one down the left side of the datasheet and the other across the top.

D

database   A tool for collecting and organizing information.

Database Documenter   Creates a report that shows details, or definitions, about a selected object and opens it in Print Preview.

database management system (DBMS)   A system for managing data that allows the user to store, retrieve, and analyze information.

database properties   Details about a file that describe or identify it.

Database Splitter   A wizard that splits a database into two files.

datasheet   A visual representation of the data contained in a table or of the results returned by a query.

data type   The kind of information a field contains—whether text, number, date/time, or some other type.

decrypting   Removing the password from a file that has been encrypted.

delete query   An action query that removes rows matching the criteria that you specify from one or more tables.

delimited file   A text file where each record appears on a separate line and the fields are separated by a single character.

delimiter   A character that separates fields in a delimited file and does not appear in the field values, such as a tab, semicolon, comma, or space.

descending   A sort order that sorts data from the end to the beginning, such as Z to A or 99 to 0. (*See also* Sort.)

desktop   The first screen you see after you start the computer.

dialog box launcher   A small arrow in the lower-right corner of a group that you click to launch a dialog box.

E

encrypting   Scrambling data in a way that can only be reconverted by an authorized user who has the password.

Expression Builder   A feature that provides the names of the fields and controls in a database, lists the operators available, and has built-in functions to help you create an expression.

F

field   A column in a database table.

field list   A window that lists all the fields in the underlying record source or database object.

File tab   A tab that displays the Backstage view and contains a menu of commands that you can use for the common tasks performed with your database files—such as opening, saving, and printing.

filter   A set of rules for determining which records will be displayed.

filter by form   A tool that creates a blank form similar to the original; useful for filtering on several fields in a form or to find a specific record.

fixed-width file   A text file where each record appears on a separate line and the width of each field remains consistent across records.

foreign key   A primary key from one table that is used in another table.

form   A database object that simplifies the process of entering, editing, and displaying data.

Form Design button   A tool that creates a new blank form in Design view.

Form tool   A tool that creates a simple form that includes all the fields from the underlying data source.

Form Wizard   A form-building tool that allows you to choose the form fields, style, and layout.

front-end file   A database that contains the queries, forms, reports, and other objects created from the tables.

G

group   Collections of records separated visually and displayed with introductory or summary information.

group footer   The section of a report where data in the group is summarized.

group header   The section of a report where the name of a grouped field is displayed and printed.

grouping field   A field by which data is grouped.

grouping intervals   The way that records are grouped together.

grouping levels   The nested arrangement of the groups in a report.

groups   Related commands within the tabs on the Ribbon.

H

hierarchical form   A form/subform combination, also called a master/detail form or a parent/child form.

I

inner join   Most common type of join; includes rows in the query only when the joined field matches records in both tables. (*See also* Join.)

innermost field   A secondary sort field in a multifield sort.

input mask   A set of placeholder characters that force you to enter data in a specific format.

J

join   A relationship between identical fields in different tables.

K

KeyTips   Small letters and numbers that appear on the Ribbon when you press Alt; used for executing commands with the keyboard.

L

Label Wizard   A wizard that asks questions about the labels you want to create and the data you want to display on them, which then creates the labels based on the answers.

left outer join   A join that includes all of the rows from the first table in the query and only those records from the second table that match the join field in the first table. (*See also* Join.)

legend   A chart element that displays a list of the colors, shapes, or patterns used as categories in the chart.

linked table   A new table created when a database is linked to an Excel worksheet.

M

main form   The primary form in a form/subform combination.

make table query   An action query that creates a new table and then creates records in it by copying records from an existing table.

Multiple Items tool   A tool that creates a customizable form that displays multiple records.

multivalued field   A field that allows you to select more than one value from a list.

N

Navigation form   A form that includes a set of navigation tabs that you can click to display forms and reports.

normal forms   The standards and guidelines of database design that can be used to determine if a database is structured correctly.

normalization   The process of applying rules to a database design to ensure that information is divided into the appropriate tables.

O

object dependencies   Describes how objects in a database are dependent on or rely on other components to function properly.

objects   Elements in a database, such as tables, queries, forms, and reports.

outer join   A join that includes all of the rows from one table and only those rows from the other table that match the join field in the first table. (*See also* Join.)

outermost field   The primary sort field in a multifield sort.

P

parameter query   A query in which the user interactively specifies one or more criteria values.

PDF   A file format that maintains the exact layout of the original file and that can easily be shared.

PivotChart   An interactive chart that shows data totals or summaries.

primary key   The column in a database that uniquely identifies each row.

Print Preview   A feature that displays a report as it will look when printed.

properties   Controls the appearance or behavior characteristics for objects and related parts like fields and controls.

Q

query   A database object that enables stored data to be searched and retrieved.

query criterion   A rule that identifies the records that you want to include in the query result.

Quick Access Toolbar   A toolbar at the top left of the screen that contains the commands that you use most often, such as Save, Undo, Redo, and Print.

Quick Start   A collection of predefined objects that you can add to your database arranged by parts for tracking things such as comments, contacts, and issues.

Quick Start field   A predefined set of characteristics and properties that describes a field, including a field name, a data type, and a number of other field properties.

R

record   A row in a database table.

record source   Tables or queries from which a query gets its data.

redundant data   Duplicate information in a database.

referential integrity   A rule that prevents orphaned records.

relational database   A group of database tables that are connected or linked by a defined relationship that ties the information together.

report   A database object that presents information in a format that is easy to read and print.

Ribbon   A graphic band located across the top of the screen that contains tabs and groups of commands.

right outer join   A join that includes all of the rows from the second table in the query and only those records from the first table that match the join field in the second table. (*See also* Join.)

S

select query   The most basic type of Access query, it creates subsets of data, displayed in Datasheet view, that can be used to answer specific questions or to supply data to other database objects.

SELECT statement   An SQL command that instructs the Microsoft Access database engine to return information from the database as a set of records.

sort   To arrange data alphabetically, numerically, or chronologically.

specification   The details of an import or export operation that contain all the information Access needs to repeat it without user input.

split form   A feature that gives you two views of your data at the same time—in both Form view and Datasheet view.

stacked layout   A layout in which the controls are arranged vertically with a label on the left and the control on the right.

subform   A form that is inserted into another form.

subquery   An SQL SELECT statement that is inside another select or action query.

T

tab   An area of activity on the Ribbon.

table   The most basic database object; stores data in categories.

Table Analyzer   A wizard that performs the normalization process by examining a table design and suggesting a way to divide the table for maximum efficiency.

tabular layout   A layout in which the controls are arranged in rows and columns like a spreadsheet, with labels across the top.

template   A ready-to-use database that contains all of the tables, queries, forms, and reports needed for performing a specific task.

Theme   A predefined combination of colors and fonts that you can select to apply to a form or report.

Totals row   A row inserted at the bottom of a table that provides a menu of functions for each column in the row.

U

unbound control   A control that displays information such as lines, shapes, or pictures; it is not bound to a field.

unequal join   A join that is not based on the equivalence of the joined fields. (*See also* Join.)

update query   An action query that changes a set of records according to specified criteria.

V

validation rule   An expression that limits the values that can be entered in the field.

validation text   The text in the error message that appears when users violate a validation rule.

W

wildcard   Characters used to find words or phrases that contain specific letters or combinations of letters.

X

XPS   A file format that preserves document formatting; it can be easily shared, printed, and archived and is more secure.

Z

zero-length string   A string that contains no characters and is used to indicate that no value exists for a field.

Credits

Index